HOME OF HARD-TO-FIND BOOKS

Rome
by John Francis Maguire

Address:
HardPress
8345 NW 66TH ST #2561
MIAMI FL 33166-2626
USA
Email: info@hardpress.net

ROME:

ITS RULER AND ITS INSTITUTIONS.

LONDON :
Printed by SPOTTISWOODE & CO.
New-street Square.

Painted by Henry Doyle, Esq.   Engraved by H. Adlard.

His Holiness Pius IX.

in the Pauline Chapel.

London, Longman & Co.

ROME:

ITS RULER AND ITS INSTITUTIONS

BY

JOHN FRANCIS MAGUIRE, M.P.

LONDON

LONGMAN, BROWN, GREEN, LONGMANS, & ROBERTS.

1857.

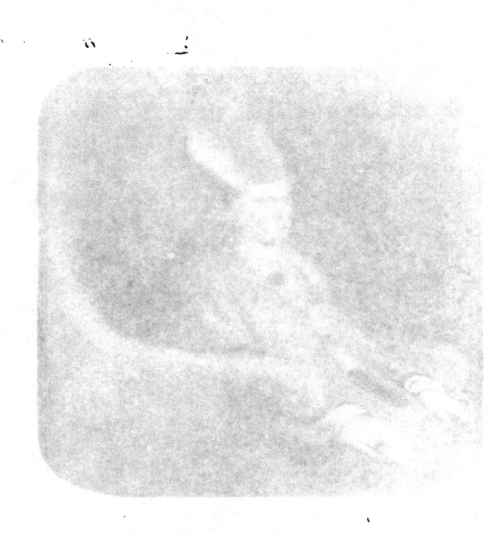

ROME:

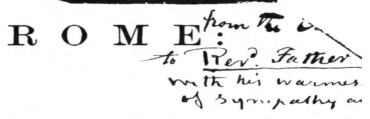

ITS RULER AND ITS INSTITUTIONS.

BY

JOHN FRANCIS MAGUIRE, M.P.

LONDON:

LONGMAN, BROWN, GREEN, LONGMANS, & ROBERTS.

1857.

TO

THE HON. AND RIGHT REV. GEORGE TALBOT,

DOMESTIC PRELATE AND
PRIVATE CHAMBERLAIN OF HIS HOLINESS PIUS IX.

THIS VOLUME IS

Dedicated

BY THE AUTHOR,

AS A TESTIMONY OF RESPECT FOR HIS CHARACTER,
AND OF GRATITUDE FOR HIS KINDNESS.

PREFACE.

THIS volume has had its origin in a series of letters, which I wrote from Rome, in the belief that the subjects of which they treated, and the information which they afforded, would prove of interest to a large circle of readers. The result justified the anticipation; for the letters were extensively copied in this country, as well as in various places in America, and were reprinted in more than one European language. The interest which they excited — or, more correctly speaking, which the information afforded by their details excited — was evidenced by almost innumerable applications made to me, to publish them in some more enduring and permanent form. Many of these applications were urged upon me with a weight of personal authority which I could not attempt to resist; and I therefore resolved to comply with a desire in which I thoroughly sympathised, and the motive of which I perfectly understood, — namely, a wish to encounter, by a representation of the true state of things in Rome, that system of falsehood and misrepresentation which has been too generally adopted with reference to all matters connected with the government and institutions of the Papal States: which system of falsehood and misrepresentation is not owing to the circumstance of the nation and government being *Italian,* but of both being *Catholic,* and of the latter being that of the Head of the Catholic Church.

At a considerable sacrifice of time, and no small interference with pressing public duty, I resolved, not on reprinting my letters, but upon using them as the groundwork of a volume in which the subjects to which they referred, but briefly treated, might be dealt with more fully and more deliberately; ample materials for their development being at my disposal, the result of what I myself saw, or what I could gather from public documents of undoubted authority. Scarcely, however, had I commenced my task, when I felt convinced of the necessity of giving a brief but sufficient sketch of the career of the reigning Pope, principally with a view of recalling to the recollection of the reader the remarkable events of the early years of his pontificate, and exhibiting the causes that of necessity arrested

the progress of those great political reforms of which
he was the author, but which evil men sought to use
to their own advantage, if not to his destruction.
A casual conversation with a friend, whose mind tena-
ciously retained all recent impressions made by the
partial statements of the enemies of the Pope, and the
traducers of his government, but from which every
recollection of the events of 1848 and 1849 had utterly
faded, determined me to carry out this resolution, and
commence the volume with a personal and historical
sketch of the career of Pius IX.   This I have done
at greater length than I had at first intended, but perhaps not so fully as the nature of the subject required.
At any rate, I trust I have done sufficient to enable
the reader to behold, in his true character, one of the
best of men, and most beneficent of rulers; and to estimate, at their right value, the accusations which have
been made against him, as a reformer of the one day,
and a reactionist of the next.

The letters to which, as I have said, this volume
owes its origin, I have but sparingly used; or where I
have used them, I have added to them considerably,—
so as to render each of the more important subjects as
full as I could afford to make it in a single volume.
For instance, I have devoted a considerable portion of
the book to a sketch of the Educational institutions of

Rome,—a subject respecting which much misconception exists in these countries.

To one portion of this book I feel it right to direct attention,—namely, to the *Appendix.* I do so for two reasons. In the first place, it contains, in the official Report furnished by the Count de Rayneval, the French Envoy at Rome, to the Minister for Foreign Affairs in Paris, the most authoritative and conclusive refutation of the charges urged against the Government of the Pope; and affords an amount of valuable information, on various points, of which it is essential that the public of these countries should be apprised. This document first appeared in its English form in the *Daily News* of the 18th of March, 1857; and while adopting this translation, I can vouch for its accuracy, as I have closely compared it with the original French, subsequently published in that journal. In no material respect does the one differ from the other; the translation, in every respect, substantially conveying the meaning of the original, and giving all its figures and facts with scrupulous fidelity. I had been in previous possession of documentary evidence, proving the truth of the statements made in this remarkable State Paper, and had even embodied many of them in my letters; but, on its appearance in the *Daily News*, I was at once convinced that I would be more likely to serve the cause which I had at heart, by abandoning what I had written, and adopting the despatch of the French Ambassador, who wrote, not only under a sense of official responsibility, but from a personal knowledge, derived alike from his long residence in Rome, and the facilities which his position afforded him of arriving at the real state of things. To this despatch I would direct the attention of every reader who desires to ascertain the truth with respect to the Papal Government.

I direct attention to the *Appendix* for this second reason,—namely, that the reader may learn, from sources of unquestionable authority, that we ourselves have very many and very important reforms to effect, both at home and in our government abroad, before we venture to become the self-appointed censor of other nations;—that, in a word, we should cast out the beam out of our own eye, before we cast out the mote out of our brother's eye.

In the chapters on the public institutions of Rome, I have been indebted, in some measure, to the able and philosophic work of the late Cardinal Morichini; which obligation I have acknowledged in more than one place. This valuable work was given to me in Rome, as containing the best and fullest information on the subjects with which I desired to become acquainted; but my letters merely contained descriptions of what *I saw*, as

I had no time, while in that city, to devote to reading. But for a fuller account, such as I now pretend to give, of the institutions which I then described, a reference to a work of the very highest authority became a matter of necessity.

I shall only add, in conclusion, the expression of a sincere and heart-felt hope, that this volume may have the effect of removing from the minds of many honest and well-intentioned readers, the dark veil with which ignorance and prejudice have obscured the truth, — and that these pages may enable the conscientious of every communion to comprehend the character and appreciate the virtues of one of the best of Men, one of the most beneficent of Rulers, and one of the most illustrious of Popes.

J. F. M.

London : July, 1857.

CONTENTS.

CHAP. XI.

CHAP. XII.

CHAP. XIII.

CHAP. XIV,

CHAP. XV.

CHAP. XVI.

CHAP. XVII.

a

ROME:

ITS RULER AND ITS INSTITUTIONS.

CHAPTER I.

Introduction.—The Pauline Chapel.—The Cardinals.—The Pope.

To no other city on the earth does the stranger direct his steps with feelings of a more varied character, or with a livelier anticipation of what awaits him on his entrance, than to Rome. No doubt, a more sacred and solemn awe fills his mind, and bows down his inmost soul, as, from some wild path amidst the mountains of Judea, he catches the first glimpse of the towers of Jerusalem—at the sight of whose holy walls the stern Crusader burst into a passion of tears, and smote his mailed breast in a paroxysm of humility and sorrow. Jerusalem is a place of one great and all-absorbing interest, being the theatre of that sublime sacrifice by which man's redemption was accomplished ; and every nodding tower and mouldering pillar of that once proud city is sacred in the eyes of the Christian of even ordinary sensibility. But Rome, while abounding in

B

sources of that deep and solemn interest which Jerusalem inspires, is also replete with attractions of a totally different kind, and offers countless objects of admiration, and subjects for inquiry and reflection, to the scholar and man of taste, the antiquarian and the philosopher. And dull must be the mind and cold the heart of him who does not experience some stir, or feel some throb, as he approaches for the first time the venerable walls, and passes beneath one of the ancient gateways, of the Eternal City. For was not this the seat and centre of that universal empire, which embraced within its circle the remotest boundaries of the known earth? — was not this the proud capital of that haughty race whose banners glistened and whose arms triumphed in every clime, and whose laws were reverenced as well by civilised nations as by savage tribes? — was not this the instructress as well as the conqueror of mankind?

It is the Rome, too, of a wider dominion and a more glorious rule than that of the greatest of the Cæsars.

If Rome were not the birthplace of Christianity, it was its nursing mother. It was the seat of the Apostles; the theatre of their trials, their sufferings, and their glory. One beholds, passing before him, as it were visibly to the sight, the long centuries of that momentous war waged between truth and error, between the powers of light and darkness. And, in spite of the vulgar dwellings, inelegant and mean, that surround him as he stands within the walls of modern Rome, he witnesses, in imagination, the solemn rites and splendid worship of that polished and attractive system of Polytheism, which, though despised by the enlightened, and scoffed at by the philosophers, still appealed, and not in vain, to the passions of a degenerate people, through its deification of the weaknesses and vices of human nature,—that claimed, as yet, the allegiance of a populace so long accustomed to its pomp and splendour, and whose temples and shrines rose on every side, in all the magnificence of their costly material, and the more inestimable beauty of their design and execution. He beholds, also, the infant Church of the True Faith hiding its timid head beneath the very highway over which the scornful polytheist strode,—crouching in cell, and crypt, and dark and tortuous labyrinth—'and, when venturing above the earth, its asylum and its refuge, appearing wicked and infamous to the Roman gaze, spite of the courage and fortitude of its apostles and its martyrs. He beholds this patient, fearless spouse of Christ weeping tears of blood, as,

"Butchered to make a Roman holiday,"

her children are torn by the jaws of ravening beasts, consumed by fire, or fall beneath the more merciful sword. He sees the red soil of the amphitheatre gradually losing its hue of carnage, and blooming with mysterious beauty, as there steals into the hearts of the thoughtful and the good a conviction of the purity of the Nazarene's faith—which, to the wonder of the scorner and the scoffer, imparts strength to tottering age, fortitude to tender youth, and the courage of the hero to the feeble virgin. He beholds how the

statues and images of the gods, so long the wor-
shipped of the masters of the world, identified with
the triumphs and the glory of a mighty race, were, at
first, carelessly regarded, next despised, then detested,
— how the crushed and trampled Church of the Catacombs emerged from the darkness to the light of day,
no longer loathed and execrated as the foe of humanity,
and the teacher of all wickedness; but hailed with enthusiasm by a softened people, and protected by the
authority, but still more by the devotion, of princes
and rulers, — and how, at length, and after long ages
of persecution and of obloquy, the Cross rose above the
temple and the shrine, to be hailed from thenceforward,
and through regions unknown to the arms or philosophy of Rome, as the symbol of man's salvation.

And here grew into maturity a power and a sovereignty greater than that of the Cæsars — the power of
the Papacy, and the sovereignty of the Church. Baptized in blood, and cradled in adversity, the Papacy
grew into strength, the citadel and the stronghold of
the Faith. From the modest throne of the first rulers
of the Church to the tribunal of the tyrant, there was,
for centuries, but a step; and from thence to the stake
and the scaffold, the road was but too well defined by
the bloody footprints of their heroic predecessors.
Wave after wave broke in fury against the rock on
which God placed His Church. Now heresy assailed
her; now schism sought to rend her asunder; now it
was the rude and warlike savage from the forests of
Germany that menaced her; and now it was the fierce

and fanatic Arab that, bursting with flaming scimitar upon the countries which, once provinces of Rome, had yielded a willing allegiance to the spiritual supremacy of the Popes, ravaged the very shrines and altars of the Apostles. But, watched over by God's providence, we behold the enemies of the Church become her friends, her assailants her protectors, her haughty revilers her humble and submissive children; till we see her striking her foundations deeper and deeper into the hearts of nations, and extending her beneficent dominion wider and wider over the face of the earth.

Then the chief events in the history of the Papacy, from the days of Charlemagne to those of Napoleon, pass before the mind in all their brilliant or gloomy colouring, as peace presided over the halls of the Vatican, or evil men sought the ruin of the successors of Peter. And there stand out from the shadowy background the striking figures of such illustrious Popes as Gregory the Great, Julius the Second, Leo the Tenth, Sixtus the Fifth, and those later Popes, Pius the Sixth and Pius the Seventh, whose sorrows and sufferings but added increased splendour to their virtues.

All kinds of associations, Pagan and Christian, crowded in confusion upon my excited memory, as I entered Rome, for the first time, on the morning of the 31st of October, 1856, the vigil of the great festival of All Saints. My great desire, paramount to all others — whether the gratification of curiosity or of taste — was that of seeing with my own eyes things of which I had, and I say it not without shame, imperfect, if not altogether erroneous notions.

This is not to be wondered at, when it is considered that the sources of information respecting all matters Roman are tainted at the very source ; and that the great body of the Catholics of these countries generally depend, certainly have hitherto almost exclusively depended, upon Protestant writers for what little they know of the Pope, and of his venerable capital.

For instance, judge the Pope by the prevailing belief of Protestant England, derived from the representations of its press, its platform, or its pulpit ; and one beholds in him a combination of the temporal despot, and the spiritual impostor, at once the scourge of an afflicted people, and the arch-priest of Satan.   Protestant credulity regards him as one whose mission and policy it is to enslave alike the bodies and the souls of men, by fettering their civil liberty with tyrannous restrictions, and darkening and stunting their intellect by the denial of a liberal education.   In their profound ignorance of the truth, many, even fair-minded and in all other respects enlightened people, look upon the Holy Father—even the gentle and merciful Pius — not merely as the stern oppressor of his own hapless subjects, but the cause of every evil which afflicts the various nations into which Italy is divided.   In their eyes, it is the Vatican which casts its baleful shadow over the fair face of the Italian Peninsula, and shuts out from that beauteous land and its gifted races the light and warmth of national freedom.   Nay, why should not this be so, when the great object of the tyrant and impostor, who sitteth on the Seven Hills of the modern Babylon, is, according to the ravings of the fanatic enemies of the Church, to trample upon the liberties of all free countries, and make of kings and princes his footstools? The ambition of Rome, say they, never sleeps; it is as dangerous now as in the days when its thunders hurled monarchs from their thrones, and brought the haughtiest warriors as suppliants to its feet. Nor was it a Julius or a Sixtus that was alone to be dreaded; for did not a Barbarossa meekly hold the stirrup of the mule on which an Alexander, then a weak and infirm old man, rode through the streets of Venice? Those who read the history of the dark and middle ages with calm and unimpassioned judgment, and are not swayed by bigotry, or bewildered by mere names, must recognise the advantages, to the peace of nations and the progress of civilisation, which had been conferred by this very influence. But that power, so often omnipotent for good, in those dark and troublous times, when might was right, and laws were far more often written in blood than ink, is now a thing of the past; being in latter years, when every country has its own well-ordered system of government, and when a well-defined compact exists between nations, by which the weak are protected from the aggression of the strong, as unnecessary as its existence is imaginary.

It will be my grateful task to exhibit to the reader a portraiture, feeble it may be in its execution, but faithful in intention, of a modern Pope — whose whole life approaches nearer to the Divine model than that of any living man.   And this I shall endeavour to do in a subsequent place.

To behold Pius IX. was my most anxious desire —which I soon took occasion to gratify; for I was not many hours in Rome before I formed one of a considerable number of persons, mostly strangers from various countries of Europe, mixed up with ecclesiastics of different nations and orders, and students of the principal Roman Colleges, that were assembled in the great hall opening into the Pauline Chapel, the Pope's private chapel in his palace of the Quirinal.   No sooner were the folding doors flung open by the officers on duty, than, with an eagerness which nearly degenerated into a rush, the well-dressed crowd possessed themselves of every vacant place.

It was curious to note the manner and bearing of the lay portion of the strange congregation thus gathered together from almost every principal nation of the world.   Generally speaking, it was respectful, and even pious; but in not a few instances curiosity was evidently combined with a supercilious contempt "for the whole thing." The French, Spaniards, Austrians, and Italians, were grave and collected, and so were several of the English; but some of the latter evidently went to the Pope's Chapel as they had gone the previous night to the Opera, to hear the music, or to "do" it, as they would the Coliseum, or the Baths of Caracalla.   I have a lively remembrance of the remarks of one young and well-dressed Englishman, who combined, in an extraordinary degree, ignorance, irreverence, and comicality ; and of the singular patience of the intelligent and courteous ecclesiastic from whom he sought information, or to whom he freely imparted his own views and opinions of what he beheld. But none so devout and so collected as the English convert, whose identity one might discern at a glance. While others held, or used, an opera-glass, he was engaged in his missal, or absorbed in his devotions.

Novelty as well as picturesqueness were imparted to the groups around me by the variety of the costume and appearance of students of different colleges, monks and friars of different orders, and priests of different countries and races. The greater number of the ecclesiastics had their hair closely cut, and the face and chin scrupulously shaven ; while others rejoiced in beards of patriarchal grandeur, descending even to the breast. Some were clad in the graceful black and white robes of the Dominican, some in the black dress of the Jesuit, some in the dark frock and embroidered emblems of the Passionist, and others in the coarse brown woollen garb of the Franciscan. Skin of every hue, eyes of every form and colour, features of every variety, marked, even to the most careless observer, striking distinctions of country, clime, and race, and illustrated the universality of that Church which has endured for nearly two thousand years, and of which Rome is the seat and centre, as it was the great nursing mother. Look at these students, and you will behold how the youth of Asia and Africa, as in the early ages of Christianity, come to learn the great truths of religion from the teacher of all nations ; and how the Greek, whose ancestors gave to Rome her arts and her philosophy, is now clad in the academic costume of that most celebrated of Roman Colleges, the Propaganda. And though speaking the same language, their marked variety of accent betrays the respective countries which have sent these youths of fairer complexion and of larger stature ; and proves that England and Scotland, as well as Ireland, are still indebted to the liberality of Rome for the training of a portion of their Priests.

On this day, as on the next morning, and on several subsequent occasions, I had the good fortune to occupy a position which afforded me an opportunity of making myself acquainted with the personal appearance of the Cardinals, who, with the exception of those immediately in attendance on the Pope, took their respective places some time previous to the commencement of the ceremonies. And taking them all, as they sat in dignified composure, the greater number of them absorbed in meditation, or devoutly reading their breviaries, a more imposing and venerable-looking body of men, or a nobler collection of intellectual heads, it would be difficult to imagine. Let me particularise a few of them.

That tall white-haired old man, who combines the apostolic sweetness of the late Archbishop Murray with the patriarchal dignity of the late venerable Dr. Egan, Catholic Bishop of Kerry, is Cardinal Tosti, for many years past the accomplished and liberal protector of that noblest of Roman institutions, the Ospizio of San

Michele. A single anecdote will best describe the man.

When the Pope and Cardinals had left Rome, after the assassination of Count Rossi, and the attack on the Quirinal, Cardinal Tosti remained at his post at San Michele. Several of the revolutionists paid him a visit, to congratulate him on his courage and devotion.

"Sirs, I refuse your praise," was his answer: "I am no more afraid of you than were any of my colleagues who are gone away. It was through love and obedience to the Holy Father that they followed him into exile. The same motives prevent my leaving this establishment; for he has desired me not to abandon so many unfortunate persons sheltered here. Besides, I am a Roman, and you are not. I shall remain at Rome without fear. If you give me a blow of a stiletto, it will only shorten my life two or three years, for I am already seventy-two."

This was in 1848; since when many additional years have rolled over that noble head, without dimming the fire of the eye that speaks of the bright intellect within.

On the same bench sits the Capuchin Cardinal; and only that the face is not so full of colour, nor the eye so keen, you might fancy that the Cardinal with the sweeping grey beard and the brown habit, now so absorbed in mental prayer, was Julius the Second, who had just walked out of the immortal canvas of Raphael. He was the Pope's confessor, is Superior of the Capuchins, and was made Cardinal a year or two ago. When the Pope was at Gaeta, this vener-

able old man, not to compromise others, put up the
Pope's decrees upon St. Peter's with his own hand.

The Dominican, in the white robes of his illustrious
order, is Cardinal Gaudi, of most agreeable countenance
and active carriage, and whose graceful and kindly manners, as I afterwards had a personal opportunity of
knowing, harmonised with his attractive appearance.
It is not long since that he came to Rome from Piedmont, where his abilities as professor had given him great
distinction. The Pope lately raised him from the rank
of simple priest to that of Cardinal.

On the same bench, and very near to where I stood,
sat Cardinal Barnabo, Prefect of the Propaganda, with
whose name the Catholics of the United Kingdom have
been familiar of late. With head solid and compact,
eye sharp and keen, gesture lively and active, the Prefect of the Propaganda looked to be, what he is, in the
fullest vigour of his faculties, of body as of mind.

That dark, little man, whose face, thoroughly Italian,
has an expression of such religious goodness, is Cardinal
Altieri. He is a prince by birth, and has held many
offices in the State.

Cardinal Picoluomini, the relative of the new queen
of the lyric stage, whose high spirit is fully equal to her
musical and dramatic genius, is that heavy, feeble man,
of large frame, massive head and dark countenance,
who limps with difficulty to his seat.

Then besides Cardinal Reisach, whose fair and florid
complexion denotes his German origin, there are Cardinals
Barberini and Medici; the latter about the finest type

of the Italian that could well be imagined, and whose marked and striking profile seemed especially suited for a medal or a coin.

A whisper is circulated — "Here is Antonelli;" and a visible stir may be observed as the celebrated Cardinal Secretary of State, and Prime Minister of the Government of Pius IX., makes his appearance. That sallow, intensely Italian face; those great black eyes, never at rest; those parted lips, that show the glittering teeth; the jet-black hair; the worn yet defiant look, so full of intelligence, power, and pride, can belong to none but Antonelli. His very walk is a kind of stride, that speaks, as it were, of the superabundant energy of one of the most remarkable men of the day — a man relied on by many as a minister of high courage, and eminent ability, but dreaded and detested by the revolutionary party.

Cardinal Ferretti, Grand Penitentiary, whose benign expression well accords with his grey hairs, is also amongst the remarkable personages of the Papal Court. This distinguished Cardinal is the cousin of the Pope, and was his prime minister previous to the revolution. He is simple in his habits, saintly in his life, and eminent for his apostolic zeal. When Cardinal Bishop of Rieti, it happened that robbers broke into one of the churches of that city, and stole from thence the pyx, adding to the guilt of their sacrilege by carrying off its sacred contents. Upon being apprised of this abominable outrage, the Cardinal, accompanied by his clergy, walked through the streets with feet bare, and

ropes round their necks, and thus proceeded in peni-
tential procession to the market-place, where he delivered a most moving discourse on the affecting text —
" *They say to her : Woman, why weepest thou ? She
saith to them : Because they have taken away my Lord:
and I know not where they have laid him.*" — John, xx.
13. The pyx was restored that night, its sacred contents untouched.

Another face, eminently Italian, attracted my attention. It was full of intelligence and animation, and
good and kindly in its expression. It was that of the Substitute Secretary of State, Monsignor Berardi, a man of
considerable ability and excellent administrative talent,
who understands several European languages, and is
thoroughly conversant with the social and political conditions of most countries.

And on this, as on subsequent occasions, I recognised
with pleasure the fair and familiar countenance of Monsignor Talbot, whom the Catholics of London may well
remember for the unaffected piety and untiring zeal with
which he discharged the laborious duties of one of the
most important of its missions; and who is known to
the " English" strangers in Rome as one of the most
obliging and courteous of their countrymen. And his
confidential position in the Papal Court, as one of the
four principal chamberlains of his Holiness, affords him
many opportunities of rendering them valuable and
timely service.

A hush now suddenly falls on the assembly, awing
into silence the whispered comments of the strangers,

who seek for information of the obliging ecclesiastics that surround them; for the Pope is about to enter. From the door at the left-hand side of the altar—in itself most simple in its decoration—there issues forth a varied and brilliant procession of the Prelates and Princes of the Church, in the midst of whom appears the imposing person and sweet and engaging countenance of Pius the Ninth, who is conducted by attendant dignitaries to the throne at the right, or Gospel side. To me, as indeed to every stranger present, the Pope was the great object of attraction—his every look and gesture being fraught with interest, even to the unbeliever and the scoffer—but how far deeper to the Catholic worshipper from a distant land, who recognised in the mild and noble figure before him the venerable head of his Church, the spiritual sovereign of the greater portion of the Christian world, whose authority is affectionately acknowledged and willingly obeyed in every country upon which the sun shines.

The features of Pius IX. have been for many years familiar to the people of most countries, through portrait and bust; and are more remarkable for gentleness, mildness, benevolence, and a rare sweetness of expression, than for any other quality or character. A face more calculated to win confidence and inspire affection I have never seen. One smile from that tender mouth, one soft beam from those mild blue eyes, and even men would come as children to his knee. Though the very opposite of those stern and haughty Pontiffs which the Protestant imagination may picture to itself, as it thinks of a Hildebrand or a Julius, I could not conceive a manner or a bearing more full of true dignity than that of the Holy Father, as he sat enthroned amidst the Princes of the Church, or rose to intone the vespers—which he did with a musical and sonorous voice—or to impart the apostolic benediction. I have elsewhere seen many pious priests in the performance of their sacred functions; but never before did I behold a countenance more expressive of profound piety, or so illumined with that heavenly brightness which outwardly manifests the working of the spirit within. It seemed, as it were, suffused with a light from above. Heart and mind and soul appeared to be absorbed, as they really were, in the ceremonies in which he assisted; and not for a second's space did his attention wander from his devotions. He communed as truly with his God, in the midst of that splendid crowd, and with hundreds of eager eyes riveted upon him, as if he were kneeling in his private chamber, and asking for another day of strength to meet the difficulties of his exalted but perilous position. I do not write this as the result of a single impression, but of one which several other opportunities only tended to confirm the more strongly. For on some seven or eight subsequent occasions I had the good fortune to be present when the Pope assisted in person at various ceremonies of the Church, more or less grand and impressive; and on each occasion I was struck by the same rapt piety, the same devout abstraction, the same beautiful expression of that holiness which irradiates the human face as with beams of celestial light.

The most prejudiced person who beholds the Holy Father engaged in any act of devotion, must give him credit for genuine piety ; but the stranger who is accustomed to regard everything Catholic with distrust, if not with aversion, compensates himself for his involuntary admiration of the bearing of the Pope, by a belief in his bigotry as a priest, and his despotic tendencies as a politician and a sovereign. Even Catholics of these countries, forgetting or overlooking the events which rendered the first years of the Pontificate of Pius IX. so full of profound and startling interest, not unfrequently fall into strange errors with respect to his character and career as a temporal ruler. It is well, on this account, that a brief history of those events in which Pius IX. bore so prominent a part, should form a portion of a volume which is chiefly written with the intention of encountering unjust prejudice, and removing injurious misconception.

Let us therefore follow this good and holy man throughout his whole career, in every stage of his life, from the hour when, as a boy, he first quitted the side of his affectionate and pious mother, to the moment when, in the ripe maturity of manhood, we at length behold him clothed with the highest earthly authority, and offering up to God, as a willing sacrifice, the sorrows and afflictions of a loving but lacerated human heart.

C

CHAP. II.

The Pope : his Birth and Education. — He studies for the Ministry.—His Malady cured.—His First Mass.—Goes to Chili.—Instance of his Charity to an English Officer.—Returns to Rome.
—Is created Archbishop of Spoleto.—Difficulties of his Position.
—Appointed Cardinal Bishop of Imola.—His charitable and
pious Works.—Is elected Pope.

GIOVANNI MARIA MASTAI FERRETTI was born in Sinigaglia on the 13th of May, 1792, of the Count Jerome
and the Countess Catherine Solazzi of the same city.
In 1803, being then in his eleventh year, he was
placed by his parents in the college of a religious body
called *Scolopii*, at Volterra, which was then justly celebrated for its course of studies, and the wise system
of instruction pursued by its gifted conductors. The
noble aspect of the youth, the sweetness of his disposition combined with the firmness of his character, the
vivacity and liveliness of his discourse, as well as the
talent which he displayed, soon gained for him the
love and esteem, not only of his companions, but also
of his masters. He was so distinguished in his studies,
that, on the occasion of the aunt of the present Emperor of France, Eloise Baciocchi, then Queen of
Etruria, visiting Volterra, and being received by its
students, he was selected to preside at what is termed

"an academy in verse," which was given in her honour, and in the name of his fellow-collegians.

In 1808, while yet pursuing his collegiate course, he was seized with violent fits of epilepsy. Nevertheless, in the following year, and in accordance with the desire of his pious mother, he received the first tonsure at the hands of Monsignor Tecontie, the bishop of Volterra; and in the October of the same year he hastened to Rome to complete his ecclesiastical studies.

This was to him the more pleasing, as his mother's wishes were wholly in accordance with his own aspirations, which ever tended to the ecclesiastical state; whilst he was also aware that nowhere as in Rome can those studies and those preparations, which train the mind and heart for the sacred duties of the priesthood, be so well attended to and completed.

In the Capital he lived with his uncle, a canon of the Vatican Basilica; but the latter being obliged to fly from Rome, in consequence of the sad events which shortly afterwards ensued, the young Mastai also, in 1810, retired from that city. In 1812, on account of his distinguished birth, he was summoned to join the guard of honour in Milan; but an exemption was accorded him because of the distressing disease to which he was then subject. From this simple fact seems to have been derived the report, which has been so currently received, but which is devoid of all reality, that Count Mastai presented himself to Pius VII. in Rome, with the intention of embracing a military life, and solicited admission to the ranks of the Noble

c 2

Guard. In truth, Mastai never adopted the military profession, nor did his disposition prompt him to such a career.

He continued in his native city till the return of Pius VII. to his States. When that sorrow-stricken Pontiff passed through Sinigaglia, Mastai had the honour of being presented to him, and soon after hastened once more to Rome, where he witnessed, in May, 1814, the enthusiastic reception given by the citizens to the Holy Father in the Piazza del Popolo. The Ecclesiastical Academy having been reopened, Mastai attended its schools, but as a layman, the disease with which he was still affected preventing his aspiring to sacred orders. But God, who intended him for the ministry, inspired him, by inward impulse, not to despair of attaining that ardently desired state; and, reassuming the ecclesiastical dress, he commenced soon after his theological studies, under the direction of the distinguished Professor Joseph Graziosi. The attacks of his malady becoming less violent, though still of occasional recurrence, he was admitted to minor orders.

In 1818, Monsignor Odescalchi, who afterwards laid aside the purple, to become a member of the order of Saint Ignatius, and was then a Prelate of the Court, invited him to take part in a mission which was about being given in his native province of Sinigaglia. Through the anxious solicitude of the Pontiff, after his return to Rome, bands of zealous missionaries were everywhere scattered throughout the provinces, to re-awaken the spirit of religion, which was, well-nigh ex-

tinct in the breasts of the people, in consequence of the
disorder which had so long and so universally prevailed.
In this mission to Sinigaglia, together with the above-
mentioned Prelate, was engaged the Bishop of Macce-
rata, Monsignor Strambi, whose cause for beatification
is now being proceeded with.   Mastai, inasmuch as his
ecclesiastical orders allowed him, engaged in the mission with singular zeal, and with the most happy results;
and returning to Rome, much improved in health, he
asked for and obtained a dispensation to be promoted to
the holy orders of sub-deacon and deacon, and was ordained subdeacon on the 18th of December, 1818.   His
aspirations were not yet satisfied; but looking forward,
ever more and more anxiously, to the priesthood, he
solicited from the Holy Father a further dispensation,
which was also granted, but with the condition that,
when offering the Holy Sacrifice, he should be assisted
by another clergyman.   The Pontiff had shown himself
so loving and paternal towards him, that he resolved to
ask for a special audience, in order, if possible, to have
even this condition removed.   In this audience the
Holy Father, with his usual benignity, taking him
affectionately by the hand, said — " Yes, we will grant
you even this favour, as I believe that for the future
you will be no longer affected with your disease." And
so indeed it has happened; as from the close of the
year 1818, to the present day, a period of nearly forty
years, he has never once been subject to it !   Thus did
Divine Providence guide the lips of the Holy Father,
to whom one might almost imagine was disclosed the

future destiny of the youthful Levite, who then knelt
before him in earnest supplication.   On the festival of
Easter, 1819, Mastai celebrated Mass for the first time,
having chosen the church of St. Anne *dei Falignami*
for that purpose.   His special motive for this selection
was, that in an adjoining orphanage he had hitherto devoted himself to the care and maintenance of about 100
poor orphans, whom he personally instructed in their
catechism and religious duties, while at the same time
they were prepared, by a suitable training, for various
branches of useful industry ; so that being thus made
good Christians, they might also one day become valuable members of society.

In 1823, a Canon of the Cathedral of St. James, in
Chili, having come to Rome to solicit from the Pontiff a
representative of the Holy See in that remote republic,
Mastai was invited by Cardinal della Genga, then Vicar
of Rome, and afterwards by Cardinal Gonsalvi, to take
part in that mission with Monsignor Muzi, afterwards
Bishop of Castello.   At that time such distant jour-
neys were not viewed without just alarm and well-
founded apprehensions of danger ; and the Countess
his mother wrote to Cardinal Gonsalvi, Secretary of
State, entreating him most forcibly not to permit her
son to undertake this remote mission.   But Mastai,
nowise affected by those dangers which a fond mother's
fancy so readily conjured up, received the invitation as
a voice from heaven, summoning him to a new and
wider field of labour.   Wherefore, yet ignorant of the
solicitations of his parent, he presented himself to the
Holy Father, who said to him,—"The Countess your

mother has written to the Secretary of State to prevent your journey ; but we have written to her, in answer, that you will surely return safe from this mission." This occurred in the month of June, 1823; and the prediction of the Pontiff was verified to the letter, as about three years afterwards Mastai revisited his friends in Sinigaglia; the Apostolic Delegate having, in consequence of the breaking out of a revolution in Chili, deemed it more prudent not to delay longer in that country. While on his route to Chili, he was obliged to stop at Monte Video and other places in South America ; and wherever he stopped he lost not a moment in exercising his ministry, to which he also untiringly devoted himself during the two years that he spent in Santiago. Besides devoting all his time and all his talents to preaching, instructing, and confessing, he gave to the poor, and applied to charitable uses, the means of which he was possessed ; so that, when afterwards made Archbishop, he had to sell some property belonging to him in Rome, in order to pay for the Bulls which are expedited on those occasions.

A circumstance of which I lately became aware is too characteristic of the illustrious object of this sketch not to be mentioned in connection with his mission to Chili. As the Apostolic Delegate and his companions and suite were on their way to the capital, they had to put up at a miserable wayside inn, far remote from any other human habitation. In this comfortless abode lay an English officer, tossing and writhing on a bed of sickness, many thousand miles away from home and friends. The sad condition of this unhappy gentleman, a stranger and a " heretic," became known to the Italian ecclesiastics; one of whom charitably remained behind his companions to watch by the sick man, whom he nursed with all the tenderness of a mother or a sister. Nor did he leave his side till he had the satisfaction of seeing him restored to health and strength. The Italian priest who so stopped by the wayside, to minister to the sick stranger, was Mastai Ferretti, now Pius IX.*

In December, 1825, on his return to Rome, he was appointed, by Leo XII., to the presidency of the vast ospizio of San Michele. The prudence and solicitude with which he discharged the laborious functions of that office are yet gratefully remembered by those who were then acquainted with the institution, and formed a prelude to the noble works which he was afterwards to achieve in a wider and more glorious field. After having for twenty months presided over this ospizio, the same Pontiff destined him to the Archiepiscopal See of Spoleto, which was the Pope's native diocese.

In this city the new Bishop founded a large orphanage for poor children intended for the mechanical arts; and in this labour of practical charity we may recognise the same untiring zeal, in ministering to the wants of the helpless and indigent, which had already marked his early priesthood. His work was the more praise-

* The name of the British officer was Miller.

worthy, as being established, not as a mere temporary institution, but as one that in future times and for future generations was to relieve the destitute orphan, and remain a perpetual monument of his benevolence and charity.

Nor was he at this early period of his career without experiencing those more public difficulties which, in a terribly aggravated form, were to cast so sad a gloom over the first years of his Pontificate. In 1831 some disturbances were excited through the States, which, however, with the aid of the Austrian troops, were soon repressed. This was a trying conjuncture for our Archbishop, as about 4000 insurgents, who, on the approach of the Austrians, had abandoned the siege of Civita Castellana, took up their quarters in Spoleto. No immediate succour could be hoped for; but still Mastai did not abandon his flock, or lose courage in the emergency. Nay, partly by entreaties and expostulations, and partly by promising some few thousand scudi to the troops, he so far succeeded with them as to induce them to return to their allegiance, and yield up their arms to the constituted authorities. These, including many thousand stand of muskets and five pieces of cannon, were transmitted to Rome. This indeed was one of those sweet and grateful triumphs which, throughout all times, men of his kind have won over passion, and even despair. At this same period, the authorities of the Provinces of Perugia and Spoleto having fled, Cardinal Bernetti, the then Secretary of State, entrusted to the Archbishop their double functions,

which during the disturbances he was *ad interim*
obliged to discharge. The band of insurgents was
headed by a certain Tercognani, to whom his followers
gave the title of General; yet such was their distrust
of him, that, on the distribution of the above-mentioned
sum, many of the under-officers, with those whom they
commanded, declared that they would not receive it
from his hands; and asked to have it distributed by
the Archbishop—a proof of how his uprightness of
character and his disinterestedness were known and
valued by all, even the armed foes of those institutions
which he represented by his office, and defended by his
authority.

We may here incidentally remark that, Spoleto
being the capital city of the province, a self-consti-
tuted committee arose in it during the revolution,
and assumed to itself the entire and uncontrolled
management of affairs. One styled himself Minister
of War, another of the Interior, and so forth. Their
sphere of action was however every day more and
more circumscribed, as each principal city of the province claimed for itself a like independence. Things
were carried on in the same manner in Perugia and
the other provinces. This may serve as an illustration
of the difficulties which are at every step to be found
in the cherished scheme of a union of the Italian States.

In the January of the ensuing year an earthquake
laid desolate a great part of the province; and thus a
new field was opened up to the charity of the good Archbishop. Everywhere he hastened to the relief of those

who were the most distressed, especially visiting and comforting those districts whose inhabitants had no shelter left save what was afforded them by rudely constructed huts.   The faithful Pastor suffered in his flock, and made their misfortunes his own.   We have, in our own times, seen heavier calamities fall upon a portion of a proud empire, whose statesmen and whose press treat with contempt the rule of ecclesiastics; but, notwithstanding the pride and power of that empire, we beheld its innocent and unoffending subjects dying like mangy dogs upon the public highways, while efforts, clumsy and unsympathising, were being tardily made for their relief.   It had been well for Ireland if, in the days of her tribulation, a Mastai had presided over the councils of her rulers — or if there had been less of the spirit of Political Economy, and more of the spirit of the Gospel.

It pleased the Sovereign Pontiff Gregory XVI. to translate the subject of our memoir, in the Consistory of December, 1832, from the Archiepiscopal See of Spoleto to the Episcopal See of Imola, in which he was successor to Cardinal Iustiniani, who had resigned its charge.   In this see he was decorated with the purple, being reserved *in petto* in the Consistory of the 23rd of December, 1839, and proclaimed Cardinal on the 14th of December, 1840.

In Imola he promoted many useful and permanent institutions.   Amongst others, a college for ecclesiastical students whose means did not allow them to complete their studies in the Episcopal Seminary; and an orphanage, or rather a society for the guardianship and maintenance of about thirty children of the poorest class destined for the mechanical arts, who were provided with their daily food, and likewise received two good suits of clothes in the year, one for winter, and the other for summer. On festival days these children were assembled by certain ecclesiastics in a small chapel, and there carefully instructed in the doctrines of the Church and in the knowledge of their religious duties. The same ecclesiastics also superintended their daily conduct, when they were sent to the shops of the city, to learn or pursue their different trades. To the care and management of the Sisters of Charity, the good Bishop entrusted a conservatorio of female orphans; and, in the same establishment, founded two female schools, one for girls of the poorer class, and the other for those of the more wealthy. He also entrusted the public hospital to the same Sisters; and, adjoining it, he erected an asylum for those who were deprived of the use of their noblest faculty.

Having accomplished these and other works, so congenial to his tender and compassionate nature, Cardinal Mastai crowned them by one of still holier humanity. To found a refuge for female penitents had long been the object of his fondest wishes. To his mind was always present the touching spectacle, to use his own expressive words, of the "lost daughters of the world soliciting admission to the fold of Jesus." For those unhappy beings his heart bled; and to afford them an asylum from the horrors of a life of misery and a death of despair, he freely sacrificed his every available resource. Out of his own private means he purchased and suitably fitted up a house for the reception of a number of these poor outcasts, as also for the accommodation of some nuns of the noble order of the Good Shepherd, who, at his urgent request, were sent from the parent house at Angiers, to take charge of the institution. That day was a proud one for Cardinal Mastai that witnessed the arrival of four Sisters at his palace; which he placed at their disposal, until their future abode was fully prepared for their reception. With indescribable joy he welcomed the good Sisters, whom he had so anxiously implored to come to his assistance in his work of charity; and the simple Nuns were filled with gratitude, at first not entirely divested of embarrassment, at the attentions lavished upon them by a Prince of the Church, who himself waited upon them while they sat at his table, and ministered to their wants with more than the humility of a servant. The feeling of delight with which Cardinal Mastai witnessed the accomplishment of an object long dear to his heart may be understood by the following letter, which he addressed to the Superior of the House of Angiers:—

"Very Reverend Mother General,—Your Reverence must already have received from your dear daughters the details of their happy arrival at Imola; but it is proper that I should myself inform you of this event, and, at the same time, that I should express to you the great consolation that I experience in seeing myself enriched with this little troop of sacred virgins, who in a few days will open

the mission for the salvation of so many poor wandering
sheep.   I feel certain that, with the grace of God, they will
reconduct them to the fold of the Prince of Pastors, Jesus
Christ.   May eternal praise be given to this God of Mercies;
and I beg your Reverence to accept the assurance of my
deepfelt gratitude.   I have the consolation of having them
with me in my palace.   I have great reason to thank the
Lord, who holds in his hands the hearts of men ; but it appears to me that he has placed those of your daughters, not
in his hands, but in his own heart.   I will not fail to render
them every assistance in their wants ; and from that thought
I pass to the pleasure of assuring you again that I am, with
deep esteem, the affectionate servant of your Maternity,

✠ JEAN MARIE, Cardinal MASTAI,
" Archbishop.
" Imola, 14th September, 1845."

Thus did the wise Prelate seek, by his new institutions, to provide for the wants and necessities of his
flock ; and it is difficult to know which most to admire,
the solicitude of the Pastor, or the generosity and
benevolence which prompted such works, embracing
all classes, and excluding none from their beneficent
operation.

To preserve in the ecclesiastics of his diocese the
spirit of their holy vocation, he opened a house for
spiritual exercises, where, at stated times, a portion of
the clergy devoted themselves for ten days to retreat—
an arrangement which, though immediately affecting the
clergy, yet exercised a beneficial influence on all his
flock, as it more fitly prepared for the duties of the
ministry those who were to be their religious guides.
He also repaired some churches, restored the episcopal

residence, and completed the front of the cathedral church, which had hitherto remained unfinished.

An incident that occurred in the February of 1846, evinced the noble courage with which the Prelate was endowed, and the singular efficacy which Providence communicated to his words. One evening of the Carnival, a little before dusk, the Cardinal was making his accustomed visit before the altar of the Holy Sacrament in the Cathedral, when the sacristan rushed towards him, crying out " to hasten for God's sake, as murder was being perpetrated in the sacristy." Invoking the Divine aid, the Cardinal at once arose, and hastening to the spot, found there, lying upon a form, a youth of about twenty years of age, who having been dangerously wounded by a bayonet thrust, had just taken refuge in the sacred building. The Cardinal had scarcely reached the sufferer, when three armed men rushed in, with the wicked intention of completing their deed of blood. But nowise dismayed by their naked weapons, and their looks of deadly hate, Mastai boldly confronted the assassins, and, presenting his pectoral cross, described to them the enormity of their crime, and commanded them to retire. His words, so full of courage, and uttered as with the authority of one commissioned by Heaven, struck terror into their breasts, and were silently and almost unconsciously obeyed.

Mastai was now about to quit the scene of so many pious labours, and so many works of charity and love, for a splendid destiny, the grandest and the loftiest which man can be called on to fulfil on this earth; but one ever fraught, if not with perils and sorrows, at least with the gravest anxieties and the profoundest cares.

In the beginning of June, 1846, being then engaged with a considerable number of his clergy in a spiritual retreat, he received the announcement of the death of Gregory XVI. Immediately on the receipt of the sad intelligence, he hastened to the episcopal residence, and having celebrated the last obsequies of the deceased Pontiff, at once proceeded to Rome, unconscious of the fate which there awaited him. He arrived in the Capital on the evening of the 12th of June; and in forty-eight hours afterwards he and his brethren of the Sacred College entered the Conclave. On the 15th, the testing of the votes commenced; the evening of the 16th saw him unanimously chosen; and on the morning of the 17th, the election of Pius IX. was proclaimed to the Christian world.

It was in these words, so truly characteristic of his modest and humble nature, that the newly-elected Pontiff announced his elevation to his brothers at Sinigaglia:—

"Rome, 16th June, at $\frac{3}{4}$ past 11, p.m.

"The blessed God, who humbles and exalts, has been pleased to raise me from insignificance to the most sublime dignity on earth. May His most holy will be ever done. I am sensible to a certain extent of the immense weight of such a charge, and I also feel my utter incapacity, not to say the entire nullity of my powers. Cause prayers to be offered, and you also pray for me. The Conclave has

lasted forty-eight hours.   If the city should wish to make
any public demonstration on the occasion, I request you will
take measures — indeed, I desire it — that the whole sum so
destined be applied to purposes which may be judged useful
to the city, by the chief magistrate and the council.   As to
yourselves, dear brothers, I embrace you with all my heart
in Jesus Christ; and, far from exulting, take pity on your
brother, who gives you all his apostolic blessing."

D

CHAP. III.

NEVER did sovereign ascend the throne with a heart more full of love for his people, or with a more fervent desire of contributing to their welfare and happiness; and rarely, if ever, did sovereign enter upon a path so abundantly bestrewn with embarrassments and with difficulties. Devoted to the Church, of which he was chosen to be head and protector, Pio Nono was not the less the friend of rational liberty, and the advocate of enlightened progress. Thoroughly acquainted with his native country, and conversant with its interests and its wants, he resolved, from the first hour of his Pontificate, to so use the power entrusted to him by Heaven, as to remedy the evils which he knew to exist, and put an end to abuses of which he could not be unconscious. Convinced that no attempt at reform could be successful so long as pains and penalties for former transgressions were still enforced against a considerable

number of his subjects, who had been connected, more
or less prominently, with revolutionary disturbances in
the reign of his predecessor; and also feeling the utmost compassion for those who suffered, whether in mind
or body— Pius IX. resolved to signalise his accession to
the throne by an act of grace which would shed a light,
as if from above, upon many sorrowing homes and de-
spairing families.   There were those who counselled the
Pope to moderate his generosity within the limits of
prudence, and to have a care how he included in a general pardon many men whose past career was no reliable
guarantee for their future loyalty.   But these cautious
advisers spoke to one whose soul was overflowing with
love and compassion, and who yearned to embrace his
entire people within the arms of a fond father.   And,
accordingly, on the 16th of July, just one month
after his election, Pius IX. published the following
decree of amnesty :—

   " Pius IX. to his faithful subjects : salutation and apostolic benediction.
   " In these days, when our heart is moved to see public
joy manifested at our being raised to the Pontificate, we
cannot refrain from a feeling of grief in thinking that a
certain number of families are unable to participate in the
common joy, because they bear the pain of some offences
committed by one of their members against society, against
the sacred rights of the legitimate Prince.
   " We now desire to cast a look of compassion on the inexperienced youth which has been led away by deceitful
hopes, in the midst of political discord, where it has been
rather the seduced than the seducer.   It is for that reason

D 2

that we wish to stretch out the hand, and offer the peace
of the heart to those misguided children who will evince
sincere repentance.   Now that our good people have shown
towards us their affection, and their constant veneration for
the Holy See, and for our person, we are persuaded that we
may pardon without danger.   We, therefore, ordain that
the commencement of our Pontificate shall be solemnised by
the following act of sovereign grace : —

"1. There is granted to all our subjects who are undergoing punishment for political offences a remission of their
sentences, provided that they make in writing a solemn
declaration*, on their honour, that they will not in any
manner or at any time abuse this grace, and will for the
future fulfil the duties of good and faithful subjects.

"2. Those of our subjects who have fled to foreign countries in consequence of political crimes, may profit by the
present resolutions in making known within the delay of one
year to our Apostolic Nuncios or other representatives of the
Holy See, their desire to profit by this act of our clemency.

"3. We equally pardon those who, for having taken part
in any conspiracies against the State, are under political surveillance, or may have been declared incapable of holding
municipal offices.

"4. It is our desire that all criminal prosecutions for
political offences which have not yet received definitive
judgment should be instantly put a stop to, and that the
prisoners be set at liberty, unless any of them may demand

* The following is the form of the required declaration: — "I, the
undersigned, acknowledge the receipt of a singular favour in the generous and spontaneous pardon which the indulgence of the Sovereign
Pontiff, Pope Pius IX., and my lawful sovereign, has accorded me for
the part which I may have taken in any manner soever in the attempts
which have disturbed public order and attacked the lawfully constituted
authority in his temporal dominions ; promise, upon my word of honour,
not to abuse in any way, nor at any time, this act of his sovereign clemency, and pledge myself, besides, to fulfil faithfully all the duties of a
loyal subject."

the continuation of their trials, in order that their innocence may be proved.

" 5. There shall not be included in the provisions of the preceding articles the small number of ecclesiastics, of military officers, and *employés* of the Government, who have been already condemned, or have fled, or are now under trial for political offences. With regard to those we reserve our decision until we shall have obtained information as to their particular position.

" 6. There are also excluded from the present amnesty crimes and ordinary offences, which are subject to the jurisdiction of the tribunal.

" We are anxious to feel a confidence that those who will avail themselves of our clemency will know how at all times to respect their duties and their honour. We hope, moreover, that their minds, softened by our pardon, will lay aside their civil hatreds, which are always the occasion and the effect of political passions, in order to draw closer those bonds of peace by which God desires that all the sons of the same father shall be united ; but if our hope be deceived, it would be with bitter pain that we should call to mind that, if clemency be the sweetest attribute of sovereignty, justice is its first duty.

" Given at Rome this 16th day of July, 1846, in the first year of our Pontificate.

(Signed) " PIUS P. P. IX."

This noble evidence of the great heart of Pius was hailed with ecstacy by a people already fascinated by the sweet countenance and modest deportment of their new ruler. Vivas rent the air ; blessings and prayers followed his steps; flowers were cast beneath his feet; and almost instinctively forming themselves into impromptu

processions, one of the most excitable and demonstrative
of the Italian people proceeded through the streets of
Rome, with music and banners, to pour out before the
palace of their sovereign an enthusiasm which appeared
to know no limit, and which could with difficulty find
an appropriate utterance.   And the solid earth seemed
to rock, and the very heavens to tremble, as peal
after peal of wild and frenzied cheering burst from
mighty masses of the populace, when, yielding repeatedly to the fond importunity of his subjects, the
Pope came forth on the balcony of the Quirinal, and
with graceful gesture imparted to them the Apostolic
benediction.   Gratitude, with pardonable vehemence,
sought a natural expression in the language of hyper-
bole ; and even the pen, more sober and less impetuous
than the tongue, became the vehicle of the most im-
passioned exaggerations.

   Very many of the political prisoners, who soon
flocked into Rome, not content with signing the
pledge of honour — the only condition imposed by the
terms of the amnesty — added, of their free accord,
such gratuitous vows as these :— " I swear by my head,
and the heads of my children, that I will, to the death,
be faithful to Pius IX." — " I swear to shed all
blood for Pius IX."— " I renounce my share of Paradise
if ever I betray the oath of honour which binds me to
Pius IX."

   But amidst this frenzy of enthusiasm there were many
who were far from being content.   The representatives
of despotic Powers witnessed with alarm and apprehen-

sion these popular ovations, but still more the beneficent acts to which they owed their origin. The cries and cheers that rang so frequently through the streets and squares of the Eternal City, in homage of the illustrious promoter of reform and exalted friend of rational liberty, sounded harshly in the ears of ministers and statesmen grown grey in the service of despotism. And ominously, too, did these wild accents fall upon the startled souls of those who, with a full knowledge of the fickle and impulsive people by whom they were uttered, and a sad experience of events still recent, shuddered as they anticipated the license to which such gatherings, processions, and demonstrations, were ultimately, and not remotely, to lead. To their alarmed fancy, the dagger of the anarchist gleamed darkly beneath the flowers of the festival. Nor were their fears without a cause. For, mixed up with the masses, consisting mainly of the honest and the well-meaning, and ostentatiously parading their enthusiasm and their gratitude, were men who, without feeling the slightest sympathy with the public joy, or the least reverence for the sovereign whose reign was inaugurated by a deed of gracious mercy, were even then planning how best to turn all this enthusiasm and all this rejoicing to their own purposes — which aimed, not at the amelioration of existing institutions, but at their overthrow.

The disciples and followers of Joseph Mazzini were even thus early at their work. And never was a more subtle and crafty policy mapped out for the guidance of a political confederation. A few extracts from the writings of Mazzini, and one or two of the more active members of his party, many of whom the amnesty permitted to enter Rome, will most fittingly display their intentions, and the nature of the means through which they sought to carry them into execution.

One of the most ardent of those who protested their gratitude to the Pope was Joseph Galletti, of Bologna, whose sentence of capital punishment, for his participation in the conspiracy of 1845, had been commuted into imprisonment for life, and the door of whose dungeon had just been flung open by the general pardon. This document had been alleged against him on his trial :—

" Our enemies are many : first of all the clergy, the nobility, many proprietors, lastly government *employés*. At the cry of liberty, shall be instituted in every city revolutionary committees, which shall make sure of the said persons the most suspected, and whose liberty or survival might bring great detriment to the cause. As a rule for the sentences of the committees, two sorts of persons are to be distinguished. 1. Those who are indifferent to the cause, but have committed no excess against its partisans, and are attached to government through love of quiet. For these you must use all zeal to interest them. 2. Those who, *employés* or not, have openly shown themselves our enemies, upsetting us in every way; and these chiefly shall be deprived of life. The manner of arrest, without violence and by night : put in prison and slain. You must use in that the greatest prudence and secrecy, giving out then either that they are hid, or exiled, or imprisoned provisionally. And all that not to excite tumults and awaken horror, as happened in the Septemberings. Their deaths to be speedy, and without torment."

Ricciardi announced that—

"To acquire independence needs revolution and war : to put aside all considerations originating in the progress of knowledge, civilisation, industry, increase of riches and public prosperity. . . . The fatal plant, born in Judæa, has only reached this high point of growth and vigour because it was watered with waves of blood.   Would you have an error take root among men, put fire and sword to it. Would you have it fall, make it the object of your gibes. . . . The question is not of a popular assembly, fluctuating, uncertain, slow to deliberate : but there needs a hand of iron, which alone can rule a people hitherto accustomed to differences of opinion, and, what is still more, a people corrupted, enervated, made vile by slavery. . . . Soon a new era will begin for men, the glorious era of a redemption quite otherwise than that announced by Christ."

But the best exponent of the process by which revolution was made a science is Joseph Mazzini.   In his address of October, 1846, issued from Paris to the friends of Italy, he says :—

"In great countries it is by the people we must go to regeneration ; in yours by the princes. We must absolutely make them of our side. It is easy. The Pope will march in reform through principle and of necessity ; the King of Piedmont through the idea of the crown of Italy ; the Grand Duke of Tuscany through inclination and irritation ; the King of Naples through force ; and the little princes will have to think of other things besides reform.   The people yet in servitude can only sing its wants. *Profit by the least concession to assemble the masses, were it only to testify gratitude.   Fêtes, songs, assemblies,* numerous relations established among men of all opinions, suffice to make ideas gush out, *to give the people the feeling of its strength, and render it exacting.* . . . . Italy is still what France was before the Revolution : she wants, then, her Mirabeau, Lafayette, and others. A great lord may be held back by his material interests, *but he may be taken by vanity.* Leave him the chief place whilst he will go with you. There are few who would go to the end. *The essential thing is, that the goal of the great revolution be unknown to them : let us never let them see more than the first step.* In Italy, the clergy is rich in the money and faith of the people. You must *manage* them in both those interests, and as much as possible make their influence of use. If you could create a Savonarola in every capital, we should make giant strides. The clergy is not the enemy of liberal institutions. Seek, then, to associate them to this first work, which must be considered as the obligatory vestibule of the temple of Equality. Without the vestibule the sanctuary remains shut. Do not attack the clergy, neither in fortune nor orthodoxy. Promise them liberty, and you will see them march with you. . . . In Italy the people is yet to be created : but it is ready to tear the envelope which holds it. Speak often, much, and everywhere of its misery and wants. The people does not understand ; but the active part of society is penetrated by these sentiments of compassion for the people, and sooner or later acts. Learned discussions are neither necessary nor opportune. There are regenerative words which contain all that need be often repeated to the people. Liberty, rights of man, progress, equality, fraternity, are what the people will understand, above all when opposed to the words, despotism, privileges, tyranny, slavery, &c. The difficulty is not to convince the people : it is to get it together. The day of its assembly will be the day of the new era. . . . Nearly two thousand years ago, a great philosopher, called Christ, preached the fraternity which the world yet seeks. Accept, then, all the help offered to you. Whoever will make one step forward, must be yours till he quits you. A king gives a more liberal law; applaud him, and ask for the one that must follow. A minister shows intention of progress; give him out as a model. A lord affects to pout at his privileges; put yourself under his direction: if he will stop, you have time to let him go: he will remain isolated and without strength against you, and you will have a thousand ways to make unpopular all who oppose your projects. All personal discontent, all deceptions, all bruised ambition, may serve the cause of progress by giving them a new direction. . . . . The army is the greatest enemy to the progress of socialism. It must be paralysed by the moral education of the people. When once public opinion has imbibed the idea, that the army, created to defend the country, must in no case meddle with internal politics, and must respect the people, you may march without it, and even against it, without danger. . . . . The clergy has only half of the social doctrine. It wishes, like us, for brotherhood, which it calls charity. But its hierarchy and habits make it the imp of authority, that is to say, despotism. We must take what good there is, and cut the bad. Try to make equality penetrate the Church, and all will go on. Clerical power is personified in the Jesuits. The odium of that name is already a power for the socialists. Make use of it . . . . Associate! associate! everything is in that word. The secret societies give irresistible strength to the party that can call upon them. Do not fear to see them split: the more the better. All go to the same end by different ways. The secret will be often violated: so much the better: the secret is necessary to give security to the members, but a certain transparency is needed to inspire fire in the stationary. When a great number of associates, receiving the word of order to spread an idea and make it public opinion, shall be able to concert a movement, they will find the old building pierced in every part, and falling, as if by miracle, at the least breath of progress. They will be astonished themselves, to see flying before the single power of opinion, kings, lords, the rich, the priests, who formed the carcass of the old social edifice. Courage, then, and perseverance!"

The transparency of danger to which Mazzini alludes, has been unveiled by Cantalupo of Naples:—

"1. The society is formed for the indispensable destruction of all the Governments of the Peninsula, and to form a single State of all Italy in republican form. . . . 30. Members who will not obey the orders of the secret society, and those who unveil its mysteries, shall be poignarded without remission. 31. The secret tribunal shall pronounce the sentence, pointing out one or two associates for its immediate execution. 32. The associate who shall refuse to execute the sentence shall be held perjured, and as such put to death on the spot. 33. If the victim succeed in escaping, he shall be pursued incessantly in every place; and the guilty shall be struck by an invisible hand, were he sheltered on the bosom of his mother, or in the tabernacle of Christ. . . . 54. Each tribunal shall be competent not only to judge guilty adepts, but to put to death all persons whom it shall devote to death."

This was the policy, these were the proposed means of action, of the men who recognised in Mazzini their apostle and leader; and a policy more ruinous to true liberty and substantial progress, it were impossible to imagine; or means more crafty, or more treacherous, not dishonesty itself could invent.

Here, on the one hand, was the large-hearted, high-souled Pontiff, abounding in love for his people, anxious to redress their grievances, to remove every just cause of discontent, and to confer upon them the largest amount of freedom compatible with safety and the preservation of interests — sacred not merely in his own eyes, but in the estimation of the Christian world; — and, on the other, a band of insane revolutionists, who, gathered from different parts of the Italian Peninsula, were sworn to subvert and destroy all forms of government that stood in the path of their reckless ambition, or that stopped short of the realisation of their utterly impracticable schemes.   These men were the worst, because the most insidious, enemies that a reforming ruler could have combined against him; for their fixed and settled plan of action was, as may be seen by the instructions of their teacher, to flatter and cajole, to seduce and corrupt, every individual or class that could serve their purpose, — to inflame the public mind by exciting the most extravagant hopes of changes which could never be soberly contemplated,—and to turn against the Pope and his government, as instruments of destruction, the very reforms which he voluntarily conceded !

These were the worst enemies of the Pope, as of true liberty; but they were not the only enemies with whom he had to contend.   Austria, that held in her grasp some of the fairest portions of Italy, experienced even more alarm than indignation, as she beheld the noble attitude of Pius IX., and saw how the spirit emanating from the Vatican was kindling a new and dangerous fire in the breast of a down-trodden people. Wily in her councils, powerful in her arms, and mighty in her resources, Austria was, from the very outset, the most formidable enemy of reforms which she had every reason to dread. Naples, too, viewed with jealousy the onward progress of the Pope, and subsequently attempted to hide from her people the knowledge of measures which he had conceded to his subjects. Smaller Powers also regarded with dismay the march of reform, and trembled for their feeble though cherished tyrannies. Nor was France, which was in a short time to be the theatre of one of the most remarkable revolutions recorded in her history, believed to be altogether sincere in her professions of approval and admiration of the benevolent acts and reforming spirit of the Pope.

Nor is it difficult to heighten the picture of the almost insurmountable difficulties which surrounded the path and followed the footsteps of Pius IX. The alarm of many of the Cardinals was great, but, taking all circumstances into consideration, by no means unfounded. They remembered the amnesty of 1831, which had only given the opportunity for violent protestations and fresh plots; and they could not believe that the amnesty of 1846 would be productive of more fortunate results. The Pope held his first Consistory on the 27th of July; when Cardinal Macchi, in replying to the allocution, thus pointed out the apprehended danger: —

" We think, at the same time, to what tempests the Church is exposed, and by what license and effrontery of opinions men, unbridled to every mischief, leave nothing untried to deprave manners with wicked boldness, to precipitate the ignorant into the abyss of error, to overthrow every power, and even the Catholic Church itself, if that were possible."

Yet, notwithstanding the complicated difficulties of his position, Pius boldly persevered in his mission of clemency and reform. He personally inquired into and improved the administration of the public departments; he rigorously examined into the management of hospitals, prisons, and religious institutions, and compelled such changes as he deemed advisable; he punished fraud and extortion, especially if practised on the poor, with the sternest severity; he promoted employment by useful works, and stimulated industry by encouragement and reward; he introduced reforms into the collection of the public revenue, and the management of the finances; he remitted taxes which pressed upon the necessities of the bulk of the population, and diminished such as interfered with their comforts; he granted " concessions " to companies for establishing railways, and aided the introduction of gas; he opened the public offices to deserving laymen; he permitted the establishment of a press, whose freedom was guaranteed by a mild system of censorship — and, to render more effective, as well as permanent, the reforms which he himself introduced, he announced, by his circular of the 19th of April, 1847, his intention of calling together a Council, chosen by the various provinces, to assist him in his administration, and give its opinion and advice on all matters of government connected with the general interests of the country.

And with all these labours he combined a sweetness

and a simplicity that won the hearts of the good, and
excited a love and a veneration that would have overcome all but the malice and the machinations of his relentless foes, who were busily occupied with their work
of " regeneration." He was to be seen, to the amazement
of the sticklers for etiquette, and to the delighted
wonder of the people, walking through the streets,
clad in a plain garb, and sparingly attended. Sorrow
had not then robbed his cheek of its freshness, or
dimmed the mild lustre of his soft blue eye; and, as
he passed through his capital, an almost adoring populace received with ecstacy the benediction of the Pontiff,
and the sweet smiles of their ruler and their father.
Children ran to him with eagerness, and artlessly made
known to him their wishes; which were ever sure to be
complied with.   One day he went on foot from the
Quirinal, to say Mass at the convent of the Visitan-
dines of St. Francis de Sales.   On leaving the church,
a little child went up to him, and said, " Art thou the
Pope?"   " Yes, my little friend, I am," replied His
Holiness.   " I have no father," said the little fellow.
" Then I will be a father to you," was the characteristic
answer of the Pope, as he embraced the child.   The
promise so given was fully redeemed; for inquiry having
satisfied the Holy Father of the truth of the child's
statement, he gave orders to have him carefully educated
and provided for, in his name and at his sole charge.

Several anecdotes are told of the Pope's gentleness
and familiarity with children.   Amongst others, the following is not the least characteristic.   One day a little

fellow, all in tears, attempted to make his way through the ranks of the Swiss guards, to present a petition. The Pope, hearing the noise, inquired as to its cause, and sent for the petition. It was in these words: — " Most Holy Father, my mother is old and infirm. I am too young to support her life and mine. Our landlord, a bad man, will turn us out to-morrow if we don't pay him the four scudi we owe him. Deign to lend them. I will pay you when I am bigger." " What is your name, my good child, and how old are you?" asked the Pope. " I am Paul; and I am ten years old." " What trade is your father?" " He's waiting in Paradise for us these ten years," answered the little fellow, with an accent of touching emotion. " And your mother?" inquired the Pope. " She embroiders and prays from morning to night." Having asked the child where he lived, and been told, the Pope desired him to come on the next day, and that he would give him what his mother wanted. In the meantime inquiries were made, which proved that the statement of the child was correct: and when he came again, the Pope gave him ten scudi. " I did not ask you for ten," said the little fellow, and he gave back six. " Take them again, my good child," said the Pope, " and tell your mother I will look after her for the future."

Not content with giving alms in the street, or to those who applied to him personally or by petition, the Pope himself visited many an abode of poverty, and ministered to the wants of its occupants with his

E

own hand. The same hand smoothed the pillow of the sick in the public hospitals (which he always visited without the possibility of his intentions being previously made known), and administered to the dying the last consolations of religion.

One night a person, in a lay habit, entered one of the public hospitals, and being attracted by the groans of a patient, approached the bed on which he lay. The sufferer was a poor French artist, who, feeling that he was dying, was most anxious to have the services of a priest. The almoner was looked for in vain; but the Pope—for it was he—administered the last Sacraments to the poor man, who died in his arms. Next day the almoner was dismissed.

Other institutions were visited in the same manner, and their abuses laid bare to the vigilant eye of one who, even in the most wretched of criminals, recognised a brother. Gentle and merciful to every form of suffering, whether the malady were of the soul, the mind, or the body, the Pope was inexorable to those who oppressed or defrauded the helpless or the poor; and many salutary examples were given, by fine or by dismissal, to officials in charge of the various public institutions, who were soon made to know that the least offence against charity or justice would not go unpunished. And no class of his subjects excited in his breast a livelier compassion than the poor imprisoned debtors, many of whom, no doubt, were the victims of their own folly and extravagance, but many more of whom were victims of the fraud or the tyranny of others. To these his visits were indeed those of an angel of mercy; for his hand flung open their prison door, and his generosity supplied them with the means of commencing a new career.

Ever alive to the great importance of educating the young—a duty to which he had already devoted so many years of his life—the Pope was determined to see with his own eyes how his wishes in that respect were carried out; and scarcely a week passed in which he did not make one of his unannounced and unexpected visits.   These visits were made by night as well as by day.

On a day in March, 1847, two priests, who had come in a hired carriage, asked permission to see the schools in a certain street.   The teachers were rather annoyed at being disturbed; and one of them said, "Certainly the Pope would not like strangers to be admitted to the school exercises without an order." "You are mistaken," said the Pope, throwing open his cloak.   He then took a seat, inquired into everything, examined the pupils, and distributed prizes to the deserving.

On another occasion he desired to witness for himself the operation of the Night Schools, which had been specially established for artisans and others who, being employed during the day, could not attend the ordinary schools; and leaving the Quirinal at night, in a hired carriage, and attended by one of his chamberlains, the Pope was enabled to judge for himself of the value of these, the most interesting, if not the most useful, of the Roman schools.

As an instance of the manner in which he corrected abuses and administered justice with his own hand, may be mentioned the following.

Shortly after his accession, as he was going into the garden of the Quirinal, a soldier on duty held out a regulation loaf. The Pope took it, and found it to be bad. "Do you always get bread like this?" asked the Holy Father. "Always, your Holiness," replied the soldier. "Well, we will look to it." Next day he asked for a loaf of the bread, and found it just the same. He sent for the purveyor, and had him at once arrested and sent to prison, to be tried for the fraud.

He was one day at the Police Palace, when, on looking out of the window, he observed a number of country people, who were kept waiting an hour for their passports, while the person in charge was lunching. The Pope sent for him, and after administering a sharp rebuke, added:—" Now you must give these poor people fifty pauls (about a pound English money) for the time you have robbed them of." "But I have not got fifty pauls," remonstrated the official. "Here they are," said the Pope; "and they shall be struck off your salary."

To love and serve his people, to render them good and happy, was the sole thought of Pius.

Fondly attached to his own family, he yet resolved, from the first moment of his election, that the natural weakness of human affection should not in the slightest degree interfere with his duty to his subjects; and, accordingly, it was soon made known to his brothers and nephews, that any hopes of preferment, to which his election to the Pontificate might have given birth, were vain and illusory. It is said that he warned one of his nephews, a young officer in the army, that he must not expect promotion at the cost of others; and exhorted another, who was living without an employment, to retire to Sinigaglia, from the ostentation of Rome. And to this policy, so widely different from that which we see practised in every court of Europe, Pius IX. has adhered to this hour. Not a single member of his family holds a public position or office, either in the Papal States, or at any foreign court; and so far from his election to the throne having served his family, it has more or less injured them — inasmuch as they have been compelled, in consequence of his elevation, to assume a greater state, and at a necessarily increased expense. In this most important respect Pius IX. has only followed the example of Gregory XVI. How splendidly does such conduct contrast with the policy pursued by every other sovereign of whom we know anything

CHAP. IV.

THE jealousy of Austria became more marked, and
her remonstrances more urgent, if not more overbearing
in their tone, as the liberal intentions of the Pope were
fully disclosed. The following passage from the *Times*
of the 28th of March, 1847, is important, being a just
appreciation of the public conduct of Pius IX., and of
the difficulties which foreign cabinets — that of Austria
especially — were determined to throw in his way : —

" The opposition of Austria has been constant and intense
from the moment of his election. The spectacle of an Italian
Prince, relying for the maintenance of his power on the affectionate regard and the national sympathies of his people
—the resolution of the Pope to pursue a course of moderate
reform, to encourage railroads, to emancipate the press, to
admit laymen to offices in the State, and to purify the law,
but, above all, the dignified independence of action manifested by the Court of Rome, have filled the Austrians with
exasperation and apprehension. There is not the least doubt
that the Cabinet of Vienna is eager to grasp at the slightest

pretext for an armed intervention south of the Po. If such a pretext do not occur, it is but too probable that it may be created; and any disturbances calculated to lead to such a result would at once betray their insidious origin. Meanwhile the Pope is menaced in Austrian notes, which have sometimes transgressed the limits of policy and decorum; and the minor Princes of Italy are terrified by extravagant intimations of hostile designs entertained against them by the national party, headed by the Pope and the house of Savoy, in order to persuade them that their only safeguard is the Austrian army. These intrigues may be thought necessary to the defence of the tottering power of Austria south of the Alps, for every step made in advance by Italy is a step towards the emancipation of the country."

It will be shortly seen that the apprehensions to which the bearing of Austria gave rise were fully justified by her subsequent acts.

In the meantime, however, the plan of promoting demonstrations was systematically persevered in; and thus was cunningly devised a kind of out-door tribunal, to which the daily course of the government was submitted, and by which its particular acts were applauded or condemned. The advice of Mazzini was followed to the letter — " Profit by the least concession to assemble the masses, were it only to testify gratitude. Fêtes, songs, assemblies, numerous relations established among men of all opinions, suffice to make ideas gush out, to give the people the *feeling of its strength, and render it more exacting.*" Care was taken to gain over the more prominent of the leaders of the populace, by working on their vanity; and amongst those was Cicerouachio, who, vain, noisy, and good-natured, was easily

persuaded that he was an orator, and who, foremost
in the expression of his boisterous homage to the Pope,
soon became distinguished as the leader of each tumultuous ovation, and eventually as the blind instrument
of his crafty flatterers.

Let it not be supposed that the Pope was either in-
toxicated or deluded by the shouts and cries, the crowds
and the processions, the music, the banners, and the
flowers, that were ready to greet his appearance on
every possible occasion.   He could not but be conscious
that — even supposing there were no lurking enemies
plotting his ruin, and whose policy it was to excite and
inflame an ardent and impulsive people—such a state of
feeling, as was naturally created by those constant and
almost daily provocations to popular excitement, must
be unsuited to a due appreciation of that rational freedom and those progressive reforms which it was his
object to promote.   Besides, placards, of a nature calculated to excite the worst apprehension of what the
future might bring, began to make their appearance on
the walls of Rome ; and in the provinces, the tumultuous
gatherings, which, according to Mazzini, were to teach
the people " its strength," and render it " more exacting," had been attended with serious disturbance.

To check an evil which was becoming too formidable
to be any longer endured, and also, if possible, to
moderate expectations which were artfully stimulated,
a proclamation was published on the 22nd of June,
1847, by Cardinal Gizzi, in the name of the Pope ; in
which his Holiness, after alluding to the reforms which

he had felt it his duty to introduce, declares that he
intends to persevere in the same course, but to observe,
in doing so, wisdom and prudence.   The proclamation
went on to say : —

"His Holiness is firmly resolved to pursue the course of
amelioration in every branch of the public administration
which may require it, but he is equally resolved to do this
only in a prudent and calculated gradation, and within the
limits which belong essentially to the sovereignty and the
temporal government of the head of the Catholic Church — a
government which cannot adopt certain forms which would
ruin even the existence of the sovereignty, or at least diminish that external liberty, that independence in the exercise
of the supreme primacy for which God willed that the Holy
See should have a temporal principality.   The Holy Father
cannot forget the sacred duties which compel him to preserve
intact the trust that has been confided to him."

The Pope then enumerates some of the reforms and
ameliorations that he had introduced, and the proclamation adds : —

"The Holy Father has not been able to see without deep
regret that certain restless minds are desirous of profiting by
the present state of things to promulgate and endeavour to
establish doctrines and ideas totally contrary to his maxims,
or to impose upon him others entirely opposed to the tranquil
and pacific nature, and the sublime character, of the person
who is the vicar of Jesus Christ, the minister of a God of
peace, and the father of all Catholics, to whatever part of
the world they may belong ; or finally to excite in the minds
of the people, by speeches or writings, desires and hopes of
reforms beyond the limits which his Holiness has indicated.
As these persons are in small number, and the good sense

and rectitude which govern the great majority of the people have hitherto rejected these insinuations and counsels, the Holy Father feels assured that they will never find a welcome among the people. But it is more easy to imagine than to describe the grief felt by his Holiness at some horrible acts which have taken place in various provinces, and which are in open opposition to the peace and concord which he was desirous of establishing among his beloved subjects, when, in the early days of his glorious pontificate, he pronounced the sweet word of pardon. Another subject of grief for his Holiness has arisen from certain assemblages of the multitude, which, under a pretext of scarcity of corn or other wants, have taken place in divers parts of the state, to the disturbance of public order, and sometimes with menace against personal security."

Cardinal Gizzi then says that the Pope does not confound these meetings with assemblies which have taken place for the manifestation of gratitude for the benefits which he has bestowed on the people, and that his Holiness is deeply sensible of such demonstrations, and implores God to bestow the most perfect blessings upon the reforms which he has granted. But he adds : —

" The paternal heart of his Holiness suffers deeply at seeing entire populations and individuals incessantly put to expense for public demonstrations, artisans abandoning their labour to the injury of their families, and youths, destined to study, losing time which is precious to them. The heart of his Holiness would suffer still more if this state of things were to continue. The first year of his pontificate is over, and in this period of time the Holy Father has been able fully to appreciate the love, gratitude, and devotedness of his well-beloved subjects. He now asks a proof of their praiseworthy sentiments ; and this proof must consist in the

cessation of all unusual popular meetings on whatever occasion, and all extraordinary manifestations, except those
for which, anterior to the present notification, permission
had been received from the competent authorities."

The effect of this proclamation was to check an enthusiasm that was rather dangerous than serviceable,
and to restore, in some measure, sobriety to the public
mind, which had become bewildered by a succession of
undue stimulants.   It, no doubt, for a time chilled the
feeling of the people, who, on some occasions subsequent
to its publication, received the Pope with a coldness
and silence that presented a remarkable contrast to the
absolute frenzy of rejoicing with which they had hailed
his appearance a few weeks before.   But who, looking
at the real state of things, as they are now presented to
their consideration, will say that this proclamation was
not absolutely indispensable, in order to dispel delusions
which it would have been in the highest degree mischievous to encourage, even by silence?   If the result
were to create a sentiment of disappointment and mistrust, its intention was honest, and its necessity im-
perative.

In a short time after (on the 17th of July), the difficulties of the Pope's position were increased by the
aggressive conduct of Austria, and the circumstances to
which it gave rise.   On the miserable pretext of protecting the Sovereign of the Papal States against con-
spirators, the city of Ferrara was occupied by Austrian
troops, 1500 strong, arrayed in order of battle, with
artillery and lighted matches.   The general in com-

mand acted under strict orders from Marshal Radetski,
then in Milan.   This gross violation of the rights and
dignity of an independent sovereign was met by a
spirited protest from Cardinal Ciacchi, the Apostolic
Legate of the city and province of Ferrara, and an indignant demand on the part of the Pope's Government,
through Cardinal Ferretti, the new Secretary of State,
for the withdrawal of the invading force.   The bold
attitude thus assumed by the Government, as well as
the natural irritation created by the insolent and
menacing conduct of Austria, in a moment excited the
military ardour of the nation, and added to the hatred
in which the foreign occupants of the soil of Italy were
held by every true Italian.   Though neither within
the province nor the disposition of Pius IX. to act
the part of an aggressor, still, as a sovereign, he had
rights to maintain, and, as a patriot, a country to defend; and, in the spirit of the one and the other, he
resolutely prepared, if negotiation should fail, to meet
the invader with his own weapons.   The people nobly
responded to their ruler; and even the cloistered monk
was not insensible to the martial ardour of the hour,
but proclaimed his readiness to don the harness of the
warrior, and wield the sword of the flesh against the
enemy.   A little while ago, and the cry was for further
reforms — now it was for battle with the Austrians;
and the press, to which liberty had been conceded, did
its utmost to stimulate to the highest point the ardour
of the nation.   All the disposable troops were ordered
to the frontiers; and the National Guard was organised

throughout the States with the utmost activity, and its banners were blessed with all the solemnity which religious ceremonial could impart. Something like the old spirit of Rome blazed out for the moment. In this critical emergency the bearing of the Pope was worthy of his position and the occasion. Thus writes the gifted contributor to a London Journal,* who witnessed what he described. " Meantime Pius, overwhelmed with the cares of his new position—isolated, so to say, among the crowned heads of Europe — has a heart and confidence in the God of justice, which nothing can daunt. He is fully prepared for every emergency." The face of Pius, says another eyewitness, " beams with the calm of a good conscience."

Even the Jews shared in the enthusiasm of the hour, and offered the homage of their gratitude to the Pope, who had not only relaxed the severity of the laws which had so long pressed upon that unhappy race, but had recently allowed them to appoint a successor to their late High Priest, then twelve years dead. On the occasion of the induction of the new High Priest, the ceremony was concluded by a hymn for the Pope, written in the choicest Hebrew.

The difference with Austria was ultimately arranged without the necessity of coming to blows.

On the 15th of November, 1847, the Council of State, promised by Pius in his circular of the 19th of April, was solemnly inaugurated, amidst the enthusiasm of the people, the earnest wishes of the moderate, the

* The Daily News.

apprehensions of the timid, and the evil expectations of the designing, whose hopes were not in reform, but in revolution — not in gradual development or judicious progress, but in anarchy and confusion.

The object of calling together the Council of State, as well as its composition and division, are explained in the following *Proprio Motu* promulgated by the Pope on the 15th of October, a month previous to its assembly :—

"When, by our circular of the 19th of April last, we announced our intention to choose and call to Rome respectable persons, from each province of the Pontifical dominions, our object was to form a Council of State, and thus endow the Pontifical Government with an institution justly appreciated by the other European Governments, and which, in former times, constituted the glory of the States of the Holy See, a glory due to the genius of the Roman Pontiffs. We are persuaded that, when assisted by the talent and experience of persons honoured with the suffrages of entire provinces, it will be easier for us boldly to take in hand the administration of the country, and impart to it a character of utility, which is the object of our solicitude. This result we are certain to attain. Our fixed determination, combined with the moderation of the public mind, must enable us to reap the fruit of the seed already sown. We will thus show the entire world, through the medium of our voices and the press, and by our attitude, that a population inspired by religion, devoted to its prince, and gifted with good sense, knows how to appreciate a political blessing, and express its gratitude with order and moderation. This is the only price we demand in recompense of our constant solicitude for the public welfare, and we confidently hope to obtain it. Trusting in the aid of Divine Providence, and wishing our sovereign resolutions to be executed, we have decreed the following of our own accord, having duly considered the matter, and in virtue of our supreme authority : —

" ORGANISATION OF THE COUNCIL OF STATE.

" The Council of State is to be composed of a cardinal-president, a prelate, vice-president, and 24 councillors, named by the provinces, and who are to have fixed salaries. Each province will return a councillor, Bologna 2, and Rome and its vicinity 4.

" The second paragraph relates to the mode of election and nomination of the councillors.

" They are to be divided into four sections : — first, of legislation ; second, of finance ; third, of internal administration, commerce, and manufactures ; fourth, of the army, public works, prisons, &c.

" The Council is instituted to assist the Pope in the administration ; to give its opinion on matters of government, connected with the general interests of the state and those of the provinces ; on the preparation of laws, their modification, and all administrative regulations ; on [the creation and redemption of public debts ; the imposition or reduction of taxes ; the alienation of the property and estates belonging to the Government ; on the cession of contracts ; on the customs' tariff and the conclusion of treaties of commerce ; on the budget of the State, the verification of the accounts and general expenditure of the administration of the State and provinces ; on the revision and reform of the present organisation of district and provincial councils," &c.

Let us not try this new concession, which was but the forerunner of one still more ample, by a false standard ; for any such mode of judging of its value or its importance would be manifestly as fallacious as unjust. We cannot attempt to test it by a comparison with the free constitution of these countries, or of any country in which popular institutions have long been established. Let us, instead of forming any comparison between it and our thoroughly defined representative system, which has been the growth of ages, and the splendid result of an unwearied and persistent struggle of the popular element against the claims and encroachments

of the kingly power and the aristocratic influence, regard it in its true light — as a bold innovation on the
established system of Papal government, and as an
eminently venturous step in the path of political change.
Surely there was enough of power in this Council of
State, if wisely and honestly directed, to bring about
the most beneficial results, by effecting improvements in
the laws and in their administration, and by a resolute
attention to the development of the material resources
of a land teeming with natural wealth, and a people
abounding in energies of which they were almost unconscious. A great reform in itself, it was intended to
be the basis of reforms far more comprehensive. It
was a mighty instrument, fashioned by the hand of a
benevolent monarch — one with which the true patriot
might have effected miracles in the way of substantial
and enduring, not vain or shadowy, improvements in all
the social and national interests of the Papal States.
But, alas! this instrument, intended for good, was
turned against the breast of its author.

That was a day of carnival in Rome which witnessed
the arrival at the Quirinal of the members of the Consulta — consisting of the President, Cardinal Antonelli;
the Vice-president, Monsignor Amici; and the twenty-
four Provincial Deputies — and beheld them take their
places in the Hall of the Throne, where they first assembled to offer their homage to the Sovereign; who, in
reply to an address from the President, spoke these
words, which were perfectly in accordance with the
intentions he had from the first expressed: —

" I thank you for your good intentions, and as regards the public welfare, I esteem them of value.   It was for the public good that since my elevation to the Pontifical throne I have, in accordance with the counsels inspired by God, accomplished all that I could ; and I am still ready, with the assistance of God, to do all for the future, without, however, retrenching in any degree the sovereignty of the Pontificate ; and, inasmuch as I received it full and entire from my predecessors, so shall I transmit this sacred deposit to my successors.   I have three millions of subjects as witnesses, that I have hitherto accomplished much to unite my subjects with me, and to ascertain and provide for their necessities. It was particularly to ascertain those wants, and to provide better for the exigencies of the public service, that I have assembled you in a permanent council.   It was to hear your opinion when necessary, to aid me in my sovereign resolutions, in which I shall consult my conscience, and confer on them with my Ministers and the Sacred College.   Anybody who would take any other view of the functions you are called to fulfil would mistake materially, as well as he that would see in the Council of State I have created the realisation of their own Utopias, and the germ of an institution incompatible with the Pontifical sovereignty."

His Holiness, having pronounced those last words with some vivacity and not a little heat, stopped a moment, and then, resuming his usual mild manner, continued in the following terms : —

" This warmth and those words are not addressed to any of you, whose social education, Christian and civil probity, as well as the loyalty of your sentiments and the rectitude of your intentions, have been known to me since the moment I proceeded to your election.   Neither do those words apply to the majority of my subjects, for I am sure of their fidelity

F

and their obedience. I know that the hearts of my subjects unite with mine in the love of order and of concord. But there exist unfortunately some persons (and though few, they still exist), who, having nothing to lose, love disturbance and revolt, and even abuse the concessions made to them. It is to those that my words are addressed, and let them well understand their signification. In the co-operation of the deputies I see only the firm support of persons who, devoid of every personal interest, will labour with me, by their advice, for the public good, and who will not be arrested by the vain language of restless men devoid of judgment. You will aid me with your wisdom to discover that which is most useful for the security of the throne and the real happiness of my subjects."

The Pope took leave of the Deputies in these words : " Proceed, with the blessing of Heaven, to commence your labours. May they prove fruitful in beneficial results, and conformable to the desires of my heart."

Amidst the heartfelt rejoicings of the population, and surrounded or accompanied by all that could gratify the eye or excite the imagination, the procession wound its imposing splendour through the streets which lay between the Quirinal and the Vatican. Brilliant tapestries ; fluttering banners, emblematic and distinctive ; gorgeous equipages ; glittering uniforms of infantry and cavalry ; costumes of all kinds, many of them in the highest degree picturesque — these, added to a dense mass of ardent and enthusiastic people, formed one of those magnificent pageants of which Rome, above all other cities, has ever been prolific. Religion lent its sacred aid, in the greatest of its earthly temples, to render solemn and memorable the inauguration of the National Council. From beneath the dome of St. Peter's, the Deputies proceeded to the chamber allotted to them in the Vatican, and there formally commenced their labours.

Of the address drawn up, in answer to the speech of the Pope, the following passages, with which it concludes, exhibit, at least, a clear perception of the motives of the sovereign, the magnitude of the work to be accomplished, and the means by which it could alone be successful : —

" But the accomplishment of an undertaking so great and so difficult will require much study, time, and calmness. We confide in the continuance of the noble tranquillity of which your subjects have given so many proofs. They will patiently await the salutary fruits of the seeds which you have sown with a generous hand.

" Your work, Holy Father, has not been undertaken to favour exclusively one order of citizens; it embraces all your subjects in a common bond of love, and that love is such that your example is admired and followed by the other sovereigns of Italy, united with their subjects in the alliance of principles, passions, and interests.

" We have often seen reforms, imposed by popular exigencies, developing themselves amidst tumults and collisions. Their conquest costs tears and blood. But, amongst us, it is the first and most venerable authority of all which wishes to initiate us in the progress of civilisation. That authority itself directs the minds in a peaceable and moderate movement, and guides us towards the supreme end, which is the reign of justice and truth on earth."

While these events were passing in Rome, the sympathies of every generous nation were drawn towards the occupant of the Chair of Peter. And on the opposite shores of the Atlantic, in the chief cities of the United States, masses of men met to express their admiration of the acts of the illustrious reformer. Amongst the most remarkable of the meetings which took place, was that held in the month of December, 1847, in the " Tabernacle," New York, at which many of the leading statesmen of America gave the warmest expression to their sympathy and admiration. The address and resolutions were proposed by Puritans, and the descendants of Puritans ; and though Catholics attended the meeting in numbers, they refrained from taking any prominent part in the demonstration, with the wise intention of rendering it the more striking and effective. The fourth resolution exhibits a thorough consciousness of the obstacles with which Pius had to contend, and the dangers by which he was menaced : —

"Resolved, — That we present our most hearty and respectful salutations to the Sovereign Pontiff for the noble part he has taken in behalf of his people; that, knowing the difficulties with which he is surrounded at home, and the attacks with which he is menaced from abroad, we honour him the more for the mild firmness with which he has overcome the one, and the true spirit with which he has repelled the other."

Nor was Ireland, even in the midst of her sorrows and her tribulations, insensible to the claims which the Holy Father had upon her sympathies ; for fresh in her gratitude was the recollection of the generous hand that had been extended towards her from the Vatican, and of those urgent appeals which were made, in her behalf, to the compassion of Christendom.   No sooner had the cry of a distressed nation reached the ear of Pius IX., than it found a ready echo in his benevolent breast ; and not only did he at once send, out of his small means, a munificent contribution towards the fund for its relief, but caused the churches of Rome to resound to the earnest solicitations of his clergy in the same cause of suffering humanity.   The Pope's feelings in behalf of Ireland are best conveyed in his own expressive words. On the 8th of February, 1847, a number of English, Scotch, and Irish gentlemen, then residing in Rome, and who had formed themselves into a Committee for the collection of subscriptions, waited on his Holiness for the purpose of expressing their thanks for his liberality.   " We desire," said the Chairman of the Committee (Mr. Harford), —

" to express to your Holiness our lively acknowledgment for the benevolent and spontaneous manner in which you have signified to us, through Dr. Cullen, your charitable and generous intention of contributing a thousand scudi to the same object.   We also beg your Holiness to permit us to express our conviction, that the sentiment which at this moment animates our hearts will be deeply felt, not only by the English now in Rome, but in every portion of the British empire."

To which, with every appearance of the most genuine emotion, the Pope replied :—

" It affords me great consolation to see so many benevo-

lent gentlemen from every part of the United Kingdom engaged in so excellent a work of charity, exerting themselves
to arrest the progress of famine, and striving to alleviate
the dreadful distress of their brethren in Ireland. Were the
means at my command more extensive, I should not limit
myself to the little I have done in a cause in which I feel the
warmest sympathy. To supply the want of a larger contribution, I shall pray with fervour to the Almighty, beseech-
ing him to look with mercy on his people, to remove the
scourge that afflicts them, and to give peace, happiness, and
abundance to the country."

But the Pope, in his Encyclical Letter of the 18th of
March, so fully expressed the compassion with which he
witnessed the increasing distress of Ireland, and his
knowledge and appreciation of the religious fidelity of its
people, as well as of their attachment to the Holy See,
that a passage from that document becomes most appropriate in this place. It is as follows : —

"Being moved by this example of our predecessors, and,
at the same time, by the inclination of our own will, when first
We learned that the kingdom of Ireland was involved in a
great dearth of corn, and a scarcity of other provisions, and
that that nation was suffering from a most dreadful compli-
cation of diseases brought on by want of food, We instantly
applied every means, as far as in us lay, to succour that
afflicted people. Therefore, we proclaimed that, in this our
city, prayers should be poured forth ; and We encouraged
the clergy, the Roman people, and those who were sojourning
in the city, to send assistance to Ireland. By which means
it was arranged, that partly by money cheerfully sent by
ourselves, and partly by that which was collected in Rome,
assistance, as far as the necessities of the time permitted,
could be forwarded to our venerable brethren the Archbishops of Ireland, which they may distribute according to

the conditions of the respective localities and of their suffering people.   But letters are still brought to us from
Ireland, and accounts are daily related to us respecting the calamities mentioned above still continuing in this
island — nay, even increasing — which afflict our mind with
incredible grief, and urgently impel us again to afford assistance to the Irish nation.   And what effort ought We not to
make to raise up that nation now suffering under such a
disaster, when We know how great the fidelity of the clergy
and people of Ireland is, and always has been, towards the
Apostolic See — how, in the most dangerous times, their firmness in the profession of the Catholic religion has been conspicuous — by what labour the clergy of Ireland have toiled
for the propagation of the Catholic religion in the remotest
regions of the world ; and, finally, with what zeal for piety
and religion the Divine Peter, whose dignity (to use the
words of Leo the Great) is not the less in an unworthy heir,
is among the Irish nation honoured and distinguished in our
humble person ! ”

By the Pope's personal contribution, as well as
through his instrumentality, a sum of about 12,000
scudi was collected, and sent to the suffering poor of
Ireland.

With such an evidence of his compassion and goodness before their eyes, it is no exaggeration to say,
that by no people were the steps of Pius in the path
of social and political amelioration watched with a more
intense and eager gaze than by the Irish, especially
those of them whose religious sympathies harmonised
with their love of rational liberty.   The Pope had also
testified his marked respect for the memory of O'Connell,
that renowned champion of the Church, whose heart,

according to his dying wish and desire, had been brought to Rome, as a last attestation of his attachment to the Holy See. The vestments used on the occasion of the solemn obsequies had been sent from the Papal Chapel, by the special orders of his Holiness.

Catholic Ireland felt towards the Pope as a child towards a father.

Towards the close of 1847, disturbances were commencing to break out in Messina; insurrection was rife in Palermo; and disaffection was hourly making itself manifest in Milan. These were the first heavings of that universal earthquake which was, ere long, to burst forth in the principal capitals of Europe. Accounts from all parts of the Italian Peninsula heralded a year of storm and convulsion.

CHAP. V.

The Year of Revolutions. — Great Excitement in Rome. — Further Reforms demanded. — Opening of the Roman Parliament. — The War of Independence. — Its disastrous Result. — Count Rossi Prime Minister. — His Assassination resolved upon.

THE year 1848 opened gloomily upon the political world, almost every country in Europe being rife with discontent, and ready for revolution. In Rome events were fast hastening to a crisis; and each new account of risings throughout the Italian States or elsewhere but added to the daring of the extreme party, now actively represented by the press, chiefly in the hands of refugees, and by the clubs, which had lately sprung into existence, and had already become the focus of intrigue, and the organs as well as the promoters of violence. By both, the crafty policy of Mazzini was persistently inculcated, and every opportunity availed of to encourage the *fêtes*, songs, processions, and gatherings of the masses, so cunningly relied on as a means of stimulating popular excitement, keeping the public mind in a state of feverish impatience, teaching the people its strength, and rendering them "more exacting." None but utterly revolutionary measures could keep pace with such a state of feeling as was artfully fostered by the enemies of rational

reform.   The deliberations of the Consulta were rudely
intruded upon by the mob-leaders, and changes demanded
with a manner not always free from menace.   To add
to the perils of the hour, the diversion of large numbers
of the people from their customary pursuits led to the
very consequences against which the Pope, in his proclamation of the 22nd of June of the previous year, had
so prophetically warned his subjects. With the abandonment of industry, idleness became general, and poverty
and distress followed as a matter of necessity; nor were
frequent acts of violence and bloodshed wanting, to impart a darker aspect to the position of affairs.

It was, then, upon a population so inflamed, that the
news of the terrible insurrection which had broken out
at Palermo, burst with electric influence. These tidings
were quickly followed by still more startling intelligence
—that a free constitution had been granted, ostensibly
of his own accord, but in reality through fear, by the
King of Naples; that movements of a revolutionary
character were apprehended in Austria and Prussia; that
barricades had been erected in the streets of Paris, and
that a Republic was established on the ruins of the Orleans dynasty.   From this moment the audacity of the
press, the clubs, and the mob-leaders, knew no bounds;
and even the most upright and well-intentioned ministers, who were constantly appearing upon and disap-
pearing from the political stage, were reluctantly compelled to flatter where they could not hope to control.

The accounts from Paris produced the most intense
excitement; and, in a short time after they were circu-

lated through Rome, the people proceeded in an immense crowd to the Quirinal to demand the promised constitution ; to frame which, with safety to the grave interests of the Church—which the Pope was specially bound to protect—seemed to their impatience a matter of trifling difficulty.   In answer to a subsequent and more formal demand, the Pope gave the following reply : —

" The events, I will not say which succeeded each other, but which have hurried on to a conclusion, justify the demand addressed to me by the senators in the name of the magistrates and the council. Everybody knows that I have been incessantly engaged in giving the government the form claimed by those gentlemen and required by the people. But everybody must understand the difficulty encountered by him who unites two supreme dignities. What can be effected in one night in a secular state cannot be accomplished without mature examination in Rome, in consequence of the necessity to fix a line of separation between the two powers. Nevertheless, I hope that in a few days the constitution will be ready, and that I shall be able to proclaim a new form of government, calculated to satisfy the people, and more particularly the Senate and the Council, who know better the state of affairs and the situation of the country. May the Almighty bless my desires and labours ! If religion derives any advantage therefrom, I will throw myself at the feet of the crucified Jesus, to thank him for the events accomplished by his will, and I will be more satisfied as Chief of the Universal Church than as a temporal prince, if they turn to the greatest glory of God."

The promise thus given was speedily fulfilled ; and on the 5th of June the Roman Parliament was opened by a speech, read by Cardinal Atlieri, in the name of the Pope ; in which, after expressing his satisfaction at having succeeded in introducing into his states the political reforms demanded by the times, his Holiness directed the attention of the Chambers to matters of pressing interest and growing emergency. The sittings were then declared to be opened. And thus was a new field offered to the activity of the party who looked upon all reforms with contempt, and regarded the most generous concessions but as a means to an end. The two Chambers contained many sincere patriots, earnestly devoted to their country, their sovereign, and their church; but their prudence and their good sense were soon overborne by the violence of those whose vanity or whose reckless ambition carried them on to every excess.

In the meanwhile the flame of insurrection had burst out in other capitals, to which the startling events at Paris had given a wild impulse. The revolution at Vienna gave new confidence to the patriots of Italy; and, after a noble struggle, the Milanese compelled the Austrians to evacuate their beautiful city. A republic was also once more proclaimed in Venice.

The Pope was not insensible to the generous influence of the hour, and no one could more sincerely desire to witness the triumph of Italian independence than he did. To accomplish this great object he made several efforts, unfortunately in vain, with a view of combining the different states into a common national league; but while he met with a cordial concurrence in some instances, his proposal was received with coldness and jealousy in others. Naples, Tuscany, and other states, entered with alacrity into the scheme; but the Sardinian Government refused to send delegates to Rome, and suggested a Congress in the North of Italy — a proposition not calculated to overcome the natural apprehensions entertained by the governments of the South of the ambitious views of Charles Albert. Had the scheme of an Italian League, under the presidency of the Pope, been carried into effect, it would, in all human probability, have effected the freedom of Italy; and while saving Rome from the machinations of anarchists, have consolidated the reforms granted to the Papal States. But such was not to be.

It would be an unnecessary task, and besides one quite foreign to the purpose of this volume, were I to follow through its vicissitudes the short War of Independence, that, commencing with an enthusiasm to which no class, and scarcely any individual, was insensible, ended in defeat and disappointment, and a more effectual riveting of the chain by which Austria held her Italian provinces in bondage. The Romans, who, on the 24th of March, witnessed the departure of General Durando from their ancient gates, at the head of a brave but not too well disciplined army, and who thought of the old times, as, with music and banners, their youth marched to resist the foes of their country, ere long received the tidings of their having capitulated at Vicenza; from which place, but three weeks before, they had gallantly repulsed the Austrians. General Durando had, in the first instance, exceeded his instructions, which were, to proceed to the frontiers, and act on the defensive;

and in an address, whose exaggeration the circumstances of the moment may explain rather than justify, pledged the Pope to a crusade of exterminations against the Austrians, as the enemies of " the Cross of Christ." The Pope's repudiation of this unwise address excited intense agitation in Rome ; but Pius resolutely adhered to his proclamation, in which, while professing his devotion to the cause of Italian independence, he at the same time declared that he could not, as Pontiff, proclaim war against a Christian power.   However, Durando was ordered to co-operate with Charles Albert ; and the unhappy result of the brief Roman campaign gave rise to a stormy debate in the Roman Commons, in which the most opposite opinions were expressed as to the conduct of the war and the courage of the officers in command. But the armies of Rome and Piedmont had other enemies to contend with besides the Austrians ; for in the camps both of Durando and Charles Albert, the emissaries of the republicans were ever actively engaged in sowing the seeds of suspicion and distrust, and amongst the very troops which, if these men were sincere in their devotion to the cause of Italian liberty, they should rather have stimulated and encouraged.

The defeat of Charles Albert under the walls of Milan put a termination to the war, the gallant monarch being compelled to retire within the boundaries of his own dominions.   And although the King had done all that man could have done, under the circumstances in which he was placed; and though the terms of the capitulation were honourable to him and favourable to the people of Milan, whose persons and property it protected, the treatment which he received from the rabble, urged on by the false and cowardly anarchists, was disgraceful in the extreme. But these men, wherever they appeared, proved themselves the worst foes of Italian freedom.

Meanwhile the press, the clubs, and mob-leaders of Rome had become more violent; while a new and more dangerous element was added to the already sufficiently excitable populace, by the return of numbers of reduced or disbanded soldiers, of questionable character, but of singular aptitude for riot and disturbance. Each hour the people—in reality the mob—grew more conscious of its strength, and consequently " more exacting " in its demands. In such a sad state of things there was only one chance for the cause of constitutional liberty against the dictation of the clubs and the lawless violence of an infuriated populace; and that was in the energy and determination of a minister of liberal policy and firm purpose.

And such a minister did Pius IX. call to his councils in the person of Count Rossi, whose abilities, as a trained and practised statesman, were only excelled by his sincere desire to see Italy restored to peace and tranquillity, and the enjoyment of national prosperity as well as true freedom. It was not in a moment like that at which things had now arrived, that a man of his stamp would lightly assume a position so abounding in difficulties, and undertake a task so fraught with hourly peril. A solemn consciousness of duty, and a chivalrous anxiety

to be of assistance to a noble but ill-used sovereign, alone
induced Count Rossi to undertake the conduct of the
government.   To the anarchists — those who looked
for the overthrow of the Pope's authority, and the
erection of a Red Republic upon its ruins—no minister
could be more hateful than Rossi; and, accordingly, his
first vigorous efforts to restore order, and put a stop to
a condition of things which no government could permit
without a virtual abdication of its functions, were
answered by a yell of rage from the revolutionary press,
and by the ferocious denunciations of the clubs. Nowise
daunted, Rossi persevered in his good work; which was
so happy in its results, that in the course of some three
weeks — for he had assumed the direction of affairs on
the 16th of August — he succeeded in the now difficult
task of inspiring confidence in the breast of a bewildered
public, and renewing hopes of ultimate success in the
minds of those who had long since surrendered themselves to despair.   With such a man there was therefore
left but one mode of dealing, and that mode was speedily
resolved upon.   The dagger of the assassin was now to
do its bloody work, not in the darkness of night, when
Nature, as it were, flings a cloak over the murderer, but
in the blaze of the noon-day sun, and in the presence
of hundreds of spectators.

CHAP. VI.

Assassination of Count Rossi. — Despatch of the French Ambassa-
dor. — Inhuman Rejoicings. — Assault on the Pope's Palace. —
The Pope's personal Liberty at an End. — No Excuse for this
Violence.

As if to prove to the world how unfitted for representative institutions were a people whom crafty or
designing men had systematically trained into licentious-
ness, the day selected for the abominable deed of blood,
which was to put an end to all hopes of constitutional
liberty, was that appointed for the re-opening of the
Chambers ; and the appropriate place selected for the
brutal murder was the very entrance to the Cancellaria,
in which the Parliament held its sittings.

Let the pen of the horrified and indignant Ambassador
of France (the Duc d'Harcourt) describe an act which
evoked one universal shout of execration in whatever
country it was heard of. The following despatch was
laid before the National Assembly of France, prepara-
tory to the debate on the proposed expedition to Civita
Vecchia :—

" Rome, November 16.

" MONSIEUR LE MINISTRE,—I have already had the honour
of announcing to you by the telegraph that M. Rossi, Mi-

G

nister of the Interior, was assassinated yesterday at 1 o'clock,
as he was alighting from his carriage to enter the Chamber
of Deputies.   He was stabbed in the throat, and died immediately.   The murderer was not arrested, nor was even
any attempt made to seize him.   Some gendarmes and National Guards, who were on the spot, did not interfere.   The
populace remained mute and cold.   It was with difficulty
that the Minister's servant could find any one to help him
in carrying the body of his master into a neighbouring
room. The Assembly, on the steps of which the murder was
committed, continued undisturbedly to read its minutes, and
not a word was mentioned of the incident during the whole
sitting.   In the evening the murderers and their adherents,
to the amount of several hundreds, with flags at their head,
fraternised with the soldiers at their barracks, and none of
the magistrates came forward to act. The Director of Police,
although urged to take some energetic measures, refused to
interfere, and withdrew. — This morning the whole of the
ministry resigned.   It is difficult to conceive any new combination possible, or any chance of re-establishing order,
after what has passed.   Such is the position of the successors of the ancient Romans! Having no packet immediately at my disposal, I have resolved to send this despatch overland.   Accept, &c.,

" HARCOURT."

The Ambassador did not add the revolting fact, that
the assassins, their accomplices, and their abettors, tra-
vestied those *fêtes* which it was the policy of the advocates of revolution to encourage ; and, gathering together all that was foul or frenzied of the population,
passed in procession through the streets, till they arrived
beneath the windows of the house in which lay the
ghastly form of its murdered owner, and there insulted,

with inhuman shouts and songs of hellish triumph, the agony of the living, and the solemn repose of the dead.

"Long live the hand which poignarded Rossi!" was the benediction pronounced upon the assassin.

That night of the fatal 15th closed in blood; but the morning of the 16th dawned on a day of horror and sacrilege, in which the guilt of the previous day was far exceeded in atrocity. The ministry of Count Rossi having been destroyed in his person, it was now determined, by those who instigated, or were resolved to profit by, his assassination, to force a ministry of their own selection upon the sovereign. The second despatch from the Duke d'Harcourt, an eyewitness to the infamous outrage, thus describes the manner in which the well-instructed rabble exhibited their "strength:"—

"Rome, Nov. 17.

"MONSIEUR LE MINISTRE, — I have had the honour to give you the account of the murder of M. Rossi. Yesterday we had a continuation of these excesses, which will make you regret, perhaps, not having given, at a certain time, some support to the Sovereign Pontiff. It would be difficult to witness a more sad spectacle for the nation, than that of which we have been ocular witnesses. Towards two o'clock a rather large crowd of the people went to the Quirinal with a programme, known beforehand, and which issued from the presses of the Popular Club. This programme demanded the dismissal of the Ministry, the formation of another, the formation of a Constituent Assembly, a solemn declaration of war, &c.— There are in the interior of the Quirinal 100 Swiss, who are alone charged with the personal guard of the Pope, with a few *gardes du corps*. When the Swiss saw this hostile demonstration, they closed the doors and prepared for a defence. The diplomatic corps had time to enter the palace, and offer to the Pope its moral support against the violence that might be attempted against him. The assemblage at first uttered menaces to obtain admission, and seeing that their desire was not complied with, they endeavoured to burn down the principal door. A few musket shots from the Swiss, and their decided attitude, soon forced the aggressors to retire to a distance. Up to this time only the populace had interposed; the attack, therefore, did not last long, and the populace were beginning to disperse when we witnessed, to our great surprise, an unexpected spectacle. The civic guard, the gendarmerie, the line, and the Roman legion, to the number of some thousands in uniform, with music and drums, came and ranged themselves in order of battle on the square of the Quirinal, and were there joined by a few of the people who had remained, and began to fire at the windows of the Palace. Some balls penetrated into the apartments, and one killed a prelate who was in his chamber. As the Swiss continued to display a bold attitude, and it was thought that a determined resistance would be offered, cannon was brought to batter down the doors of the Palace of the Pope, who is mildness itself, and who had only a hundred Swiss to defend him. It is generally thought that there were only a few hundred plotters, who had laid the plan of this conspiracy. There were near the Pope, during the whole of the day, only the diplomatic corps. The Pope, all this time, showed much *sang froid* and firmness; but as it was impossible to oppose resistance, — and, besides, as he was less able and disposed than anybody to shed blood — it was necessary to do whatever was demanded by his own troops, who besieged him in his palace. Negotiations were entered into, and a list of ministers was proposed to him, at the head of which figure MM. Mamiani, Sterbini, Galleti, &c. This he accepted, protesting, however, against the violence which was practised, and declaring that he would refer to the Chambers the other measures which were demanded of him. The authority of the Pope is now absolutely null. It exists only in name, and none of his acts will be free and voluntary.

"HARCOURT."

The statement of the French Ambassador omits the fact, of which perhaps he was not aware at the time he wrote his despatch, that the motley rabble, amongst whom, to their shame, men who called themselves soldiers were mixed up, had proceeded in the first instance to the Chamber of Deputies, and insisted on several members of that body accompanying them, as their organ and mouthpiece, to the palace of the Pope. To his eternal honour be it recorded, the insulted Sovereign declared, in spite of the hoarse and savage shouts which reached his ears, that "he would not grant anything to violence." This was his reply to the second demand made by the dishonoured Deputies, in the name of a frenzied mob. But the brutal violence to which his Holiness eventually, though under protest, did yield, will be even more fully understood from the following passages of a letter which appeared in the *Daily News*, written by a gentleman whose communications to that journal excited the greatest attention at the time : —

"At this stage of the proceedings it was evident that the die was cast. From the back streets men emerged bearing aloft long ladders wherewith to scale the pontifical abode ; carts and waggons were dragged up and ranged within musket-shot of the windows to protect the assailants in

G 3

their determined attack on the palace; the cry was, 'to arms! to arms!' and musketry began to bristle in the approaches from every direction; faggots were produced and piled up against one of the condemned gates of the building, to which the mob was in the act of setting fire when a brisk discharge of firelocks scattered the besiegers in that quarter.

" The multitude began now to perceive that there would be a determined resistance to their further operation, but were confident that the Quirinal, if not taken by storm, must yield to progressive inroad. The drums were now beating throughout the city, and the disbanded groups of regular troops and carabineers reinforcing the hostile display of assailants, and rendering it truly formidable. Random shots were aimed at the windows, and duly responded to ; the outposts, one after another, taken by the people, the garrison within being too scanty to man the outworks. The belfry of St. Carlino, which commands the structure, was occupied. From behind the equestrian statues of Castor and Pollux a group of sharpshooters plied their rifles, and about four o'clock Monsignor Palma, private secretary to his Holiness, was killed by a bullet penetrating his forehead.

" As if upwards of 6,000 troops of all ranks were not considered enough to reduce the little garrison of a couple of dozen Swiss, two six-pounders now appeared on the scene, and were drawn up and duly pointed against the main gate, and, a truce having been proclaimed, another deputation claimed entrance and audience of the Pope, which the monarch ordered to be allowed. The deputation were bearers of the people's *ultimatum*, which was a reproduction of the five points before stated, and they now declared that they would allow his Holiness *one hour to consider ;* after which, if *not* adopted, *they announced their firm purpose to break into the Quirinal, and put to death every inmate thereof, with the sole and single exception of his Holiness himself."

Who will attempt, on rational grounds, to account for this abominable outrage? If, indeed, the palace assailed with such savage fury had been the dwelling-place of some foul tyrant, stained with the blood of his people — of some hardened monster, to whose ears the cries and groans of his subjects were as sweet music— of some wretch, dead to every good and generous emotion, and whose greatest delight it was to oppress and trample upon those unhappily subject to his sway, — then might the world comprehend and account for the dark doings of this day of shame and terror. But the monarch thus brutally outraged, was the best as well as the most exalted of living men, — in whose breast ever welled a fountain of love, and charity, and compassion, — whose every thought, from the moment that he rose in the morning, till he last knelt to his God at night, was of doing good — how he could improve and elevate his people — how he could promote their temporal and eternal interests — how he could most effectually minister to the necessities of the poor, the suffering, and the sick— how he could most securely train the young in intelligence and virtue, raise up the fallen, and restore the erring to the right path. His was a brow that never contracted in resentment — his an eye that never flashed with anger — his a mouth that never uttered words of scorn or contempt; but, ever gentle, ever merciful, ever good, Pius IX. seemed born to attract towards him the hearts and win the confidence of mankind. But the base and bad took advantage of those qualities which command the respect of the good, and despised the gentle and benign sovereign for the lack of that sternness and that rigour which they could alone appreciate, but which formed no element in the sweet character of the Vicar of Christ.

The plotters had done their work too effectually to allow of hope for their return to reason. The moderate were shocked at the excesses perpetrated in the prostituted name of liberty; but they were powerless in this hour of frenzy, nor could their voice be heard in the wild storm of popular commotion. The power of the Pope was utterly paralysed, and his personal safety in danger. To repeat the words of the Duke d'Harcourt, "The authority of the Pope is now absolutely null. It exists only in name, *and none of his acts will be free and voluntary.*"

CHAP. VII.

The personal Liberty of the Pope at an End. — He resolves to abandon Rome. — His Flight from the Quirinal. — He reaches Gaeta. — His Reception by the King and Queen of Naples.

SUCH being the case — all power and authority being centred in the very men who had been all along plotting his overthrow, and who now gloried in their achievement — there was but one course left to the outraged sovereign — namely, *flight;* and this he was soon induced to adopt. One consideration more than another was powerful with the Pope — that the direction of those affairs which related to the Church was not only interfered with, but was rendered wholly impossible.

At first, he was doubtful as to the course which he should take, or the resolution to which he should come; and in this state of suspense he remained for two or three days, when he received a letter from France, from the Bishop of Valence. In this letter the Bishop acquainted His Holiness that a little silver case having come into his possession, which had served Pius VII.

of blessed memory to keep therein a consecrated particle, in order that he might have the most Holy Sacrament as a solace during the sad exile to which tyranny and infidelity had condemned him; he was happy to have it conveyed to Pope Pius IX., as a memorial of one of his holy predecessors, and as an object perhaps not useless during the events that were taking place in those days. On the receipt of this precious memorial, the Pope no longer delayed, or hesitated as to the course which he should take; and he accordingly resolved upon abandoning Rome. At first, he deliberated upon what place to select for his stay; but as the Spanish Court had offered him their hospitality, and as the Ambassador, Signor Martinez della Rosa, assured him of the immediate arrival of a steamer belonging to that nation in the harbour of Civita Vecchia, the Pope thought that this would be an opportune means whereby to effect his escape. But the Spanish steamer being retarded from day to day, and the state of affairs in Rome becoming more and more alarming, the Pope intimated to the Spanish Ambassador that he purposed setting out at once, and that orders might be given to the captain of the steamer, when he should arrive at Civita Vecchia, to sail to the port of Gaeta, whither he had determined to proceed. The intended flight had been already communicated to upwards of fifty persons, ecclesiastics and seculars, and everything was in readiness for its accomplishment. It took place in the following manner:—

Count Spaur, Minister of His Majesty the King of Bavaria, wished to take upon himself the duty of accompanying the Pope on his secret journey. Meanwhile, the Palace of the Quirinal, which had witnessed the savage assault of the 16th, was surrounded on all sides by armed men, and guarded by a great number of sentinels; so that the escape of the Pope seemed to be a matter of impossibility — at least, beyond his power, or that of his faithful friends, to accomplish. But Providence was on the side of the good, and against the wicked. It was about the dusk of the evening when, in pursuance of the plan that had been adopted, the Duke of Harcourt, whose despatches have been quoted, came to visit the Pope, leaving his carriage at the foot of the stairs by which all those who are about to have an audience with the Holy Father must ascend. After a short communication with the Duke, the Pope asked him to remain in his cabinet, in order that he himself might retire to another apartment, and, laying aside his white robes, assume the dress of an ordinary priest. This humble toilet was completed in a few minutes; and the Holy Father, who throughout preserved the greatest calmness and tranquillity of mind, took his leave of the Duke, who was deeply affected, but who was compelled to remain awhile in the cabinet, in order to give the fugitives time to pass through the secret apartments, and descend into the Cortile by another staircase. The Cavalier Filippani a Roman, who had a carriage in readiness in the cortile, accompanied the Pope through the spacious halls along which they had to pass, their footsteps lighted only by a single taper, which was borne by the Cavalier. As they passed through one of the apartments, the taper was suddenly extinguished, and both the Pope and his attendant were left in total darkness. To proceed further without light was impossible; so Filippani was obliged, in order to re-light the taper, to return to the same cabinet in which the French Ambassador had been purposely left waiting. On seeing Filippani return, the Duke was seized with astonishment and terror, believing that some untoward occurrence had occasioned the extinction of the taper, and deranged the entire plan of escape; but his mind was immediately relieved, and his apprehensions of danger removed, by the assurance that it had occurred through mere accident. All cause of apprehension was not yet over; for just as the Pope was about stepping into the carriage prepared for him, a domestic, accustomed to show respect to his illustrious master, and totally forgetful of impending danger, cast himself upon his knees to receive the blessing. Fortunately, however, he instantly arose upon a sign to that effect being rapidly made to him.

The Cavalier Filippani got into the carriage along with the Pope, and the carriage crossed the Piazza and Cortile of the Quirinal, which was full of guards, whose attention was so engaged at that very moment—one might almost say miraculously so—that they did not perceive who it was that passed; and Pius thus escaped, through the midst of armed men, from the palace in which he had been held and treated as an actual prisoner. Having passed the Piazza del Quirinale, the carriage descended by the Via delle tre Canelle into the Piazza degli SS. Apostili, and having traversed a portion of the Corso, proceeded through different streets to the Coliseum, and thence by the Via or Strada Labicana, from whence the Pope arrived on foot at the monastery of SS. Marcellino e Pietro, where Count Spaur, with another conveyance, was awaiting him. Having passed through the adjoining gate of S. Giovanni, he arrived without any mishap at the gate of Albano, and, in accordance with the plan previously arranged, went somewhat out of his way by the so-called Gallerie di Castel Gondolfo, where he was to meet the post-chaise which was to carry him to Gaeta, and which fortunately was there in readiness to receive him. The Pope descended from the conveyance in which he had arrived, and rested against a paling during the short space of time in which they were adjusting his trifling baggage; and at this very moment three gendarmes on patrole happened to pass by, and halted between the carriage and the Pope. But he calmly saluted them, by wishing them "a good night." His dress, that of an ordinary priest, saved him from their recognition. Count Spaur now mounted to the box seat; and the Holy Father, with the Countess and her son Maximilian, then about the age of eighteen, and a Bavarian priest, D. Sebastian Liebel, entered the carriage. At dawn, on the 25th, they arrived safely at Fondi, and continued their route to Mola di Gaeta, where they met Cardinal Antonelli and Count Arnan,

Secretary to the Spanish Embassy; whose exertions and zeal, in conjunction with those of the Ambassador Martinez della Rosa, cannot be too highly praised, directed as they were to assist the Supreme Pontiff in this afflicting emergency. Here the Pope rested for some hours, and then, accompanied by the same retinue, proceeded to the neighbouring Gaeta, expecting that he should there find the diocesan Bishop. Before parting, however, he wrote a letter to the King of Naples, and Count Spaur offered himself to be its bearer. In this letter the Pope informed King Ferdinand, that, having been compelled to abandon Rome, he felt himself bound to announce to him that he had entered his kingdom; but that he did not wish, by his presence, to cause him the least trouble during the stay which he would be obliged to make, whilst waiting for the vessel which should carry him to Spain. The Nuncio of the Pope, who had left the King a little time before, returned again to the Royal Palace with the Bavarian Minister, who about midnight presented to his Majesty the letter of which he was the bearer. Scarcely had the King read it, when, with a promptitude and alacrity that displayed alike his generosity and attachment to the Vicar of Christ, he gave orders that a vessel should on the instant be got in readiness, and such matters placed in it as his own mind suggested would be most necessary to supply the wants of the Pope and the companions of his exile. Then he himself, with the Queen and the entire Royal family, going on board, sailed immediately for Gaeta, where the vessel arrived about mid-day. In the meantime, the Pope, not having found the Bishop at his residence, betook himself to an humble inn, without having been recognised; and there he passed the night.   On the King's arrival at Gaeta, he caused the Queen to be conveyed to one of the palaces, and then taking another route, in order to escape the observation of the curious crowd, prevailed upon the Pope to leave his humble dwelling unobserved, and come to the Royal palace; which invitation, warmly and affectionately urged, was accepted by the Holy Father.   On the Pope's arrival at the palace, he was met by the Queen, who received him, on bended knees, at the foot of the staircase.   Much affected at this reception, the Pope gave his blessing to the good Queen, and, raising her up, he ascended the stairs in company with her, and conversed with her Majesty until the arrival of the King, who could not speak through emotion, as he beheld the illustrious fugitive beneath his roof, and thought of the indignities and outrages which he had endured.   And it must be said, in justice to the King of Naples, that he maintained throughout the entire of the Pope's long stay in his dominions — a period of nearly seventeen months—the same generous solicitude for his comfort, and the same veneration and affection which he displayed from the very first moment, when he found the loftiest Majesty of the Christian world sheltered in a lowly inn, a fugitive from the rage of enemies who had turned his capital into a Pandemonium.

Before referring to subsequent events, it may be well to say something of the feeling which the flight of the Pope excited, wherever the sad story was heard.

CHAP. VIII.

The Flight of the Pope supposed to be the Downfall of the Papacy.
— Former Popes driven from Rome — Pius VI. and Pius VII.
— General Cavaignac's Letter. — Testimony of the " Times."—
Addresses pour in on the Pope. — Offers of Hospitality.

" THE Pope has fled — the Papacy is at an end!"
This was the cry which, uttered by the vainglorious
revolutionists of Rome, was repeated, with more or
less of exaggeration, by every thoughtless enemy of the
Church. From press, and platform, and pulpit, the
ominous announcement rang forth — " The Papacy is
at an end!" Bigots piously congratulated each other
as they met, on the happy overthrow of the too long-en-
dured abominations of the Vatican. Never more was
the Scarlet Lady to sit upon the Seven Hills of the
modern Babylon! The reign of Antichrist was at
an end! The miserable fabric of pasteboard and paint
had been swept to everlasting ruin by the strong
breath of Public Opinion! Let " alleluias " ascend to
heaven, for man was once more free! Such were the
tidings of gladness which thrilled the soul of the fanatic,

and led astray the judgment of the shallow. People who thus rejoiced in what seemed to be the fulfilment of their own prophecies, knew little of the Church, little of her history, and much less of the political agencies by which, for a longer time than any existing monarchy has endured, Providence has protected the Papacy, and guarded from spoliation its temporal possessions.

Pius IX. was not the first Pope who was compelled to leave Rome, whether through the ingratitude of a deluded people, or the hostility of a foreign foe; nor, in all human probability, will he be the last. Of the past, let a few instances suffice to show, that, although Popes have been driven from their Capital, not only was the Papacy untouched, and its temporal possessions secure, but that persecution gave new life and imparted greater energy to the Church.

Gelasius the Second was forced to leave Rome by the Emperor Henry the Fifth, and to fly for refuge to France — a country even at that period (A. D. 1118) offering a ready asylum to the Sovereign Pontiffs. On his journey, all the nobility and clergy of Provence came to meet him; and the King of France fell prostrate at his feet.

Eugenius the Third, like our Pius, was compelled to leave Rome through the conduct of his people, instigated to rebellion by Arnold da Brescia; and in his flight this Pontiff was met by deputations representing the majority of the bishops and people of Armenia, who,

H

shaking off the Nestorian heresy, became reconciled to the Church.

Alexander the Third was exposed to the outrages of the faction of the Emperor Frederick (Barbarossa)— to escape whose fury the venerable Pontiff wandered a fugitive through Italy, France, and Germany. But his long exile was one continued ovation. The princes and people of all Christian nations rivalled each other to do him honour. Messages and gifts flowed in from the King of Jerusalem, and even from Emanuel Comnenus, Emperor of Constantinople, who was a supporter of the Greek heresy; and the Kings of France and England esteemed it an honour to wait upon the illustrious exile. The Catholic Bishops of all countries, including St. Thomas of Canterbury, tendered him their homage, and addressed him letters of affectionate sympathy. And, finally, a league was formed, by the Venetians and the different cities of Lombardy, to protect him against Frederick; who, at last, was forced to throw himself as a suppliant before the outraged Pontiff, and, upon his knees, to beg for mercy and pardon. This struggle, one of the most protracted and perilous which the Papacy ever had to encounter, terminated in the establishment of the See of Rome on a much firmer basis than before.

Coming down to late times, we behold Pius VI. exposed to danger and persecution, and eventually dying in exile. He is compelled to deliver up, by extorted treaty, important portions of his possessions, and to submit to see the priceless treasures of art with

which he had enriched his galleries, made the spoil of
the conqueror. His capital is occupied by a French
army — his authority is superseded — a Republic, on
the model of that of France, is established in its stead;
and because he will not acknowledge the usurpation, he
is compelled to leave the Vatican, and seek shelter in
a convent near Florence, in which he is allowed to remain but a short time. Treated like a criminal, and
transmitted from fortress to fortress, Pius VI. at last
yields up a life of suffering, most heroically endured.
Still the Papacy was not destroyed, nor was its temporal sovereignty at an end.

In Venice, not in Rome, was his successor, Pius VII.,
elected. Alike in name, he was also similar to him in his
sufferings. There are many yet living who remember
the persecutions to which this saintly Pope was subjected. The policy of the Directory was to uproot the
Papacy — that of Napoleon was to maintain it, but in
complete subjection to his authority. "All Italy,"
said Napoleon, writing to Pius, in the year 1805,
"must be subject to *my* laws. Your situation requires
that you should pay me the same respect in temporal,
which I do you in spiritual matters. You are sovereign
of Rome, but I am its emperor. All my enemies must
be its enemies. No Sardinian, English, Russian, or
Swedish envoy may be permitted to reside at your
capital." The reply of Pius to that extraordinary,
being who already aimed at universal dominion, and
whose star of destiny then rose high in the ascendant,
was dignified and firm; the more so, that his position

placed him at the mercy of the conqueror. Pius thus writes : —

" Your Majesty lays it down as a fundamental principle that you are Sovereign of Rome. The supreme Pontiff admits no such authority, nor any power superior in temporal matters to his own. There is no Emperor of Rome. It is not thus that Charlemagne treated our predecessors. The demand to dismiss the envoys of Russia, England, and Sweden, is positively refused : the Father of the faithful is bound to remain at peace with all, without distinction of Catholics or heretics."

Every one acquainted with the events of those times knows how Buonaparte gradually stripped the Pope of his dominions — how the excommunication boldly launched at him by Pius, was resented by the armed invasion of his palace, and the seizure of his person — how for years he was kept as a prisoner in the fortress of Fenestrelles, and, when ultimately brought to Fontainebleau, compelled to submit to terms which seemed to place the independence of the Church beneath the armed heel of the conqueror, and render the Vicar of Christ the subject, if not the slave, of an earthly monarch. Still the Papacy was not at an end ; and Rome once again hailed with grateful affection its long-suffering and saintly sovereign, Pius VII. And, as in previous instances, the trials and humiliations to which the august Head of the Church was subjected, only drew more strongly towards the Chair of Peter the sympathy and allegiance of the faithful throughout the Christian world.

Look now to the last instance in which foolish men beheld the downfal of the Papacy.

"Pius IX. has seen the last of Rome," said one eye-witness of the events of 1848. "We have beheld the end of the reign of the Popes," said another. And thus writes one of the inspired madmen of the hour—"The Republic is erected on the ruins of the throne of the Popes, which the shout of all Europe, the maledictions of all people, and the spirit of the Gospel, have trampled in the dust." The wretch who wrote this lied and raved at the same time.

Every generous nation of the earth sympathised with the illustrious victim of human fickleness and ingratitude; and from the midst of every Catholic people came the most ardent expressions of homage and devotion. The sovereigns and princes of Europe wrote to Pius in terms of the greatest respect and affection; and the chief Catholic Powers vied with each other for the honour of receiving him within their dominions. The most eloquent orators in the French Assembly and the Spanish Cortez, while eulogizing his virtues and enumerating his many acts of liberality, enforced the necessity of the Pope having absolute independence in the government of his territories.

It was in the following language, so earnest and so full of warmth, that the heroic Cavaignac, then at the head of the French Republic, wrote to His Holiness, in the very hour which was declared by false prophets to be that of his "downfal:"—

"Paris, Dec. 3.

"Very Holy Father—I address this dispatch and another from the Archbishop of Nicea, your Nuncio to the government of the Republic, to your Holiness, by one of my aides-de-camp.

"The French nation, deeply afflicted at the troubles with which your Holiness has been assailed within a short period, has been moreover profoundly affected at the sentiment of paternal confidence which induced your Holiness to demand, temporarily, hospitality in France; which it will be happy and proud to secure to you, and which it will render worthy of itself and of your Holiness. I write to you therefore in order that no feeling of uneasiness or unfounded apprehension may divert your Holiness from your first resolution. The Republic, the existence of which is already consecrated by the mature, persevering, and sovereign will of the French nation, will see with pride your Holiness give to the world the spectacle of that exclusively religious consecration which your presence in the midst of it announces, and it will receive you with the dignity and the religious respect which becomes this great and generous nation. I have felt the necessity of giving your Holiness this assurance, and I heartily desire that your arrival may take place without much delay.

"It is with those sentiments, Very Holy Father, that I am your respectful son,

"GENERAL CAVAIGNAC."

And on the following Christmas Day the diplomatic body, then assembled at Gaeta—and including the Russian Ambassador at Naples — waited on the Pope, and thus addressed His Holiness through the Ambassador of Spain:—

"Holy Father, on this solemn day, consecrated by religion, the diplomatic body performs a duty in laying at the feet of your Holiness its most respectful and sincere homage. Having witnessed the virtues which your Holiness displayed in circumstances too striking ever to be forgotten, we are happy to express on this occasion the same sentiments of admiration and devotedness, as unalterable as the virtues they inspire.   In wishing your Holiness the peace and happiness of which you are so worthy, we are only faithful interpreters of the wishes of our Governments, who all take a lively interest in the fate of the Sovereign Pontiff, whose cause is too just, too holy, not to be protected by Him, who holds in His powerful hand the destinies of nations and kings."

While that section of the public press of these countries, which represents the extreme anti-Catholic portion of the population, laboured to prove that the flight of the Pope was not only the destruction of his temporal sovereignty, but the ruin of his spiritual influence, there were some writers who, either fairer or more far-seeing, took quite a different view of the real position of Catholic affairs.   Amongst those who did not suffer their judgment to be blinded by their prejudices, was a writer in the *Times* of December 4th ; a passage from whose able and generally well-toned article on the great event of the hour, is a striking testimony against the ravings of bigotry : —

"It is a matter of history, however singular and unwelcome such an assertion may sound, that in the very hour of his flight and his fall, Pius IX. was and is more entirely and essentially pope and head of the Latin Church than many hundreds of his predecessors have been amidst all the

splendour of the Lateran.   Personally the deposed Pontiff
has exhibited to the world no common share of evangelical
virtues ; and though his political abilities proved inadequate
to execute the moderate reforms he had entered upon, from
the unworthiness of his subjects and the infelicity of these
times, yet the apparition of so benignant and conscientious
a man on the Papal throne, in the midst of the turmoil of
Europe, has forcibly struck the imagination and won the
affection of the whole Roman Catholic population of Europe.   Accordingly, at a crisis when every other constituted
authority has been more or less shaken, and every other
institution tried, the Romish hierarchy has, in all countries
where it exists, extended its influence, and more displayed
its power."

At no period of his Pontificate did Pius IX. command
a greater degree of influence throughout the Catholic
world than during his stay at Gaeta.   With a lowlier
reverence, and a more profound devotion, Catholic
nations bowed before the venerable Father of the
Church; no longer enthroned amidst the splendours of
the Vatican. but an exile, driven from his capital by
violence and treason.   Declarations of attachment, professions of admiration and sympathy, offers of assistance, and presents of money, poured in upon the Pope.
And it may be here properly remarked, that of the vast
sums which he has since expended in works of utility
and charity in Rome, the larger portion was then derived from the generous and spontaneous offerings of the
faithful.   In every living language did sympathy convey
its sweet consolation to the wounded heart of Pius.
And perhaps one of the most touching letters received
by the Holy Father was one sent to him by a Lutheran

Protestant, named Christian Freytag, of Lubec, enclosing thirty ducats, and concluding in these words : —

" Permit me, Holy Father, who am penetrated with the most profound respect for your holy person, to continue my prayers for you to our Saviour, Christ Jesus. Deign, in return, to bless my family, who, although Protestant Lutherans, implore for you the choicest blessings from the hands of our Father in Heaven, who Himself is Love and Holiness."

Addresses poured in upon the Royal Exile from the Archbishops and Bishops of Martinique, Oregon, Agra, the Mexican Confederation, Auckland, Bosnia (in the Ottoman Empire), Japan, Lima, Melbourne, Pondicherry, Sydney, Santiago; and, without enumerating the places or dioceses throughout the world from which there flowed one great tide of sympathy, it is enough to say, that on whatever spot of the earth a Catholic altar was raised, or in which a Catholic community existed, there was experienced a filial sense of horror at the outrages perpetrated on the Holy Father—and that the entire Church felt aggrieved in the sacred person of the Supreme Pontiff.

But in no country did the events which terminated in the flight of the Pope excite a more profound feeling of regret, or a keener sense of indignation, than in Ireland; and by no people was attachment to the person of the Pope, and devotion to the Holy See, more ardently and emphatically expressed, than by the Catholic population of that country. Loving liberty with passionate ardour, and sympathising with every generous effort made by the oppressed nations of Europe to shake off the yoke of the stranger, they looked with horror upon the brutal and sacrilegious outrages with which the most illustrious, as well as the most enlightened and well-intentioned reformer of the age, had been rewarded for his large and liberal concessions. They had followed every step of his political progress with the deepest interest, enhanced by a consciousness of the dangers which he had to encounter, and a knowledge of the complicated obstacles that lay in his path; and they sickened with disgust as they read of the murder of the Pope's minister, and the assault upon the Quirinal. For independently of the ingratitude which such atrocities evinced, they saw how the dagger and the bullet of the assassin struck at that very Liberty whose prostituted name he invoked. The people of Ireland well knew that such excesses, which delivered up Rome to a reign of anarchy, afforded a ready excuse to every despotism, and a plea against all concessions to popular demands.

At any rate, at no time in the history of the Church did a sentiment of more complete identity exist, than that which now bound so many wide-spread nations and races to the Chair of Peter. The rock on which the hand of God had placed the Church was never stronger than in this hour, when the storm howled, and the waves of human passion dashed against it in their fury. Neither was the Papacy at an end; nor were its temporal power and possessions to be torn from it. For — such was the will of Providence — the de-

scendants of the same race that, through their sovereign
Charlemagne, restored the keys of the cities of the
Exarchate, which were torn from the grasp of the Lombard invader, and placed them on the altar of St. Peter,
were, in a few brief months from the hour of the flight of
Pius, to lay at his feet the keys of his liberated capital.
And, most wonderful dispensation of Providence! the
same nation that would have blotted out the Papacy
under the Great Revolution, or held it in bondage beneath the armed power of the First Napoleon, now
rushed to its rescue under a Republic, whose President
gloried in the fact that he was the nephew of the very
Emperor who had held in captivity the sacred person
of Pius VII. And yet there were those who shouted—
" The Papacy is at an end!"

During the Pope's sojourn at Gaeta, that port was
frequented by vessels from many nations — including
France, Portugal, Spain, Piedmont, and America, —
who sent deputations to the Holy Father, offering him
their hospitality, and the homage of their respect. The
Protestant King of Prussia placed at the Pope's disposal a castle in his own dominions; and on the part of
England, Admiral Parker came twice to Gaeta, offering him an asylum in the island of Malta. But overcome by the cordial and generous reception which the
King of Naples had given him, and by the desire
which that monarch expressed of his remaining in his
territory, Pius resolved upon doing so, more especially
as the vicinity of Gaeta to Rome afforded just grounds
for its being preferred to the other States.

CHAP. IX.

Confusion in Rome at the Flight of the Pope. — His Protest from
Gaeta. — The Constituent Assembly convoked. — Arrival of
Mazzini. — State of Rome. — Pius appeals to the Catholic
Powers.—His Appeal responded to.

IT is not necessary to enter into a detail of the events
which followed the departure of the Pope; nor to justify a course which, though irritating to a ministry
who had been absolutely forced upon His Holiness with
fire and sword, was inevitable, if the personal freedom
of the Sovereign were to be preserved. "The Pope,"
said the proclamation of this bewildered ministry,
" ceding to fatal counsels, quitted Rome this night."
Rifle-bullets, scaling ladders, combustibles, and pointed
cannon, must have meant "fatal counsels;" for to
these the Holy Father certainly did yield. The protest
made by the Pope at Gaeta will sufficiently describe
what took place since his quitting Rome on the 25th of
November. It also briefly refers to the efforts which
he had made to satisfy the demands and promote the
happiness of his subjects. This protest was made on
the 17th of December : —

" Raised by Divine dispensation, in a manner almost miraculous, in spite of our unworthiness, to the Sovereign Pontificate, one of my first cares was to endeavour to establish a union between the subjects of the temporal state of the Church, to make peace between families, to do them good in all ways, and, as far as depended upon us, to render the state peaceable and flourishing. But the benefits which we did all in our power to heap upon our subjects, the wide founded institutions which we have granted to their desires, far, as we must in all candour declare, from inspiring that acknowledgment and gratitude which we had every right to expect, have occasioned to our heart only reiterated pain and bitterness, caused by those ungrateful men whom our paternal eye wished to see daily diminishing in number. All the world can now tell how our benefits have been answered, what abuse has been made of our concessions, how, by denaturalizing them, and perverting the meaning of our words, they have sought to mislead the multitude, so that these very benefits and institutions have been turned by certain men into arms, with which they have committed the most violent outrages upon our sovereign authority, and against the temporal rights of the Holy See. Our heart refuses to repeat in detail the events which have taken place since November 15, the day on which a minister who had our confidence was barbarously murdered by the hand of an assassin, applauded with a still greater barbarity by a troop of infuriated enemies to God, to man, and to every just political institution. This first crime opened the way to a series of crimes committed the following day, with sacrilegious audacity. They have already incurred the execration of every upright mind in our state, in Italy, and in Europe; they have incurred execration in all parts of the earth. This is the reason why we can spare our heart the intense pain of recapitulating them here.

" We were constrained to withdraw from the place in which they were committed — from that place where vio-

lence prevented us from applying any remedy, reduced
to weep over and deplore with good men those sad events,
and still more lamentable want of power in justice to act
against the perpetrators of these abominable crimes.   Providence has conducted us to this town of Gaeta, where, finding ourselves at full liberty, we have, against the authors of
the aforesaid attempts and acts of violence, solemnly renewed the protests which we issued at Rome at the first
moment, in the presence of the representatives accredited
to us of the Courts of Europe, and of other and distant
nations.   By the same act, without in any manner departing
from the institutions we had created, we took care to give
temporarily to our states a legitimate governmental representation, in order that in the capital and throughout the
State provision should be made for the regular and ordinary
course of public affairs, as well as for the protection of the
persons and property of our subjects.   By us, moreover, has
been prorogued the session of the High Council and the
Council of Deputies, who had recently been called to resume
their interrupted sitting.   But these determinations of our
authority, instead of causing the perturbators and the
authors of the acts of sacrilegious violence of which we
have spoken to return into the path of duty, have urged them
to make still greater attempts.   Arrogating to themselves
the rights of sovereignty, which belong only to us, they have,
by means of the two councils, instituted in the capital an
illegitimate governmental representation, under the title of
Provisional Supreme Junta of the State, which they have
published by an Act dated the 12th of the present month.
The duties of our sovereignty, in which we cannot fail, the
solemn oaths with which we have, in the presence of God,
promised to preserve the patrimony of the Holy See, and to
transmit it in all its integrity to our successors, obliges us to
raise our voice solemnly, and protest before God, and in the
face of the whole universe, against this gross and sacrilegious attempt.   Therefore we declare to be null, and of no

force or effect in law, all the acts which have followed the violence committed upon us, protesting above all that the Junta of State established at Rome is an usurpation of our sovereign powers, and that the said Junta has not and cannot have any authority.   Be it known, then, to all our subjects, whatever may be their rank or condition, that at Rome, and throughout the whole extent of the Pontifical State, there is not and cannot be any legitimate power which does not emanate expressly from us ; that we have by the sovereign *motu propria* of the 27th November, instituted a temporary commission of government, and that to it alone belongs exclusively the government of the nation during our absence, and until we ourselves shall have otherwise ordained.   " PIUS PAPA IX."

This protest, when published in Rome, was torn down and trampled upon ; and the " Supreme Junta," in the belief, or on the plea, that by such a course alone could the horrors of impending anarchy and dissolution be prevented, called on the ministry to present to the Chamber of Deputies a project of law for the convocation of a Constituent Assembly.   This proposal was adopted ; and a Roman journal of the day thus describes the intended character of the new constitution :—

" It consists of fifteen articles, and explains the mode of election and qualification of the members and electors.   The elections are to be by electoral colleges.   This Bill for the summoning of a Constituent Assembly at Rome, as presented to the Roman Parliament, proposed to enact that the election to the Assembly should take place on the 25th of January, by universal suffrage and ballot ; that the Assembly should be of two hundred members, paid at the rate of two crowns a day, without property qualification ; and, finally, that the Assembly should meet at Rome on the 5th of February."

The Constituent Assembly, thus chosen and thus constituted, was formally opened on the day appointed; and its first act was to declare the Roman Republic, and depose the Pope.   One of the most prominent actors on this occasion was Sterbini, who, having come to Rome after the publication of the amnesty with which Pius IX. inaugurated his reign, and taken advantage of the relaxation of the laws relating to the press, established the *Contemporaneo*, under the affectation of promoting moral and social reforms; and increasing in audacity as time progressed, and as " the people " grew more and more " exacting, " he became the promoter of disaffection, and the organ of sedition.   There were some men of character and prudence in the Assembly, such as Mamiani, who endeavoured to prevent, if possible, the adoption of this extreme course; but they were overborne by the vehemence of those who had nothing to lose, and everything to gain; by the ardour of the young, the rash, and the inexperienced; and by the cries and shouts of the gallery — the Roman " Mountain," which was to be from henceforward the chief power of the Assembly, and the capricious despot whose approval was to be propitiated by gross flattery, or by coward submission to its violence.

The same " Mountain " thundered forth its loudest peal of welcome, as Mazzini, in a month after the opening of the Constituent Assembly, was conducted to a seat of honour beside the President.   The wildest exultation filled the breasts of his disciples and followers, as the High Priest of Insurrection at length arrived, to witness the splendid result of his machinations, and enjoy the short-lived triumph of an impracticable republic. From the Capitol of Rome — once again to be the Teacher, if not the Mistress, of the world — was freedom to be proclaimed to the whole human race!

But soon did those who assumed the task of governing a people whom they had systematically educated to a disgust of every restraint whatsoever, begin to appreciate the difficulties of their position. Having themselves given a flagrant example of disregard for the respect which is due to legitimate authority, it was not to be expected that their influence with an excited and turbulent populace would be of much avail. In vain were pompous proclamations, appealing to republican virtue, placarded on the walls; in vain did orators, once demagogues and incendiaries, now preach peace and patience, and expatiate, in stilted phrases, on the beauty of order. These fine words did not stay the uplifted hand of the assassin, or scare the noonday robber from his spoil. Rome became the attraction and refuge of the scattered vagabondage of Italy; and the peaceful portion of the population beheld, with consternation, their city, their property, and their lives, at the mercy of lawless wretches, whose utterly desperate fortunes fitted them for every deed of violence and rapine. Now indeed might the well-intentioned deplore the loss of a mild and benevolent sovereign, the recollection of whose light and gentle rule rendered the iron pressure of a brutal yoke more odious and intolerable. Industry paralysed, trade destroyed, employment hopeless, credit

I

annihilated, houses untenanted, hotels deserted, and the streets swarming with an idle, starving, and desperate population, Rome presented a miserable spectacle to the civilised world, notwithstanding her enjoyment of her newborn freedom, and her emancipation from the thraldom of a " priestling," as one of the orators of the Assembly indecently described the Supreme Pontiff.

In such a state of things, what course was left to the Pope but to demand aid from the Catholic Powers, and obtain, through armed intervention, the restoration of his dominions? Was he to return alone to the captivity from which he had almost miraculously escaped, and trust himself to the tender mercies of a rabble brutified by idleness, by turbulence, and by crime ? Or was he to submit himself to the disposal of the men who, since the very hour when they availed themselves of his freely-bestowed pardon, had been plotting his downfal? In all probability, had Pius IX. been rash enough to return to Rome, or not to have fled from Rome, the world might have heard, with new horror, that the Vicar of Christ was the occupant of a dungeon in the fortress of St. Angelo.

The Pope appealed, wisely appealed, to the great Catholic Powers, and demanded their armed assistance. This he did, by his Cardinal Secretary of State (Antorelli), in a note of singular ability and power, dated from Gaeta, the 18th of February, 1849. In it were recapitulated the reforms and concessions that he had granted, as well as the various machinations by

which his efforts were neutralised, and the good he
intended was converted into sources of evil.

The document is one of considerable length ; but the
following passages will sufficiently describe its character,
and indicate its purpose :—

" After the most iniquitous malversations to reward their
accomplices, and get rid of honest and God-fearing men —
after so many assassinations committed under their guidance
—after having let loose rebellion, immorality, irreligion—
after having seduced the imprudent youths, desecrating
even the places consecrated to public worship by converting
them into dens of most licentious soldiery, formed of runa-
ways and criminals from foreign countries — the anarchists
wished to reduce the capital of the Catholic world, the See
of the Pontiff, to a sink of impiety, destroying, if they could,
all idea of sovereignty for him who is destined by Providence to govern the Universal Church ; and who, precisely
to exercise freely his authority over all the Catholic world,
enjoyed as an estate the patrimony of the Church. At sight
of such desolations and massacres the Holy Father could not
but be profoundly grieved, and at the same time moved to
weep over his faithful subjects, who claimed his aid and his
succour to be delivered from the most atrocious tyranny.

. . . .

" The decree called fundamental, emanating on the 9th
inst. (February) from the Roman Constituent Assembly, is an
act which is the essence of the blackest felony and most
abominable impiety. It declares, principally, the Pope deposed by fact and by right from the temporal government of
the Roman State ; it proclaims a Republic ; and by another
act is decreed the confiscation of the armoury of St. Peter.
His Holiness, seeing that it disgraces his supreme dignity of
Pontiff and Sovereign, protests before all the sovereigns,
before all nations, and before the Catholics of the entire

world, against this excess of irreligion, against so violent an attempt, which despoils him of his sacred and incontestible rights.   If a proper remedy is not applied to this state of things, succour will arrive only when the States of the Church, at present a prey to their most cruel enemies, will be reduced to ashes.

" The Holy Father having meanwhile exhausted all the means in his power, obliged, by his duty to the Catholic world, to preserve in its entirety the patrimony of the Church and the sovereignty which is annexed to it, so indispensable to maintain his liberty and independence as Supreme Chief of the Church herself, moved by the sighs of his faithful subjects, who loudly implore his aid to deliver them from the iron yoke of tyranny which they cannot endure, addresses himself to the Foreign Powers, and in a particular manner to those Catholic Powers who, with such generosity of soul and in so glorious a manner, have manifested their firm intention to defend his cause.   He has confidence that they will concur with solicitude, by their moral intervention, to re-establish him in his See, in the capital of his dominions, which have been piously allotted for his support in full liberty and independence, and which have been guaranteed by the treaties that form the basis of European nationality.

"And since Austria, France, Spain, and the kingdom of the Two Sicilies, are, by their geographical position, in a situation to be able efficaciously to concur by their armies in re-establishing in the Holy See the order which has been destroyed by a band of sectarians, the Holy Father, relying in the religious feeling of those powerful children of the Church, demands with full confidence their armed intervention to deliver the States of the Church from this band of wretches, who, by every sort of crime, have practised the most atrocious despotism."

To this appeal, which it pained the heart of Pius to make, but which the madness of his enemies rendered

a matter of necessity, the Catholic Powers responded
with a generous alacrity, and a filial ardour; and,
ere many weeks had passed, Rome witnessed the
approach of the army of France—this time come, not to
assail the Papacy, nor to rifle of their priceless treasures
the galleries and temples of the Eternal City: but to
restore to the Pope his venerable Capital, and rescue its
people from the horrors of anarchy and confusion.

Some few instances may best represent the state to
which the special friends of human liberty had succeeded
in bringing things in Rome, the centre of their Model
Republic.

CHAP. X.

Profane Rites in St. Peter's. — Atrocities of the Republic. —
Delusion of the Republicans. — Lord Palmerston's Advice. —
Appeals to France and England. — Armed Intervention indis-
pensable.

THE Triumvirs — Mazzini, Armanelli, and Saffi —
determined to celebrate the great festival of Easter with
all the religious pomp which could be obtained in the
absence of the Supreme Pontiff; and, accordingly, they
commanded the Canons of St. Peter's to prepare for the
same magnificent worship which the Pope had usually
celebrated, and which had hitherto attracted the Catholic faithful from all parts of the world to the centre of
Catholic unity.   The good priests, loyal to their duty
as ministers of God, refused to play the ignominious
part of political showmen, more especially in this sad
hour of the Church's desolation.   Compelled by the
honourable refusal of the Canons to look elsewhere
for a celebrant of rites which, to many, had an air of impiety, the Triumvirs were content to avail themselves
of the assistance of a priest alleged to be under inter-
dict, and who celebrated pontifically at one of the four
altars of St. Peter's, at which only the Pope and
the Dean of the Sacred College, appointed by Papal

Bull, are authorised to offer the Holy Sacrifice. The sublime church was dressed in all its festal splendour; but instead of the Pope, the Cardinals, and the Prelates, there were present the Triumvirs, the Deputies, public officials, and the Clubs; while the Tuscan, Swiss, American, and English consuls also graced the motley assembly by their presence. Military music was substituted for the glorious chaunt of the Papal choir. At the conclusion of the Mass, the presumptuous priest went in procession to the great balcony, from which on that day twelve-month the Holy Father had given his benediction to his people; and, bearing the Blessed Sacrament in his hand, and surrounded by the banners of the Republic, he imparted his blessing to a kneeling multitude, amidst the pealing of bells and the roar of cannon. Mazzini, too, presented himself to the deluded people, who shouted for him, and the liberty which, through him and his followers, they then enjoyed. This solemn mockery, according to one of the organs of the revolution, was the festival of the " New Pasch." " The Vicar of Christ was wanted," said the writer, who added, " but not by our fault; and, though he was away, we had the people and God." For their courageous resistance to the commands of the Triumvirs, the Canons were condemned to pay each a fine of 120 scudi; not indeed solely for this offence, but also for having refused to sing the *Te Deum* for the Republic! The reason given for this sentence was, " That the Canons had grievously offended the dignity of religion, and excited scandal; and that it was the duty of the govern-

ment to preserve religion from contamination."* Their
punishment was, however, a very trifling one, when compared with that which was inflicted on the Provost of the
Cathedral of Sinigaglia, who was murdered on the
21st of March, 1849, for having guiltily refused to sing
Te Deum for the proclamation of the Republic !

The celebration of the festival of *Corpus Domini* was
even more glaringly profaned; the Republican leaders
playing a still more prominent part, to the indignation of
the faithful.

In times of civil commotion, when the authority of
the executive is subservient to the caprice or fury of
the populace, all kinds of excesses may be calculated
upon with certainty; for in such moments it happens,
either that acts of individual ferocity pass for proofs of
a zeal perhaps too exaggerated in its manifestation, or
that those entrusted with the administration of the laws
find themselves too weak to arrest, or too much compromised to punish, their perpetrators. The short-lived
Roman Republic was not unfruitful of monsters, some
of whom, for savagery and blood-thirstiness, would not
have suffered by comparison with the most ferocious
" Reds " of the Reign of Terror, in the first French
Revolution. Amongst those who earned for themselves
an infamous notoriety was Lambianchi, who appeared
to have had a special mission — namely, to hunt down
and kill all kinds of ecclesiastics. This mild patriot was
indignant at the absurd leniency of the government,

* Stato Romano, book v. cap. 6.

that released, after a short imprisonment, a number of priests and civilians, whom, on account of their dislike to the Republic, he had sent as prisoners and criminals to Rome. In the estimation of this zealot, hostility to the Republic was the greatest of all offences, and, as such, richly merited death. He was then stationed on the confines of Naples, on duty with the Revenue Police; and from thence he had forwarded his prisoners to Rome, in the full belief that the bullet or the sword was to be the reward of their monstrous guilt. Disgusted with what he held to be the criminal weakness of the authorities, he swore that in future, not only would he act the part of the officer of justice, but that of judge and executioner. And he kept his oath with exemplary exactness; for when, on his return to Rome, he encountered, on the road of Monte Maria, the parish priest, Father Sghirla, a Dominican, he slew him on the spot, and afterwards made a boast of his meritorious act! Having commenced so happily, he determined to render still greater service to the Republic. He took up his residence near Santa Maria, in Trastevere; and having "suspected" that priests and monks were conspiring the ruin of the Republic, he prowled about in quest of his prey, and, having succeeded in seizing several, shut them up in San Callisto, and commenced slaughtering them at his pleasure. It is not known how many such proofs he thus gave of the strictness of his republican principles; but he himself afterwards boasted that they were "very many." Neither are the names of his victims accurately known; but amongst those who thus fell by the hand

of this monster, was another Dominican, Father
Pelliciajo, the priest of Santa Maria sopra Minerva.
It was said that fourteen were found half-buried in the
convent garden; but it is certain that, having information
of these assassinations, the government sent its officers
to save the prisoners who remained alive, and that twelve
were rescued in spite of the resistance of the executioners.
Those who were thus rescued were either priests or
monks.*

A still bloodier tragedy was enacted in the noon-
day, on one of the most public spots in Rome, and in
the presence of a considerable multitude.   Two unfortunate men had been seized, and were conducted into
Rome in the midst of a threatening mob.   They were
clad as vine-dressers, but the cry was raised that they
were Jesuits!   To be a Jesuit was to be an enemy of the
Republic, and to be an enemy of the Republic was to
deserve death.   Shouts and imprecations rose on every
side; eyes flashed and daggers gleamed; furious hands
were thrust forth to clutch the innocent victims of
popular rage.   "At them! At them!"—" Kill, kill!"—
" They are Jesuits!"—were the cries with which the sanguinary mob lashed itself into frenzy; and, on the Bridge
of Saint Angelo, the wretched victims were literally torn
to pieces by blood-thirsty savages — an immense multitude being spectators of the tragedy!

To this public butchery might be added a long list
of atrocious murders at Rome, Ancona, Sinigaglia,
Bologna, and throughout the Papal States.

* Farini, Stato Romano.

Notwithstanding the affectation of respect for religion which the Government, or the Triumvirs, exhibited, they made no successful effort to check the fury of the unbridled and licentious faction which held dominion in the streets, and which lost no opportunity of inflicting injury upon the priests.   While hymns of liberty were sung, and greetings of brotherhood were interchanged, dwellings were broken into, villas were plundered, property was stolen, and every opportunity was availed of for violence or rapine.   No doubt, the Government desired, and in many instances made attempts, to restrain this lawlessness; but what could it do against numbers — especially against those who had been too well taught the lesson of their " strength ?"   Besides, its energies were now required for the defence of the Capital against the advancing armies of indignant Christendom.

Perhaps the strangest delusion common to this period, was the belief entertained of the stability and permanence of the Republic, and of the sympathy and support which it was certain to receive from the principal nations of Europe, if not from their governments.   The Rome of the Popes being, according to the boastful assertion of the revolutionists, as much a thing of the past as the Rome of the Cæsars, the Rome of the People was now to have its career of glory and renown.   These enthusiasts saw the future from the historic hill of the Capitol; but an English minister, not averse to foreign commotion, viewed it from a less elevated position, but through a clearer atmosphere.   Lord Palmerston, then Foreign Minister, assured those who successively waited

upon him on behalf of the Republic, that it was advisable
to come to terms with the Pope, for that it was certain
he would be restored in spite of all opposition.   This
was the advice which he offered from the beginning;
and even after a gleam of transitory success, the result
of the repulse of the French in their first serious assault
on Rome, had flung a ray of hope over the fortunes of
the Republic, the same advice was more emphatically
urged by his Lordship, with the assurance that, no
matter what might be the form of government in
France, even should it be that of a Red Republic,
still France would restore the Pope to his dominions,
under some title, or name, or colour.

The French Assembly as well as the English Parliament
were addressed in a manifesto issuing from the Roman
Assembly, who began at length to understand that the
Catholic Powers would not refrain from active interference in the Pope's behalf.   The Roman Republic
was, indeed, willing to recognise the spiritual jurisdiction of the Holy Father, but unwilling to restore his
temporal authority; which latter would be much better
retained in the hands of the Triumvirate — Mazzini, Armanelli, and Saffi.   What the power of the Pope, for the
free exercise of his spiritual authority, would be under
the rule of those gentlemen, and coexistent with the
revolutionary zeal of the Assembly, the tyranny of the
gallery, the activity of the clubs, the ferocity or enthusiasm of the press, and the sanguinary and unchecked
license of the streets, it would be absurd to speculate
upon.   In fact, in such a state of things, the Pope would

be nothing better than a state prisoner, at the mercy of a reckless faction, the more insolent because of their success; and the dearest interests of the Church would be hourly imperilled through the machinations or the violence of its most inveterate opponents.

As matters stood, mere negotiation was useless; and nothing but the sword could put an end to the complicated difficulties of the question. If the Pope were to be restored, it should be as an independent sovereign, not as a puppet or a slave.

The other Catholic Powers eagerly responded to the appeal from Gaeta; but to France, the eldest born of the Church, belongs the glory of restoring the Vicar of Christ to his throne of the Vatican.

CHAP. XI.

The French occupy Civita Vecchia, and march on Rome. — First
Assault unsuccessful. — Bravery of the Besieged. — Rome sur-
renders. — The Pope's grateful Letter.

ON the 25th of April, 1849, the French squadron
anchored before Civita Vecchia; and on the day following, at noon, that city was occupied, without resistance,
by 1800 men of the expeditionary army.   On the 28th,
General Oudinot commenced his march on the capital;
and on the 30th, the armies of the two Republics first
came into hostile collision.

The Triumvirate and the Assembly had not been idle
in the meantime, but had adopted every available means
of preparation.   They endeavoured to render the venerable walls of Aurelian capable of resisting a modern foe;
they organised bands of volunteers, in aid of the regular military force which had been gathered together;
they drilled and they disciplined all who could or would
bear arms; they excited the passions of the populace by
animated appeals; and, by placards and manifestoes,
distributed along the line of the French march, they
sought to enlist the sympathies of their republican as-

sailants in behalf of a republican cause. The first attack of the French general was not successful; and his retreat, which was accompanied by severe loss, was hailed with frantic joy by those who favoured the new order of things. The fabric of the Roman Republic was now cemented by the blood of its defenders, who died in vanquishing the armed ambassadors of Despotism! The attention of the civilised world was fixed on the victorious standard waving from the Castle of St. Angelo; and the Rome of the People was to prove itself worthy of its ancient fame as the Rome of the Cæsars!

The story of this first assault was thus given in a letter from Toulon, dated the 4th of May, and which was published at the time :—

"It is known that after having organised Civita Vecchia, of which the command had been given to Colonel Blanchard, of the 36th, General Oudinot took up a position within a few leagues of Rome, hoping, no doubt, that the presence of the expeditionary corps would determine a movement against the Triumviral Government. His expectations were not realised. A company of the first battalion of tirailleurs, sent on to the gates of Rome, having been received with musket shots, retired in good order, and soon after part of the division advanced and penetrated without much difficulty into the *enceinte* of the capital, of which the streets were barricaded; but they were received by a well-fed fire of musketry, and a storm of missiles from the windows and roofs of the houses. The 20th of the line, which was in the front, was severely treated; a company of voltigeurs of that regiment was almost totally destroyed. At last, seeing the impossibility of continuing a struggle which became fatal, General Oudinot ordered the retreat, and the expeditionary corps occupies at this moment a strong position near Rome.   We had about 200 men killed, of whom some are officers; amongst them is M. Farras, aide-de-camp of General Oudinot, and several hundreds wounded."

This victory inspired the republicans with increased confidence in that dashing soldier of fortune, Garibaldi, to whom the command had been entrusted.   Oudinot, taught not to despise the valour of the Italians, at once demanded of his government strong reinforcements for his little army.   In the meantime more fervent appeals were made to the defenders of Rome and its populace, to resist the stranger, and thus not only cover the new-born Republic with immortal glory, but save Rome from the reimposition of an authority which, as the orators of the Assembly and the press declared anew, was contrary to the Gospel, and execrated by mankind.   The enthusiasm of the mob was kept alive by such agreeable diversion as hacking and hewing to pieces some three or four superfluous carriages of the Cardinals, which had been left after the remainder had been converted into street barricades.   The work of demolition having been completed to the satisfaction of the mob, the fragments were borne in procession to the Piazza del Popolo, and there, amidst shouts, yells, and savage rejoicings, converted into a flaming bonfire.   But, this time, the shouts of triumph and hymns of rejoicing had not the same terrible meaning as when, a few months before, they were heard beneath the windows of the room in which lay the body of the murdered Rossi.   The pay of the soldiery was increased, bread was distributed,

rewards were freely promised; and those whose dwellings were in reach of the enemy's fire, were allowed to
occupy the deserted palaces and other great houses
which were beyond the range of the French artillery.
The grim portraits of the mailed and ermined ancestors
of those princely families, whose mansions were thus
occupied, might be supposed to frown down upon the
strange intruders, who strutted amidst their splendid
galleries, so rich in treasures of immortal art, with
more than the pride of genuine possession.

A skirmish with the Neapolitans, in which the inde-
fatigable Garibaldi was successful, further increased the
confidence of the revolutionary party in Rome. Some
slight subsequent successes added to that general's fame,
and brought to his ranks an accession of desperadoes,
whose influencing motive was far more that of plunder
than of glory. Well might Rome look with apprehension on these her new defenders !

The struggle which followed certainly did honour to
the courage and endurance of the besieged. On the
12th of June, the investment of the city was complete ;
and on the 29th of the same month, in consequence of
the continued refusal of the Assembly to yield, the final
attack was made. From the 24th to the 29th, the struggle
had become more deadly, the French steadily gaining
the advantage, but not without the utmost exertion,
the defenders performing miracles of valour. Some
young men who had thrown themselves into the Casino
Barberini were surrounded by the enemy, and all slain,
after a struggle so obstinate and furious, that one is

K

said to have received no less than twenty-five wounds, —honourable testimonies of his courage. The legion known as the Medici were particularly distinguished by their heroism; for though numbers of that corps were buried beneath the ruins of the Vascello Palace, which fell on the 26th, the survivors stood out valiantly against the foe. Other strong places fell on the 27th and 28th beneath the furious fire of the French artillery; but such was the desperation which the struggle with the "foreigner" had enkindled in the fiery Italian heart, that the wounded crawled from the hospitals, to assist, with their feeble arms, in the hopeless task of defending the crumbling walls of the Rome of the Cæsars. On the night of the 29th, the roar of the artillery mingled with peals of thunder; and the flashes of the guns gleamed more redly by contrast with the white glare of the flaming lightning. On the morning of the 30th the fate of Rome was decided. The French rushed through the breach, and were there met by the defenders; when a desperate hand-to-hand conflict ensued, the officers giving an example to their men, fighting with muskets, and even striking with their clenched hands. Four hundred of the besieged were bayoneted on the bastion which they defended with such resolute valour; and such was the determination " to do or die," that many of the artillerymen were found lashed to their guns, which they would not abandon in life, and which they grimly guarded in death.*

It was Garibaldi himself who declared, in reply to the Assembly, that all further attempts at defence were

* Farini.

useless; and as this opinion coincided with the feelings or apprehensions of the majority, negociations with the victors were decided upon, notwithstanding the opposition of Mazzini, who now saw his short-lived authority at an end.   Oudinot would listen to no terms short of unconditional surrender; and on the 2nd of July he entered Rome with his army, Garibaldi having quitted it on the previous night with some 5000 men.

The French General at once sent the tidings of his victory to Gaeta, by Colonel Niel, who was entrusted with the grateful duty of laying the keys of the liberated city at the feet of the Supreme Pontiff; who thus expressed, in an autograph letter, the gratitude which he felt to the gallant victor, and to the great and generous nation whose valour and whose fidelity to the Holy See he so well represented : —

"Monsieur le General, — The well-known valour of the French arms, supported by the justice of the cause which they defend, has reaped the fruit due to such arms — victory. Accept, Monsieur le General, my congratulations for the principal part which is due to you in this event — congratulations not for the blood which has been shed, for that my heart abhors, but for the triumph of order over anarchy, for liberty restored to honest and Christian persons, for whom it will not henceforth be a crime to enjoy the property which God has divided among them, and to worship with religious pomp, without incurring the danger of loss of life or property.   With regard to the grave difficulties which may hereafter occur, I rely on the Divine protection.   I think it will not be without use to the French army to be made acquainted with the history of the events which occurred

during my Pontificate; they are traced out in my allocution, with which you are doubtless acquainted, but of
which I nevertheless send you a certain number of copies,
in order that they may be read by those whom you may
think it useful that they should be acquainted with them.
This document will sufficiently prove that the triumph of the
French army has been gained over the enemies of human
society, and will of itself awaken sentiments in the mind of
every right-thinking man in Europe, and in the whole world.
Colonel Niel, who, with your honoured despatch, presented
to me the keys of one of the gates of Rome, will hand you
this letter.   It is with much satisfaction I avail myself of
this opportunity to express to you my sentiments of paternal
affection, and the assurance that I continually offer up prayers
to the Almighty for you, for the French army, for the government, and for all France.

"Receive the Apostolic benediction, which I give you
from my heart.

(Signed)   "PIUS, P.P., IX.
"Gaeta, July 5."

Thus terminated a contest which the Catholic world
deplored with anguish, yet in the result of which it
could not but rejoice; for Rome, the Eternal City,
the Seat of the Apostles, the cradle in which the
Church of God was rocked amidst the storm and fury
of Pagan persecution, was restored to the venerable
successor of Peter — the good, the holy, the benevolent Pius.   Those, too, who loved rational liberty,
not license, were glad that the tyranny of the clubs
and their organs of the press was at an end; and that
a stop was put to the system of spoliation and outrage
which had so long spread terror through the streets of
the Capital of the Christian World.

CHAP. XII.

The Pope's Edict published in Rome. — Another Amnesty. — Rome reassumes its old Appearance. — General Reaction. —The Pope's Return announced. — His Journey.—He re-enters his Capital.— Enthusiasm of the People.

On the 20th of September, 1849, the Papal Commission, which consisted of four of the Cardinals, published an edict of the Pope, dated from Portici the 12th of the same month; by which his Holiness granted a Council of State—to give its advice on all projects of law before being submitted to the sovereign sanction, and on all questions of importance in every branch of the public administration — a Consulta for finances — Provincial Councils — and in which was confirmed the existing municipal institutions. The two concluding articles announce important reforms, and proclaim an amnesty : —

" Art. 5. The reforms and improvements will extend to the judicial order, and to the civil, criminal, and administrative legislation. A commission will be named to examine this question immediately.

" Art. 6. Finally, being always inclined to indulgence and pardon by the inclination of our paternal heart, we still wish to be clement towards the men who have been drawn into treason and revolt by the seduction, the hesitation, and perhaps also the weakness of others. On the other hand, taking into consideration what is required of us by justice, which is the foundation of kingdoms, the right of others violated or set aside, the duty incumbent on us of protecting you against a renewal of the evils which you have suffered, and the obligation of keeping you from the pernicious influence of the corrupters of all morality, and the enemies of the Catholic religion, which, being the inexhaustible source of all good and social prosperity, was your glory, and caused you to be remarked as the elected family which God favoured with his more particular gifts, we have ordered that an amnesty should be published in our name for all those who are not excepted in this decree of amnesty.

" Such are the dispositions which, in the presence of God, we have thought it our duty to publish for your good. They are compatible with your dignity, and we are convinced that, being faithfully executed, they may produce that good result which is the honourable wish of wise minds. The good sense of all of you who aspire to good, in proportion to the evil they have suffered, are to us our ample guarantee. But let us be careful to put our confidence in God, who, even in the midst of his just designs, never fails in mercy.

  " Given at Naples, in the suburb of Portici, on the
   12th of September, 1849, fourth year of our
   Pontificate."

Accompanying this edict, was a notification from the Papal Commissioners, in which were explained the terms and limitations of the amnesty announced in Article 6:—

" To those who have taken part in the last revolution in the Pontifical States is granted the pardon of the penalty to which they shall be liable for the political offences for which they shall be responsible. The members of the Provisional Government, the members of the Constituent Assembly who have taken part in the deliberations of that Assembly, the members of the Triumvirate, and of the Government of the Republic, the chiefs of the military corps, all those who, having already on former occasions enjoyed the benefit of the amnesty granted by his Holiness, have forfeited their word of honour in joining in the late political movements; in fine, those who, in addition to political offences, have rendered themselves guilty of other crimes provided against by the laws now in force, are excluded from the benefit of this amnesty. The present amnesty does not imply the maintenance in the employment of the Government, or in provincial or municipal posts, of those who have rendered themselves unworthy of them by their conduct during the late events. The same reservation is applicable to the military and *employés* of all arms."

Rome now began to breathe freely, as one who awakes from a horrible dream, in which images of terror mingle in wild disorder, and to whose startled soul the light of morning brings a delightful consciousness of security. The streets began, by degrees, to assume their wonted appearance, and the shops their former air of business. Workmen were again employed in various branches of industry; and even the cleansing, painting, and decoration of palaces, villas, hotels, and lodging-houses, absorbed a considerable amount of labour. The churches were again visited, and even thronged by worshippers; for the observance of religious duty was no longer regarded with suspicion, nor was piety to be classed in the same category with treason. Ecclesiastics once more freely walked through the streets; for though fierce eyes might flash, and dark brows gather in a frown, as the religious habit was

recognised by the scattered and panic-stricken disciples
of revolution, its wearer had no longer an apprehension
of being rushed upon by a noon-day murderer, or
torn limb from limb by infuriated bloodhounds.   The
painter again resumed his pencil, and the sculptor his
chisel; for Rome was once more an object of attraction
to people of distant nations — to the religious, to the
curious, to the idle, to the wealthy — almost every one
of whom, by whatsoever motive attracted within its
walls, was sure to benefit one or other section of the
community, whether by daily expenditure, by purchase,
or by the giving of an order for the execution of some
work of art.   The population, which recent events had
caused to dwindle down to that of a third-rate Italian
city, began to flow in with a daily increasing stream; and
by the latter end of the year 1849, or the commencement of 1850, the Corso was again instinct with life;
and equipages of all kinds, from the hackney carriage
of the stranger and sight-seer to the chariot of the
prince, once more rattled and flashed through the
streets and public places of Rome.

Many there were, no doubt, who regretted the absence of that license which they had enjoyed during
the brief existence of the Republic, and who looked
with disgust upon the restoration of order; but the
vast majority of the population — even including those
who had been seduced from their allegiance by specious
words, wild hopes, or a restless craving for change —
longed earnestly for the return of the Pope, the recollection of whose gentle virtues and paternal dis-

position was now only the more enhanced by his trials' and his sorrows. The reaction in favour of a restoration to the old order of things — or to the rule of the Holy Father — was rapid, and pervaded all classes; for independently of the anxiety to behold once more that familiar countenance, which never looked but with love upon the people, there was no class, no interest, no industry, that had not suffered from the wild and stormy period which, commencing with the flight to Gaeta, did not end till the Pope's government was fully restored. To have him once more in his own palace, was now the most anxious wish of his people; and this feeling was frequently expressed through deputations earnestly praying his return.

If Pius IX. appeared to some rather reluctant to hasten the moment of his return, it was not to be wondered at if he were so; for, living in tranquillity, in one of the most beautiful spots of the earth, with the lovely Mediterranean sparkling and murmuring beneath the balconies of his palace, and the delightful influence of a delicious climate wooing his spirit to peace, he might well have looked back with horror to that dreadful day when the Quirinal was besieged by a furious mob, whose savage cries were even more fearful than their murderous violence.

At length, however, the time of the Pope's return was announced to an expectant people, and great was the joy which it caused.

If manifestations of popular enthusiasm could have satisfied the heart of Pio Nono, he had ample cause for congratulation in his progress through the Neapolitan and Roman States. From his departure from Portici on the 4th of April, to his arrival in the great Square of the Lateran, his journey was one continous triumph. The people, clad in their holiday attire, met him everywhere with beaming eyes, with blessings, and with shouts of joy; flowers were strewn beneath his feet by beautiful maidens and graceful youths; banners, bearing mottoes expressive of welcome and homage, rustled in the gentle breeze; the prince vied with the peasant in testifying veneration and love for his person; and as his carriage passed along through city or through highway, multitudes reverently knelt to receive his benediction.

So long as the journey was performed in the Neapolitan dominions, the Pope was accompanied by his generous host, Ferdinand, King of the Two Sicilies, who thus gracefully terminated his hospitality, the munificence of which was only surpassed by its delicacy.

A very simple but beautiful description of illumination welcomed the arrival of the Holy Father at Terracina. No sooner had the sun sank beneath the waves, than the sea seemed at once lit up, as if by enchantment. Millions of orange rinds had been converted into lamps, with oil and wick; and these being simultaneously lighted and set afloat, the effect of the sudden and strange illumination was beautiful, beyond the power of language to describe.

In his own dominions, his welcome was even more enthusiastic than that given by the lively and impulsive

Neapolitans; for here there was an atonement to be made, and a bitter memory to be wiped out. At Frosinone, Velletri, and along his route, great preparations were made to receive the Sovereign befittingly; and at the former place houses had been pulled down, to widen the street through which he was to pass. The Church, no longer widowed, but now joyful as a bride, everywhere assumed her brightest attire, and put forth her most imposing pomp, to express the gratitude and exultation with which she hailed the return of Christ's Vicar to the Chair of Peter.

. At Velletri, where his reception was equally splendid and enthusiastic, the Holy Father was met by General Baraguay Hilliers, who had come thither to offer him his homage.

The crowning spectacle of the whole was witnessed on the 14th of April, when Pius IX. presented himself to his now repentant capital. The whole population had been from an early hour in the streets, and every spot was occupied from which the first glimpse of the Holy Father could be obtained. Amidst a waving sea of human beings, through which French and Roman troops with difficulty preserved an open space, Pius made his entry. Such was the enthusiasm now manifested, that one unacquainted with the Italian character might have supposed that the population had suddenly gone delirious. And yet many who now, with wild and vehement gesture, called down blessings on the Holy Father, had, not very long before, as wildly and as vehemently shouted, "Long live Mazzini!"—nay, perhaps, had yelled their coarse imprecations against the Pope on the 16th of November, 1848, because he would not accept a revolutionary ministry at the demand of an armed mob.   But now, flowers, and smiles, and blessings were flung over the past; and those were a small minority who did not feel genuine satisfaction at beholding the return of their good and gentle Sovereign. With illuminations, and music, and joyous cries, were renewed, at night, the rejoicings of the day.

The exulting strains of the *Te Deum* — that glorious anthem of kings and conquerors — which now echoed through the superb dome of St. Peter's, were answered from the Churches of Christendom; for the Catholic world rejoiced in the triumph of good over evil, of order over anarchy.

CHAP. XIII.

Disastrous Effects of the Revolution. — The Pope's Efforts to remedy them. — His daily Life. — His Audiences. — Petitions. — The Pope's Charity. — His Munificence.

RETURNED to his dominion, Pius IX. strenuously devoted himself to the difficult duties of his position, and endeavoured, by the application of wise remedies, to repair the injury which had been inflicted on the Papal States—in their trade, their industry, their finance, as well as in their intellectual progress and moral condition — by the fury and paralysis of the Revolution. In its paper money and its debts, the Republic left a legacy of serious embarrassment to the Pope ; but this difficulty has at length been happily and completely overcome ; and the finances of the Pontifical Government may now stand comparison with those of many prosperous European States. To educate youth, to reform the criminal, to comfort the sick, to protect the widow and the orphan, to shield old age from want, to encourage industry, to reform abuses, and to re-awaken in the hearts of his people the spirit of religion — these have been the principal cares of Pius IX. since the hour of his return to Rome. And to these duties, to which he was equally impelled

as a temporal sovereign and a spiritual father, were
added those of the Supreme Pontiff, who has to watch
over the widely-spread branches of the Catholic Church
throughout the world, and to apply to the wants and
necessities of each such remedies as its condition and its
circumstances demand.   It was not to be supposed that
the revolutionary embers would not, now and then, emit
a sullen spark; but though plot and conspiracy have
since then been attempted and detected, the feeling of
the people — even of the fickle populace — is, year by
year, becoming more in favour of the Pope, and less in
favour of those wild schemes which brought such misery
and suffering upon the country.   If, as yet, Pius IX.
has not renewed the experiment with which he commenced his reign, let those who read the story of the
past say, if the present system—of gradual reform and
steady amelioration—should not be preferred to a more
ambitious achievement, when attended with a more
certain risk?

Let us now enquire more minutely than we have as
yet done into the character of the Holy Father; and we
shall behold his simple and laborious life—his universal
benevolence—his active and unceasing charity—his enlightened liberality—his splendid munificence—his great
and continual efforts to render Rome the chief object
of attraction to the pious, the polished, the learned, and
the philosophic, of every civilised nation of the earth.
Judge, from his daily life, how different is the real
Pope from the imaginary portraiture which fiction has
drawn, and which prejudice has accepted.

He rises before six o'clock, and celebrates Mass every morning in the year. Not content with this act of priestly devotion, he hears another Mass. He then gives audience to his Secretary of State, on matters of public importance, and next to his Major Domo, on the affairs of his household. He next receives the letters addressed to him, which, as I shall have reason to show, are of the most varied character. These he carefully reads, and places in the hands of his Private Secretary, for further information, or to be at once acted upon, as the case might require. At ten, his audiences, properly so called, commence, and generally last till two. He then dines, his fare being of the simplest kind. At three he frequently drives out, his excursion usually occupying till five. At five the audiences are resumed, and continue till nine, or even to ten, at night. The audiences being over, he then reads his office, just as any ordinary priest, and retires to a bed as simple and plain as belongs to the humblest student in Rome. Besides special audiences, which may occur at any moment, each day is set apart for those of a particular kind, and the transaction of certain classes of business, connected either with the internal administration of the Papal States, or appertaining to those no less grave matters which demand the constant consideration of the Supreme Pontiff. The various fixed audiences which are given at present on each day in the week, may be thus particularised : —

MONDAY.

Morning. — His Eminence the Secretary of Memorials, and the Minister of Arms. The first Monday of the month, the President of the Academy of Noble Ecclesiastics, and the Secretary of Regular Discipline, who has audience also on the third Monday. The second Monday, the Promoter of the Faith. The fourth Monday, the Advocate of the Poor.

Evening. — Cardinal Prefect of the Segnatura, Secretary of the Council, Administrator and Secretary of St. Peter's, and the Secretary of Briefs to Princes.

TUESDAY.

Morning. — Cardinal Secretary of Briefs, Cardinal Pro-Datario, and the Under Datario. On the first and third Tuesdays of the month, the Cardinal Visitor of the Apostolical Ospizio of San Michele, and Monsignor the Almoner.

Evening. — The Master of the Apostolic Palace, and Monsig. the Commendatore di S. Spirito. The second Tuesday of every month, Monsig. President of the Consulta, which is one of the principal tribunals of Rome.

WEDNESDAY.

Morning. — Minister of the Public Works, Minister of the Interior and of the Police, and Minister of Finance.

Evening. — Monsig. the Assessor of the Holy Office, Monsig. the Secretary of the Consistory, Monsig. Secretary of Ecclesiastical Affairs, and Monsig. Secretary of Latin Letters.

THURSDAY.

Morning. — Congregation of the Holy Office.

Evening. — Monsig. the Auditor of His Holiness, and the Secretary of Briefs to Princes. Every first Thursday evening, the Secretary of Holy Rites.

FRIDAY.

Morning. — Cardinal Secretary of Briefs, Cardinal Pro Datario, and Under Datario, Cardinal Secretary of Memorials, and Monsig. Secretary of Sacred Rites.

Evening. — Cardinal Penitentiary, and Monsig. Secretary of Bishops and Regulars.

SATURDAY.

Morning. — Minister of the Interior and of the Police, and Minister of Finance.

Evening. — Cardinal Vicar of Rome, Monsig. Secretary of Latin Letters, Monsig. Secretary of the Apostolic Visit. The last of these on the third Saturday of every month.

SUNDAY.

Evening. — Monsig. Secretary of Propaganda, Monsig. Auditor of His Holiness, and Monsig. the Secretary of Studies.

Before the above-mentioned morning audiences commence, the Holy Father receives, about half-past eight o'clock, every day of the year, his Eminence the Secre-

L

tary of State, or, in his place, Monsig. the Under Secretary of State.

These are the audiences which are fixed and settled as I have particularised; and, I venture to say, they do not allow of much leisure time to His Holiness.

It may be asserted, with perfect truth, that the Pope is the sovereign who, of all others in the world, is the most accessible to his subjects. Even the humblest applicant may approach his person; nor is the blackest criminal in the States debarred from the privilege of addressing him by petition. Hence the innumerable claims for audiences; and hence the flood of appeals, on every imaginable subject, that pours in on His Holiness, either directly, or through a multitude of channels, official or otherwise. A petition to the Pope is no idle mockery, but an appeal that, in one shape or other, is certain to reach the ear, if not touch the heart, of the most merciful and benevolent of living men. No matter for what offence a prisoner may have been incarcerated, that prisoner may appeal directly to the Pope; and no officer or person in charge of a prison dares to stand between the criminal and the seat of mercy. As in all other places in the world, but perhaps more peculiarly in southern countries, there are crimes, even terrible ones, which are almost wholly the result of passion and excitement; and if, upon inquiry through the proper channel, which inquiry is unfailingly made, the Pope feel convinced that mercy may be beneficially extended, it is so extended, and the punishment either greatly lessened, or a free pardon granted. As I shall have to treat elsewhere of the public prisons of Rome, which I have personally examined in detail, I shall not further allude to this portion of the subject at present, but content myself with the statement of a fact, which will afford the best idea of the real value of this privilege of petition,—that no fewer than from 50 to 60 pardons are granted by the Pope every month of the year,—and therefore, that from 600 to 700 persons, who have been condemned for various offences, are annually restored to freedom by the exercise of that noblest prerogative of Princes, mercy.

The charity of the Holy Father is also hourly appealed to, and scarcely ever in vain. If he walk through the streets, hands may be seen stretched forth, holding letters of supplication — perhaps complaints of injustice, or of wrong inflicted, but more generally appeals for alms; and these are taken by one of the Noble Guard (a few of whom accompany His Holiness), and are afterwards handed to himself personally. Then the Post-office is a constant means of communicating directly, and without any intermediate agency, with the Pope; and there is no letter or petition which he receives, be it from the humblest, the meanest, or the most guilty, that he does not read, and into the subject-matter of which he does not inquire. The official channels of communication are the following. The Cardinal Prefect of Subsidies receives communications on matters immediately connected with his office, as well as upon others; and he has a fixed day in every week for an audience of the Pope, to whom he refers

them.　The Cardinal Secretary of Memorials also receives petitions, as well as complaints, on almost every
subject respecting which appeal or remonstrance could
be made.　Every petition is examined by his Secretaries, then referred to him, and by him submitted to
the Pope, of whom he has an audience every Tuesday
and Friday.　Then there is Monsignor the Almoner of
the Pope, who has crowds of petitioners at his door, and
who has appointed days for hearing and receiving appeals,
which are similarly transmitted as all the rest.　Monsignor the Almoner accompanies the Pope when he
goes abroad, and invariably brings with him a bag of
money, for distribution amongst the poor who may be
met with on the way.　The Minister of the Interior dis-
charges the functions of the Minister of Grace and
Justice, which latter office is merged in the former;
and this officer is likewise made the medium of appeals
for mercy.　Then there are the Secretary of State, and
the Under Secretary, whose duty it is to receive, inquire into, and submit petitions to His Holiness.　The
Cardinal Vicar is also an important channel of communication; so is every Cardinal, each of whom, according to his particular position, has constant claims
made upon his influence; so are all who hold offices
about the person, and may be said to have the ear, of
His Holiness,—so also are the Parish Priests, to whom
vast numbers, especially of the poor, first address their
complaints, or make their necessities known.　Through
these and other channels the people communicate with
their Sovereign, the poor and the needy with a compas-

sionate and bountiful benefactor. I stated an important fact, which strikingly illustrated the value of the privilege of petition to the prisoner, and the merciful and clement disposition of the Pope; and I shall now mention one which as conclusively displays his benevolent and charitable nature. Since his accession to the Pontificate, in 1846, Pius the Ninth has spent, in charitable and pious works, no less a sum than 1,500,000 scudi —a sum fabulous in amount, when taking into consideration the extent of his *private* resources. These consist of 355 scudi a month, or about 4,200 scudi in the year; which would be about equal to 1000*l.* a year of English money. What a revenue for a Sovereign Prince! How, then, it may be asked, were the 1,500,000 scudi obtained?—from what source was this enormous fund derived? The answer, which I have elsewhere anticipated, is significant, and affords a lesson to those who foolishly imagine that the Papacy would be destroyed the moment that, by revolution or plunder, the Pope should be deprived of his temporal power; that is, of his sovereignty over the Papal States. The greater portion of this wealth, which the Pope so generously devoted to works of piety and charity, poured in upon him at Gaeta, while he was an exile from his country and his throne—poured in upon the Father of the Christian Church from *all* quarters of Christendom, at the very moment when thoughtless persons were frantically shouting out—" the Papacy is at an end !" There are those in Rome and throughout the States who long for a change of Government—for *any* change, by which they might hope to realise their dreams, or accomplish their personal objects—and who, therefore, are hostile to the existing state of things ; but in the great breast of the people — the mass of the people—there exists a sincere loyalty to the throne and person of the Pope, and a profound conviction of those virtues which adorn his character as a Man, a Ruler, and a Priest.

CHAP. XIV.

Instances of the Pope's Charity. — More Instances. — Curious Applications.—Protestant Opinions of his Character.—He gives Audience to a Negro Slave. — His Affability to Students.— The Holy Father on foot.

As a proof of the benevolent and merciful character of His Holiness, I stated that he distributed, during his reign, no less than 1,500,000 scudi in pious and charitable works, at the same time mentioning that his own private income did not exceed 4,200 scudi, or about 1000*l.* a-year. Perhaps I might illustrate, by an interesting fact, that intense love of the poor, and sympathy for the suffering, which the Holy Father has invariably displayed.

Shortly after his return to Rome, from his temporary exile at Gaeta, the Queen of Spain sent him, as a mark of her respect, a splendid tiara, which was valued at 50,000 scudi — a very large sum, even when represented by English money. The Pope accepted the princely gift, but gave immediate orders that its value, to the full amount, should be distributed to the poor, to the aged, and the sick, and in such a manner and through such channels as would be certain to produce the most beneficial results.

I have heard of numbers of instances of the impulsive generosity with which he responds to appeals to his compassion, all equally indicative of the charity of his disposition.

In the month of October last, a poor family fell into distress, in consequence of the illness of one of its principal members, and were unable to bear up against the expenses in which they necessarily became involved. In their affliction they appealed to the Pope — applied by petition ; and the answer, after inquiry made into the facts of the case, was a prompt gift of 50 scudi. Similar appeals, daily and hourly made, produce similar or even greater results.

A little time before that, a certain person applied to the Holy Father for an office of some importance, that would have been of the greater consequence to him, from the reduced circumstances into which he and his family had fallen. Unfortunately, the office, which was in the gift of the Holy Father, had been previously promised to another ; but so keenly did the Pope feel for the disappointment which a refusal must inevitably inflict on his suitor, that he sent him 1000 scudi as a compensation for his loss, and as a means of relieving his necessities.

Not more than a few days previous to my arrival in Rome, a venerable pensioner, who had once held some small office, not being able to provide himself with certain comforts suited to his extreme age and ailing condition, without involving himself inextricably in debt, applied to the Pope for assistance, and, to his surprise, at once received *eight years'* amount of his pension *in advance;* although no insurance company in the world would have valued his life at more than a year's purchase.

I had an opportunity of witnessing the manner in which the alms given from the private purse of the Holy Father are distributed, and the gratitude with which they are received. Speaking on one occasion to a kind friend, to whose courtesy and whose intelligent mode of communicating information I had been equally indebted, on a subject interesting to us both — namely, the character of the Pope, and especially his charity and benevolence—he suddenly said, — " Perhaps you would have no objection to discharge for me a little commission with which I have been intrusted. It is to give a small sum from His Holiness to a poor family. The father, an old man, sent a petition some time since to the Quirinal, imploring assistance ; and, on inquiry being made, the case was found to be a deserving one." We — for I was accompanied by a young Irish clergyman — immediately expressed our willingness to act as temporary almoners of the Papal bounty ; and the sum of 15 scudi — more than 3*l.* — was handed to us. At our earliest convenience, we proceeded to the house, which was in one of the narrowest streets of the city — the very description of street that Tacitus tells us was considered the most agreeable to the Romans of his day, with lofty houses on each side, affording ample protection against the raging heat of the noonday sun. Ascending massive

stone steps, which seemed to go to the top floor of the
building, we came to the landing indicated in our instructions.   The door was freely opened to our sum-
mons ; and on entering, we were at once convinced
that the necessity was as pressing as the aid was timely.
There was nothing of that squalid poverty which as
often exhibits the absence of all self-respect as the
presence of intense destitution ; on the contrary, the
apartments, while most scantily furnished, were scrupulously clean.   But the head of the family, a fine
venerable old man, who might have sat to a painter as
a model for one of the Apostles, was past the years of
labour ; and a daughter seemed, from the supernatural
brightness of her eye, the peculiar hollowness of her
cheek, and her wasted mouth, to be far on the road to
a happier world.   We explained the object of our visit,
and produced the little roll of gold pieces with which
we had been intrusted.   The glitter of the gold brought
happiness to the heart of that poor family, for it spoke
of unaccustomed comforts and momentary abundance ;
and food and clothing are positive happiness to the
poor.   In an ecstasy of gratitude, the mother and her
children flung aside the needle-work with which they had
been employed, rushed to us, seized our hands, and
kissed them with graceful gestures ; at the same time
murmuring blessings on the head of their good and merciful Father and Pope.   We felt convinced that the
family, thus temporarily relieved, would be cared for by
one of those noble charitable confraternities which
abound in Rome, and are the glory of the Church.

I was told of a somewhat curious application made to the Pope by a poor countryman of my own.   Writing to His Holiness from England, he informed him that he had lost the use of his limbs, and that he wished him, as the successor of St. Peter, to bid him " Stand up and walk," as Saint Peter did to the lame man, as recorded in the Acts of the Apostles.   This singular letter was referred to the Pope, who immediately sent ten dollars to the writer, at the same time informing him that he had not the miraculous powers of Saint Peter.

And in an audience with which I was honoured by the Holy Father, I had a good opportunity of understanding the strange and varied character of the petitions poured in upon him daily, to the very necessary exercise of his exhaustless patience.   In the course of the audience, the Pope took up a large package or bundle of papers from the desk-table by which he stood for the whole time, and, with a smile full of singular sweetness, not however unmingled with humour, he said, — " These are all I have got this morning."   And surely they were sufficient, and rather more than a first-rate London barrister could conveniently " read up" before going to court.   Two or three of the documents were, in fact, as bulky and voluminous as chancery briefs.   And the most voluminous of these was the contribution of a lady, who evidently desired to take the Holy Father into her confidence upon the most delicate of all questions to her sex — marriage.   Her inclinations tended decidedly in that direction; but there were " difficulties" in the way — and with these she managed to fill sheet after sheet of respectably-sized paper. The Pope read several passages of this formidable petition, and glanced at its various heads, and then laid it aside with a meaning smile, and a gesture expressive of more than a suspicion of his correspondent's state of mind.   Another petition was for no less a sum than 150 dollars ; and this " very moderate demand," as, with quiet humour, the Holy Father termed it, appeared to be based upon no other justification than the alleged fact, that such a sum would be just then particularly convenient to the petitioner.   But there were others, praying for mercy, or asking for assistance in cases of real distress.   And as the good Pope glanced at these, a look of tender compassion chased away for the moment the sweet smile that played about his mouth, and the light of genuine humour that sparkled in his mild blue eye.   It evidently was an easy matter to touch the heart of Pius IX.   These petitions were to be handed over to a confidential secretary, by whom a *résumé* of their contents was to be prepared for the future inspection and decision of the Pope.   And this he explained in the simplest and most unaffected manner — in fact, as if he were the equal of those who then regarded him with reverential homage, the more profound because of his virtues, of his pure and noble nature, than on account of his exalted temporal rank, as the first of Christian Sovereigns, or of his sublime spiritual dignity, as Vicar of Christ.

I could fill a volume with well authenticated facts illustrative of the tender and compassionate disposition

OPINIONS OF THE POPE'S CHARACTER.

of one who, in this as in many other respects, is recognised by all who know him to be a type and model of the noblest of Christian virtues. Let it not be imagined that my information is by any means exclusively derived from those whose personal veneration for the Holy Father might be considered to influence their judgment. Such is not the fact; for I have heard English Protestants, who have not a single feeling in common with the religion of which he is the head, and whose prejudices are strongly opposed to the form of government now existing in Rome, speak of the Pope with the utmost respect and veneration. A most intelligent Englishman, of the class I indicate, was speaking to me with respect to certain reforms which he deemed absolutely necessary—not great organic changes, but reforms in administration—and he wound up by saying: "But as for the Pope, I verily believe there is not a kinder, or better, or purer man living on the earth—there can be only one opinion about him."

Then as to his personal bearing, even to the humblest, no other Sovereign approaches him in this respect. No matter what may be the object for which an audience is sought of the Pope, whether of business or charity— to prefer a charge, or obtain a favour—no matter for what it may be, the same kindness and courtesy are exhibited to all persons, and on all occasions.

A most remarkable case in point occurred in the course of the last year, which, in its simple and unaffected goodness, puts to shame those exhibitions of mock sympathy for the poor African slave in which it is the fashion now-a-days to indulge. A family of French extraction brought with them from New Orleans a female slave of pure African blood. Had this poor woman desired to do so, she might have made herself free; for long before the cry for the emancipation of the Negro was heard in England, a Pope had declared that in the Roman States " no slaves could be." Having been brought up a Catholic, she wished to be confirmed ; which she eventually was, in the chapel of the French Nuns of the Sacred Heart, by Archbishop Bedini. It afterwards occurred to her mistress that it would be a great comfort to the good creature if she were allowed to stand somewhere so as to get the Pope's blessing as he passed. His Holiness was informed of the matter; to which he replied,— " I will think about it." The next day, a papal dragoon was seen riding up and down the Via Condotti, making inquiries at various places for " Mademoiselle Marguerite," for whom he had a letter of audience with the first Sovereign of the world ! Not finding Mademoiselle Marguerite in the Via Condotti, the dragoon became somewhat perplexed how to execute his commission. At last he said to himself, — " Oh, this is one of those French or English devotees, and they will know something of her at the convent of Trinità di Marti." To that convent he accordingly proceeded, and was there told that his letter would be safely delivered to the right person. At the appointed hour, the sable-visaged Marguerite found herself in the midst of a company of the high-born, the rich, and the beautiful, who were waiting to pay their Easter homage.   The Pope was long and privately engaged.   But when he was at length free, the first name called was that of "Mademoiselle Marguerite."   One may imagine the feelings of awe and reverence with which the poor despised child of Africa prostrated herself at the feet of the successor of Peter.   A voice of touching sweetness and gentleness soon inspired her with confidence.   "My child," said the Pope, "there are many great people waiting, but I wish to speak to you the first.   Though you are the least upon earth, you may be the greatest in the sight of God."   He then conversed with her for twenty minutes.   He asked her about her condition, her fellow slaves, her hardships.   "I have many hardships," she replied; "but since I was confirmed, I have learned to accept them as the will of God."   He exhorted her to persevere, and to do good in the condition in which she was placed; and he then gave her his blessing.   He blessed her, and blessed " all those about her; " so that this poor despised slave carried with her, from that memorable interview, greater courage and stronger fortitude to bear up against her yoke of suffering and humiliation.

A beautiful feature in the character of Pius IX. is his benignity.   From it springs that thoughtful consideration for the feelings of others which ever distinguishes him, and of which an instance has been given in the case of one whom prejudice—aye, and prejudice deep-rooted in the breasts of those who boast of their Christianity — accounts, if not actually infamous, at least destined by nature for persecution and degradation.

To children especially he is gentleness itself. He delights to engage them in conversation, as he meets them in his walks outside the city, or in its more retired districts. But he never fails to inquire as to their knowledge of the catechism, and their progress in education; and if he find that the object of his scrutiny is ignorant, or in danger of falling into an evil course, either through having bad or negligent parents, or from being unprotected, he at once gives orders to one of his attendants,—which orders ensure to the child the benefit of a good education, or the protection of a safe asylum.

To students he is as affable and familiar as he was in his bishopric of Imola, or while yet a simple priest. In the early part of last Autumn he had a number of the students of every ecclesiastical college in Rome to dine with him. This was an act of condescension altogether unusual, as the Pope almost invariably dines alone; but such is the special kindness which he feels towards the students of the Irish College, that more of their body enjoyed the distinction than of any other college, that is, in proportion to their relative numbers.

One afternoon, I was returning from a ramble over the charming Pincian Hill, from whose various elevations exquisite views of Rome and the country beyond it may be enjoyed, when the friend who accompanied me cried out,—" See! there is the Pope!" I accordingly looked in the direction to which he pointed my attention, and I saw a figure clad in a white cloth sutane, with a cape and belt of the same colour, and wearing a wide-brimmed crimson hat, adorned with a gold cord, which encircled it, and which terminated in large tassels of the same costly material. At each side walked two persons, dressed as the students of the Apolonari College; and behind came three or four officers of the household, one of whom acted as Almoner, as is the custom when the Pope goes abroad. These were followed, at some distance, by a few of the Noble Guard; and then two carriages of a plain description, the one for His Holiness, the other for his attendants. My friend and I did not hesitate long about forming part of the *cortége* that accompanied the illustrious pedestrian from the foot of the Pincian Hill, across the Piazza del Popolo, through the gate of the same name, and for nearly two miles along the Flaminian Way, which the prevalence of a strong wind had rendered more than usually dusty. Divested of the splendid robes in which I last beheld the Pope, and clad in the simple dress which I have described, his figure appeared stout and robust, but by no means unduly full for a man of sixty-three — which is about his age at present. He walked vigorously and well, freely using his arms as those do who desire to give the benefit of the healthful exercise to all their limbs. As he was descending the hill, he met a group of students of the Propaganda, amongst whom I instantly recognised one of the dark faces which I had previously seen in the Pauline Chapel.

M

The Pope at once stopped, and conversed with them for a few moments. In the same way he spoke to some children who had been enjoying themselves in innocent sport, but who, on being addressed by the Holy Father, evinced towards him respect, not bashfulness. For two miles, or even more, he stoutly pursued his way along the road, walking in the very centre of it, and little regarding the dust which rose before a breeze that was robbing many a tree on each side of its russet leaves. Every human being whom he met on his way knelt to receive his blessing. There was no exception whatever — old as well as young, rich as well as poor, the rude driver of the quaint-looking market-cart, as well as the noble equestrian—all knelt as he approached, and with an utter disregard of the mode or place in which they knelt. I particularly remarked that a group of gentlemen, some of whom were named to me as members of well-known noble families, at once dismounted, and knelt with just the same alacrity as the very poorest. The latter had more than one motive for their act of homage; for they knew that the Almoner, or his substitute, was among the attendants of the Holy Father, and that he bore with him a purse, which had been replenished specially for them, and whose contents were in rapid process of distribution. The dress of the Holy Father was different indeed from that in which I beheld him on several previous occasions; but there could be no change in the unalterable mildness and benevolence which nature and character had impressed upon his features. There was nothing in that face to awe or repel, but everything to attract. In its general character—I do not mean its lines and curves, but its spirit—there is in the face of Pius IX. much that would recall to the memory the sweet countenance of another most benevolent Priest, the illustrious and lamented Father Mathew. Nor is the resemblance merely external; for, in considerateness and kindness of manner to all persons, without distinction of rank; in compassion and tenderness for the poor and the suffering, and in unfailing gentleness to youth, there is much similarity of character and disposition between these two great and good men. In their boundless charity— the desire to convert their every possession into the means of relieving others—I can see a still stronger and more touching resemblance.

The Pope, as might be supposed, receives many beautiful and costly presents, not alone from the faithful, but even from those who, while they regard his church with aversion, admire his character, and do honour to his virtues. Amongst other presents received, not long since, by the Holy Father, was a sumptuous saddle, studded with precious stones, and enriched with all the barbaric magnificence of the East. This costly gift was the offering of the present Sultan, who has frequently, and in many ways, manifested his personal respect for the Pope. By the sale of its gems and other ornaments, he was enabled to carry out a favourite work of charity. With their produce, he fed and clad and consoled the poor. The Queen of Spain also sent him a gorgeous golden chalice, which blazed with jewels ; but the Pope had it divested of its precious stones, broken up, and sold — and with the proceeds he was enabled to establish in Rome additional public bakeries, in which bread is sold to the poorer classes at a low price.   There were, last year, six of such valuable institutions established in the most convenient districts of the city ; and not only do they confer an immediate benefit on those for whose especial use they are intended, but they also confer great good on the community generally, by helping to keep down the price of this most important article of daily food.   From many causes, the past year has been one of serious privation in most parts of Italy, as well as in Rome and throughout the Papal States.   The vintage has been generally unfavourable, owing to the continual prevalence of that mysterious blight which has for years ravaged the wine-producing countries of Europe ; the grain crops have also suffered materially ; and oil, which is an article of primary necessity to the Italians, has increased immensely in value, in consequence of the more than partial failure of the olive.

In connection with the public bakeries, there may be mentioned another work of benevolence commenced by the Pope, out of compassion to the poorer classes.   He has lately caused to be constructed a number of small houses, in which the working man, or the poor family, can have good accommodation, and even considerable comfort, at small expense.   This attempt is, in Rome as in most other places in which it has been made, only in its infancy ; but it is to be made on a larger scale, according as circumstances render it convenient or possible.   These houses have been erected at the sole cost of the Holy Father, and out of his private purse.

CHAP. XV.

Personal Courage of His Holiness. — His Presence of Mind in the Hour of Danger. — His Visits to the Cholera Hospitals. — Not afraid of his Subjects. — Evidence of his Fearlessness.

I SHALL have ample occasion to exhibit still further the merciful disposition, as well as the enlightened character, of Pius IX.; but it may not be out of place to refer to one trait in his character, for which, owing to misrepresentations of its real nature, many people may not give him credit — namely, *courage.* In moments of the greatest danger, he has displayed a calmness and a presence of mind that are not always associated with the more vulgar quality of mere physical bravery. Mild and gentle as he is by nature, there is no danger which he would not face, when called upon by a consciousness of duty to do so. Remember how boldly he braved, and how effectually he awed, the furious assassins in the sacristy of the Cathedral of Imola. Also, how, amidst the horrors of the fearful 16th of November, 1848, he maintained his position with unshrinking courage, declaring that "he would yield nothing to violence." If, at length, he did affect to yield, it was to save his faithful guards and personal attendants from being butchered, and the streets of his capital from being deluged with innocent blood. Again, during his flight, he exhibited a coolness and a courage which those interested in his safety could with difficulty emulate.   And bravely, too, on another critical occasion, but one of a far different kind, did his nerves withstand a shock that made many a stout heart tremble at the time. This was on the 12th of April, 1855, when the flooring of a hall in the Monastery of St. Agnes gave way beneath the unaccustomed weight of some hundred and fifty persons ; and Pope, cardinals, prelates, generals, soldiers, monks, and students, were whirled through the yawning ruin, amidst falling beams, fragments of masonry, and clouds of dust.   Not a few were hurt, some more or less seriously, by the fall and the consequent crush ; but the Pope was untouched — his escape, under the circumstances, appearing to be something miraculous.   Not the least miracle was the wonderful presence of mind which he displayed at such a fearful moment.   By cheerful words he dispelled the panic with which nearly all were seized.   And, in gratitude to God for such an escape, he invited those who were unhurt to follow him to the church ; where, in a full and firm voice, he intoned a thanksgiving to the Almighty for His great mercy.

I shall not dwell upon his courage in braving the perils of the Cholera Hospital ; for there is not to be found a Roman Catholic Priest who, however naturally timid or apprehensive he may be, is not at any moment ready to incur the danger of visiting and administer-

ing to the sick, no matter by what malignant disease
they might be stricken down, and whether in the wards
of an hospital, or in the fetid atmosphere of a garret
or a cellar.   But the difference between the two cases
is this — the Priest goes to the cholera hospital in the
discharge of his duty ; but the Pope did so with the view
of allaying the wild apprehensions of his people, and
giving an example of fearlessness to others.   Indeed,
it would be impossible to describe the dismay and
horror of the lower classes of the Roman people at the
last visitation of this terrible disease.   As the poor
were in general its victims, and as the rich mostly escaped
—just as has been the case in all other places—it was
madly supposed that there was a hellish conspiracy of
the rich against the poor !   They even fancied that the
doctors were bribed to administer poisoned medicines to
the class marked out for sacrifice.   In moments of terror
men and women go back to childhood, and are slaves to
its wildest credulity.   The subject of the cholera swal-
lowed up all other topics, and entirely absorbed the public mind.   " Who is dead to-day? — how many cases since
last night?" were the questions almost universally asked.
In a word, the panic was at its height.   And such was
the mortal terror caused by the spread of this disease,
pronounced to be " contagious," that the nearest and
dearest ties of affection and of blood were appealed to
in vain, and the sick were fled from in dismay.   In
the midst of this panic, when all who could have done
so, had left Rome, the Holy Father himself publicly
visited the great hospital of Santo Spirito ; and going

from bed to bed, he blessed and consoled the patients, taking many of them by the hand; and, with the utmost tenderness and compassion, he assisted one man in his last agony. He then visited the convalescents, and spoke to them, and blessed them, and cheered them by his gentle voice and hopeful words. A few days afterwards he went to the female cholera hospital at Saint John Lateran, and there imparted consolation to the last moments of a poor Jewess, who actually died in his arms. On another occasion he visited the French soldiers who were attacked by the disease, and in the same pious offices displayed at once his compassion and his courage. Of course, these visits produced a profound sensation and most beneficial effect throughout Rome; and in a short time the wild panic subsided, and the community was restored to tranquillity and confidence.

It has been freely and frequently stated that the life of the Pope is in constant danger from his own subjects, and that he dares not venture abroad. That he does go out, and that, too, in the most public places in Rome, I was a witness of on more than one occasion. He is frequently to be seen walking on the Pincian Hill, and on some days even in the streets of the city. But he necessarily prefers more retired and less populous districts, for other reasons than those of apprehension or mistrust; for he is so hemmed in by the people, asking his blessing, imploring alms, or presenting petitions, that it is with the utmost difficulty he can make his way through the crowd which his appearance in the more populous districts is at once sure to attract. Certainly, one thing is true beyond doubt, — that, if any of his people be so utterly abandoned as to entertain evil designs against the sacred person of their Sovereign, they have numberless opportunities of carrying their designs into execution, or, at least, of making the attempt with every probability of success. At any rate, if danger exist, the Pope looks and acts as if it did not exist; and that it does not, is the conviction of those who are best acquainted with the feelings of the people. On the contrary, the Holy Father is personally beloved by his subjects; and any outrage, or even insult, offered to him would be followed by summary vengeance from the hands of those who witnessed it. To give a striking instance of the confidence which the Pope manifests in his people — or of his fearlessness — I may mention that having gone, a short time since, by chance into a field in which five battalions of Roman infantry were going through their exercises, he allowed them to fire blank cartridge right in his face; although there was a report then rife in Rome, that the Papal army was full of " dangerous democrats."

Gentle, merciful, compassionate, and paternal, Pius IX. is; but there is no sacrifice which he would not be prepared to make, no danger which he would not cheerfully encounter, in the vindication of the truth, or in the discharge of what he felt to be his duty. " I am prepared to go to-morrow to the Catacombs, as many of my predecessors have done, if the interests of the Church of God require it," were words which he uttered in my presence; and with such simple dignity, such an unconscious nobleness of gesture, such a quick flushing of the face and lighting up of the eye——that there rose up before my mind those fearless martyrs of the early Church, who, though holy and gentle and mild as Pius, could yet meet the sword of the slayer without the betrayal of a single emotion of human weakness.

The Pope's immediate connection with the principal institutions of Rome will still further illustrate the benignity of his nature, and the paternal character of his rule.

CHAP. XVI.

The Roman Hospitals. — La Consolazione. — San Giovanni di Calabita. — San Galicano. — San Giacomo. — Santissima Salvatore. — Santissima Trinita di Pellegrini.

I HAVE ever held the belief, that no institutions reflect greater credit on a ruler, or a higher honour on a country, than really good and efficient hospitals, to which the poor may have immediate recourse, without a sense of personal degradation, and with full confidence in the ability and zeal of those by whom they are managed. It cannot be said that the greater portion of the magnificent hospitals of Rome are the work of the present Pope; for, were it true, it would be a sad reflection on his illustrious predecessors. But this I can assert, from having beheld the result with my own eyes, as well as instituted minute and repeated inquiries, — that Pius IX. has not only added largely and munificently to those valuable monuments of the zeal and humanity of former Popes, and in several instances out of his own private resources, or such means as were at his immediate disposal; but that he has most rigorously reformed the whole system, and brought it, or is engaged in bringing it, to a condition as near perfection as it is possible to render institutions of human origin. Some hospitals have been entirely, and others almost wholly, rebuilt; more have been added to, so as to double the extent of their accommodation; new and improved arrangements have been adopted in many — and in *all* the influence of a vigilant eye is plainly manifest, even to the most casual visitor. I use no mere phrase, when I allude to the influence of this well-known vigilance; for the administrators of the Roman hospitals have already had frequent proofs of the watchfulness of His Holiness, in visits unannounced and unexpected. It is his invariable practice not to give the slightest notice of his intention to visit those institutions until he is actually seated in his carriage, and is leaving the gates of the palace; and he only then communicates his intention to one of the Noble Guard, who rides on before, not to announce the Pope's coming, but in order that the gates might be at once opened on his arrival. In this manner he has visited and inspected all the hospitals of Rome; and many of the improvements and reforms already adopted, or in actual progress, are the valuable results of those visits, and the fruits of the experience thus acquired. Nor have the visits of His Holiness been alone made at times when the health of the city was good, and no danger could have been apprehended; for, as I have elsewhere stated, when cholera broke out in Rome, and the usual alarm accompanied its mysterious and appalling presence, the Pope publicly visited the hospitals then open for the treatment of this terrible disease: and this he did, not merely to allay the terror of the people, but to excite to greater activity the zeal and self-devotion of those

who were then entrusted with their care, from the
most distinguished physician down to the humblest
attendant.

The result of the munificent additions which the
Pope has made to the hospitals of Rome, as well as of
the constant solicitude with which he watches over their
management, is this — that not only is the amplest accommodation now offered for the treatment of every
possible form of human malady, but there are means
ever at hand to meet any exigency which could arise ;
such, for instance, as the prevalence of a dangerous epi-
demic.   The first hospital which I visited will sufficiently
illustrate the power of expansion that may be said to
be common to all the hospitals of Rome.

La Consolazione.

This was *La Consolazione*, built very close to the Tar-
peian Rock, which place of tragic interest has now almost to be looked for, though not in vain ; as nearly
thirty feet of the once dreaded precipice are yet visible
above the constantly encroaching soil.   Still Byron
might well have asked —

> ".   .   .   .   .   .   where the steep
> Tarpeian ? fittest goal for Treason's race,
> The promontory whence the Traitor's Leap
> Cured all ambition."

This hospital, which was founded and afterwards enlarged by Cæsar Borgia, was the smallest of the many

through which I went, and yet, to me, its size appeared very great; for the chief ward in the establishment for the men was about 200 feet in length, and contained 62 beds. To this great hall the present Pope lately added a new wing, in which 16 beds were placed, ready for use; but of the 78 beds then made up, and ready at a moment's notice, not more than 21 were occupied. Such, however, is the great width of the principal hall, or ward, that a double row of beds might be easily placed at each side, as is done in the great hospital of *Santo Spirito*, and to a certain extent in the other hospitals. The width being about 40 feet, two rows of beds at each side—the head of the second bed being placed up to the foot of that next the wall—would not occupy more than 24 or 25 feet, thus leaving a great passage, of at least 15 feet, in the centre; so that in this hospital there might, at any moment, be 156 beds ready for the reception of patients. It was at the time entirely devoted to surgical cases, such as fractures, wounds, burns, &c. I carefully noted that, not only was the building lofty in proportion to its length, and thoroughly ventilated, but that a most liberal allowance of space was preserved between each bed—generally, an average of 5 feet. Of course, the curtailment of this space between the beds would still further add to the power of accommodation, in case of necessity. The beds looked good, clean, and comfortable, and the entire building partook of the same character; although, to the eye of one accustomed to timber flooring, a dull red brick, or tile, while eminently useful in a warm country, does not at first sight make the most favourable impression. Six secular clergymen constantly reside in a house attached to the hospital, which is also attended by Jesuits, and other religious orders. A number of novices are likewise in unceasing attendance upon the sick. In this, as in all the Roman hospitals, there is a little Chapel — the altar of which is visible from every side — in which mass is daily offered up for the benefit of the patients, who also assist at the rosary, and other religious exercises. It is scarcely necessary to remark how much this salutary provision for the comfort and consolation of the sick aids the efforts of human skill in the favourable treatment of disease, and to what extent it assists in the operation of the cure. To the patient, whose body is tortured by pain, or whose mind is prostrated by the effects of the malady, the consolation of hourly spiritual ministration is a blessing great beyond expression, — such, indeed, as those in rude health cannot by possibility appreciate. It is at a moment of the kind that the gentle voice reaches his heart, and the word of whispered counsel touches his inmost soul.

The hospital for women is divided by a street from that of the men. It had 24 beds in immediate readiness, besides ample resources in case of necessity; but of the beds so prepared, not more than 9 were then occupied. The low wailing moans of one poor woman, whose breast had been fearfully scalded, and who had been only that day taken in, were most painful to hear. The unhappy sufferer evidently struggled with her anguish; but it frequently overmastered her, and a sharp cry occasionally testified to its severity. A religious community had the charge of this branch of the hospital, and several of its members were busy about the beds of the patients, or employed in various duties necessary for their comfort. The beds were neat and well kept, and the place quite clean.

SAN GIOVANNI DI CALABITA.

This hospital particularly interested me, it being intended for a class of cases entitled to the greatest sympathy, and for which, in my judgment, every state, or government, should make the most ample provision, — namely, those afflicted with temporary maladies. It is built on the island of St. Bartholomew, in the Tiber, and upon a most appropriate site—the very spot on which, in Pagan times, stood an hospital attached to the temple of Esculapius. It was founded in the Pontificate of Gregory XIII., in 1581; and is under the care of the Brothers of St. John of God, an order specially instituted by its holy founder for attendance on the sick. This order, which is of Spanish origin, is popularly known by the name *Benefratelli*, from the fact of their having, on their institution in Rome, gone about soliciting alms, and using the words — " *Fate bene fratelli per l'amor di Dio* " — " Brethren, do good for the love of God." Seven of the brothers were in the hospital as I entered, and were engaged in attendance on the sick. The principal hall is about 200 feet in length, and

N

contained fifty beds in a state of immediate preparation ; but of this number not more than sixteen were occupied at that time.   One of the patients, a singularly interesting young man, a native of Switzerland, whose malady was an affection of the chest, was surrounded by the female members of his family, whose holiday attire imparted a cheerful aspect to the place.   He was evidently of a somewhat better class, and, in conversation with a friend by whom I was accompanied, he expressed himself most grateful for the attention which he had received.   The capability of expansion, acoording to circumstances, was as manifest in this as in the other hospitals.   I found the beds to be neat, comfortable, and well ordered.

An adjoining hospital, for women, was in the care of a number of Italian nuns.   Not more than eighteen of the beds were then occupied, though the great hall in which they were placed might be easily made to ac-commodate five times that number of patients.   Yet another hall, or ward, had been recently added to it by the present Pope.

San Galicano.

The Hospital of San Galicano is interesting in many respects, but in this respect more than in any other — that it exhibits, in a very striking manner, the ad-mirable solicitude which the Church evinces towards the young.   This hospital was established for, or is de-voted to, the treatment of cutaneous diseases of all kinds. Originally, it was an hospital for leprosy — a disease of which, happily, little is now known in Rome. It was founded in 1722 by a pious priest, Emilio Lami; was enlarged in 1754 by Benedict XIV.; and owes many of its improvements to the benevolence and vigilance of Pius IX. Its present accommodation is for 60 men, 54 women, and 30 boys—in all 144; but the number of patients at the time of my visit did not exceed 104, of which number the boys constituted more than one-third. The latter were then engaged in play, in a spacious yard; and if I were to judge of their condition by their vivacity, I might safely predict for them a speedy restoration to health. The disease seemed principally to have assumed, with them, the character of "scald," as they all wore on the head a close-fitting linen cap. Their dress was dark and serviceable, and decidedly comfortable. Some persons may deem it a great calamity, that the treatment of the disease with which these children are afflicted generally extends to the term of a year, or even a year and a half; but their ideas might undergo a change if they learned that the education of the young patients was as strictly looked to, as if they were attending a seminary, instead of being the inmates of an hospital. The boys are placed under the care of the Brothers of St. John of God, by whom they are taught reading, writing, and arithmetic, and are thoroughly grounded in catechism and Christian doctrine. In fact, they undergo a course of education and a course of physic at one and the same time; and when they leave the hospital cured, they also leave it educated. The same may be said of the girls; with this

N 2

difference, that, in addition to the literary and religious instruction which they receive, they are also taught useful work of various kinds. At the time I visited the institution, I saw about thirty girls, whose ages varied from three to fourteen years, receiving instruction in catechism from one of the Sisters of Charity, to whose management they are happily entrusted. Some of the children had been sent in from the country, for the advantage of the better treatment which the hospital afforded, and, being the offspring of poor parents, living in remote and sequestered districts, were generally ignorant at the time of their admission; but, thanks to the care taken of them by their excellent teachers, they were then progressing in intelligence as in health. Old and young hear Mass every morning, and attend the rosary and other devotions during the day. The two establishments — male and female — presented a pleasing appearance of neatness and cleanliness, valuable as a remedial adjunct, but perhaps still more valuable in its influence on the tastes and habits of its youthful inmates. I was shown the separate bath-rooms for the children of both sexes. In the boys' department there were six baths of white marble, over one of which was carved the ominous word " *Leprosia* ; " but as there had been no case of that frightful malady in the hospital for two years before, that bath enjoyed a state of fortunate exemption from use.

SAN GIACOMO.

The most beautiful of the Roman hospitals, though not the largest in its accommodation, or the vastest in its extent, is that of San Giacomo in Augusta. It is likewise one of the noblest monuments of the munificence and humanity of Pius IX. Originally founded in 1339, by the executors of Cardinal Pietro Colonna, in compliance with his testamentary wishes, it was improved and enlarged in the present century by Pius VII. and Leo XII. It was instituted for the poor who were afflicted with ulcers, or other loathsome diseases that rendered them objects of aversion; and in 1515 Leo X. specially destined it for the treatment of leprosy and syphilitic diseases. But the whole building was splendidly restored by Pius IX.—in fact, was re-erected. Completed in August 1856, it was in full operation when I visited it in the following November; and, from the perfection of all its arrangements, as well as from the care taken to provide for the cure and comfort of the patients, it may be termed a model hospital.

The length of the great hall is 340 feet; and, as I entered it at an hour when the day was drawing to a close, it seemed to me something wonderful in its extent. But viewed at any time, or under any circumstances, it would be impossible to behold a more imposing, or a nobler hall. Its width as well as its loftiness are in proportion to its length; so that there may at any time be two rows of beds at each side, and still an ample space preserved between the outer rows. In the centre there is laid down, for the entire length of 340 feet, a pavement of pure white marble, fully six feet in width, and of fine quality. A light gallery divides the height of the walls on each side; its object being to afford greater facility in the management of the windows. This hospital had been opened with 108 beds, but it then contained 130, and at any moment might be made to accommodate 200. In case of an emergency, the lower hall, over which the one I describe has been erected, could be at once restored to usefulness; whereas now it is abandoned for the new and beautiful building. There is a large staff of experienced physicians and surgeons, besides twelve or fourteen attendants, also professional men, but some of them with a reputation yet to achieve. Three visits daily are regularly paid to all the patients in the hospital —the first in the morning, the second at noon, and the third in the afternoon. As the surgeons went their rounds on the occasion of my visit, many a wound or ulcer was bared, and many a moan was uttered, as the attendant dressed it under the direction of the head surgeon, or he himself, rapidly and with practised hand, used the knife, or applied the caustic. This institution is called the Hospital of Incurables; but while, unhappily, a large proportion of its inmates may come within that dismal category, the term incurable would not apply to others, the former rules of admission having been relaxed, for purposes of greater utility. Its spiritual care is entrusted to the Brothers of St. John of God, who are likewise assisted by members of other religious orders.

A short time previous to my visit, the Pope had carefully gone through this hospital, and personally examined into all its details. He went to the bed-side of the patients, inquired into their condition and the nature of their malady, and blessed, consoled, or admonished them. I was shown a most interesting-looking boy, who was at the moment engaged in reading his prayer-book, by the light of a lamp; and as the light fell upon his youthful features, wasted by sickness, and spiritualised by an expression of intense piety, a painter might have borrowed from his countenance and attitude an idea of angelic purity and sanctity. He was suffering from an aggravated spine disease, and no hope was entertained of his recovery. The compassion of the Pope had been greatly excited by the sweet and gentle resignation with which the little fellow bore his sufferings; and tears of tender pity fell from the eyes of the Holy Father upon the pale cheek of the child, as he kissed him and pressed him in his paternal arms, after he had confessed and absolved him. There seemed, as it were, a radiance of holiness around the sweet head of that dying boy.

In another part of the building, there is a department for women, but, though of nearly equal accommodation, not at all similar in its construction and arrangement. And here, as in the hospital which I have described, surgical cases are relieved irrespective of the age, country, or religion of the patient. Several charitable congregations of both sexes minister to the religious wants of the suffering. This hospital was a favourite resort of St. Philip Neri. And very frequently, at the present day, many of the unhappy females who are driven, by their vicious lives, to seek relief within its walls, owe their thorough reclamation to the exertions of pious ladies — many of them of the noblest families of Rome — who constantly attend it.

Besides this hospital for women, there is the important one of

SANTISSIMA SALVATORE.

This great hospital, which consists of two piles of buildings, separated by the street leading from the Lateran to the Coliseum, was founded in 1216 by Cardinal Giovanni Colonna, and was at first called after St. Andrew, but soon after by its present name, from the confraternity to whose care it was committed. This confraternity was composed of twelve noble Romans, who had charge of the Chapel called Sancta Sanctorum, near the Lateran Palace. The hospital is chiefly intended for women requiring medical treatment, and receives patients of any country, age, rank, or religion. It has also a male department, principally for those who have suffered from violent accidents; and the average number of beds in both is over 500. Great care has been taken of late years in the management of this hospital, which is now remarkable for its cleanliness and neatness. Its ordinary or smallest staff consists of two principal physicians, and one principal surgeon, with two assistant

physicians, and two assistant surgeons; besides its
attendants and dressers. The regular visits are made
twice a day; but professional assistance is to be had at
any moment of the day or night. A religious order
called *Cruciferi*, from the red cross borne on its habit,
attends to the spiritual wants of the patients.

In 1821 Pius VII. transferred to this hospital a community of Sisters of Charity who had dedicated themselves to visiting the sick in another district. Leo XII.
and Gregory XVI. were both conscious of the value of
this noble order, and conceded important privileges to
it. The vows [(those of poverty, chastity, obedience,
and hospitality), last only for a year, and are renewed at
the end of that time; but when the Sisters attain the
age of forty, they can make the vows perpetual.

The cost of a patient in this hospital averages a shilling
a day of our money.

Santissima Trinita di Pellegrini.

This hospital was founded by St. Philip Neri in
1550. It is destined for the relief of pilgrims, and is
used for convalescents from the other great institutions.
It contains about 500 beds, and affords relief to more
than 11,000 persons in the year. The institution of the
Jubilee, which has been the great source of pilgrimage
to Rome, originated, in the year 1300, with Boniface
VIII., and serves to bind Catholics of all nations by the
closest ties to the See of Rome. At first, it was to
have taken place every hundred years; but Clement VI.,

whose seat of government was at Avignon, shortened
the period, and ordained its celebration in the year 1350 ;
and it was further shortened to a quarter of a century
in 1475, by Paul II. St. Philip Neri, in 1550, founded
the Confraternity of the Holy Trinity, to succour and
relieve pilgrims, and also to receive convalescents from
the other hospitals.   Paul IV. granted the confraternity
a convenient building for an hospital, and Clement XII.
added refectories in which about 1000 persons can receive their meals at the same time. In Jubilee years the
number of pilgrims is immense ; and even in ordinary
years, especially at Easter, it is considerable.   To be received, they must have come from a distance of at least
sixty miles, and have brought with them certificates from
their bishop and parish priest to the effect that their
journey was for visiting the Holy Places.   Italians are
entertained for one day, Ultramontanes two, Portuguese
five, and so on.   In the Jubilee of 1825 the number of
pilgrims who received hospitality was 263,592 : and the
expenses of that year, under this head, amounted to
64,644 scudi.

    Passing over a number of smaller hospitals, and all
those which may be described as private, I come to the
most important, if not the most interesting, of all.

CHAP. XVII.

Great Hospital of Santo Spirito. — Its Extent and Importance.—
Its Foundling Hospital. — Foundlings not necessarily illegitimate. — Reasons why legitimate Children are sent in.

SANTO SPIRITO.

To go through this magnificent hospital, which is not
only the greatest but the most ancient of the existing
Roman hospitals, was the work of several hours.   It is
said that it owes its origin to the patriotic charity of a
Saxon King, who, having abdicated his throne and become a convert, took up his abode in Rome in 728,
and there founded an hospital for the relief of his countrymen.   It was restored by Innocent III., who confided it to the Brothers of the order of S. Spirito, from
which it derived its name. To enlarge and enrich it, was
the grateful task of many successive Popes.   Benedict
XIV., in 1751, added a museum and anatomical theatre:
Pius VI. endowed the museum liberally with the choicest
specimens;   and   Pius   VII. added   dissecting   rooms,
baths, and many other requisites.   The present Pope
has made this noble institution the object of his special
solicitude, and effected the most important reforms in

its management and administration.   Amongst the
most valuable of the reforms effected by Pius IX., was
the appointment of twenty Capuchin Priests to its
spiritual assistance.   To render their connection with
the hospital complete, he had a house built for them
within the enclosure; so that at all hours, of the night
as well as of the day, some members of the body might
be in the wards, and in attendance on the sick. A community of Sisters of Charity also aid in the pious work,
as well as manage the working details of the vast
institution — which, besides the hospital for the sick,
also contains an hospital for the reception of deserted
children, and a conservatorio for children of the same
class, who, after being nursed outside, are restored to
its care.   The magnitude of the hospital, properly so
called, may be best understood when I state that there
were 780 patients in its extensive wards on the day
that I passed through them; that there is accommodation for twice that number; and that in case of an
emergency — such as might arise from the sudden out-
break of disease — it could be made to receive 2000
patients!   I took the number then in the hospital from
the register, which was courteously exhibited to me by
the Sister in whose charge it was, and by whom it was
kept in a manner to excite admiration even in a London banker. Two of the Sisters were at the same desk;
and both kept an account of every article given out of
the storerooms, or supplied from the kitchen — itself a
curiosity — and, in fact, of every detail connected with
the daily management of the vast establishment.   In

another part of the building, the Prelate in charge has his apartments, and to him the officers in charge communicate all necessary particulars, as well as receive orders and instructions at his hands.   My application, to be permitted to go through the different departments, found him in the midst of his affairs, giving audiences and despatching business — business involving the welfare of not less than 2000 human beings.   No sooner was the request made than it was granted, and orders were at once given that every part of the immense establishment should be thrown open to my inspection — a permission of which I fully availed myself.

The halls in this hospital are of enormous size, and afford space to two rows of beds on each side, leaving from fifteen to eighteen feet in the centre.   Here, as in other hospitals which I had seen, the beds were clean and comfortable ; and such was the effect of good ventilation, that I failed to perceive the least unpleasantness of odour, such as is a matter of common occurrence even in hospitals of great pretension.   The same remark I can safely make of the other Roman hospitals which I visited ; and in a quick perception of offence to the sense of smell, I am too painfully acute for my own comfort.   I did not consider the mortality by any means in excess, but rather the contrary ; for in an hospital of 800 patients, many of whom, both medical and surgical, had been received in a bad state, the deaths for the last three days were but eleven — that is, four on the first day, four on the second, and three on the day of my visit.   The medical and surgical staff is fully in proportion to its requirements, care being specially taken that professional aid may be had at a moment's notice, during every hour of the four-and-twenty.   It would be quite unnecessary to represent in detail the several features of this hospital: and it will therefore be sufficient to say, that they are adapted to the great ends proposed — the comfort, the consolation, and the cure of the patient.

I must not, however, omit referring to its really fine museum, abounding with the most beautiful preparations, natural as well as in wax, of all parts of the human frame, and exemplifying the effects of various kinds of disease on its principal organs.   I was particularly struck with some preparations which displayed in the most startling manner the virulence of what I may unprofessionally term the *poison* of cholera.   Two or three of the great organs of the human body were, in one place, represented in their normal or healthful condition; and similar organs, which, having discharged their separate functions regularly and healthfully before they were blasted by this fell disease, were shown dried, like leather, and shrivelled up to a tenth of their original size.   But a further and still more striking illustration of the terrific power of the disease was exhibited in the skull and great bones of a patient who had fallen a victim to it in 1853 — which were as blue as if they had been purposely dyed of that colour.   The poison had not only withered up cartilage and muscle, but had penetrated to the very bone.

Curiously enough, these preparations, as well as the

other interesting objects that enriched the museum, were pointed out to me by one who had covered himself with distinction, by the skill, humanity, and untiring zeal which he displayed in his treatment of cholera patients in the year to which I refer. At that time Dr. Ceccarelli was a young man in his profession; but such was his skilful treatment of the disease, that he effected many cures which at the moment appeared wonderful. At length, he himself yielded to its force, and the effects of almost matchless exertion; but to the bedside of the now illustrious patient rushed numbers of his brethren, to watch over a life eminently precious to humanity and science; and ere long the Holy Father had the satisfaction of rewarding, with his own hand, merit and worth to which he was keenly and gratefully sensible. The particular preparations of which I have spoken bore upon them the name "Ceccarelli;" but it was not until I had parted from my courteous guide, that I learned by whom I had been accompanied.

In another part of the building is a great military hospital, the hall or corridor of which seemed of enormous magnitude. It was much occupied, but entirely by Italian soldiers.

I was most anxious to judge for myself of the condition of the Foundling Hospital, which, as I have stated, forms an important branch of this vast institution; for I had heard different opinions as to its management. A kindly, cheerful-looking Sister was directed to act as our guide; and she at once led the way, through many courts and corridors, to that part of the building.

The average number of children received during the year is about 900 ; but of these, not more than 600, or two-thirds, are illegitimate——the remaining 300 are the offspring of poor and needy, perhaps in some instances of heartless parents, who, from various causes and motives, adopt this ready mode of providing for them, or getting rid of them.

If it happen, as it very often does with people in the humblest condition of life, that their family exceeds their means of supporting them, one of the children is committed to the wheel of the Foundling Hospital of *Santo Spirito*——it might be, with some mark on its dress, by which it could be registered in the hospital, and its identity afterwards proved ; in case, for instance, of its being claimed by the parents, which is by no means of uncommon occurrence. Another frequent cause of having recourse to this institution, for the maintenance of legitimate offspring, is, either the delicacy of the mother, or the delicacy of the child. The mother has no nourishment to give the infant, and she is too poor to provide a nurse for it ; therefore she sends it, or bears it, to an asylum where that aliment, which nature has refused to her, will be provided for it. Or it is a rickety, miserable little thing from its birth, stunted, mal-formed, or so delicate that, in the rude hut of its parents, it has no chance of ever doing well ; then, too, in its case, the wheel of the hospital is a safe resource, and with parents of hard hearts takes the place of many an evil suggestion, such as is too often present in the homes and the breasts of the destitute. Frequently, the parent is known to argue that the infirm or malformed child, who is thus got rid of, has the best chance of recovery, and certainly of being provided for, where eminent medical attendance is always to be had, and where the greatest care is taken of the training and future interests of the foundling.   It may be said, that this facility of getting rid of legitimate offspring leads to a disregard for the manifest obligations of a parent's duty; but to this fair objection I can only offer a pre-ponderating advantage, — that it does away with that awful proneness to infanticide which distinguishes other countries, but pre-eminently England.   In England, a mother—a mother by lawful wedlock, too — is starving, or her poverty has assumed a degree which renders her desperate ; and she makes away with her children secretly, or slays them more openly, and consummates her frantic guilt by destroying her own life.   No cases of this nature occur in the Papal States ; not because intense poverty is not experienced there by classes as well as individuals, but that the State has afforded a means of provision which leaves no room for fierce suggestion and terrible temptation.   It may also happen that a man's wife dies in giving birth to a child, or from some other cause ; and that the poor bewildered father, not knowing what to do with the helpless little creature, consigns it to the shelter of the Foundling Hospital, which, he well knows, is under the protection of the State, and managed by a body of religious women whose lives are devoted to its duties.   These are some of the causes which induce the parents of legitimate offspring

o

to adopt this mode of providing for them. As to the causes which influence the parents of illegitimate off-spring to rid themselves of the living evidences of their shame, they are too obvious to be particularised.

The number of 900 may seem very great, as repre-senting the annual average received; but it should be stated that the hospital of Santo Spirito affords an asylum not only to the foundlings of Rome, but to those of the provinces of Sabina, Frosinone, Velletri, and the Comarca, and also districts on the borders of the king-dom of Naples.

Not more than fifty of the children recently sent in were in the house when I went through it ; the remainder had been sent off to the country, for the benefit of better nursing, and a more healthful atmosphere, than the city could furnish. Several of the wretched little beings were known to be the children of wedlock, from certain precautions taken by those who had sent them in ; and, from the state in which I saw but too many of them, I could well understand the pressure under which their parents had acted. Some of them were evidently suffering from transmitted disease ; others were shrouded from the light, their sight being grievously affected ; more were evidently passing away to a happier world, and lay still and cold in the cot, or feebly moaned in the arms of a nurse ; while not a few were exhibited with pride by their nurses, and crowed and bawled as merrily and lustily as if they had been born heirs to princes, and were cradled in royal luxury. One special " *bambino* " was really a noble fellow, and, were it not that he was swathed and strapped and bandaged, so that he resembled a juvenile mummy, he might have fairly rivalled any authentic feat of the Infant Hercules.

I had heard a great deal of the mortality of this institution, and was quite prepared to have such statements confirmed ; but, taking all circumstances into consideration, especially the condition in which the children are sent in, the actual percentage of deaths was far less than I had been led to anticipate, and, in fact, had been informed it was. I made particular inquiry on this head, and was informed, on the best possible authority, that, of late years—during which much has been done by the present Pope for the better management and administration of the hospital—the mortality did not exceed *ten* per cent. Had it been much more, it could not have been a matter of reasonable surprise. For only imagine a poor little being brought, in a basket, a distance of sixty miles or more, under the rays of a burning sun, or in the depth of winter, perhaps in the midst of rain and snow ; and then judge in what condition it must be ere it reaches the wheel of the hospital !

The nurses are kept with great care, and never leave their young charge. They are well fed, and well paid, and every inducement is held out to them to discharge their duty honestly and faithfully. The constant presence of one of the Sisters is a guarantee for as much care and attention as can be expected from such a class to such a class—from the mercenary hireling to the miserable foundling, the offspring of shame, or, at best, the child of poverty. I should not report truly, however, if I did not state, as the result of my visit, and a by no means careless inspection, that the nurseries were in good order, that the cots of the children were clean, and that all the other requisites for such an establishment were ample and comfortable. The beds of the nurses were also neatly made up; and the women themselves looked to be healthy, and competent for their task. Still I would defy any one, who had not a heart of iron, to pass unmoved through the rows of cots, in which many a pale and sickly little face unconsciously appealed to his compassion, and from which there came low, feeble moans, that were but too eloquent of pain. For my part, I felt more acutely when passing through those dormitories, occupied by their miserable little tenants, than I did when witnessing the grown man shudder as the surgeon's knife touched his shrinking flesh, or as the sharp shriek of agony gave evidence of torture too great for human nature to endure in silence.

Some particulars with respect to the reception and care of the foundlings may be added. But, first, as to the origin of the system.

The protection of exposed or abandoned children, whether the offspring of lawful wedlock or the fruit of illicit connection, has occupied the attention of the Church from its earliest ages, and was made the subject of discussion in various councils so far back as the fourth century. In this aspect, as in many others, Christianity offered a striking contrast to Paganism; the one so full of tenderness and compassion, the other selfish, stern, and remorseless. Constantine, the first Christian Emperor, evidently with a view of preventing the system of child-murder, which was common at the time, and which had long existed in more polished Greece, made known his desire to assist those who, from their poverty, or other cause, could not support their children.   The first regular asylum for exposed infants was established in Milan, in the year 795, in the house of an archbishop, who left his wealth for its support, with the direction that the children should be maintained till the age of seven, and then taught a trade.   Innocent III., in the twelfth century, collected all abandoned children, either legitimate or of poor or unnatural parents, in the place where he opened an hospital for the sick.   A similar institution was established in Paris, in 1638, by that Prince of Humanity, St. Vincent de Paul; and in the following century London followed the merciful example.

Particular care is taken in noting down everything connected with the reception of the child.   Of course, the day of the year and month are noted, as well as the very hour; and, if the person bringing the child have no difficulty in telling them, also the name and origin.   The official in charge makes a slight incision, in the shape of the cross of Santo Spirito, on the right foot, and introduces into it a dark dye, in order to render the mark indelible.   The child is then carried to the nursery, where it is taken charge of by the Superior, who examines the clothes, to ascertain if there be any mark, writing, coin, medal, or ribbon: and if there be any such, she makes a note of it, which she fastens to the clothes.   In fine, every particular by which the identity of the child can be described, is carefully put aside and registered. If there be no certificate of baptism, the little one is carried to the church, and there baptised conditionally. The nurseries consist of three rooms, capable of containing fifty beds for the nurses; and each bed has two cradles near it. Two of the rooms are for the healthy children, and one for the sick.

The children are not long retained in the hospital, the rule being to send them to the country as quickly as possible. In fact, on certain days nurses apply for the children, bringing testimonies from the Parish Priest and Deputy, as to age, health, and capability, and also as to the birth and death of their own children; in order that they should not ask for their own offspring, and support them at the expense of the institution. The nurse receives a present of clothes, marked with the cross of S. Spirito, and is paid at the rate of one scudo a month for fourteen months. Then commences the nursing *a pane*, which lasts till twelve years for boys, and ten for girls. For the first six months of the dry-nursing, the pay is sixty bajocchi a month, and after that forty bajocchi till the end. Morichini, from whom I take these particulars, states that it is remarked in Rome that nurses entertain a greater affection for boys; which is principally accounted for because of the advantage to be gained from the boy when he grows up, in case of the family adopting him. It even frequently happens that the foundling is the most cherished member of the poor family into which he is received. The boys, when they return from their nurses, are sent to the orphanage of the City of Viterbo, called S. Maria della Providenza, where, for a certain monthly pension, they are maintained, clothed, educated, and instructed in some trade or art, until the age of twenty-one, when they are dismissed with a present of ten scudi. If the boy be taken by any person, he must be educated and trained in the same manner, and until the same age, when, having received the allotted sum, he may remain in the family, or go where he pleases.

The girl who is kept by a family must be maintained decently till she is married, or enters a convent; and in case of her marriage, which is her usual destiny, she receives a certain sum of twenty scudi; but as there are various dowries established for illegitimate girls, she may receive even 100 scudi — a small fortune in Italy. The girls are restored to the institution after being nursed, and form a great establishment, amounting to somewhat about 600 in number. Their dowry, on leaving the conservatorio for the home of a husband, is 100 scudi.

The manufacture of wool and hemp was introduced at a very early period into this institution; and since then all kinds of feminine work, including sewing, embroidery, lace, &c.

If my visit to the infant dormitories occasioned a feeling of sadness, a walk through the department for the grown female foundlings replaced it by one of real satisfaction. The entire establishment was a model of neatness and good order, and its numerous inmates seemed to be cheerful and happy. In one large and airy room,

a number of girls were prosecuting their daily studies;
in another, they were employed at work of different
kinds; and in a third, they were receiving religious instruction from one of the nuns, between whom and
their pupils the strongest affection subsists. Carefully
watched over, well instructed, usefully trained, and provided with a suitable dowry on their quitting the asylum, it cannot be said but that the hand of charity has
done what it could to compensate the foundling for the
want of a parent's love, if not to efface the ignominy of
an origin of shame. Formed and trained by such holy
and gentle teachers, and brought up in the practice of
every virtue, it certainly is not the fault of the institution, or of its system of management, should the foundling of Santo Spirito, in her married life, not be a good
wife and a good mother — the virtuous companion of her
husband, and the watchful guardian of her children.

HOSPITAL OF SAN ROCCO.

In connection with the Foundling Hospital, which
has been alluded to at such length, may be noticed the
remarkable hospital of San Rocco.

It was originally established in the year 1500, with
50 beds, partly for medical and partly for surgical
cases; but, in the year 1770, Clement XIV. devoted
it exclusively to its present purpose—a lying-in hospital, in which female frailty is hidden from the scorn
of the world, and by which the honour of families is
protected. It has one great hall, and several chambers,

one of which is for births. The average number of beds is about 20, but these may be increased if necessary. Each bed has its curtains and a screen, by which it is effectually separated from the other beds, and, of course, from their occupants. Those who present themselves for admission are received without any question being made; and should they wish to cover their faces with a veil, so as to preclude the possibility of recognition, this measure of precaution is permitted them. In the register of the hospital the patient is alone distinguished by a number. To insure the secrecy so desirable in an institution of the kind, no one is allowed to enter its walls save the physicians, midwives, nurses, and attendants. When recovered, the patient can leave the hospital without any apprehension of danger, as the door does not open on a public road, but near an unfrequented way. Those who dare not admit their condition, without ruin to their character, are received a considerable time before the period of delivery; and, if not poor, they pay a small pension, which is increased if they desire better accommodation. The children are sent to Santo Spirito; but those mothers who desire to reclaim their offspring at a future time, put some distinguishing mark upon them, by which they could be afterwards recognised. Morichini, who wrote in 1841, states that the average number of annual admissions, from 1831 to 1840, was 165. Generally, the applicants are received from seven to eight days before the time of delivery, and are kept until as long after as may be necessary; but some have been known

to have remained but a few hours! The average time,
however, is from four to five days in all. This, like
the other charitable institutions of Rome, is partly supported by its own revenues, and partly by the State.
I was informed that, in nearly all respects, its condition
at present is similar to what it was ten or twenty years
since.

I know it will be said, by people who look at only
one side of the question, that such institutions as those
last described necessarily lead to immorality, inasmuch
as they afford a ready asylum to shame, and a convenient oblivion of its consequences. No doubt, there
would be much force in this objection, if it could be
viewed by itself only. But, on the other hand, is there
not a road thus left open to moral and social redemption,
which is closed against the frail one in other countries?
— and are not greater and more terrible evils obviated,
not by the toleration, but by the prudent recognition,
of the one evil? The State, by its support of S. Spirito or S. Rocco, does not proclaim its toleration of
immorality, and its consequences; but it wisely admits
their existence, and the utter impossibility of their total
prevention; and it meets them in a manner equally consistent with wisdom and humanity. If, indeed, the
State did no more than merely establish a foundling
hospital, or a secret lying-in hospital, the soundness of
its policy might be questioned. But it does more, — it
openly discourages and denounces vice, — it banishes it
from the streets and highways, — it preaches against it, —
it educates against it, — it takes numberless precautions

against it.   Still, in spite of every effort which religion can inspire, or human wisdom adopt, it is impossible to guard against the commission of certain offences; and, acting on this admitted fact, it is even commonly prudent to render them as little hurtful to society generally as possible.   The great object of human laws should be rather the reformation than the punishment of the offender; and, applying this principle to the particular evil with which we now deal, let us ask, whether is the open acknowledgment of unchastity more calculated to deprave the woman who makes it, or the hiding of her shame, through such means as these institutions offer to her in her hour of misery? Is it nothing that the honour of a family, hitherto without stain, should be saved?—is it nothing that the unhappy woman, oftentimes the victim of another's treachery, or of her own unsuspecting innocence, should have the means of redeeming her character, if not of recovering, by a future of penitence and virtue, her self-respect?   Is it nothing that the innocent offspring should be rescued from the desperation of its mother's frenzy, and the mother from the damning guilt of its murder?   Shame and despair are fearful prompters to a weak woman, who hears, in her anguish, the fiery hiss of the world's scorn, and beholds its mocking finger pointing her out as a lost one.   And many a tender and gentle woman, whose soft white hand never before inflicted injury on a living thing, has, in a moment of mental agony and moral bewilderment, clutched, with a grasp of frenzy, the neck of her

infant, and crushed out its little life in the mad hope
of hiding one crime by the commission of a greater.
No, no; the austere virtue which turns away its offended eyes from the infant dormitories of S. Spirito,
and the closely-curtained beds of S. Rocco, is a mere
prude, wanting alike in wisdom and in charity.

HOSPITAL FOR LUNATICS.

Adjoining the great hospital of San. Spirito, is situate
an extensive hospital, or asylum, for lunatics, divided
into two branches, one for male and the other for female patients. It is subject to the authority of the
prelate in charge of San. Spirito, but it enjoys a separate administration. To Father Lanez, the second
General of the Jesuits, it principally owes its origin,
in 1548; and amongst those holy men who assisted in
the good work, was the illustrious Boromeo, upon whom
every institution of a charitable nature possessed an
irresistible claim. At an early period it was placed
under the charge of a religious confraternity, with the
sanction and approbation of Pius IV. The present
hospital may be yet improved in the extent of its accommodation, or its patients may be fittingly transferred to a building which would have the advantage of
a rural position, and of extensive grounds. But, so far
as the treatment of the inmates is concerned, there is
nothing at present to be desired. For many years past,
the mode of treatment has been that which humanity
suggests, and of which reason approves. Gentleness

and persuasion have long taken the place of that barbarous coercion, and that cruel system of restraint, which were at one time universal, more through ignorance of the real nature of the malady, than from any want of compassion for the condition of its unhappy victims. In Rome, restraint, which is most sparingly applied, is used only in particular and extreme cases, and then only when paroxysms of fury are apprehended, which might be dangerous to the patient as well as to others; and then, instead of irons, and chains, and hand-cuffs, a strap or a waistcoat is alone employed. The beds are of a good description, their covering being specially attended to in the colder months of the year. The dress of the patients is in every way sufficient, and their diet is generous in its quality and its quantity. They are carefully visited every day by the medical staff of the hospital, which consists of men of the highest reputation for their skill in the treatment of the disease. Religion is also employed with great success, as a means of tranquilising the mind, and assisting the progress of the cure. The patients attend mass daily, and join in other religious exercises; and during lucid intervals, they are instructed in spiritual matters by a number of clergymen, who constantly visit the institution. To a community of Sisters of Charity is entrusted the management of the hospital; and these nuns attend both departments — that for men, as well as that for women. Morichini states that the institution was visited in 1835 by the late celebrated Dr. Esquirol, who had applied all his life to the study of the disease, and the best mode of its treatment; and that this distinguished authority spoke highly in praise of the system then adopted, and of the general management of the hospital.

However, since then there have been considerable improvements attempted and carried out: and whatever might be said of the Roman Lunatic Asylum some years since, it may now be spoken of in terms of just approval. The present Pope has carried out very important reforms in its management, through the aid and assistance of the gentleman now at the head of the institution. Dr. Gualandi, of Bologna, specially visited the hospitals of France and England, some years since, with the view of inquiring into their management, and studying such improvements in the treatment of the disease as modern science had invented, or experience had proved to be those most successful. He returned to Rome, after a prolonged tour and careful inspection of the principal hospitals of the two great countries mentioned; and, on his arrival, he presented himself to the Pope, and laid before the Holy Father his plan for the management of the Roman hospital. This plan was at once adopted by the Pope, who placed its author at the head of the institution, with full authority to carry it into immediate operation. Dr. Gualandi availed himself of the permission thus given to him, and at once effected some very important changes. He dismissed several of the officials, and replaced them by persons of approved humanity and intelligence; and in many other ways he carried into execution his own designs and the benevolent wishes of Pius IX.

It may be mentioned, that throughout the Papal States there are some of the best asylums for insane persons which are to be found in Europe. For instance, that of Perugia is spoken of in the highest terms by all who visit it : and in Ferrara the treatment is the mildest that can be imagined — in fact, there appears to be no restraint whatever, save that which the gentlest authority imposes. In Bologna, Ancona, Faenza, Pesaro, and Macerata, the treatment of lunatics is equally humane and intelligent. At any rate, it may be safely said, that there is no suggestion which may be made to the Pope, having for its object the improvement of these institutions, and the amelioration of the condition of their inmates, that will not command his sympathy and insure his co-operation.

The Brothers of St. John of God, amongst their other good works, devote themselves to the care of the insane, and are very successful in their management of them.

I have referred only to the *Public* Hospitals of Rome in the foregoing chapter ; but, besides those, there are several private institutions, also affording a large amount of relief. The total accommodation which the entire of the Roman hospitals is capable of affording, under ordinary circumstances, is not far from 5,000 beds. The average number of beds daily occupied may be set down at 2,000. But this average number either diminishes or increases, according to the time of the year, and the state of the public health.

CHAP. XVIII.

The Roman Prisons —In a State of Transition —Beneficial Change
in their Management — Religious *versus* Lay Officials.

I MUST premise that it is not my intention to attempt
an elaborate account of the Roman Prisons; I desire
rather, by a description of a few of those institutions,
to exhibit the value of an important change recently
made in the character of their management, and the
practical and successful efforts of Pius IX. towards a
steady reform in the system of their government.   Some
of the prisons are old, and not well adapted to an improved system of classification, or to the carrying on of
such works as are regarded as a useful aid to the reformation of the prisoner.   But the spirit of progress is
manifested in various ways; for instance, in the alteration
of an inconveniently constructed building — in the en-
largement of one found to be too small for a judicious
separation of certain classes of offenders — or in the
erection of new and really splendid institutions, in which
all the modern improvements are adopted, or about to
be so.   In more than one instance, I witnessed the
alterations actually being carried out ; and I visited and
went through the different departments of prisons which

had been completed but a short time before. In a word, it may be said, with the most perfect truth, that the prisons of Rome are *in a state of transition ;* and that, in a very short time, every such institution will experience the advantage of that wise and humane policy which characterises the rule of Pius IX. If the stranger who visits Rome do not find all its prisons in the same condition in which he might wish to see them, he must, in the first place, recollect, that the resources at the disposal of the state are but small, and that the income of the sovereign is less than that of a third-rate country gentleman in England ; and he must remember, in the second place, the confusion and trouble caused by the Revolution of 1848, and its subsequent events—by which many useful public undertakings were entirely suspended, and many valuable reforms rendered for a time impossible. Indeed, with such causes for discouragement, the wonder is, not that so much remains to be done, but that so much has been accomplished. Besides, it should be borne in mind, that the most important changes effected in the prisons of the United Kingdom are of recent date ; and that their condition, not very long since, was a cause of scandal and reproach to a people calling themselves Christian.* Even at this day, in spite of the enormous wealth of England, and her unlimited facility of applying public money to the erection of such institutions, the prison system of England will not for a moment stand comparison with that of Belgium. Nor must it be

* See Appendix.

P

forgotten that England, as well as other countries, is
indebted to Rome for the improvement of the separate
system — which dates so far back as the pontificate of
Clement XI., fully a century and a half since. And those
Reformatories, too, which are so recent in this country,
are of old date in Rome ; in which city, under various
denominations, many such now exist, and have existed
for a considerable period.   In many of the schools and
orphanages of Rome are to be seen the best possible
models of the modern " Reformatory ; " for in them the
youthful vagrant, or incipient criminal, is rescued from
ignorance, idleness, and vice, and trained to knowledge,
industry, and virtue.

The important change in the Roman prisons, which
I propose as the principal object of the present notice,
is the gradual substitution of members of religious orders
for the ordinary staff of jailors, turnkeys, and guards —
which change also fitly typifies the substitution of persuasion for force.

In all humane systems, the thorough reformation
of the criminal ought to be the great object aimed at.
Punishment, no doubt, is essential, as a means of
deterring others from the commission of similar offences, as well as arresting the offender in his career
of guilt ; but unless the improvement of the prisoner
be insisted upon as an object of primary importance,
it were better, perhaps, for society that he was got
rid of altogether — for he is restored to it hardened,
corrupted, and desperate, and thus unfitted for any
useful or creditable employment.   To effect the refor-

mation of the unfortunate criminal is certainly the first wish of the paternal heart of Pius IX.; and, with this object in view, he has of late entrusted several of the prisons of Rome to the sole and unrestricted management of religious orders. Jailors and turnkeys, however excellent many of them personally may be, are not usually inspired by very pure or lofty motives in the discharge of their functions. To suppose they were, would be to expect too much from human nature. So the prisoner is docile, and does not give much trouble, they are satisfied. Besides, their first duty is to retain in safe custody those committed to their charge ; their next is to compel a rigid compliance with the prison rules ; and satisfied in these respects, they generally think of little else. The mere stipendiary — save in rare and noble instances — serves mechanically, and from the hope of pecuniary reward, or personal advancement; or if he display unusual and remarkable activity and zeal, it is mostly from the same impelling motive. But the religious serves out of pure charity, and from the love of God. Thus, while the one is a jailor, and nothing but a jailor, the other is a friend and a benefactor. The whole and only object of persons devoted to a religious life is to serve God, by doing the greatest possible good to their fellow-creatures, no matter how degraded they may be, no matter into what depths of physical misery or moral depravity they may have fallen. It does not require much penetration to determine which of those two classes of persons is the more calculated to inspire the prisoner with confidence, and thus achieve the very first step towards real, not mock, reformation.

In the first prison which I visited, I had the opportunity of understanding the value of the substitution of the new system for the old. This was a prison for women, called

The Termini.

The door was opened by a Lay Sister of the order to which the control of the establishment has been entirely confided. The order is that of the *Sœurs de Providence*, one of those noble institutions of which Catholic Belgium has been so gloriously fruitful. It is specially devoted to the care of jails, hospitals, and schools; its mission being to reclaim the erring, to succour and console the sick, and to enlighten the ignorant. I had the advantage of an introduction to the Rev. Mother, whose honest, kindly, and most intelligent countenance was a passport to immediate confidence. Under her guidance, we—for I was accompanied by friends, some of whom were deeply interested in the object of the visit— were conducted through the building. We first passed into a great open space, in which the prisoners are allowed to take exercise and recreation at regulated hours. And if those who have formed to themselves fearful notions of Italian prisons and Italian "dungeons," had only stood within that vast enclosure—certainly two English acres in extent— and beheld it so warm and cheerful as I saw it, overhung by a cloudless sky, and lit up by a bright sun,

their preconceived notions would have received somewhat of a shock; for a place more *un*prison-like I never
beheld. A few of the prisoners were at that moment
sauntering about this open space; others were in the
chapel; more were confined in the infirmary; but the
great body of them were assembled in a vast apartment,
arranged in the manner of an ordinary school, and were
engaged in various descriptions of female work, from
the making and repair of the clothes of the inmates, to
the fabrication of the most beautiful and costly varieties
of lace. Three or four Sisters superintended the employment of the prisoners, and completely controlled
them by their presence. When I first visited the prison,
no regular uniform had been attempted, although it
was in immediate contemplation, and was to have been
adopted in a few days; and, therefore, had I been suddenly introduced, without having previously known the
nature of the establishment, I should have at once pronounced it to be an industrial school for adults, under
the superintendence of a religious community — so little
did there *appear* of any system of punishment, or even
of restraint. But, here and there, amongst those silent
rows of quiet-looking women, there were some whose
hands had once been red with blood, and who, in their
forced seclusion from the world, were then expiating the
gravest offences against the laws; offences prompted,
in most instances, by fierce and sudden passion. I was
pointed out two in particular, who had been guilty
of " assassination; " and their dark and sullen features
were in terrible harmony with their crime. For three

P 3

years the Sisters have had the management of this institution, with its average of more than 200 inmates; and beyond their own unaided influence, and the protection of a solitary sentinel, who keeps guard over the gate, there is no means of controlling this large body of women, who in Ireland would certainly, and with propriety, be classed as " able-bodied." There was some difficulty experienced at first, and not a little serious danger either. In fact, there was a regular rebellion on the occasion of the Nuns undertaking the management, as the prisoners fiercely resisted their authority. To such lengths did the prisoners proceed, that one of the Sisters was thrown down by them, and another was struck violently on the face. Fortunately for the cause of order, and the future peace of the prison, the presence of mind displayed by the Sister who had been struck, speedily put an end to the tumult. She quietly said to the excited woman by whose blow her cheek had been reddened — " You have slapped me on the one cheek; now slap me on the other," at the same time deliberately turning her cheek to her furious assailant. In an instant, there were two parties in the prison, whereas there was but one a moment before. The gentleness and courage of the Sister were irresistible in their appeal to the better part of their rude nature, and a majority at once ranged themselves on the side of order; and from that moment to the present, the authority and influence of the Nuns have been complete and undisturbed.

At the time of my visit, there was but one of the

prisoners in solitary confinement. Her immediate offence was that of striking another prisoner. On our expressing a wish to see the cell and its inmate, it was cheerfully complied with. The bolt of the exterior door was withdrawn, though not without some difficulty, by the small hand of the Sister who accompanied the Superior; and, as we entered the cell, which was well lighted, we saw a young woman sitting on a low bed, working, with a cushion and bobbins, at a fine description of lace. She at once respectfully stood up, and smiled brightly at the Reverend Mother, who addressed some words of remonstrance to her in a frank and kindly manner. Her features were regular, and her eyes peculiarly bright, imparting to the face the appearance of one liable to strong and violent excitement. One of the party interceded for her with the Superior; and upon his intercession having been favourably received, his hand was eagerly and respectfully seized by the liberated captive, and kissed after the fashion so common in Italy when acknowledging an obligation. In answer to an inquiry as to the nature of her offence, we were informed that she had assassinated some person in a moment of terrible excitement. But I afterwards learned that she was a married woman, and that, having discovered, under peculiar and aggravating circumstances, that her husband was unfaithful, she suddenly caught up a knife that lay within her reach, and stabbed his paramour to the heart. We did not perhaps expect such a revelation; but the impulsive manner and easily-lighted-up countenance of the woman made one readily comprehend with what rapidity the mind might have prompted and the hand executed even a deed of blood. Indeed she afterwards thanked the Superior for having placed her in solitary confinement, and thus afforded her time for reflection; for such was the frenzy roused in her by her quarrel with the fellow-prisoner whom she struck, that she said she could no longer control her passions, and that, had she not been forced away, she would certainly have done her a mortal injury.

We were shown through the various dormitories, which were of immense size, lofty, airy, and well-lighted. In one room, which was over 40 feet square, there were but 18 beds, neatly arranged, and cleanly in their appearance, as well as comfortable in their materials; and in another, which was 60 feet in length by 40 in width, there were not more than 25 beds. The infirmary, chapel, and refectory, were large in proportion, and kept in a condition of perfect cleanliness,—the necessary result of such superintendence and such control as the wisdom and humanity of His Holiness had provided for this important institution.

When it was first handed over to the Nuns, a few of the prisoners were in a state of great ignorance, some of them being unable to read. But since then their proficiency in reading and writing, as well as in useful and ornamental needle-work, has been most remarkable; and their conduct has also been almost uniformly good. The Superior stated that nothing could be more edifying than the piety of their demeanour when assisting at the death-bed of a fellow prisoner, or their eagerness in sharing in the religious ceremonies appointed for that solemn moment.   In fact, a dozen feeble women, acting under a sense of religious obligation, and animated by tender compassion for human misery in its most painful form, have succeeded in acquiring the most salutary control over more than 200 of their ruder fellow-creatures, not a few of whom are expiating offences of great enormity, and who perhaps at one time recognised no law but that of their fierce and untutored natures.   It is unnecessary to say that *religion* is the potent agent by which gentleness and docility are insured, and amendment is being steadily accomplished.

The influence of the Nuns was submitted to a severe test in carrying out, on a subsequent day, the change of dress which had been in contemplation at the time of my first visit.   Then, as I have stated, their dress might have led a stranger to suppose that the institution was a school, or a factory, rather than a prison ; and not only were many of the prisoners possessed of clothes, but also of various other articles.   Indeed I had particularly remarked the number of boxes or trunks in some of the dormitories.   The time being come for the meditated change, it was announced that from a certain day — then named — the prisoners should cease to wear their ordinary clothes, and were to assume a regular costume instead ; and that they should likewise surrender everything which they possessed.   To prepare for the new state of things, the Sunday — the day previous to that of the intended change —

was to be celebrated as a festival, in a religious as well as in a more mundane sense; and such was the influence which the devotions of the day produced upon their minds, that, although some of the unhappy women wept bitterly as they parted with their clothes, or surrendered their little effects, the most complete and perfect obedience was manifested by all, without an exception. The costume was universally assumed, and boxes and money were quietly yielded up. One of the prisoners surrendered eighty-three dollars, which she had kept in a belt, till then concealed about her person. The Nuns looked forward to the enforcement of the new rule with considerable apprehension, not knowing how the prisoners would receive it; but, happily, the result has afforded another and striking instance of the power and influence of an authority which, while commanding respect, also inspires affection. Even this prison is still only in a state of progress; and many other reforms — especially a separate system of cells for sleeping — are in contemplation, and will be adopted with as little delay as possible.

The Brothers of Mercy have got the control of a prison for men in the adjoining building, but only for the last twelve months; and though some of the officers of the former staff are still retained, the *three* brothers to whom its care has been entrusted, would not, as they stated, be in the least degree afraid of having it left entirely to their own custody and management. Their influence — the influence of a mild and gentle, but firm rule — is already most wonderful, and productive of the best results, in the improved tone, manner, and feeling of the prisoners. This prison, at the time I visited it, was undergoing considerable material alterations, mainly undertaken for the more easy and speedy adoption of a better system; but, so far as it was possible, in the condition of evident transition in which our visit found it, even industrial and literary training was sedulously promoted. The moral improvement of the prisoner is, of necessity, the first object, and is never, under any circumstances, neglected. The brothers under whose care this prison is placed belong to a Belgian community, established by a distinguished ecclesiastic, Canon Scheppers, of Malins, who has been recently appointed one of the Chamberlains of His Holiness; though his sense of duty may to a certain extent render his appointment an honorary distinction.

SANTA BALBINA.

A number of the same valuable brotherhood preside over an interesting institution, intended for the reformation of juvenile offenders, and vagrants of the worst class — the prison of Santa Balbina. Visiting it after the hours appointed for labour or study, I saw several of the boys in the play-ground, a large open space, in which they roamed about freely, and indulged in harmless sport; but under the watchful eye of a brother, whose manner towards them was of that paternal kind which, while exciting confidence, also commands respect and ensures obedience. The entire number of young prisoners was 97 on the day I went through the institution. But, really, the term "prisoner" does not exactly describe their condition, save so far as they are under a certain restraint, and cannot leave until permitted to do so. They are all taught to read and write; many of them are employed in a vineyard and garden belonging to the establishment; and the rest are occupied in various industrial pursuits, suited to their state in life. The rule by which they are governed, and which they cheerfully obey, is that of all others best calculated to effect their reformation. The separate cell system is in a great measure carried out in this prison; the extensive dormitories being divided by rows of small apartments, perhaps about 6 feet by 5, wired in at the top, and in front. By this arrangement ventilation and thorough separation are obtained at the same time. This plan has been also adopted in the Catholic Reformatory now in operation at Hammersmith. The boys much prefer this separate system to that of open dormitories, the idea of the little room being *their own*, as well as the duty of keeping it in order, in some degree exciting a feeling of self-respect. The Brothers say " they can do anything " with the boys; such is the influence which they possess, and, above all, the confidence which their motives inspire, even in the breasts of the most corrupted. The severest punishment, unless for an attempt at escape, is confinement for a short period; and it may be mentioned that there is but one " guardian " attached to the prison, and that he is stationed at the outer door.

The Brothers have been connected with this asylum for three years.

Another of the many reformatories existing in Rome may be here fittingly introduced. It is that of

Santa Maria della Misericordia.

This institution owes its origin to the humanity of a private individual, Paola Campa, who established it in the year 1841. It combines in it many interesting features; being at once an orphan asylum, a reformatory, and a school for agriculture. Its worthy founder, nowise dismayed by the smallness of his means—which had been saved from his income in a public office —or by the failure of other attempts, determined to gather together a number of poor abandoned orphan children—in fact, vagrants—and to educate them in religion and virtue, and in a knowledge of agriculture; for the general complaint was, that too many poor boys had been reared to trades. He selected a salubrious part of the suburbs, in which he procured a vineyard of three *rubbia*, to which he added seventeen more— in all, twenty. Complete success crowned his charitable efforts; for in a very short time there were 147 boys of various ages, from five to eighteen years, in the institution; 103 of whom had been sent by the Police authorities, 33 by the Commission of Subsidies, and the rest by private individuals. The first were paid for by the police, at the rate of 20 scudi a year each; private persons paid at the rate of 24 scudi for those whom they sent in; and some of them were at the entire charge of

the generous founder himself.   The number of boys was
limited to 200, as a single *rubbia* of land only gives work
to 10 pupils.   The boys are divided into small companies, each of which has for its head an agriculturist
of experience and good conduct, who never leaves his
pupils, but sleeps with them in their dormitory, eats
with them at the same table, and instructs them in the
field.   The other officers have separate duties, and all
are presided over by an ecclesiastic, as Superior.   The
pupils are taught catechism, reading, writing, arithmetic, and the principles of agriculture; and their
practical training includes the cultivation and management of vines, olives, corn and vegetables, meadows,
and grass fields.   They likewise have bees, silkworms,
and also a few cattle for their instruction in pastoral
occupations.   And, in order to stimulate their zeal, a
portion of the profits is reserved for them, and placed
in the savings bank, there to increase by interest.
They rise early, arrange their dormitories, assist at
Mass, and then eat their first meal; and after singing
pious hymns, they go in companies to their work, under
the escort of their respective chiefs.   The principal
meals are taken in common in the refectory, and are
eaten in silence, a good book being read during the
time.   Bread is freely given them while at work, little
time being allowed for idling; but on festival days,
after the performance of their religious duties, they are
suffered to indulge in harmless sports in the beautiful
and varied grounds of the institution, which is near the
Villa Albano, whose trees shelter it from the hot wind.

Watched over day and night (the dormitories being well lighted); controlled by a discipline at once mild and firm; and constantly occupied in rural labour, in study, in pious practices of religion, and in healthful recreation—it may be easily understood that punishment is rarely necessary, and that reformation is the certain result of a system which developes the finest qualities of the mind and heart, and finds a free scope for the energies of the body. MORICHINI gives a touching instance of the affection entertained by the boys for their benefactor. On the occasion of CAMPA returning to the institution, after his recovery from a severe fit of sickness, the boys, by a spontaneous impulse, formed a circle round him, and on their knees offered an *Ave* to the Virgin Mother, the Protectress of the Institution, in thanksgiving for his safety.

Pius IX. has established more than one of this class of institutions; and amongst others, a valuable and flourishing one for vagrant children of more tender years, who receive in it a religious, a literary, and an agricultural training. To found and maintain this reformatory, which is known as that *della Vigna Pia*, the Pope devoted to it three vineyards, his own private property. This single fact is indicative of his zeal for the instruction and reformation of the young.

CHAP. XIX.

Prisons of San Michele. — The Cellular and Silent Systems long
practised in Rome. — The Political Prison — very unlike an
Italian Dungeon.

AT San Michele, one of the greatest establishments
in Rome, embracing within its vast extent a grand
college, an hospital, more than one asylum for the poor,
and three prisons — there is a prison for males, in which
the separate system has been strictly carried out for
150 years, or since the time of Clement XI. In some
respects it is very similar to the modern military prisons
of Ireland, one of the most perfect, if not best managed,
of which is that of Cork. In all cases that it can be
enforced, the silent system is maintained; but there are
times when speaking is allowed, and occupations, — for
instance, particular descriptions of work, — during which
it cannot be judiciously prevented. The cells, as in the
military prison to which I have referred, rise tier over
tier, or story above story — all looking into, and lighted
by, a vast hall, in which various kinds of industrial
employment are carried on. The prisoners eat their

food in their cells; and as I entered the great hall of the prison, I beheld them walk quietly and silently from their cells to where an officer was serving out to each a fair allowance of a soup that looked well to the eye, and that a curious friend assured me was not at all unpalatable to the taste.   On Sundays they are allowed to talk to each other for half an hour.   They rise every morning at half-past five o'clock, dress, and arrange their cells; at half-past six, they attend Mass; they then breakfast; at half-past seven, they proceed to their various occupations, always of an industrial kind, at which they continue till half-past eleven; they then get their dinner, and remain in their cells till half-past one; when they resume their work, which lasts till five.   At five they sup; after which they immediately attend school, which lasts till half-past seven; when instruction of a religious nature is given, and the night prayers are said.   They then return to their cells, into which they are shut up till the next morning commences another day of melancholy drudgery, irksome, no doubt, but by no means unimproving.   Several of the prisoners had been sentenced to various terms of imprisonment, some even for life; but the greater number, if not all, of this class had their sentences commuted to twenty years on the occasion of the last anniversary of the Pope's accession to the throne.

This prison was designed and constructed by the celebrated architect Carlo Fontana, at the command of Clement XI., by whom it was originally intended for the reformation of a more youthful class of offenders.

Q

Each cell is twelve palms in length and ten in width, and is lofty in proportion.   An iron balcony runs before each row of cells, the upper rows being reached by a circular, or winding, stairs.*

It will be perceived that the separate and the silent systems, which are now regarded in these countries as modern inventions in prison discipline, are carried out in a Roman prison whose origin dates back a century and a half; and that both those systems are applied within rational and humane limits — neither being maintained as a matter of inflexible rule, but both being judiciously modified and departed from, equally to the advantage of the prisoner and the institution.

Four Brothers have the sole charge of this prison. By one of them, a young man of gentle manner and prepossessing appearance, I was conducted through its various departments, the details of which he explained with equal courtesy and intelligence.

THE POLITICAL PRISON.

Passing over the prison for women, which forms part of the vast collection of buildings, I may refer to that in which persons convicted or accused of political offences were then confined.   To this department of the building I turned with considerable anxiety, being desirous of judging, by what I should myself see, how far the statements of certain of the English journals, with respect to the treatment of political prisoners, were

* The illustrious Howard specially procured a plan of this prison for his great work; it being, as he says, " different from any I had before seen."

true or false. I expected, at the least, to behold gloomy and noisome cells; to see the victims of Papal tyranny lying on scanty bundles of straw flung on stone couches, and to hear the clanking of the galling fetter and the ponderous chain. In fact, to realise the picture of a " Roman dungeon" which English writers have made familiar to my mind, the prison into which I was about being admitted should, as nearly as possible, resemble those fearful dungeons that are shown to the stranger in Venice, and which, in their horrid gloom and tomb-like aspect, speak with terrible eloquence of the mysterious tyranny of its departed Republic. But as the guardian turned the key, and flung open the door of the great hall of the prison, my thick-coming fancies and dark associations were at once dispelled. For, instead of gloom, and horror, and noisome dungeons, I beheld a large, well-lighted, well-ventilated, and — could such a word be properly applied to any place of confinement — cheerful-looking hall. The bright sun streamed in through several windows, placed rather high from the ground, on one side of this vast hall; and on the other side, and facing the light, the cells were constructed, row above row, their doors and windows opening into this large enclosure. There was no clanking of chains to be heard, but, instead, the hum of conversation, as some twenty or twenty-five men were, at the moment, either walking up and down, or engaged in a game of dominoes. They all wore their ordinary clothes, and might have passed for a number of persons who had been confined for debt. A glance into the interior of the cells of this Roman dungeon was quite sufficient to show that, not only had they ample air and light, but that they differed from ordinary cells in the great superiority of their size and arrangement. In size alone, they were considerably larger than the cells of an ordinary prison.   They also differed from the ordinary cell in a much more remarkable manner ; for in those into which I looked, there were drinking-glasses of different kinds, some ornaments, and other articles not to be expected in such places.   So far as a sense of delicacy would permit of my doing so, I saw enough to discredit the statements which I had been accustomed to read ; and to convince me, that, at least in this prison — the only prison in Rome in which political prisoners were then detained — there was no feature, whether of degradation or of cruelty, which could in any way justify those descriptions of " Italian dungeons " so familiar to the public of the United Kingdom.   I passed through a room, or ward, of considerable size, in which there were several men, the greater number of whom were sitting on their beds ; which beds appeared to be of the description usually found in a public hospital.   Light and air were fully supplied to this as to the other compartment which I have described.

This prison is entirely in the hands, and under the management, of the police.   At the time of my visit, somewhere about the middle of last November, the number of prisoners within its walls was under fifty ; and of this number but a small proportion was undergoing punishment for what are, in Rome, classed under the head of purely political offences.   At first, I was unable to understand the distinction between offences "*purely political*," and offences "*arising out of party-spirit.*" It was, however, a distinction easily explained. The former class of offence is defined by its own term, and comprehends conspiracies and other attempts against the sovereign authority of the state. But the other class of offences has its origin in the vehemence of party-feeling, and the quarrels and violence to which it leads. Perhaps I could not better indicate the character of those offences, as a means of distinguishing them from such as are purely political, than by a reference to those outrages to which party-spirit annually leads in the North of Ireland, and which, though arising out of party-spirit, are not purely political in their character, and in no way imply an attempt against the government. Where such offences involve injury to property, and even to life, as they very frequently do in the Roman States, they must be punished, or society would at once become disorganised. And this class of offenders formed more than two-thirds of the entire number suffering punishment, or under arrest, for offences in any way arising out of politics. In fact, at the time of my visit to Rome, there were not more than 70 "purely political" offenders in *all* the prisons of the States; while of the other class, who had committed offences "arising out of party-spirit," the gross number was about 200—which figures exhibited a very different state of things from what, in common with the general public of these countries, I had been led to believe.*

* See Appendix.

Q 3

CHAP. XX.

Asylum and Prison of the Good Shepherd. — Singular Influence
of the Nuns over the Prisoners. — Model Prison of Fossombrone. — The Pope a Prison Reformer. — His Advice to Bishop
Wilson.

I WOULD desire to notice somewhat in detail one of the
most interesting of the Roman reformatory institutions
— the Asylum and Prison of the Good Shepherd.   It is
a splendid establishment, of immense size, quite modern
in its construction, being one of the many grand monuments which the Pope has erected during his reign.
There formerly existed here an institution for female
penitents, who had voluntarily sought an asylum from the
misery and horror of a profligate life, which was under the
direction of a community of Augustinian Nuns; but
within the last three years the vast building erected by
Pius IX. has been completed, and handed over to the
Nuns of the order of the Good Shepherd, twenty of
whom entirely govern and control its three distinct
and separate departments, — one called the Preservation
Class — the other, the Voluntary Penitents — the third,
the Prison for those condemned to various terms of
confinement.   At the time I visited the institution,
there were sixty of the first class, fifty-five of the second,

and sixty-five of the third — in all 180. There was not even a sentinel stationed at the gate, as is almost universally the case with establishments in which condemned persons are detained; and not a single man, or indeed guard of any kind, was to be seen within the walls. The exterior door was opened by one of the Nuns, who summoned the Superioress; by whom, personally, every portion of the vast building was readily and courteously exhibited, and fully explained.

In the first large apartment which we entered, there were assembled between thirty and forty of the young persons comprehended in the Preservation Class, and whose ages ranged from four to upwards of twenty years. Several of them were orphans; others were children of parents then in prison for offences of various kinds; and a few were the children of depraved parents, from whom they were rescued by being placed in this asylum. Special care is taken that no really bad characters are admitted into this part of the establishment, lest they should have an opportunity of corrupting those old enough to receive the moral contagion; and, indeed, the appearance and manners of the girls, as they stood silently and respectfully before one of the Sisters, from whom they were then receiving religious instruction, was calculated to impress even the casual visitor with an idea of their innocence. They were nearly all pleasing-looking, and not a few had faces full of actual beauty, and that of the true Roman type. These children and young girls are taught to read and write, to make up accounts, to be expert in plain and other

Q 4

work; and it is scarcely necessary to add, that their moral and religious training is the first care of their gentle and affectionate guardians. Many of the girls wore collars of merit suspended round their necks, and to some of them was delegated the authority of Monitresses. Their dormitories, through which I passed, were large, lofty, cheerful, admirably ventilated, and kept in a state of the most perfect neatness. A well-kept and sufficiently spacious garden is attached to this branch of the establishment, for the exclusive use of this class—a high wall separating the garden appropriated to the second class, or Voluntary Penitents.

Perhaps the term Voluntary Penitent does not strictly apply to the entire of this second class; for a considerable number of them had been brought in by their parents, in the hope of checking them in a course of folly or of guilt. The rest had, of their own choice, sought a refuge in the asylum; and a number of both were then in the infirmary ward. Should a parent desire to place an erring daughter in this asylum, application is made to the Cardinal Vicar, within whose jurisdiction it is, and, upon his consent being given, compulsion might be had recourse to, in case resistance were attempted.

A description of the daily existence of this class of inmates may be interesting, as illustrative of the system adopted for their reformation.*—They rise in summer

---

* A similar system is adopted, perhaps with some modifications, in most of the Houses of Refuge in Rome.

at five, and in winter at half-past five. After a short time spent in mental prayer, they hear Mass, and then commence work—always of a useful and profitable character. During their work they frequently sing pious hymns, which lighten their labour, and keep the mind away from thoughts which it would not be well to encourage. Before breakfast—which is invariably eaten in silence—they make an examination of conscience; and, during the repast, a chapter of a good work is read. One of the Sisters overlooks this as well as the other meals, which always commence and terminate with prayer. After dinner, the Penitents enjoy an hour of innocent recreation, a Sister being present. They are not allowed to speak in whispers, nor are they permitted to indulge in vain or idle discourse, much less to allude to improper or dangerous subjects. After recreation, prayers, reading, and study, follow. They then resume work, at which they continue till the time arrives for saying the rosary, which is said in common. At half-past six or seven, they sup, equally in silence, and during the reading of a pious book. Another hour of recreation follows; and at nine o'clock they say their night prayers, and retire to rest. Silence is observed in the dormitories, and indeed always, except during the hours of recreation. The Penitents do not speak to any visitor, other than a father, mother, guardian, or person who has placed them in the institution, except in the presence of a Sister. They practice humility, obedience, and mortification; they have the use of good books; they confess weekly, and communicate monthly:

they control even their gestures, and comport themselves with grave and modest demeanour. When going from one place to another, they walk two and two; they call each other "sister," and they each serve in their turn. The profit of their work is all their own.

In each dormitory, as in all the dormitories of the establishment, one of the Sisters has her bed placed; so that, as a lamp is kept burning throughout the night, her watchfulness over her charge may be said never to cease.

The third compartment is the Prison, which has its chapel, its refectory, its work-rooms, its hospital, its dormitories, its schools, and, of course, its kitchen. In the hospital, there were several wretched women, of different ages, expiating, in various stages of physical suffering, their career of vice. The women in this side of the building were all prisoners, having been condemned by the tribunal of the Cardinal Vicar to various terms of imprisonment, from six months even to twenty years. The only woman then condemned for this latter period was remarkable for her tall stature, and a certain wildness of the eye. Her offence was that of infanticide — a very rare and exceptional crime in the Papal States, and one which excites peculiar horror when it does happen. It may be also said that it is one to which the precautionary policy of the government allows no kind of excuse; for the establishment of a great Foundling Hospital affords an easy opportunity of disposing of illegitimate offspring, otherwise than by assassination, as is too commonly the case in

England. Upon this important question the most opposite opinions are entertained — some holding that the facility of getting rid of the shame and the burden of maintaining the offspring of illicit connexion is an incentive and a boon to immorality ; while, on the other hand, the singular infrequency of the crime of child-murder is triumphantly appealed to as the result of a policy as merciful as it is indispensable. Several of the women, then in the prison, had been condemned for periods of five, and even ten years. In the infirmary ward were some elderly women, who had been detected keeping houses of bad character, and ensnaring young girls to their destruction ; and these venerable sinners had been each condemned to imprisonment for a period of five years. One old and rather repulsive-looking woman, who had been convicted of selling her own daughter to infamy, was undergoing a sentence of imprisonment for *ten* years. I mention the offence and the punishment, as indicating the vigilance and rigour of the tribunal presided over by the Cardinal Vicar, who, as the Guardian of Morals, takes cognizance of all glaring instances of their infraction. Among the other prisoners, were wives against whom charges of incontinence had been made and proved by their husbands. Considering, then, the character of many of the prisoners, it was a matter of amazement to learn with what facility they were controlled, and to see the flimsy nature of the locks by which alone the doors of the work-rooms and dormitories were fastened. I examined several of them with curiosity ; and, on drawing the key from the lock of one of the principal wards, I found it was just about the size of that used for an ordinary bed-room of a private house in England or Ireland! In each dormitory was placed the bed of the Nun, little more than its curtains distinguishing it from the beds of the prisoners. In one dormitory I counted as many as twenty-eight beds. And to maintain authority over, and ensure the obedience of, their twenty-eight occupants, there was but that one Sister; unless the aid of a "guardian"—one of the prisoners, raised to that rank for good conduct—might be relied on in case of necessity. But though some difficulty had been experienced in the commencement, when the institution was first handed over to the Sisters, none whatever is felt at present; for the rudeness, and even violence, of the past has altogether disappeared, and the entire of the prisoners are remarkable for their docility and ready obedience to the orders of the Nuns. The Superioress stated that there never was an attempt made to escape; and, on being asked what she could do in case a number of the prisoners determined to set themselves free, she answered, with a quiet little shrug, —" There would still be no fear, for the majority, being well disposed, would at once take part with the Sisters."

In this prison it is deemed unnecessary to adopt the separate or cellular system, from the fact that one of the Nuns is always on the watch, and may at a moment obviate any inconvenience which could arise from a number of the prisoners sleeping in the same apartment. In conclusion, I may safely assert that, in all respects, this prison — in which the same industrial, literary, moral, and religious training is carried out as in the two other departments of the establishment — will stand comparison with the very best in the United Kingdom. Of itself, it is an admirable illustration of that reformatory spirit of which PIUS IX. is the origin and the inspiration.

The grand new prison near Fossombrone may be also incidentally referred to. It is now ready for 250 inmates, and is to be rendered capable of containing 500. This will be the Model Prison of the States, in which every improvement that experience has proved to be useful, or that humanity can suggest, will have a fair trial. In the other prisons there is change as well as progress; but in this there will be the most perfect adaptation of the means employed to the object to be accomplished. The penitentiary system, which combines cellular separation at night, and silent work under inspectors by day — and which has been in operation in the prison of San Michele since the year 1704 — will be applied to adults in the new institution of Fossombrone. The construction of this prison is an additional evidence of the humanity and reformatory zeal of Pius IX.

It would be only tedious if I were to refer to the other prisons in Rome, especially as I have given sufficient to justify my assertion, that they are *in a state of transition,* and the expression of a confident hope that, in the course of a very short time, they will be inferior in no respects, save in the expense of their construction, maintenance, and management, to the boasted prisons

of England. I do believe that in some respects they will
be vastly superior in their results; above all, in the great
work of reformation — in the real improvement of their
unhappy inmates, whose guilt is, in the Roman States,
as in other countries, most frequently caused either by
poverty and ignorance, or by temptations against which
poverty and ignorance are but a poor protection. To
no subject has the Pope devoted more attention than to
this most important one of the treatment of criminals;
and the gradual changes which are being effected, or
which are already planned, have been entirely inspired
by the zeal and humanity of His Holiness, whose chief,
as well as most enthusiastic, agent in the good work is
his principal Chamberlain, Monsignor de Merode *, the
brother-in-law of the Count de Montalembert. Monsignor Talbot, who also holds the office of Chamberlain to
His Holiness, is equally most zealous and earnest in the
great work of prison reform. So that the Pope has the
advantage of the assistance and sympathy of two men
who are singularly suited to the promotion of this great
and humane object; for while Monsignor de Merode has
had extensive experience of the prison-system of Belgium, which is perhaps superior to that of any in the
world, Monsignor Talbot is thoroughly acquainted with
all those improvements which have been recently adopted
in England. The former distinguished person has the
official charge of the Roman prisons; while the latter
visits them several times in the week, but in a capacity

* See Appendix.

more immediately spiritual.   The Pope was not satisfied with hearing of the state of those institutions, and he resolved to see with his own eyes into their actual condition.   Accordingly, in October 1855, he made several visits to the Roman prisons, going through their different departments, the dormitories, the cells, the workshops, the infirmaries, and the kitchens, in which he carefully examined into the quantity and quality of the food distributed to the prisoners.   And of these he asked various questions — as to the offence which they had committed — the length of their imprisonment — and the manner in which they were treated.   This visit was one of entire surprise to the authorities, and at the time excited the greatest interest throughout Rome, as no such visits had been made since the year 1824, when Leo XII. personally inspected the prisons in the same manner.   Many of the reforms which are being carried out, as well as those which are now in contemplation, are in a great measure the fruit of that memorable inspection.

In concluding my notice of the Roman Prisons, I may repeat, that, while the greater number of those institutions would bear no comparison to the magnificent and costly establishments of England, they are, in general, in a state of *hopeful transition*, not to costliness and magnificence, but to more practical efficiency, and more certain success.   It would be strange, indeed, if the condition and treatment of the prisoner did not command the attention of one of the most benevolent of

men, whose feelings with reference to this unhappy
class were touchingly expressed on the occasion of his
giving a final audience to Bishop Wilson, when that
prelate was about to return to his distant diocese. —
" Be kind, my son," said the Pope, " to all your flock
at Hobart Town, but *be kindest to the condemned!* "

CHAP. XXI.

Houses of Refuge. — Charitable Associations for the Defence of the Poor and the Imprisoned. — Society of S. Giovanni Decollato. — Society della Morte.

ROME also possesses several Houses of Refuge for women, who have left the prison or the hospital, and who anxiously desire to atone, by a future of virtue, for the crime and scandal of the past. Some of these date so far back as the time of Leo X., in 1520; and others have associated with them the illustrious names of St. Ignatius of Loyola, St. Charles Borromeo, and St. Philip Neri, who have either been their founders or their patrons. Similar institutions, of a recent date, have had their origin in the charity of a Pope, a cardinal, a simple priest, or even a lay person of either sex. And as a founder, promoter, or patron of such charities, Pius IX. has, to say the least, equalled even the most munificent of his predecessors.

In connection with the Roman Prisons may be noted some few of the more remarkable charitable associations which have been founded for the comfort and relief of their unhappy inmates. The first of those to which I refer is that for the —

R

DEFENCE OF THE POOR AND IMPRISONED.

To protect the poor, and defend the weak against the aggressions of the strong, has been at all times a leading principle of the Church; which has given birth, in Rome as elsewhere, to many institutions animated by her spirit, and devoted to her cherished objects. The Arch Confraternity of St. Ivo is one of these. But so early as the year 563, Gregory the Great instituted seven *difensori* in different portions of the city; and in 1340 the College of the Procuratori assumed the title of "*diritti de' poveri.*" Urban VIII. instituted the office of Advocate of the Poor in civil cases, to which a noble citizen was nominated. The Congregation of St. Ivo, which was established in the beginning of the 16th century, was thus called after its founder, a saint of that name, who, a lawyer by profession, had consecrated his life to the gratuitous advocacy of the poor, especially orphans and widows. The society consisted of advocates and prelates of the Sacra Rota, who met on Sundays in the Church of S. Paolo Decollato; and who, after having performed their religious duties, assembled at an appointed place, and listened to the questions which the poor submitted to their consideration. When convinced of the justice of a case, they at once undertook its defence. The society was created into an arch confraternity by Paul V., in 1616. It has a Cardinal Protector, and a Prefect, who is a prelate of the Curia Romana. The members of the confraternity are all lawyers. The defence of each case is intrusted to a brother, after it has been inquired into, and the poverty of the client clearly established. The society pays all its expenses; for, besides having small but sufficient revenues at its disposal, it commands the gratuitous services of the procurators and advocates who are members of its own body. It defends the causes of poor strangers as well as others. Many great and illustrious names have been enrolled in this noble association, which has received special honours and privileges from various Popes.

The Arch Confraternity of *S. Girolamo della Carita* also undertakes the defence of prisoners and poor persons, especially widows. It has the administration of a legacy left by Felice Amadori, a noble Florentine, who died in the year 1639. This confraternity owes its origin to Clement VII., while he was still Cardinal Giulio de' Medici. It was raised to the dignity of an arch confraternity by Leo X., who conceded to it the Church of St. Girolamo, in 1524. It has been, since then, an object of peculiar interest to successive Pontiffs, from whom it has received important privileges, all tending to increase its usefulness to the poor and the distressed. The principal objects of their solicitude are persons confined in prison; and these they visit, comfort, clothe, and frequently liberate, either by paying the fine imposed on them as a penalty for their offence, or by arranging matters with their creditors. They have access to all the criminal offices in Rome, and thus ascertain the number and amount of penalties imposed.   With a wise charity, they endeavour to simplify and shorten causes; and they employ a solicitor, who assists in arranging disputes, and thus putting an end to litigation.   Some of the most important prisons, including the New Prisons, have been confided to their superintendence; and, besides examining the food of the prisoners daily, they defend their interests and maintain their rights with the zeal of humanity and religion. This confraternity embraces the flower of the Roman Prelacy, of the Patrician order, and of the Priesthood. Like most of the other charitable bodies, it possesses revenues of its own, and is further assisted in its pious work by assistance from the State.

A kindred confraternity is that of *Pieta de Carcerata*, which was founded in 1575 by a French Jesuit, who, on going to confess prisoners, ascertained their great want of charitable assistance.   It was raised to an arch confraternity by Gregory XIII.; and Sixtus V. endowed it with peculiar privileges.   The Church of St. John, in the district of Pigna, was conceded to it by the former Pontiff.   The members visit, comfort, exhort, and give alms to the prisoners; they also give food and clothing, pay debts, and endeavour to reconcile creditors.   This confraternity consists of persons of rank, both lay and clerical, to whom is freely permitted the privilege of visiting the prisons.   The Capitoline Prison is specially intrusted to their pious ministrations; and those condemned to the "galleys" are objects of their merciful compassion.

Arch Confraternity of S. Giovanni Decollato.

Morichini gives an interesting account of this confraternity, whose mission is one of singular charity,—to bring comfort and consolation to the last moments of the condemned. It appears that on the 8th of May, 1488, some good Florentines, then in Rome, considering that those who died by the hand of justice had no one to visit and comfort them in their last hours, instituted a confraternity which was at first called *Della Misericordia*, and afterwards by its present name, from the church of their patron. Pope Innocent VIII. granted the society a place under the Campidolio, in which they erected a church to St. John the Baptist; and here they were allowed to bury the remains of those who had been executed. Their objects were sympathised with, and their efforts assisted, by successive Pontiffs. Tuscans only, or their descendants to the third generation, are received into the society.

On the day previous to the execution of a criminal, they invite, by public placard, prayers for his happy passage to the other life. In the night of that day, the brothers, some half dozen in number, including priests, assemble in the church of S. Giovanni di Fiorentini, not far from the New Prisons. Here they recite prayers, imploring the Divine assistance in the melancholy office which they are about to perform. They then proceed to the prisons, walking, two by two, in silence, some of the brothers bearing lanthorns in their hands. On entering the chamber called *conforteria*, they assume

R 3

the sack and cord, in which they appear to the prisoner as well as to the public. They divide between them the pious labours. Two perform the office of consolers; one acts as the *sagrestano*; and another makes a record of all that happens from the moment of the intimation of the sentence to that of the execution. These dismal annals are carefully preserved. At midnight the guardians of the prison go to the cell of the condemned, and lead him, by a staircase, to the chapel of the *conforteria*. At the foot of the stairs, the condemned is met by the notary, who formally intimates to him the sentence of death. The unhappy man is then delivered up to the two "comforters," who embrace him, and, with the crucifix and the image of the Sorrowful Mother presented to him, offer all the consolation which religion and charity can suggest in that terrible moment. The others assist in alleviating his misery, and, without being importunate, endeavour to dispose him to confess, and receive the Holy Communion. Should he be ignorant of the truths of Christianity, they instruct him in them in a simple manner. If the condemned manifest a disposition to impenitence, they not only themselves use every effort which the circumstances of his case render necessary, but call in the aid of other clergymen. The other members of the confraternity employ the hours preceding the execution in the recital of appropriate prayers, and confess and communicate at a mass celebrated two hours before dawn. Clad in the *sacco*, they proceed, two by two, to the prison, the procession being headed by a cross-bearer with a great cross, and a torch-bearer at each side, carrying a torch of yellow wax. The procession having arrived at the prison, the condemned descends the steps; the first object which meets his gaze being an image of the Blessed Virgin, before which he kneels, and, proceeding on, does the same before the crucifix, which is near the gate that he now leaves for ever. Here he ascends the car which awaits him, accompanied by the " comforters," who console and assist him to the last; and the procession moves on to the place of execution, the members of the confraternity going in advance. Arrived at the fatal spot, the condemned descends from the car, and is led into a chamber of an adjoining building, which is hung with black, where the last acts of devotion are performed, or, if he be impenitent, where the last efforts are made to move him to a better spirit. The hour being come, the executioner bandages his eyes, and places him upon the block; and thus, while supported by his *confortori*, and repeating the sacred name and invoking the mercy of Jesus, the axe descends upon the criminal, and human justice is satisfied. The brothers then take charge of the body, lay it on a bier, and, carrying it to their church, decently inter it. Finally, they conclude their pious work by prayer.

The Confraternity " della Morte."

Frequently, towards night, does the stranger in Rome hear in the streets the sad chaunt of the *Miserere*; and on approaching the place whence the solemn sounds proceed, he beholds a long procession of figures clad entirely in black, and headed by a cross-bearer ; many of the figures bearing large waxen torches, which fling a wild glare upon the bier, on which is borne the body of the deceased.   It is the confraternity *della Morte*, dedicated to the pious office of providing burial for the poor.   It was first instituted in 1551, and finally established by Pius IV. in 1560.   It is composed mostly of citizens of good position, some of whom are of high rank.   The members are distinguished by a habit of black, and a hood of the same colour, with apertures for the eyes.   When they hear of a death, they meet, and having put on their habits, go out in pairs ; and when they arrive at the house where the body lies, they place it on a bier, and take it to a church, singing the *Miserere* as the mournful procession winds through the streets.   Even should they be apprised of a death which had occurred twenty, or even thirty, miles distant from Rome, no matter what may be the time or the season, the burial of their poor fellow-creature is at once attended by this excellent society.   In the Pontificate of Clement VIII., a terrible inundation was caused by the rise of the Tiber—a calamity ever to be dreaded, and ever attended with the greatest misery and danger to the poor ; and the brethren were seen employed, as far as Ostia and Fiumicino, in extricating dead bodies from the water.

Another confraternity—*della Perseveranza*—which is composed of pious men, visit and relieve poor strangers who are domiciled in inns and lodging-houses, and minister to their different wants. This confraternity was established under Alexander VII., in 1663; and besides its duty of ministering to the necessities of the living, it also provides decent sepulture for the dead — poor strangers being in both cases the objects of their special care.

A fatal accident, which occurred near Tivoli, in September 1856, afforded a melancholy occasion for the exercise of the charity of one of those institutions, and severely tested the humanity and courage of its brotherhood. An Irish clergyman, whose name it is not necessary to mention, was unfortunately drowned while bathing in the sulphur lake below Tivoli. After three days, the body was recovered; but it was found to be in an advanced stage of decomposition, in a great measure owing to the highly impregnated character of the water. The members of the confraternity *della Morte*, established in the Church of the Carita, in Tivoli, laid the body in a coffin, which they had provided for the purpose; and though the day was intensely hot, and the odour from the body was in the highest degree offensive, they bore it, for a distance of five miles, to the Cathedral, where, after the last offices of religion being paid to it, it was buried in the grave set apart for the deceased canons of the church. Here were a number of men, the majority of them artisans, encountering this fearful danger, and undergoing this perilous toil, beneath the raging heat of an Italian sun; not only without hope of fee or reward, but freely sacrificing their day's employment to the performance of a pious work. The number of the brethren to whom this duty was allotted was twenty-four; and they relieved each other by turns — those not engaged in bearing the body chanting sacred hymns, the dirge-like tones of which fall upon the ear of the stranger with such solemn effect.

CHAP. XXII.

Education in Rome. — The Old Calumny against the Catholic
Church refuted by the Educational Institutions of Rome. —
Its Schools more numerous than its Fountains. — Elementary
Education. — Gratuitous Education originated by Ecclesiastics.
— Religious Orders devoted to the Gratuitous Education of the
Poor.—The Brothers of the Christian Schools.—Their admirable
System of Education.

THE old and long-standing calumny against the Catholic Church is, that she hates, because she dreads, the
light; and that darkness being her congenial element, and
indeed essential to her safety, it has been, as it ever will
be, her policy to discourage the progress of education,
and thus retain the human mind in a convenient state
of intellectual twilight. This is no worn-out and ob-
solete accusation, which one has to search for in some
musty volume, or dig out of some rust-eaten record of a
past age. On the contrary, it is the one most frequently made at this very day, by those who desire
to misrepresent the Church; and it is the one, of all
others, most readily credited by the Protestant public
of these countries. Now if this accusation — that the
Church is the friend of ignorance, and the enemy of
education — be at all true, to no better place within the
wide circle of Christendom could we look for the exem-
plification of this barbarous and benighting policy, than

to Rome; for there, not only has the Pope to maintain
his spiritual supremacy by the force and power of ignorance, but his temporal power has also to be upheld
by the same potent agency.   Therefore, schools ought
to be very rare in Rome, and systematically discouraged
by its ruler and his government.   Or, if they exist in any
number, they should be such only as were intended for
the training of ecclesiastics, whose chief object would be
the perpetuation of the same state of popular debasement,
which, according to the calumny, is the very foundation
and stronghold of the influence and authority of the
Church, — its influence and authority over the darkened
mind of man.   If London, Liverpool, and Manchester
swarmed with schools and seminaries of every kind, and
suited to every want and necessity of the population;
and if these schools were flung open gratuitously to the
children of the poor, so that there ought not to be an
ignorant child left in either of those great communities,
it might be said, with justice, that London, Liverpool,
and Manchester were marching on the high-road of
civilisation, and were entitled to the respect and admiration of all other communities.   If the same can be
said of Rome, is not Rome equally entitled to the
same admiration and the same respect?   Let us see
if Rome really merit praise on this account.

It may be said of Rome, that she possesses, even at
this day, and notwithstanding the ruin of many of the
magnificent aqueducts of the olden time, a greater
number of public fountains, from which her population
may draw an abundant and unceasing supply of the

purest water, than any other city in the world. And yet her schools are more numerous than her fountains, and quite as accessible to *all* classes, from the youth of her nobility to the offspring of the porter and the wood-cutter; and not more pure and unpolluted is the spring from which the young intellect draws its first nourishment in the seminaries of the " modern Babylon," than are those streams which bring health and daily comfort to the poorest of her people.   Pass through its streets, and at every turn you hear the plash, plash, of water, falling gratefully on the ear; and so may be heard the unmistakeable hum and buzz of the regional and the parish schools.   But these, great in number as I shall show them to be, form but a small portion of the educational institutions of calumniated Rome.

First, of Elementary Education.

Until the year 1597, when the illustrious Saint, Giuseppe Calasanzio, opened the first gratuitous school for the poor, which he did in the neglected district of Trastevere, elementary education in Rome was entirely in the hands of the masters of the regionary, or district, schools, who were then partly paid by the State, and partly by a small weekly stipend from their pupils. Miserable, however, as the payment of the regionary teachers was, they stoutly resisted the benevolent exertions of the Saint in favour of gratuitous education; nor could he have overcome the many difficulties which were placed in his path, and which were attributable to various causes, if he were animated by a less ardent zeal, or were endowed with a less energetic spirit.   In

the course of his charitable ministrations to the poor, he
saw that which we all see at this present day — namely,
that ignorance was the fruitful source of misery and
vice; and, Catholic Priest as he was, he resolutely
girded his loins to encounter that very evil of intellectual darkness which *he* believed to be the worst
enemy of the Church.   His efforts were attended with
the success which they merited; and to those efforts,
followed, as they have been, to this hour, by the exertions and sacrifices of numberless successive benefactors
of youth, are due that noble system of *gratuitous instruction* which forms one of the most striking and
hopeful features of modern Roman civilisation.

Leo XII. placed the elementary schools under the
control and jurisdiction of the Cardinal Vicar; and, by
his bull of 1825, the private schools, otherwise the
regionary schools, were subjected to a strict system of
supervision.   These latter are held in the private
houses of the masters, who, if the number of their pupils
happen to be sixty—beyond which number no one
school can contain—must employ the services of an assistant; the calculation being, that one teacher cannot properly attend to more than thirty scholars.   The course
of education varies in different schools, according to the
age, condition, or necessities of the pupils.   In general,
besides the usual system of reading, writing, arithmetic, and catechism, are included the elements of the
Italian and French languages, Latin grammar, geography, sacred and profane history, &c.   The religious
education of the child is never overlooked in these

schools, though under the management of laymen; for not only do the pupils attend mass every morning, but there are various religious practices observed during the day. Punishment, which is strictly limited to beating on the hand with a small rod, is rarely administered, and is in many schools absolutely dispensed with. The masters must submit themselves to an examination, in order to test their competency; and the duty of making this examination is entrusted to a Committee of Ecclesiastics, delegated by the Cardinal Vicar.* The same Committee likewise exercise a general superintendence over the schools, their discipline, and their system of education. In case of the illness of a master, a substitute, paid by the State, attends in his place; and the State also contributes an annual sum to provide rewards for deserving pupils. The number of the regionary schools is rather on the decrease than otherwise; but this decrease is owing to a cause in the highest degree favourable to a more widely-diffused system of education — namely, *the increase of gratuitous schools.* The average, for some time past, has been somewhere about 50 schools for boys of the private

* It would be advisable if the example of Rome had been followed in England; for it appears, by the last Census Report, that such an examination of teachers as I have above referred to, is much required in the private schools of the latter country. Mr. Horace Mann says —

" In the case of 708 out of 13,879 schools, the returns were respectively signed by the master or mistress with a *mark.* The same is noticeable with respect to 35 public schools, most of which had small endowments." Mr. Mann truly remarks, that " the efficiency of a school depends unquestionably more upon the efficiency of the *teacher* than upon any other circumstance."

and paying class, with 80 masters and assistants, and less than 2000 scholars.   The exact number of regionary schools at present is 49.

The saintly founder of the gratuitous schools was actively assisted by other ecclesiastics —who were equally determined foes to ignorance; and before God called him to his reward, in the ripeness of a glorious old age, he had the happiness of beholding many free schools crowded with the children of the poor, and the organisation of a number of religious and charitable associations devoted to their care.

From those "Pious Schools" many others sprang; and now, in every part of Rome, there are gratuitous elementary schools suited to the wants and necessities of the population, with systems of education adapted to various occupations and different branches of industry. Among the most prominent and successful conductors of elementary education, are the Fathers Scolopi, the Fathers Somaschi, the Fathers of the Christian Doctrine, and the Christian Brothers — all of whom have a number of flourishing schools under their charge.

There are then the Parish Schools, one of which, at least, is to be found in every parish of Rome.   These schools are under the immediate control and direction of the Rector, or Parish Priest, who uses his best influence to induce the attendance of pupils.   These schools alone afford a vast educational provision for the children of the poorer class.

Besides these, there are several schools in the care of societies of various kinds, but whose chief object is the education of youth. Of these, may be mentioned the Society *degli Asili d' Infanzia*, which has two asylums, or educational establishments, for boys; one in Trastevere, and the other in Regola. Also, the Society of Private Benefactors, amongst the principal of whom is Prince Doria; and they have an admirable institution entirely maintained at their own charge.

The Roman Conference of the Society of St. Vincent de Paul has lately opened a flourishing school for the education of boys; and it is certain to use every exertion to extend the sphere of its operations.

The Christian Brothers, or Brothers of the Christian Schools, have taken strong root in Rome, and are there, as in all other countries where they have been established, amongst the most zealous and successful of the teachers of youth. To the Catholic reader of these countries, more especially of Ireland, their wonderful success, in elevating the tone and character of the working classes, is well known; and in Rome, their reputation, for the possession of all those attributes which can constitute zealous and conscientious teachers, is fully as high as it is elsewhere. These men are the very chivalry of the intellectual army of modern times; and yet their order is one of the many educational institutions which have sprung from the bosom of the Catholic Church — the reputed friend of darkness, and champion of ignorance! Some notice of the origin of this order may fitly introduce an allusion to their success in Rome.

The Christian Schools of France owe their origin to the zeal and piety of the Abbé de la Salle. This distin-

s

guished ecclesiastic was born at Rheims on the 30th of April, 1651, of parents of the highest respectability. Resolving to devote himself to the service of religion, he accepted a canonry in the Cathedral of Rheims, and, at a suitable age, was raised to the priesthood. Seeing the spiritual destitution of the children of the poor, and the very inefficient means for their instruction which the existing schools afforded, he determined on devoting to their reformation all the time which his other duties left at his disposal. He assembled a small number of teachers, induced them to adopt a kind of community life, presided at their studies, and used every effort to qualify them for the discharge of their important and onerous obligations. He soon found, however, that his new undertaking would demand all his time and attention. He therefore resigned his canonry, sold his patrimony, and distributed its proceeds to the poor; brought the teachers to reside with him in his own house, and laboured with them in the conducting of the schools. The fruits of his teaching soon became manifest; the schools attained a high reputation, and numerous applications poured in on the good Abbé for communities of such efficient teachers. A noviciate, or House of Probation, was established, in which the junior members of the society were educated and trained to their respective duties; and in a very short period the Institute spread itself throughout the principal parts of the kingdom.

Rules and constitutions for its permanent government were now drawn up; religious engagements for a limited time entered into; and the title of " Brothers of the Christian Schools" adopted. In 1702 the saintly founder sent two of his brothers to Rome, in order to form an establishment in the Holy City. His object in doing so was (according to his own declaration) to place his Institute under the auspices of the Holy See; to have more ready access to the feet of Christ's Vicar, for the approbation of its rules and constitutions; to attach it for ever to the imperishable and infallible Church; and to give testimony of his inviolable attachment to the Centre of Unity, at a time when so many were found ready to limit its prerogatives, and question its authority. The undertaking was, after some time, successful. An establishment was formed. Another was given by Pope Benedict XIII., by whom the society was approved and confirmed in 1715. From that time it continued to flourish until the disastrous period of the Revolution, when the decrees of the National Assembly, which proscribed religious societies, compelled the brothers to disperse, and scatter themselves throughout the kingdom. Some took refuge in Italy, and were received into the houses existing in that country; but the success of the French arms in that peninsula deprived them of even this protection. Of the numerous establishments which had been possessed by the society, two only, those of Ferrara and of Orvietto, now remained; and to their existence was owing the revival of the body, when the decree of the French Consul permitted the brothers again to assemble in community.

In 1801 they opened an establishment in Lyons.

Other establishments followed.   In 1815 they reas-
sumed the religious dress ; and from that period to the
present, they have been increasing in numbers and
efficiency, diffusing blessings around them in every
locality which has been favoured with their pious and
edifying labours.*

Actively patronised by successive Popes, including
Leo XII. and Pius IX., the brotherhood, having been
reinforced from France, greatly extended the sphere of
their labours.   They now, in 1857, possess five houses
in Rome ; in each of which there are 500 pupils, or, in
all, 2,500.   They have, besides, a school for the sons
of the French soldiers ; and also a boarding-house for
boys who are intended to fill situations in shops and
other places of business.

Morichini bears the highest testimony to the value
of these schools, and commends the zeal and ability of
the masters, and the docility and affection exhibited by
the scholars.   Indeed, he goes so far, in his praise of the
schools of the Christian Brothers, and of the manner in
which they are conducted, as to assert that the boys
have been known to go home grieving when the following day happened to be a holiday !   If this be so, never
was there a more eloquent tribute offered by pupils

* By the latest authoritative returns we possess (those of 1844), we
find that in France they have 658 schools ; in Belgium 41 ; in Savoy
28 Piedmont 30 ;   Pontifical States 20 ;   Canada 6 ;   Turkey 2 ;
Switzerland 2 ; besides several in the United States of America.   The
number of children in daily attendance at their schools exceeds 200,000.
Since the date of this return, the number of their schools and scholars
has been greatly increased.   The schools of this order in the United
Kingdom afford education to somewhere about 30,000 boys.

to their teachers. The Brothers do not confine their labours exclusively to their own schools, but attend to some others which have been lately established, either by the act of the Pope, or by the assistance of private individuals.

Kay (the Travelling Bachelor of Cambridge), in his *Education of the Poor in England and Europe*, published in 1846, says of the educational system of the Brothers of the Christian Schools :—

"The education given in their schools is very liberal, and their books very good. The Brothers consider that *if they neglect to develop the intellect of their pupils, they cannot advance their religious education satisfactorily ;* they consequently spare no pains to attain the former development, in order that the latter, which is the great end of their teaching, and of all instruction whatsoever, may not be retarded." *

To many of the Roman monasteries there are colleges or schools attached, in which the students, during their course of study, assume the dress of the order, without however becoming members of it. Thus the Benedictines, at S. Calisto ; the Regular Canons, at S. Pietro in Vinculi; and the Greek Basilians, at Grotto Ferrata, in the neighbourhood of Rome, whose schools are frequented by many children from Rome.

Adjoining the Mamertine Prison, there is a School of Design for those who are preparing for any branch of the carpenter trade. This school is of very ancient date, and was founded by the Arch Confraternity of St. Joseph.

* For a practical illustration of their system of education, see Appendix.

CHAP. XXIII.

The Roman Night Schools. — The Deaf and Dumb. — Asylum of
Tata Giovanni. — San Michele, a School of Industry and Art.

PASSING over a number of other day schools, to which
allusion might be profitably made, we come to a class of
schools which, owing their origin to the charity of a humane and religious mechanic, are increasing yearly
in number and in usefulness.   These are the Night
Schools, which are specially intended for and devoted to
the education of young artizans, and others engaged in
various laborious pursuits, and who, from their constant
employment during the day, are deprived of the
ordinary means of intellectual and moral instruction.
In fact, no other class of pupils can obtain admission
to them save those so circumstanced as I describe.
These schools are thirteen in number; eleven being under
one institution, and two under separate institutions.
Each school consists of four classes, the number of pupils
attending each school being, at the lowest estimate,
about 120; which would give a total attendance of
pupils at not less than 1,600.   These schools are sustained by various means and resources — by private
contributions, by grants through the Commission of

Supplies, and by certain ecclesiastical funds temporarily conceded to them by the present Pope; taken from the treasury of the Dataria Apostolica, and from the Office of Briefs and Memorials. Amongst the benefactors of those valuable institutions, His Holiness is the principal; he gives to them 120 scudi annually, out of his *private* purse. The example of the Pope is imitated by the cardinals, the nobility, the clergy, and other classes of the community.

The ordinary teaching comprises reading, writing, and arithmetic; with a knowledge of the principles of design and practical geometry, both of which latter are applied to the ornamental, useful, and mechanical arts. Eight years of age is the earliest period at which a boy can enter the school, but he may attend it until he is established in life. In their mere educational character and results, these schools will stand a fair comparison with schools of a somewhat similar but more ambitious character in France and Belgium; but in one respect — the moral and religious training of the young workman — the Roman Night School stands by itself. In most of the schools elsewhere, religion is not even thought of; but in Rome it is made a primary consideration; and the most efficacious means are adopted, especially through religious societies, or congregations, under the guidance of clergymen, not only to ensure to the Night Scholar a thorough knowledge of the principles of his religion, but to induce him to the fulfilment of its obligations.

The cost of each school is about twenty scudi per month, or 240 scudi a year. This sum serves to procure oil for the lamps, paper, ink, and books — all of which are given gratuitously to the scholars. The principal items of expense are the rent, the furniture, and the salary of the " guardian."

The first of those schools was established in the year 1819, by a poor artizan, Giacomo Casoglio, a carver in wood, who gathered together a few idle boys who were playing on the banks of the Tiber, and whom he induced, by kind words and little presents, to follow him to his home. There he communicated to them what little he himself knew of the rudiments of secular knowledge, and also instructed them in the truths of religion. He was aided in his pious efforts by some good ecclesiastics, who threw themselves with ardour into the work; and, ere long, the humble artizan had many imitators, who excelled him in knowledge and influence, though they could not in charity.

In 1841, the number of schools was eight, and of scholars 1,000; but, in 1856, the schools had increased to thirteen, and the scholars to 1,600. Pius IX., from the first year of his pontificate to the present time, has ever evinced the greatest anxiety for the spread and progress of those schools, the number of which he has personally assisted to extend. And not only does he contribute liberally to their support, but he has on several occasions visited them, without having given any previous notice of his intention; and minutely enquired into their system of education, their discipline, and their operation, and also examined several of the pupils, the best of whom he distinguished by rewards given with his own hand.

It may be added, that the utmost care is taken by the masters that the pupils do not ramble about the streets at the conclusion of their studies. In general, they are accompanied to their homes by the masters, as is the custom in the Pious Schools. Examinations are held every year, with a public distribution of prizes by the hands of eminent persons; and the prizes are always of a useful character, so as to assist the humble parents of the pupils. The elder boys are conducted to the public hospitals, and there encouraged to the pious duty of ministering to and comforting the sick. In fine, every effort is made by those who are entrusted with the management of these schools, as teachers, directors, or superintendents, to fit the pupil for a life of industry, honesty, piety, and active benevolence.

DEAF AND DUMB.

Rome, among its other educational institutions, possesses an admirable one for that most afflicted class, the deaf and dumb. It owes its origin to the benevolence of an advocate, Don Pasquale di Pietro, who established it in the year 1794, on the system so successfully adopted in Paris. It has since, with the consent of the family of the founder, been taken in charge by the Congregation of Studies, and is now under the protection of the

Cardinal President of the Commission of Subsidies, and of a deputy, and is managed by a competent staff. Every improvement which science and humanity have invented or devised for the benefit of these sufferers, has been adopted by the conductors of the Roman institution ; and with such success, that the utmost admiration is excited by its public examinations, in which the pupils display the greatest intelligence, and a thorough knowledge of the many subjects embraced in a system of education in the highest degree liberal and comprehensive. They are even instructed in various branches of the sciences. Persuasion is the only means used to obtain obedience, there being no punishment or disgrace other than that involved in the loss of a reward. This institution was lately visited by the Holy Father, to the intense delight of its inmates.

There are three colleges or seminaries for artizans — namely, those of the Termini, Tata Giovanni, and San Michele. The two latter deserve special notice. First, the

ASYLUM OF TATA GIOVANNI.

Princes and prelates, great merchants and successful professional men, have not been, as we have already shown, the only founders of institutions for the relief of suffering humanity, the shelter of the widow and protection of the orphan, or the education of the ignorant; for, in all ages of the Church, and in all Catholic countries, we find the Divine spirit of benevolence animating some poor, unknown, and perhaps despised person, to undertake and successfully accomplish a great work of charity. And it would be difficult, indeed, to find a more signal instance of energy and humanity than was displayed by an illiterate journeyman-mason, by whose more familiar name one of the most useful of the Roman educational institutions of Rome has been long known. The history of its foundation is this :—

Towards the close of the last century, there worked at the sacristy of the Vatican Basilica, as a mason, an humble and illiterate, but religious man, Giovanni Borgi, who, after his day's toil, was in the constant habit of attending the sick in the hospital of *Santo Spirito*, which lies in the same direction. Indeed, such was the zeal with which he performed this office of charity, that he spent entire nights by the bedside of the sick, and frequently fell asleep over his work in the day. On one evening, as he accompanied a procession of a religious confraternity through the city, his attention was attracted to a number of wretched boys whom he saw lying on the steps of the Pantheon, and crouching under the benches of the fowl market near that building, after having wandered about all day, barefooted and in rags. These were partly vagrant children, who had run away from their parents; children whom their parents had abandoned; or poor orphans, who were utterly destitute. Commiserating their unhappy state, Borgi took some of them to the ground floor of the house in which he himself resided; and having clad them, with the aid of alms which he collected, he apprenticed them to useful trades. Two good ecclesi-

astics having observed his conduct with admiration,
assisted him, as well by counsel as by money.   The
little asylum soon afforded shelter to forty boys, when
it was removed to a convenient house, one of the
friendly priests paying the rent.   It was now assisted
by a society, which was formed to aid it, and which, by
voluntary subscription, contributed more than 100 scudi
a month for its support.   Thus aided, its organization
was further developed in 1784.   Giovanni called the
boys "sons," and they called him "Tata," which
is a vulgar word for father; and hence the name of
" *Tata Giovanni* " given to the institution.   Pius VI.
highly approved of the good work, and having purchased
for the institution the Palazzo Ruggia, became its
principal protector, and was most kind to Giovanni —
who now frequently took up idle and dissolute youths
by force ; which so alarmed the beggars, that one
had only to say to the importunate — " Fly, fly ! here
is Tata Giovanni ! " in order to scatter them at once.
The institution was now increased to 100 boys.   They
rose at an early hour, heard mass, and then received a
loaf of bread, after which they went to their respective
shops ; to which TATA frequently went round himself,
in order to enquire how his " sons " were going on.   At
the *ave maria* he stood at the entrance door, with a bag
in his hand, into which the boys dropped what they had
earned during the day.   Though ignorant himself, TATA
knew the value of learning ; and he induced a number
of benevolent persons, lay and clerical, to teach the boys
in the evening.   The school lessons were followed by the

rosary ; and then came the frugal supper—at which, through humility, Princes of the Church frequently served as the attendants of these poor children. The rule of TATA was strict ; nor had the proverb, " Spare the rod and spoil the child," a more firm believer than himself. His care of the boys was unceasing. He walked through their dormitories all night, and did not seek repose till the morning. During this time he did not by any means neglect the sick at *Santo Spirito ;* and if he could not contrive to go himself to the hospital, he was sure to send some of the older pupils to perform that office of charity. TATA, though strict, was also considerate ; and frequently, especially on festival days, accompanied his " sons " to the country, where — though old, short, and thick-set, blind of one eye, and his quaint head covered by a scratch wig — he was not ashamed to join in their sports. After fifteen years of sublime perseverance, this good man died ; but not until he saw his labour crowned with success, and his cherished institution established on a firm and lasting basis. The work, so nobly begun, was well followed up by patrons of rank and influence ; and though the place was changed, and another institution amalgamated with it, it preserves to this day the familiar name of its founder, *Tata Giovanni.* The plan of sending the boys out to work having been found inconvenient, workshops were formed in the establishment ; but the old system was again restored. TATA, rude and illiterate as he was, was endowed with great good sense ; and in no respect did he more strikingly manifest this fine quality than in the wisdom with which he allowed the boys to select the trade to which they had the greatest inclination, for which they evinced the greatest aptitude, and that best suited their capacity and strength. The soundness of this principle is practically recognised by its continued adoption. At twenty years of age, the inmates of the asylum are dismissed ; and not only are they well educated, carefully trained, and thoroughly practised in their respective trades; but they have, in their savings, —being the surplus over a certain daily charge for their support,— the means not only of providing tools and instruments necessary for their calling, but for the purchase of clothes, a bed, and other necessary articles. Besides the elementary studies, in which the boys are thoroughly grounded, they are also taught geometry and the principles of design. Well may the orphan boy bless the memory of that poor ignorant mason, who, under a rough exterior and even repulsive manner, con- cealed a heart of the tenderest compassion and the loftiest charity. May the name of TATA GIOVANNI be long honoured on this earth !

Pius IX., while yet a simple priest, presided over this admirable school, from motives of the purest charity, and in order to do good to a class for whom he ever felt the profoundest sympathy. It was his ordinary cus- tom to dine off the humble fare provided for the boys, as he sat at the head of their table.

SAN MICHELE.

San Michele, now a Conservatorio di Belle Arti, is

one of the most interesting institutions in Rome, and
will amply repay the trouble of a visit. Besides training a number of boys to different branches of the purely
mechanical arts, it frequently contributes to the great
world of art some of its most distinguished ornaments.
For instance, it was a former pupil of San Michele
who lately completed the beautiful monument to Gregory XVI., now in its place in St. Peter's, and which
no one can regard without a feeling of genuine admiration, for the exquisite grace of the figures that adorn
it. In the vast and comprehensive seminary the visitor
may observe its pupils engaged in the most varied and
opposite pursuits. Here, they are learning some simple
handicraft — there, the highest branches of art. In one
hall, a number of boys are weaving carpets, of the most
costly texture and elaborate design ; in another department, other classes are cutting cameos, engraving on
steel and copper, or engaged in modelling a bust or a
group, or chiselling it into its enduring form out of the
pure marble of Carrara. You leave the hall where
some incipient Canova is learning the first principles of
his immortal art, and, passing to another part of the
building, you hear the quick stroke of the carpenter's
hammer, or see, drying in the open air, a piece of cloth
that has lately received its colour in the dye-vat. The
wise principle of this noble institution is to allow the
boy to adopt the pursuit most congenial to his tastes, or
best suited to his capacity — not compelling the youth
who feels within him an instinctive longing for the
beautiful in art, to toil and drudge at some mere me-

chanical pursuit; nor training another to the profession of an artist, instead of conferring on him a purely mechanical trade. The illustrious Howard, who speaks of "this large and noble edifice" with admiration, remarks that when he visited San Michele, there were in it about 200 boys — "all learning different trades according to their different abilities and genius."

To secure admission to this institution, a boy must be an orphan, a native of the Roman States, and not over twelve years of age. Occasionally, boys are admitted for a small pension, not exceeding sixteen or seventeen shillings a month; and for this small sum they are fed, clothed, and given a sound literary education, a trade, or perhaps a profession. Intercourse is freely allowed with their relatives, so that family ties, where they exist, should be kept up. The education given to the boys is that which best adapts them to the situation in life which they are destined to fill. Besides other branches, music is carefully taught; and perhaps the stranger, who visits Rome, could enjoy no greater treat than that afforded on the occasion of the great festival in honour of the Patron Saint of the institution, when the choir, entirely composed of the pupils, performs the splendid music selected for the day, which is celebrated with unusual pomp.

The boys seemed to be happy and contented, as indeed they well might be; for the treatment which they receive from their superiors is kind and affectionate in the extreme. Persuasion, not force, is the rule of the institution. That they were fine healthy-looking little fellows,

I can say with certainty; and the manner with which they replied to such observations as were addressed to them by the ecclesiastic who kindly conducted me through the greater portion of the vast building, was frank, self-possessed, and most respectful — which manner was in itself a good test of the training of the pupil, and the conduct of the master.

To understand the value, or the result, of that artistic training which the higher classes of the pupils receive, one had but to pass through the stately apartments of the Cardinal Protector, the learned and venerable Tosti. These apartments principally consist of a number of halls and galleries, enriched by a splendid collection of works of art and articles of vertu — a great number of the former having been executed by the pupils of the institution. Besides paintings and engravings, many of evident merit, were some beautiful busts, groups, and bas-reliefs. A lovely little chapel, all of the purest marble, was also the work of their hands. Amongst the most exquisite of the works of art, not of modern execution, was a group in silver, representing the scourging of the Redeemer in the hall of Pilate. It stood about nine inches high, and one glance was sufficient to tell that it came from the hands of a master; for genius was stamped upon it most unmistakably. The artist was the famous Benvenuto Cellini.

Writing of this noble institution, Morichini justly says: — " The hospital is a perfect polytechnic school, a perfect conservatory for arts and trades, and which

T

the genius of the Popes had established a century in advance of the most cultivated nations of Europe."

In another branch of the same establishment, there is an extensive conservatory for girls, who are gratuitously maintained, and taught everything necessary to their future condition. They are carefully trained in a knowledge of the more domestic duties,

CHAP. XXIV.

Female Education. — Ample Provision for it. — Colleges and Seminaries. — English and Irish Colleges. — The Propaganda. —
The Roman College. — Educational Statistics of Rome. — Its
high Standard.

IT is not necessary to refer again to the system of
education carried on in prisons, reformatories, and even
hospitals for the treatment of disease; sufficient has
been shown, in the Prison of S. Michele, the Reformatory of Santa Balbina, and the Hospital of San Galicano, to prove that the education of the young is
considered in Rome as a matter, not of secondary, but
of primary importance.

Nor is it advisable to go through a list of the schools
for female children, which are intended for those of
every class and condition in life, from the daughter of
the prince, to the poor deserted child of the street.
The conservatories alone would make a long list, to say
nothing of the public schools under the care of the
Maestre Pie, one of which, at least, is to be found in
every parish. There are several other religious orders
specially devoted to the instruction of youth, including
the following:—the Ursuline, the Presentation, the
Sacred Heart, the Divine Love, the Providence, the
S. Giuseppe, and the Holy Name of Jesus. In fact,

it may be said, that wherever there is a convent of nuns, there is also attached to it a school for some one class or other of female children.   Not a few of the institutions for girls were originally intended as reforma- tories, or asylums for the protection of young persons in danger of growing up in ignorance or vice.   For in- stance, that known as *Il Borromeo* was founded by Car- dinal Borromeo, who purchased a house on the Esquiline, and placed in it many poor abandoned girls, who were so utterly destitute, that they were commonly called " censiose," or *ragged*.   So that the " ragged school " is by no means of that recent origin which, in England, many persons suppose it to be.   The children maintained in this institution, as in all the conservatories, are trained up in *industry*, as well as instructed in the usual course of knowledge suited to their position.   In- deed, industrial training is a necessary element in the education which girls receive in all such institutions; as the profits of their work go in some degree to meet the charge of maintaining the establishment; the rest being generally supplied either from revenues attached to the original foundation, or by a contribution from the State, administered by a particular commission, or controlling body.   A favourite form of Roman charity is that of establishing asylums for children " in danger," no matter whether the danger arise from their orphan condition, or from the neglect of careless or the ex- ample of bad parents; and at the present day, there are to be found zealous clergymen, benevolent laymen, and charitable women, ready to imitate the holy ex- ample of a Borromeo or a Neri.   When I come to give the total of scholars of all ages and both sexes, it will be seen that the education of the female child is as carefully provided for as that of the boy.

I now proceed to notice, or rather enumerate, the educational institutions of a higher class.

The colleges or seminaries for the higher studies are the Orfani, the Panfili—for ecclesiastics from the estates of the house of Doria—the Capranica, for Romans or the natives of some dioceses of the Marche ; the Seminary of St. Peter, the Roman Seminary, the Seminario Pio ; the secular Colleges of Ghislieri, Clementino, Nazareno, and Borromeo, specially for the sons of the nobility.

The Seminario Pio was founded and endowed by Pius IX., out of *his private purse,* and may be mentioned as another proof of his zeal for education. The students of this ecclesiastical seminary are chosen, by examination, from the dioceses of the Papal States. The result is, that the best student of each diocese is enabled to perfect his education in Rome, and thus carry back to his native place somewhat of the apostolic spirit of the Holy City.

Besides these, there are the colleges of the Benedictines in S. Calisto, and of Regular Canons Lateran, in S. Pietro in Vinculi.

The following are colleges for foreign ecclesiastical students : —

The Propaganda ; and the colleges of the English, Irish, Scotch, Greek, Belgian, French, German, and Hungarian nations.

T 3

The English College was founded and endowed by
Gregory XIII.; but the funds are not equal to the
support of more than 20 or 25 students.   However,
Pius IX. has recently joined to this institution a new
college founded by himself, and bearing his own name.
The Collegio Pio must not be confounded with the
Seminario Pio, mentioned above.   The Collegio Pio
has been established by the Pope, not alone to meet
the growing wants of the Catholic Church in England,
but to provide a place of study for the numerous con-
verts that of late years have quitted the Protestant
Church, and returned to the venerable Church of their
fathers.

A new French college has also been established by
the present Pope; and it is probable that, before long,
an American college will be also opened in Rome.   By
such acts as these does Pius IX. exhibit, as Supreme
Pontiff, "his care for all the churches."

The number of pupils in the Scotch College is not
very great at present; but it is progressing.

The students of the Irish College are steadily increasing in number.   Of this fact I was myself a witness.   On
my first visit to the ecclesiastical college of my own
nation, the number of students was forty-six; but before
I left Rome it was increased to fifty-four, by accessions
from various dioceses in Ireland.   Indeed, I had travelled
to Rome with two students whom I accidentally met on
the platform of the railway in Paris; and they were
from the diocese of Cloyne, in the county of Cork.

My first visit to the college found the students just

terminating a "retreat," which was conducted by a priest of the order of the Passionists, whose picturesque convent forms so prominent a feature on the Celian Hill. I was introduced into a long narrow chamber, from which the bright sun was excluded by dark blinds, and which, indeed, received its only light from the candles burning on the altar. The students, who were clad in the usual academic costume, were seated in silent rows, listening with the most profound attention to the eloquent exhortations of the Passionist, who appeared to put forth all his fervour and all his impressiveness in his concluding appeal. His voice was rich and melodious, and adapted itself to every style ; and his action was eminently natural — that is, it corresponded with the words which he uttered, and the emotion which he felt. In fact, he was an orator, appealing, too, to the most favourable audience — to young, pure hearts, glowing with piety, and full of enthusiasm for the sacred profession to which they aspired. The devotions of the day were concluded by the students approaching the altar, and, kneeling before a large cross, which lay at its steps, kissing the feet of the image of the crucified Redeemer, — an act of pious homage, not to the insensible ivory, but to the Divine Being, whose sublime charity and compassion for fallen man it visibly and strikingly represented.

The more I saw of this college — and I was a frequent visitor — the more I was impressed with its discipline, its management, and its system of education. Certain portions of the necessary course are taught within its walls ; but the students also attend the lectures of the

Roman College, and the Propaganda. In a short time they become thoroughly acquainted with the Italian language, which is indispensable to them as a medium of instruction. The gravity and decorum of the students, as they walk, in groups of ten or twelve, through the streets of Rome, is only exceeded by their piety and collectedness in their devotions, whether performed in the adjoining church of St. Agata, or in whatever church they happen to visit. Indeed, they are fortunate in their superiors, the Rector and Vice-Rector *; than whom it would be difficult to find two men of gentler nature, of a solicitude more truly paternal, or who are more profoundly impressed with a sense of their great responsibility. The natural consequence is, that the students honour and love their superiors. For certain months in the summer they reside altogether at the establishment in the country; and, at other times, a visit to the vineyard which the college possesses outside the city affords them the opportunity of healthful exercise.

The church attached to the *Irish* College was that appropriately selected as the resting-place of the heart of Daniel O'Connell; and a very graceful mural monument — erected at the sole cost of Charles Bianconi, to the memory of his illustrious friend — marks out the spot, and commemorates the fame of the great champion of Catholic liberty. This monument was one of the first works which brought the artist Benzoni into notice,

* Monsignor Kirby and the Rev. Dr. Moran. The latter, a scholar of distinguished merit, is nephew to the Most Rev. Dr. Cullen, the predecessor of Dr. Kirby, and now the Catholic Archbishop of Dublin.

and assisted him to attain the deservedly high position which he now enjoys.

There are several Irish students in the famous Propaganda; and the Irish branches of the Dominican, Augustinian, and Franciscan orders, have each a house in Rome.

The Propaganda, as is well known, is the celebrated college in which students intended for foreign missions are educated. Here meet all nations, and are spoken all tongues; and from this great institution annually go forth brave and devoted soldiers of the Cross, not a few of whom seal with their blood their fidelity to the faith of the Gospel. This college has its own staff of professors, who deliver lectures of the highest character, which are attended by students of many other colleges. At the annual Polyglot Academy held this year, the pupils recited compositions in no less than *forty-four* different languages. Fourteen of these were Asiatic, four African, twenty-four European, and two Oceanic. The last were spoken by natives of Uvea and Tonga. All nations and all races of the human family are represented in the pious and heroic youth of this great Catholic University, which strictly fulfils the sublime mission of the Church, to "go and teach all nations."

The public schools are the Roman College, the Appolinare, and, so far as rhetoric, the College of St. Maria in Montecelli. Of one only of these — the Roman College — a brief notice is required.

To give anything like a complete account of the

Roman College would require a separate treatise in itself. A sketch of a single Faculty will, however, give some idea of the extent of its curriculum, and of the method of instruction. As it is upon the Faculty of Philosophy that the character of a university will be generally found to depend, it will be convenient to take it in this case as an example. This Faculty is conducted by nine professors. The course of instruction extends over a period of three years, and includes the following subjects:—

LOGIC AND MATHEMATICS,	MORAL PHILOSOPHY,
ELEMENTARY MATHEMATICS,	PHYSICO-CHEMISTRY,
MATHEMATICAL PHYSICS,	ANALYTICAL GEOMETRY,
PHILOSOPHY OF RELIGION,	ASTRONOMY,
DIFFERENTIAL AND INTEGRAL CALCULUS.	

In the first year of this course of Philosophy, the student has to attend lectures on two subjects; Logic and Metaphysics, and Elementary Mathematics. There are three lectures, of an hour each, every day; two being devoted to the Logic and Metaphysics, and one to the Mathematics. In the second year of Philosophy, the student attends four courses of lectures; Moral Philosophy, Physico-Chemistry, and Mathematical Physics, for an hour each every day, and Analytical Geometry for half-an-hour every second day. In the third year, the student attends three courses,—the Philosophy of Religion, Astronomy, and the Calculus; lectures being delivered on each of these subjects every day.

From this statement it will be seen that, as far as the machinery of professorial instruction is concerned, the faculty of philosophy in the Roman College is superior to that of any university or college in Great Britain or Ireland, not excepting Oxford or Cambridge. In some of the universities lately established in this country, great stress is laid upon the importance of mathematical studies. Yet we find that even in these institutions, such, for instance, as the Queen's University in Ireland, a single professor is expected to teach *every* branch of mathematics; whilst in the Roman College there are in general four distinct chairs appropriated to mathematical subjects. It is worthy of remark that many of the text books are written by the Jesuits themselves. Some of these are well known in England; such as the *Principia Calculi Differentialis et Integralis, itemque, Calculi Differentiarum finitarum: auctore Andreâ Caraffa. S. J.*

The metaphysical course is very extensive. It is principally devoted to a critical examination of the various theories of Psychology. The British writers who attract most notice are Locke and Reid; but the greater part of the Psychological course appears to be devoted to combating the fallacies of the German Metaphysicians.

The course of Astronomy possesses many points of interest. In the first place, it is based, to a great extent, on the lithographed treatise which the late celebrated Father De Vico prepared for his class. This gives it a marked character of originality. In the second place, many brilliant discoveries have of late years, as well as centuries ago, been associated with the name of the Collegio Romana; and its observatory has long been acknowledged to be one of the best in Europe. In studying that important part of astronomy which treats of the measurement of time, the student remembers with pride that it was to the founder of the College, to Gregory XIII., we owe the correction of the Calendar. The extent of the astronomical course may be judged from the fact, that it enters fully into such questions as the Lunar Theory, the stability of the Solar System, the Secular and Periodic Variations, the effect of a resisting medium, and the figures of the planets; all these questions, as a matter of course, requiring a familiarity with the highest branches of mathematics.

In the course of Physico-Chemistry, after going through Chemistry proper, and the theories of Light and Heat, the class is occupied with experiments in Electricity, Magnetism, and Galvanism. These experiments are, however, but of secondary importance; the main part of the lectures in these latter subjects being devoted to discussing the investigations of Ampère, Arago, Faraday, &c., and developing the several formulæ which bring magnetism and electricity into the domain of mathematics.

The Roman College is entirely under the management and in the hands of the Jesuit Fathers, who fill the different chairs in such a manner as to maintain the high reputation of that illustrious order. In the Ap-

pendix of this volume is given one more proof of the
services which members of this body have conferred
on the cause of science. I allude to the measurement
of the base line, for a trigonometrical survey, by Father
Angelo Secchi.*

The great University, the Sapienza, closes my list
of institutions for public instruction in Rome. This
college was founded in the year 1244, by Innocent IV.,
and has been entirely remodelled in the course of the
present century by Leo XII. The present Pope has
added to the number of its chairs.

Cardinal Morichini states that, in 1841, there were
in Rome 27 institutions and 387 schools for the instruction of the children of the poorer portion of the
public. Of these, 180 were for children, or infants,
of both sexes; and, of the remainder, 94 were exclusively devoted to males, and 113 to females. The
total number of scholars in *elementary schools* amounted,
at that time, to 14,157. Of these, 3,790 were of the
infant class; and of those of more advanced years,
5,544 were males, and 4,823 were females. In *gratuitous*
elementary schools, 7,579 received their education ;
namely, 3,952 boys, and 3,627 girls. In schools *paying
a small pension*, there were 1,592 males, and 1,196
females — making a total in such schools of 2,788.
Of the 387 schools referred to, 26 belonged to religious communities of men, and 23 to religious communities of women. The rest belonged to, or were
conducted by, seculars. In addition, 2,213 children,

* See Appendix.

of both sexes, learned the rudiments of education in special conservatories and hospitals.

The figures which are given exclude students in the
universities and higher colleges.   Including these, however, with the classes already mentioned, the student
population of Rome, as compared with the total population of the city, was, in the year 1842, as *one in eight.*
But since then, as I have shown, the schools and the
scholars have considerably increased.   For instance, not
to go beyond the Night Schools and the schools of the
Christian Brothers, the increase is very marked since
the time when Morichini wrote.   The schools of the
former description have increased from eight to thirteen,
and their scholars from 1,000 to 1,600.   Besides, the present Pope has himself established a number of schools for
children of both sexes, and does all in his power, by pecuniary aid as well as by other modes of encouragement,
to promote new schools throughout the Papal States,
and to enlarge, or otherwise improve, those already in
existence.   He also impresses on his clergy a duty
which they zealously perform — that of urging parents
to send their children to school, and thus take advantage
of that great humanising agent which is brought to the
very doors of the humblest and poorest.   So that, it
may be fairly asserted, if a single Roman child grow
up in ignorance, or without the benefit of a sound and
useful education, the fault lies with the parents of the
child, and not with the government of Pius IX., or
with those institutions which redound so much to the
honour of the Eternal City.   If, then, the educational

standard were *one in eight* when Morichini wrote, it must now closely approximate to *one in six,* which is, perhaps, the highest standard at which any State can reasonably hope to attain.＊

＊ Mr. Horace Mann, in his celebrated Report attached to the Census Tables of 1851, — which Report was published in March, 1854, — says, at page 21 : — " Most competent writers are now inclined to assume that *one in eight* would be a satisfactory proportion, after making due allowance for practical impediments." At the same time, Mr. Mann adverts to the opinion of Mr. Edward Baines — the acknowledged leader and organ of the voluntary party — who, after a careful course of reasoning, says that *one in nine* would be a proportion quite as high as the condition of society in England would permit. One in eight is, therefore, the highest educational standard at which any party, even those holding the most advanced views, aspire. In 1851, *one in eight and a third* was the *nominal* educational position of England.

For conclusive information as to the real or nominal character of elementary education in Great Britain, the reader is referred to the Appendix.

CHAP. XXV.

Universities in the Papal States. — Their Courses and Museums.
— Valuable Libraries. — Admission gratuitous. — Elementary
Instruction. — Communal Schools. — Number of Students in
the Universities. — The Church not afraid of the Diffusion of
Education. — Mr. Macaulay quoted.

HAVING given a general idea of the educational resources of Rome, it may be well to add some few
particulars with respect to the provision made for the
instruction of youth throughout the Pontifical States ;
inasmuch as it must tend to show, to those who are
believers in that imaginary policy of intellectual darkness attributed to the Church, that in the very dominions of the Church, where the Church may be said to
possess more direct influence and authority over temporal matters than in any other part of Christendom, it
preserves its influence and maintains its authority in
spite of the intelligence it persistently awakens, and
the knowledge it so anxiously and laboriously promotes.

There are seven Universities in the Papal States —
namely, those of Ferrara, Bologna, Urbino, Macerata,
Camerino, Perugia, and Rome. In each there is taught
a complete course of Theology, Jurisprudence, Philosophy, Medicine and Surgery, besides other branches.
The Universities of Rome and Bologna are of the first

class, and in these is taught, in addition, a complete course of mathematics. They are also supplied with a number of other chairs which do not exist in the universities of the second class. It is the rule, I believe, that in the first-class universities there must be thirty-eight chairs; but in Rome there are forty-five, and two additional chairs were recently instituted.

The secondary as well as the first-class universities are supplied with museums of a comprehensive character, illustrating the various sciences, such as zoology, mineralogy, anatomy, chemistry, mechanics, &c. ; and, as for the museums of the first class universities, it may be said, with justice, that they rival those of any European capital, in the variety and value of their collections. Thus, for instance, the museum of mineralogy in the Roman University, as well as its collection of birds, excel, in their completeness and extent, those of any other Italian city. The same may be said of the museum of Bologna, some idea of the magnitude and value of which may be afforded by the fact, that its anatomical collection contains 60,000 preparations!

Each university is also supplied with an ample library, in some of which may be found works of great antiquity and of rare value. In the two great universities there is an excellent observatory, well provided with the best, the newest, and most costly instruments. Four of the universities — those of Rome, Perugia, Bologna, and Ferrara — possess each a chair of Agriculture; and in order that experiment and practice might be combined with theory, certain grounds are

U

attached to each of these universities, for the practical study of this most valuable and ancient of all the sciences.

The admission of the student to the University is *gratuitous*, the salary of the professors being either at the expense of the State, or, as in some of the secondary institutions, at that of the Province, or provided for out of special funds destined to the purpose. At one period only is there any charge made to the university student, though by no means in the majority of cases; and that is, on his attaining to and taking out his academical degrees — namely, of Bachelor, Licentiate, and Doctor; and the entire cost for *all* the degrees does not exceed 60 scudi, or about 13*l.* And in many instances, especially where the student is in a humble position of life, and cannot afford this very moderate charge, it is either partly or wholly remitted. It is also remitted in cases of signal merit, as where the student reaches to the honours of the Laureate.

Then, with respect to elementary instruction, the amplest provision is made for it; for not only in the first-class cities, but in general in all cities — in Ireland we should call them towns — containing from 2,000 to 5,000 inhabitants, there is a Gymnasium, or a Lyceum, for the instruction of youth. In the gymnasium are taught, besides other matters, reading, writing, arithmetic, elementary philosophy, and the principles of jurisprudence; and, as an invariable rule, the boys are well grounded in a knowledge of their religion. Some of these institutions are under the care of religious bodies, specially

devoted to the instruction of youth ; others are conducted by secular priests ; and more are confided to laymen.   The appointment of teachers belongs generally
to the local municipality, and is made with the approbation of the bishop of the diocese, and the sanction of
the Congregation of Studies, to which department belongs
the superintendence of all the educational institutions
of the Pontifical States.   The Roman College may be
termed the Gymnasium of Rome ; but besides the arts
or sciences above mentioned, there is also taught in
it a complete course of theology.

To those institutions, as to the universities, the
students are admitted *without any charge whatever*, and
they can enter them with the utmost facility.

They attend Mass every morning, and are instructed
in catechism, either every day, or on certain fixed days,
according to their class.   On festivals, they assemble in
their societies, or congregations, when they approach the
sacraments, and receive religious instruction from their
spiritual director ; and every year, towards Easter, they
make a spiritual " retreat " for some days.

Where the gymnasium, or lyceum, does not exist,
there is to be found a Communal School, for boys—which
Communal School may be seen, not merely in every
small town, but even in every village.   Similar schools
are established for girls, conducted by the *Maestre Pie*,
and other religious orders devoted to the promotion of
education.   It may be again repeated, that all these
schools are *wholly gratuitous* ; the State, or the respective municipality, defraying the charge, where it is

not otherwise provided for by old foundations, or by special funds.

Even from the incomplete list of educational institutions which I have given, it may be supposed that the number of students receiving a first-class education in the great Universities and in the principal Seminaries is considerable. By the latest returns, I find that the number of this class of students amounts to 28,899 — a vast number indeed, especially when contrasted with the smallness of the aggregate population of the Papal States. Attending the Roman University, the number is 1,051 — that of Bologna, 1,050 — Macerata, 1,313 — Perugia, 1,137 — Pesaro and Urbino, 5,178 — Ferrara, 3,706. Then Ancona has 2,515 scholars of the higher grade, and Ascoli, 2,253 — and so on, until the gross number of 28,899 is made up.

These details, imperfect as they are, render utterly ridiculous the accusation levelled, by malice or by prejudice, against the Catholic Church, which is said to owe the preservation of its authority to the ignorance, and therefore to the mental debasement, of its followers. If the Church be really afraid of the general diffusion of education, she must be said to adopt an extraordinary mode of evincing her alarm. You apprehend that a certain enemy has a design on your life — that he meditates your destruction with a deadly weapon. Prudence tells you to avoid him, or to deprive him of the means of effecting his purpose. At any rate, whether you fly or resist, there is one thing which, unless you be an idiot, you do not do, — you do not yourself select the weapon, and place it in his hand, with an invitation to its murderous use. If the Church dreaded the light, how comes it that it is she who draws back the veil which shrouds the intellect, and reveals to the inquiring spirit of youth the choicest treasures of knowledge, human and divine ? Trace her history throughout all ages in which she has exercised influence over man, and you ever find her the most zealous as the most successful promoter of education, and, above all, dispensing it with unstinting liberality to those classes of the community who have been considered, even of late years, and in many states and by many statesmen, as not entitled to its advantages. One proposition, however, is clear beyond question — if the progress of enlightenment be so certain to ensure the downfall of the Church, and necessarily of the Papacy, as we are confidently told it is, then Rome is deliberately, and with great trouble, devoting both herself and the Pope to destruction.

But to those who look to the progress of human enlightenment as the means of ensuring the destruction of the Church, may be commended the following deliberate statement, written by Mr. Macaulay, who certainly is not open to the charge of partiality on the side of the Catholics : —

"We often hear it said, that the world is constantly becoming more and more enlightened, and that this enlightenment must be favourable to Protestantism, and unfavourable to Catholicism. We wish that we could think so. But we see great reason to doubt whether this is a well-founded expectation. *We see that during the last two*

*hundred and fifty years the human mind has been in the
highest degree active;* that it has made great advances in
every branch of natural philosophy ; that it has produced
innumerable inventions tending to promote the convenience
of life ; that medicine, surgery, chemistry, engineering, have
been very greatly improved ; that government, police, and
law, have been improved, though not to so great an extent
as the physical sciences.   Yet we see that, during these two
hundred and fifty years, Protestantism has made no conquests worth speaking of.   Nay, we believe that, *as far as
there has been change, that change has, on the whole, been
in favour of the Church of Rome.*   We cannot, therefore,
feel confident that the progress of knowledge will necessarily
be fatal to a system, which has, to say the least, *stood its
ground in spite of the immense progress made by the human
race in knowledge since the days of Queen Elizabeth.*"

CHAP. XXVI.

Relief of the Poor. — Poverty not treated as a Crime. — Vagrancy and Imposture sternly dealt with by the Popes. — Efforts to suppress idle Mendicancy.— Modes of Relief. — Commission of Subsidies. — Charitable Institutions. — Industrial Relief.

IT is no exaggeration to assert, that the wants of the poor are nowhere more effectually relieved than in Rome. Charity, springing from the very bosom of the Church, where it has ever existed pure and undefiled, flows through numberless channels upon those whose wants, whose necessities, and whose sufferings, render them objects deserving of sympathy and compassion. And though its seeming superabundance may, and not unreasonably, be supposed to inflict a certain amount of injury on the community, by rendering the humbler classes less self-reliant than they would be under a different state of things; still, no one can deny that relief — food, clothing, and shelter — is successfully applied to all who stand in need of such assistance. Indeed, one often hears it made a matter of creditable pride, that so great a calamity as a " death from starvation" is one of those things never heard of in Rome, or in the Papal States. Morichini only follows the example of other writers, when he says, at the conclusion of one of

u 4

his chapters — " Thanks be to God! we did not know that any one died of hunger in Rome, even in the worst times." And the same grateful boast is commonly made use of by those who defend the government and institutions of the States of the Church from the accusations of prejudice or of ignorance. It would be well if the same could be said of more prosperous countries, and more powerful nations.*

It certainly does appear to be a matter next to an impossibility that any one should die of starvation in Rome; for not only are the most ample resources applicable to every human want, and to which the poor may have immediate access; but there exist all kinds of charitable associations, devoted to the sacred duty of feeding the hungry, clothing the naked, visiting the sick, and comforting the afflicted. Then there are many well-known public institutions, always open to the poor person in distress, and from whose doors want and destitution are never driven by surly porters, representing rather the selfishness of the rate-payer than the charity of the Christian. Besides, as a general rule, one, of course, admitting of exceptions, the Italian Catholic does not feel any hesitation in making known his wants to his neighbour — to his fellow-man — or in asking for his assistance. In these countries, and espe-

* I could not avoid regarding, as rather a curious coincidence, the fact, that, just after I looked over my note-book, in which I had specially recorded this creditable boast, which is so frequently made to the stranger visiting Rome, I glanced through the " *Times* " of the same day (Feb. 21st, 1857), in which I saw it stated that *three* persons had *died of starvation*, on the previous day, in one district of London !

cially in England, poverty is certainly not regarded with a sentiment of reverence, as it is in Rome.   There, voluntary poverty is held a virtue ; and therefore, natural or accidental poverty cannot be treated as a vice.   The Church that has canonised beggars will not imprison the poor in a workhouse, merely to spare the sensitive nerves of the fastidious.

But though poverty is not regarded as a crime in Rome, as I have heard it stated, on competent authority, it is elsewhere *, still there is no sanction whatever given to mere vagrants and impostors — those who simulate woes with a view to extort alms from the bene-

* In the *Times* of Friday, June 26th, Mr. Alderman Copeland is reported to have said, in his place in the House of Commons, on the previous night— " That his experience, as a citizen of London and a magistrate, had long convinced him that here (in London) *poverty was regarded as a crime, and treated as a crime."*   The question before the House was on a motion, by Viscount Raynham, in reference to the administration of the Poor-law in certain metropolitan workhouses.

This statement, so deliberately made by Mr. Alderman Copeland, and which Sir John Pakington hoped was " rather the expression of warm feeling than of deliberate conviction," is thoroughly confirmed by the Editor of the London *Standard,* in an article of that paper of the 2nd of July.   The writer says : —

" That the large amount of the prison element in the discipline and management of workhouses has been fruitful of evil ; it has produced the impression that poverty itself is a crime.   *Workhouse authorities regard every application for relief as an attempt to swindle ; every workhouse inmate as a rogue and a vagabond.*   No wonder is it that the only principle of management, if principle it can be called, is to render the workhouse as forbidding as possible, as much like a prison as is compatible with a workhouse.   On this principle they allow the inmates to grow up idle and disorderly, because labour is of itself a relief. * * * Unlike the true Christian principle of sound legislation, workhouse management is not ' a terror to evil-doers,' but a terror to those who do well.   The bold, the unscrupulous, and the incorrigible find their account in it ; *and the Devil finds his, too."*

See Appendix for a proof that poverty is treated *worse* than crime.

volent.　No doubt, the giving of alms in the streets, and at the doors of churches, does something to encourage the lazy and the indolent to prefer a life of mendicancy to a life of honest labour.　But, to obviate this evil, the most rigorous measures have been adopted by successive Popes, from the time of Pius V., in the sixteenth century, to Pius IX. in the nineteenth, to suppress vagrancy, and defeat and punish imposture.　Even the mildest pontiffs and the holiest saints have sternly set their faces against loose and disorderly beggars, while their hearts overflowed with compassion for real suffering. St. Charles Borromeo issued a severe edict, prohibiting mendicancy in the churches of his arch-diocese of Milan; for in his time the importunities and audacity of the beggars, who swarmed in the churches, was such, in Milan as well as in Rome, that great scandal was thereby caused to religion.　Gregory XIII., Sixtus V., and subsequent pontiffs, vigorously struggled with this evil; and to their efforts, as well as to those of private individuals, inspired by their example, are owing many of the public asylums and orphanages that flourish in the present day, and which, at the time of their original foundation, were intended for the succour of the aged and infirm, or for the protection of destitute and abandoned children, who would otherwise have grown up in ignorance and vice.　Gregory XIII. provided the monastery of St. Sixtus for the reception of the destitute; and Sixtus V. assigned some houses near the Ponte Sisto to form an asylum for the relief and seclusion of mendicants.　Innocent XII. issued bulls for the suppression of that mendicancy which fostered idleness and led to disorder; while at the same time he extended the means of affording relief to the really deserving, by founding one general institute, calling it, *Ospizio Generale di Poveri Invalidi.* The pontifical palace of the Lateran was assigned to some as an asylum; while others—those who were married and had families — were relieved in their own houses. The magnificent institution of S. Michele—which, as I have before stated, now combines within its walls a school of art and trade for boys, a conservatory for girls, two asylums for men and women, and three prisons, including that for the reformation of the young—mainly owes its origin to the determination of Clement XI. to imitate the example of his energetic predecessors, and free Rome from the evils of importunate and turbulent mendicants. Pius VII., Leo XII., and Pius IX. have followed in the same path—each founding one or more institution for the reception of the really destitute; and also either increasing the number, or adding to the accommodation, of the existing orphan asylums, industrial schools, and reformatories. It has been the constant practice of the Popes, from the time of Sixtus V. to the present, to send foreign vagrants to their own country, and, by stringent measures, to compel those capable of work to do so. The same has been done by the present Pope, who, while full of compassion for undoubted distress, is as much opposed as any of his predecessors to that sturdy idle mendicancy which is so demoralising wherever it is tolerated.

To render the relief of the meritorious poor more
systematic and effectual, Leo XII. established, in 1826,
the Commission of Subsidies; and to this body is entrusted the management of the greater number of the
public charities, and the administration of revenues
which had previously been distributed through a number of channels.   This important body is composed of
a Cardinal President, and fifteen other members — including the Treasurer General of the Camera, and the
Almoner of the Pope.   Twelve of the " deputies " preside over the distribution of alms in the city.   These
deputies are nominated by the Pope, and chosen partly
from the prelacy, and partly from the nobility, and
hold office for six years.   The city is divided into
twelve districts, or regions, and each region is still
further subdivided into parishes; each parish having its
own organisation, consisting of the parish priest and
two parochial deputies (a citizen and a *dama di carita*),
who are nominated by the Cardinal President, and
hold office for three years.   These parochial congregations, with a physician and a surgeon, form the *congre-
gazione regionaria,* at whose meetings one of the deputies of the Commission presides.   All these give their
services *gratuitously;* but each of the district associations
has a secretary and a bailiff or steward, both of whom
are paid.   The Commission also has its necessary staff,
who are likewise paid for their services.   The alms are
given personally, and by domiciliary visits — by which
means the really poor are known.   The *motu proprio*
of Leo XII. divided these alms under different heads—

ordinary, extraordinary, and urgent; and not only do they include money, granted for periods of six and even of twelve months, but also clothing, beds, and working tools.   All these articles are manufactured in the asylum of Santa Maria degli Angeli, which is a *house of industry*, in the best sense of the word, and one of those many institutions which owe their origin to the wise efforts of late Popes to substitute useful labour for idle mendicancy.   These articles are stamped, and cannot be sold or bought, under a penalty of ten days' imprisonment, and the forfeiture of the article.   Applications for relief are sent in to the parochial deputies, and addressed to the Cardinal President.   The case is at once visited, in order to test the truth of the statement; and a report upon its merits is made to the parochial congregation, or to the district prefect.   The granting of " urgent " aid, or aid in clothing, and like matters, is in the power of the latter; but applications for other descriptions of relief are discussed by the parochial congregation, who transmit them to the district congregation, with a recommendation as to the quality and amount of the aid to be given.   These are again examined by the district congregation; and the prefect presents the deserving cases to the Commission, by whom finally the proposed aid is approved.   Assistance is also given by the Cardinal President directly, or through the Parish Priests.

The reports presented by the Commission to the Pope are documents of much importance, as they not only contain an audit of their expenditure, but supply information respecting the moral and material condition of the poor, and offer valuable suggestions as to the best mode of their improvement.

But there are those in Rome, as in other cities, who are " ashamed to beg," and who would rather endure the greatest extremity of want than make their distress known to others.   With some, especially those who have seen better days, pride is the influencing motive of this reserve ; with others, that bashfulness and timidity which so frequently accompany decent poverty.   The sympathising spirit of charity overlooks not, but specially considers, this class of sufferers ; and the Church has, from time to time, given birth to associations whose object it is to *seek out* the poor who blush to make their wants known, and who hide their misery from the gaze of the world.   Rome boasts of many such institutions. Amongst them, may be mentioned the Arch-Confraternity of the Twelve Apostles ; the Congregation called " Urbana," from Pope Urban VIII. ; and the Congregation of Divine Piety.

The first-mentioned association employ a number of physicians, who visit the sick whom the members have found to stand in need of such succour.   They also provide professional assistance for the defence of the poor ; and they specially protect orphans and widows, and procure a safe shelter for girls "in danger."   They likewise arrange disputes and reconcile enemies.   The brothers, who are called " deputies," are all of noble or wealthy families, and include some lawyers.

The second, besides performing many works of piety, devote themselves to the assistance of poor nobles who have fallen into distress, and to whom they allow a monthly stipend.

The Congregation of Divine Piety was founded by Giovanni Stanchi, Priest of Castel Nuovo, in 1679. This noble society seeks for objects deserving of its charity; and when convinced, by visit and enquiry, of the existence of real distress, it relieves the individual, or the family, by the most timely succour — sometimes by food; sometimes by money and food; sometimes by a present of beds and clothing; and sometimes by the payment of an arrear of rent, or by the redemption of articles pawned through the pressure of want. Its largest aid is given when it is apprised of the urgent necessity of a poor and respectable family. These special alms are administered through four members, who are not required to give an account of the sums confided to them, so that the names of the persons assisted might not appear on the register. In many instances, succour comes unexpectedly to a reduced family, who never know their benefactor; so that they have only to thank Divine Providence for their timely relief. An unknown person presents himself at the house of a family in distress, makes the offering, and disappears. Well might the Society be called by the beautiful and expressive title of " Divine Mercy."

Morichini says truly, there is not a religious association or institution that does not dispense relief — not a convent or monastery that does not give some kind of food — not a noble or wealthy house that has not its fixed assignment for the poor.

But one of the most important branches of the charity administered to the poor of Rome, is the employment afforded by certain " public works," which are principally undertaken with a view to the industrial relief of those who would otherwise be idle, if not utterly destitute. These works are undertaken even more for this charitable object, than for the purpose of beautifying the city, or maintaining in preservation the remains of the ancient monuments; though, as I shall show in a subsequent chapter, the Pope devotes the greatest attention to the safety of objects so dear to the scholar and the man of taste.

The stranger may behold a number of men, certainly not of the able-bodied class, languidly wielding the pickaxe, or slowly trundling the wheelbarrow, at the base of some ancient monument; removing obstructions, directing dangerous streamlets into a safe channel, and carting away rubbish which centuries had accumulated, — thereby frequently revealing to modern curiosity a choice bas-relief, or more valuable inscription. These workmen form a considerable portion of the number to whom employment, of various kinds, but generally with the same object in view, is thus mercifully afforded.

This system of industrial relief is by no means of modern invention, having been originally established and adopted by Sixtus V. and Innocent XII. The French Administration made use of it with considerable advantage, as well as a means of employment, as of restoring to view many half-buried monuments of ancient art.

Leo XII. also employed the same means towards the same ends; and Gregory XVI. greatly increased the annual sum devoted to this creditable purpose. But Pius IX. has still further improved on the liberality of his predecessors, as witness the many important works which he has of late years undertaken and carried out.

In the winter the pressure is greater than in summer; employment, through private enterprise, being more general in the latter period of the year, when the wants of Italian life are fewer, and the poor are enabled to eke out a subsistence by selling fruit and other small merchandise. Healthy and able-bodied men are not employed on these works, unless they are proved to be in absolute want; such employment being reserved for those whom private persons would not be likely to select, and who, in fact, are really fitting objects for assistance. Masons and bricklayers are found to be the most frequent applicants for this species of relief; while carpenters, smiths, hatters, and shoemakers, are very rarely so. A period of severe pressure, which diminishes the means of employment afforded through private enterprise, necessarily enhances the value of this resource to the really industrious; and according to the necessity of the moment, so is the amount of employment increased.

A certain proportion of this means of employment is reserved for those who have come out of prison, and have not been able to find work in the ordinary way. These are under the *surveillance* of the police, and are, at first, paid a smaller sum for their labour than is given to all others; but if it be found that they conduct themselves

x

properly, and do their work diligently, they are then put upon a level with the rest, and receive the usual pay, which is fifteen bajocchi a day. This would be a miserable rate of payment in these countries, but it is not so in countries where the wants of life are few, and where they are cheaply provided for.

Besides the numerous asylums in which old age and infirmity are sheltered, there are hospitals provided for temporary relief; such as those of S. Galla and S. Luigi, which receive all those who have no other place of shelter during the night.

I had an opportunity of seeing a number of old men sitting down to a comfortable repast in the refectory of the noble asylum of S. Michele. The hall was of considerable size, with tables ranged on each side. The tables were decently furnished with linen and other requisites; and before each old gentleman was placed a most excellent dinner, consisting of soup, meat, vegetables, and bread, with a fair proportion of wine. And composedly and respectably sat those old gentlemen before their meal — not one which was grudged to them by selfish ratepayers and pinching "guardians of the poor," but to which they felt, because they had been so taught, that age and infirmity gave them an indefeasible right. There was no badge of degradation — nothing to denote that they were outcasts from "respectable" society; — on the contrary, such was the grave composure and dignity of those "ancient Romans," that a stranger who beheld them, might have readily supposed that he was in the dining-hall of a hotel, and not in the refectory of a poor-house. From what I saw of their manner to my guide—one of the clergymen having the care of the establishment—I could well understand how different, in its influence on the mind and heart of the recipient, is that charity which springs from the love of God, and that which is the offspring of mere State expediency. The one cherishes the best feelings of the heart; the other chills and deadens, if it do not kill, them.*

My gradually diminishing space will not admit of any further reference to this subject. I shall only add, that the severity of the laws against street mendicants has been relaxed, since the year 1837, in favour of certain invalids and infirm persons, who procure a licence and a badge. They are to be met with in most places in Rome, as, indeed, others who have not obtained this legal *status* ; but I cannot say that I have found them unduly importunate. At any rate, if a stranger happen to express a feeling of annoyance at the prevalence of the practice of soliciting alms, he is very likely to be reminded of the words of the Redeemer, who said, in reply to the hypocritical remonstrance of Judas, when Mary anointed the feet of Christ, " *For the poor you have always with you; but me you have not always*" (John xxii. 8).

* I find, by referring to the great work of John Howard, the philanthropist, who visited Rome towards the close of the last century, that he was favourably impressed by this institution. He thus writes:—

" Adjoining to another court are apartments for the aged and infirm, in which were 260 men and 226 women. Here they find *a comfortable retreat,* having *clean* rooms and a refectory. I conversed with some of them, and they appeared *happy and thankful.*"

x 2

CHAP. XXVII.

Dowries. — Monte di Pieta. — The Roman Savings' Bank. — Its
Origin, its Operations, and its Success.

AMONG the other charities of Rome, those which have
been established, whether by associations or individuals,
for giving *dowries* to young girls, especially orphans, are
peculiarly interesting. This has at all times been deemed
a work of great merit ; and hence we find Popes, cardinals, princes, nobles, merchants, lawyers, and others,
bequeathing funds, with the object of making an honourable provision for those who, without such provision being made for them, might be exposed to danger,
if not to destruction. The number of dowries now
given in Rome, of which there can be any public record, is about 1200 annually ; and this has been the
average for the last fifteen or twenty years. In the
year 1789 there was published a little volume on this
subject, in which it was stated that the sum which was
then annually distributed was 60,000 scudi ; which
gross sum, at an average of 40 scudi each dowry, would
provide 1500 portions — then, as now, given to young
girls on their marriage, or on their entering a convent.
To this pious work several confraternities, or religious
associations, are entirely devoted. Of these, the Arch-

Confraternity of the Holy Annunciation might be mentioned. In the year 1460 a society, consisting of 200 Roman gentlemen, was formed; the first motive of this association being, by the practice of piety and good works, to do honour to the Annunciation of the Blessed Virgin. It was then united to the Church of S. Maria, now commonly known as the Minerva, from its having been built on the site of an ancient temple erected to the worship of the Daughter of Jove. In 1486 the society was dedicated to the gathering of alms, with a view to the portioning of poor girls, so as to save them from danger of seduction. It was constituted an arch-confraternity by Gregory XIII. in 1581; and Pope Urban left it heir to his wealth. As early as the year 1600, it portioned 200 girls annually, the greater portion of whom received 50, and some 100, scudi. In 1700 it gave about 400 portions; and at this day the average is about the same, at a gross disbursement of 16,000 scudi. It still consists of Roman gentlemen, a certain number of whom are ecclesiastics, the Cardinal Vicar being its Protector. The objects of its bounty must be of good character, and born in wedlock; but this latter condition is overlooked in special cases. And in order that its charity should not be given to an undeserving person, a probation of three years is insisted upon, during which time the girl is watched over by the society; nor is the dowry given until the moment when she becomes a wife or a religious. This period of probation is of great advantage to the girl herself, as well as to the community generally.

The arch-confraternity just described is not of so ancient a date as the arch-confraternity of *Gonfalone,* from which sprang several others, also dedicated to the same objects — the protection of poor girls, whom they assisted to establish in life.

Morichini states that there were, when he wrote, no less than thirteen institutions or associations in Rome by which dowries were provided. And in his work he alludes to no fewer than sixty-two, by which relief, of one kind or other, was administered.

Pius IX. has at all times esteemed this giving of dowries to young girls a great charity; and has accordingly expended, and continues to expend, a considerable portion of his private means in the good work.

This description of charity is very common throughout Italy, and is practised to a considerable extent by noble and wealthy families and by pious individuals. Sums of money are commonly bequeathed for this purpose; and the bridal festivities of the rich are gracefully availed of as a fitting occasion of conferring happiness on the poor.

A brief notice of what was intended as a useful charity may be here added: the —

MONTE DI PIETA.

This institution, which was originally established so early as the year 1539, when it received the sanction of Paul III., was intended as a remedy against the prevailing evil of usury. Extinguished in the troubles which marked the close of the last century, it was resuscitated in 1803 by Pius VII. The loan was then limited to one scudo, or crown; in 1814 it was increased to three; but from that time it was extended to fifty, and ultimately it has had no fixed limit. The office is opened at an early hour, and is not closed till all the business is done. The loan is always one-third less than the value of the article pledged; and articles of gold and silver are estimated at their intrinsic value, the work of the artist not being taken into consideration. Each loan or pledge is carefully registered, and the goods are laid aside in large halls specially adapted to the purpose, and arranged with the utmost care for their safety and preservation. The goods are retained from six to seven months; after which time, if the interest (which is limited to 5 per cent.) be not paid, they are sold *in canto;* and if there be any surplus after the loan and interest, it is kept for the persons who have pledged the articles. *Pledges to the value of a crown are received and renewed gratuitously, and without interest;* which is, of course, intended for the accommodation of the poor, who avail themselves of it very freely. These free pledges frequently amount to a considerable number daily. They increase in October and in the time of the Carnival, and diminish at Christmas and in August. The daily loans amount to nearly 4000 crowns, and the capital in circulation amounts to more than half a million of crowns. The number of pledges at the time when MORICHINI wrote, was more than 100,000; and the annual revenue derived from the transactions of the institution was then about

40,000 scudi.   All kinds of articles, with the exception
of those belonging to public institutions, and which are
marked, are received; and it frequently happens that
objects of the greatest value are deposited as pledges,
more for the sake of securing their protection, than with
a view to pecuniary convenience.   In all respects the
arrangements are admirable, and excite the interest of
those who witness the operations of the institution;
which is administered by a prelate, a treasurer-general,
and a confraternity.

In natural connection with the *Monte di Pieta*, may
be noticed the

Cassa di Risparmio, or Savings' Bank.

Savings' Banks are of comparatively recent origin; the
earliest — that established in Hamburg—dating no further
back than the year 1778.   Before the close of the century, the example of Hamburg was followed in several
European countries, England included. The first in Italy
was established in Milan in 1823 ; but it was not until
the year 1836, when the experiment had been satisfactorily tested in many other places, that it was attempted in
Rome.   In that year, four Roman gentlemen of rank
met together to discuss the subject in all its bearings—
the advantages and dangers of such an institution, and
its adaptation to the genius and character of the people.
Satisfied of its usefulness as a promoter of industry and
frugality, they resolved on the attempt to establish it
in Rome, and drew up rules for its management.   They
secured the Prince Francesco Borghese as its Pre-

sident, and obtained the sanction and assistance of Gregory XVI., who highly approved of its 'principles. No sooner was the public announcement made of the intention to establish the bank, than one hundred associates were enrolled, including the first names of Rome. A Council, of twelve persons, was next formed, including the President, Vice-President, the Secretary, five Councillors, a Director, an Auditor, a Cashier, &c. A popular explanation of the object of the bank, its advantages and its usefulness, was drawn up by the Secretary, Monsignor Morichini, one of its four originators, and was generally distributed. The President (Prince Borghese) gave rooms in his own palace; by which act he increased the confidence already created in the public mind. On Sunday, the 4th of August, 1836, the bank was solemnly opened; and its rapid success was the best reward of its benevolent promoters, and the best commentary upon the soundness of their judgment. The bank is opened on Sundays and Wednesdays at nine o'clock in the morning, and is not closed until the business is at an end. Deposits are received on Sunday, and drawn on Wednesday. The sum received at one time may range from one paolo, or five-pence, to 20 scudi, or somewhat more than 4l. Interest, at the rate of 4 per cent., is paid on deposits of more than 20 bajocchi, or a little more than tenpence. Payment of interest is made twice a year, in June and December. If the interest be left undrawn, it is also liable to interest. A notice of fifteen days is required for drawing sums above 10 scudi.; but any demand under that sum is paid at once.   The Council assemble twice a month to discuss the affairs of the bank, and are especially solicitous as to the best mode of investing the money deposited, respecting which some difficulty may at times be experienced.   The accounts are published annually. As a means of realising funds, current accounts are opened with persons of wealth and approved character. The public funds that offer a European guarantee, and afford a ready facility of purchase and sale, are another means of investment.   Mortgages, at a moderate rate of interest — a boon to many an encumbered proprietor, who thus is enabled to exchange a heavy liability for one easy to bear — also afford a means of investment. Shares are likewise bought in approved projects, according to the best discretion of the Council.   The sum contributed by the persons who associated with the purpose of establishing this valuable institute, was 5000 scudi ; and with this small sum and the moneys of the depositors, it was almost immediately in successful operation.   Monsignor Morichini, its original Secretary, gives an account of what it did within the period of six years from the day it was opened.   The deposits for that time amounted to 1,653,659 scudi ; and the money taken out amounted to 769,852 scudi.   The number of pass-books issued was 16,364, in which 158, 647 deposits had been entered.   The cancelled pass-books were 6,249.   For an entirely new institution, this was a highly successful result.   The comparatively low rate of interest prevents speculation,. which, if encouraged, would interfere with the manifest intentions of the founders, and risk public confidence in its usefulness. But several benefit and charitable societies use the bank as a legitimate means of increasing their income, and extending their utility.

The Roman Savings' Bank, though established only twenty years since, has already received about four millions of scudi, or nearly one million of our money, in deposits. For the year 1856 there was an increase in the number of depositors and in the amount of deposits over those of 1855. The increase in the number of depositors was 216 — and in the amount of deposits, 80,000 scudi. These figures are of themselves no trifling indication of increasing prosperity.

CHAP. XXVIII.

Religious Character of the Roman people. — Attendance in the
Churches. — Roman Churches not merely Local. — Attendance
at the Forty Hours' Adoration. — Religious Retreat for the
Poor. — Festivals of the Church. — The Pope at San Carlo. —
The Monastery of the Passionists. — Church of St. Clement. —
Church of St. Isidore.

An erroneous notion with respect to the religious character of the Roman people, is commonly entertained
by strangers who casually visit the churches of Rome.
They imagine, because they do not behold the churches
crowded with worshippers, that therefore the Romans
are not a religious people. As a general rule, the
idler in Rome is not an early riser; while, in order to
be able to form a fair idea of the devotional character
of the people, he should be so; for it is at the very
hour when he is still buried in peaceful slumber, that the
people are to be found in great numbers in the parish
churches, or in those attached to the convents, and are
even seen crowding round the rails of the altar as com-
municants. This description applies to the week days,
but of course in a much greater degree to the Sunday.
Before commencing the business of the day, the shop-
keeper and the trader punctually attend Mass; and
the workman sanctifies his coming toil by the same pious

practice.   Strangers almost invariably go to the High
Mass, to witness the more imposing ceremonial, and
enjoy the treat which the fine singing affords ; but the
Roman people go at the earliest hours to the "low
Mass" — the feeling of religious obligation being, with
them, a sufficient inducement.   Thus the great churches,
such as the Jesu and the Minerva, may be seen
crowded at an early hour in the morning by devout
congregations ; and so may other churches, which, on
many accounts, are held in special favour — for example, the Church of the Capuchins, in the Piazza
Barberini.   Besides, notwithstanding the occupation of
the people during the hours of business and labour, it
is almost impossible for a visitor to enter any one
of the 300 or 400 churches of Rome, no matter at what
hour of the day, without perceiving at least two or three
persons kneeling before the altar of the Blessed Sacrament ; which altar is indeed as conspicuous from the
worshippers who are absorbed in devotion before its
rails, as by the lights which are constantly kept burning upon it.   I myself must have visited very nearly one-
half of the Roman churches, and certainly all those considered the most remarkable ; and I have never seen any
one church entirely destitute of worshippers ; whereas,
on many occasions, I have seen considerable congregations both at Mass and at Vespers.   But, after all, how
is it possible that any number of the churches of Rome
could appear to be well filled?   Remember, the population, according to the last census, was about 172,000,
and that the number of churches is between 300 and

400; and that amongst them are included St. Peter's, St. Paul's, Santa Maria Maggiore, the Lateran, Santa Croce, and a number of other stupendous buildings. Why, it would require a far larger population than London possesses to fill the churches of Rome; half a dozen of the largest of which might hold every man, woman, and child of the population in the midst of which they are erected.

"But why," asks the utilitarian, in the true parochial spirit, "has Rome so many churches, when there are no congregations to fill them?" The answer is, the Roman churches are not local churches, for local purposes, and local wants; they belong to Catholic Christendom — to the Church of the whole world — and not to Rome alone. From the fourth to the nineteenth century, the great churches of Rome have been the splendid evidences of the piety and liberality of rulers and of nations; and, even at this day, the contributions of the faithful throughout the wide extent of the earth have assisted Pius IX. to bring to a state of completion the great Basilica of St. Paul's, which, originally commenced by Constantine, and finished by Theodosius and his son Honorius, has risen from the ashes of the great fire of 1823 in almost unparalleled grandeur and magnificence. All the churches of Rome have been erected with the great and paramount object of giving glory to the Supreme Being; but many have been founded with the additional object of honouring the Virgin Mother of God, and the apostles and martyrs of the Church — of commemorating those glorious deeds by which the religion of the Gospel was firmly established, and recording those signal events by which the Church was protected from the violence or the machinations of her enemies. Surely, St. Peter's is not a mere Roman Church — but the Church of the Christian World ; for beneath its sublime dome repose the bodies of the two greatest of the Apostles — Paul and Peter. Thus many of the churches, which the utilitarian may deem superfluous and unnecessary, rise above the hallowed relics of some saint or martyr, whose preachings, whose labours, or whose sufferings, caused them to belong, not to any country or to any race, but to the world and mankind. And where, more fittingly than in Rome, could Catholic piety have erected, or Catholic munificence have adorned, such splendid memorials to the honour of the heroes of God's Church ? In fact, in the Christian temples of Rome, you may trace the chequered history of the Church throughout all ages, from the gloomiest days of its persecution, to those of its proudest triumphs and most splendid conquests. Popes, emperors, kings, princes, cardinals, and bishops, as well as empresses, queens, and princesses, have ever sought, through the magnificence of architecture, the charms of painting, and the more spiritual beauty of sculpture, as well as by the lavish use of the rarest and most costly productions of nature, to render Rome, as it were more visibly and strikingly to the eye of the stranger, the Centre of Catholic Unity — the City of Holy Places.

The immense number of churches in Rome may be

further accounted for by the many parishes into which
the city is divided; each parish having a church of its
own; by the fact, that to each convent or monastery
a church is almost invariably attached; and, also, by the
number of national churches belonging to Catholic
nations in various parts of the world.

But I was alluding to the devotion of the modern
Romans. To really understand the religious character
of the people, one ought to see them at the devotion of
the *Quarant Ore,* or the forty hours' adoration. The
spectacle is most impressive, — the church, purposely
darkened, crowded at all hours with kneeling worshippers — the outlines of the building dimly traced, and
the congregation but faintly illumined, by the lights
which burn on the altar on which the Blessed Sacrament is exposed. Then the deep, earnest devotion,
the reverent air, the prayerful attitude, so humble and
so pious, must satisfy any one who is not an arrant
scoffer, that those who kneel before that altar do so in
the spirit of the liveliest faith and the sincerest piety.
The prince and the peasant meet here on a perfect
equality; the one receiving new impulses to that
charity in which the Roman noble so truly proves
himself to be a son of the Church — the other bor-
rowing strength and fortitude to meet and endure the
difficulties of his lot in life.

Space will not permit of my alluding to, much less
dwelling upon, the many means by which a religious
spirit is cherished amongst all classes of the people; and
I shall only therefore attempt, by a single illustration,

to afford the reader an idea of that solicitude which is ever felt for their spiritual welfare.

About forty years ago, Michelini, a curate in the Trastevere, obtained, for the purpose of prayer and temporary retreat, the family house of the Ponziani, which was then a granary. In this retreat the poor prepare themselves for their first communion, by a seclusion of eight days; during which time they are provided gratuitously with every necessary, and ministered to and instructed by ecclesiastics who shut themselves up so long as the retreat lasts. Seventeen of these retreats, to sixty persons each retreat, take place in the year; so that each year 1020 Christians are fully prepared for the greatest act of their spiritual life; and these are not the rich — who enjoy the possessions of the world — but the poor. Pius IX. evinced his interest in this most valuable charity, by presenting himself unexpectedly, about three years since, and administering communion to the temporary inmates of the building. The whole thing is beautiful. A cheerful little court, for recreation, adorned with plants and orange trees; and the modest refectory at the side. Upstairs, the wards, plain and exquisitely neat, each with a bed for a priest who presides, and over the door the name of a saint. Several chapels for the different exercises, one set apart for the Communion, and a room for an hour's conversation — all singularly tasteful and attractive. In one of the chapels are beheld an eloquent testimony to the efficacy of this good work — the pistols, stilettoes, and knives, voluntarily

Y

abandoned.   In this house of touching kindness, food, lodging, instruction — everything, as I have said, is *gratuitous* ; given by the devotion of the priests, and the alms of the faithful.   We have praise for the hospital and for the well-ordered prison ; but in such an asylum as this, the poor find a greater mercy — the silent supernatural bringing of man's soul to God.

A corresponding place for women is established at San Pasquale.

To prepare the young for their First Communion has ever been one of the most cherished objects of the Pope, who has done much to render its influence more lasting on the mind and heart of the youthful communicant. It is his frequent habit to administer the Sacrament to them himself.

The Festivals of the Church afford the religious people of Rome abundant opportunities of indulging their piety.   I had an opportunity of witnessing the celebration of several, and at the same time of convincing myself of the devotional character of the modern Romans.

On Tuesday, the 4th of November, the Feast of St. Charles Borromeo, I formed one of a vast crowd who had assembled in and about the Church of San Carlo, in the Corso, to witness the imposing spectacle of his Holiness coming in state to that fine church.   Having heard and read so much as to the indifference of the Romans to such spectacles, to which use too had rendered them so familiar, I was amazed at the eagerness so vigorously manifested, not by strangers, but by citizens,

to catch a glimpse of the Holy Father. To me, who
witnessed it for the first time, the whole pageant was
as striking as impressive ; nor was its effect diminished,
but greatly enhanced, by the graceful and elegant
manner in which the inhabitants of the palaces and
houses on each side of the Corso evinced their respect
for the Pope.   From every window and balcony was
suspended a piece of drapery, or tapestry of some kind ;
and, in many instances, judicious contrast and tasteful
arrangement added much to the general effect.   The
picturesque street, so full of architectural variety — the
eager crowd, including the representatives of many
countries, attracted to Rome by various motives — the
uniforms and accoutrements of the troops that lined the
streets — some French, some Italian, some Swiss —
infantry as well as horse — the flashing of the gorgeous
equipages of the cardinals — the clash of arms, and the
grand burst of two full bands, as the more magnificent
state coach of his Holiness, preceded and followed by
his guards, was driven to the door, and he himself
alighted in the midst of a kneeling crowd, to whom
he imparted the apostolic benediction, — all seen, too,
beneath a beautiful Italian sky and a bright Italian
sun, formed a picture brilliant and striking to any eye,
but one in the highest degree interesting and impressive
to a Catholic from a distant land.

The appearance which the interior of the fine Church
of San Carlo presented, was most imposing.   It was
decorated, according to the custom on such occasions,
with a rich drapery of crimson damask with a gold

border, relieved by a blended drapery of white silk
similarly ornamented.   With this drapery, the piers,
pillars, and pilasters, were concealed ; and where arches
occurred, they were gracefully festooned with the same
elegant material — the effect being further heightened
by flowers tastefully disposed, and by a profusion of
wax lights in every variety of candelabrum.   The
swelling notes of the grand organ, the glorious burst
of the full choir, consisting of the best singers of Rome,
and the splendid ceremonials with which the Church
did honour to one of the most illustrious of her children
— all realised to the eye and to the imagination a grand
picture of Catholic worship.

I was rather surprised to hear it said that this visit
of the Pope's was only in *mezzo gala,* or half state.

The rush to witness the departure of the Holy
Father was quite equal to that which marked his arrival.

During my stay in Rome, I was present at many
celebrations of the great annual festivals, and in some
of the most interesting of its churches.   For instance, the Church of St. John and Paul, belonging to
the Passionists ; the Church of St. Clement, belonging
to the Irish Dominicans ; and the Church of St. Cecilia,
in Trastevere, to which is attached the convent of the
Benedictine Nuns.

The monastery and church of the Passionists are replete with interest.   The body of the " Blessed Paul,"
the founder of the order, lies under an altar of one of the
side chapels, and could be seen, through the glass cover-

ing in front, on the day of the festival. I was shown
the rooms, or cells, which he occupied during his life-
time, and in which are preserved with religious veneration, not only his missal, his crucifix, and his chalice, and
the furniture of his little oratory, but even the smallest
and most insignificant article of daily use. The hair-
shirt which he wore, and the instruments of " discipline" which he used, were eloquent evidences of his
mortification and self-subjection.

The grand ceremonies of the day are, on most occasions of the kind, followed by a repast, in which, out of
special honour to the festival, some departure is permitted from the simplicity, if not austerity, of the
general and almost invariable rule.

The appearance of the refectory of this monastery, in
which the entire of the community, nearly eighty in
number, and several guests — including the cardinal celebrant, some foreign bishops, and a few lay gentlemen —
were assembled, was very striking. The same silence
was strictly observed during the meal on this day as on
ordinary occasions. Some two or three of the brothers
were of very advanced age, and of the most venerable
aspect, their silver hairs imparting a more spiritual
beauty to features refined by study, and wasted by
vigil and mortification. A modern painter could here
have found living studies for saints and martyrs of other
days; nor would he have looked in vain for the bloom
and fulness of manly beauty amongst those dark-robed
soldiers of the faith.

An agreeable hour, spent in cheerful conversation, filled up the interval between the conclusion of the meal and the commencement of Vespers — to which crowds of people, clad in their holiday attire, might be seen coming from different directions. I greatly enjoyed a saunter in the delightful shade of the gardens of the monastery, and still more the grand and varied prospect spread out before me, as I stood at the boundary wall overlooking the Colosseum, the warm travertine stone of which glowed like amber in the bright sunlight. One of the brothers, Father Luigi, had known and loved a dear and valued friend of mine — the late lamented Frederick Lucas, the distinguished member for Meath; and our mutual friendship and respect for that brave-hearted champion of the Church united us in sympathy, as we spoke of his courage, his manliness, and his genius.

The Church of St. Clement seemed to wake up to life, as, on the day of the high festival, its ancient tribune was crowded with priests of every rank, from the cardinal to the deacon, and as gorgeous vestments contrasted with the pale cold marble of its beautiful choir. A cardinal-bishop celebrated the High Mass; and a grand choir chaunted the solemn and majestic music in a manner that, far from distracting the attention, inspired that devotional feeling which it is the intention, or should be the object, of sacred music to assist in producing. The epistle and gospel were read from the marble pulpits, or *ambones,* which occupy each side of the choir, and which, with the choir itself, are of great antiquity.

I subjoin a description of this remarkable church, written, many years since, by Eustace, in his *Classical Tour ;* and merely add, that the tribune is enriched with mosaics of the thirteenth century, and that the Chapel of the Passion is adorned with the fine frescoes of Masaccio—most important, not only for their intrinsic merit, but as exemplifying the history of the art.*

---

* This church is thus fully described by Eustace : —

" The church of St. Clement, in the great street that leads to St. John Lateran, is the most ancient church in Rome. It was built on the site, and was probably at first one of the great apartments of the house of the holy bishop whose name it bears. It is mentioned as ancient by authors of the fourth century (St. Jerome, Pope Zozimus, &c.), and is justly considered as one of the best models that now exist of the ancient form of Christian churches. It has frequently been repaired and decorated, but always with a religious respect for its primitive shape and fashion. In front of it is a court with galleries, supported by eighteen granite pillars, and paved with pieces of shattered marble, among which I observed several fragments of beautiful *verde antico.* The portico of the church is formed of four columns of the same materials as the pillars of the gallery, and its interior is divided into a nave and aisles by twenty pillars of various marbles. The choir commences about the centre of the nave, and extends to the steps of the sanctuary ; there are two pulpits, anciently called *ambones,* at each side of the choir. A flight of steps leads to the sanctuary or chancel, which is terminated by a semicircle, in the middle of which stands the episcopal chair, and on each side of it two marble ranges of seats border the walls, for the accommodation of the priests ; the inferior clergy with the singers occupied the choir. In front of the episcopal throne, and between it and the choir, just above the steps of the sanctuary, rises the altar, unencumbered by screens, and conspicuous on all sides. The aisles terminated in two semicircles, now used as chapels, called anciently *Exedræ* or *Cellæ,* and appropriated to private devotion in prayer or meditation. Such is the form of St. Clement's, which, though not

Y 4

A splendid entertainment evinced the hospitality —
the national hospitality — of the kind-hearted prior and
his most interesting community. It was partaken of by
a goodly company, including cardinals, prelates, and
many foreign ecclesiastics and laymen.

The fine library of this convent is much used by the
community, which consists of several students as well
as priests ; and from the intelligence and cultivation of
the former, I could well judge that the Irish branch of
the illustrious order of St. Dominick, which boasts of
so many eminent divines, is not likely to degenerate in
the present age.

The Church of St. Isidore, attached to the convent
of the Irish Franciscans, was fast approaching to a state
of restoration as I was about leaving Rome. I had
no opportunity of seeing this beautiful church ; but
I have since learned that its restoration and embellish-
ment do equal credit to the zeal and energy of the
community, and to the liberality of the faithful. One of
the good priests told me, with feelings of the liveliest
gratitude, of his interview with the Holy Father, to
whom he applied for assistance in the undertaking ; and

originally a basilica, is evidently modelled upon such buildings ; as
may be seen not only by the description given of them by Vitruvius,
but also by several other churches in Rome, which having actually been
basilicæ, still retain their original form with slight modifications. The
same form has been retained or imitated in all the great Roman
churches, and indeed in almost all the cathedral and abbey churches
in Italy ; a form without doubt far better calculated both for the beauty
of perspective, and for the convenience of public worship, than the
arrangement of Gothic fabrics, divided by screens and terminating in
gloomy chapels."

of the kindness with which he was received — the sweet simplicity of the good Pope — the warm interest which he manifested in the object of the application — and the generosity with which he contributed even to the last scudo then in his possession.

CHAP. XXIX.

THOUGH this volume is written with a far different
object from that with which a guide-book is compiled,
still it might seem to many readers an unpardonable
omission, if a work in any way referring to Rome did
not contain some allusion to the Queen of Churches —
St. Peter's.

This sublimest of temples was perhaps never better
described than by the most majestic of modern prose
writers, and the greatest of poets—Gibbon and Byron.
The former describes St. Peter's as—" the most glorious
structure that ever has been applied to the use of
religion." And in this noble apostrophe does the *Childe*
pour forth his admiration : —

> " But thou, of temples old, or altars new,
>   Standest alone — with nothing like to thee —
>   Worthiest of God, the holy and the true.
>   Since Zion's desolation, when that He
>   Forsook his former city, what could be,
>   Of earthly structures, in his honour piled,

Of a sublimer aspect ?   Majesty,
Power, glory, strength, and beauty — all are aisled
In this eternal ark of worship undefiled.
Enter : its grandeur overwhelms thee not ;
And why ?   It is not lessened ; but thy mind,
Expanded by the glories of the spot,
Has grown colossal, and can only find
A fit abode wherein appear enshrined
Thy hopes of immortality ; and thou
Shalt one day, if found worthy, so defined,
See thy God face to face, as thou dost now
His Holy of Holies, nor be blasted by His brow."

An extract from a diary which I kept while in Rome, and in which I hurriedly jotted down the impressions of each day, will best convey the feelings with which I for the first time approached and quitted St. Peter's:—

"The Church of Churches, the great Christian Temple, was first to be seen — seen before the eye rested on any other object, whose interest was of the present or of the past. St. Peter's — the true type of Christian Rome — of its greatest glory and widest sovereignty — of its piety and its splendour, its religion and its art — St. Peter's, to which the longing of the Catholic heart is instinctively directed.

"As I approached this glorious fabric — across the wide area half-enclosed within the outstretching arms of the magnificent double colonnade, which adds to its external splendour, and which of itself is unrivalled by any similar construction — my eye grasped it in too eagerly, with too great a desire to be astonished — to feel amazed at its stupendous proportions ; and, I must confess it, I at first felt disappointed.   In vain I was

told that the figures which surmount the attic of the
front were nearly twenty feet high, and that they stood
150 feet from the ground.   Still I experienced a sense
of disappointment, because, as I approached the building, the dome gradually sank from my view, and the
façade, though vast in extent, being 368 feet wide, is more
heavy and monotonous than striking.   But as I crossed
the threshold, and stood within a vast hall, stretch-
ing nearly 200 feet on either side, and saw that this was
only the vestibule of the temple — and yet larger than
many great churches — the true idea of St. Peter's
began first to break upon me. With a slower step and a
deeper reverence, I entered the church itself.   Again,
though but for a moment, a sense of disappointment
came across my mind.   My eye glanced so rapidly to the
tribune, which bounds the view, that I lost all idea of
distance, although the bronze figures which support the
chair of Peter were about 600 feet from the place where
I then stood.   I was involuntarily thinking of the limited
nature of the works of man, however vast his concep-
tions or mighty his means of realising them ; but man
himself assisted in dispelling a thought injurious to the
sublime genius of Michael Angelo.   A few French
soldiers were scattered over the church, and the vastness of the majestic structure dwarfed them into mere
atoms.   The fact is, the very perfection of its proportions, the harmony of all its parts, the freshness and
beauty of its colouring, and the bright clear atmosphere,
so different from the religious gloom which forms one of
the leading characteristics of Gothic temples — prevent

St. Peter's from producing on the mind that immediate impression of its vastness, which its enormous length and its noble height might be supposed to do. Gigantic as it is, it is too beautiful to astound, and too bright to awe, the mind of the beholder. But as you walk up the glorious nave, spanned over by its lofty arched roof, rich in carving and blazing with gold, and approach the wide circle of the uplifted dome, and your eye springs giddily into its sublime elevation — then do you really comprehend the glory of St. Peter's, and then do you bow in homage before the grandeur of human genius. With a sense of relief, I dropped my gaze upon the marble pavement beneath my feet; but a glance at the wide-spreading transepts did not do much to weaken the impression which the unrivalled splendour of the dome had produced. I quitted the temple with even greater reverence than I entered it."

That first visit, which I thus faintly attempted to describe, I followed up by at least ten more; and each time that I walked through the building, the more was my admiration increased—more by the grandeur of its dimensions and the harmony of its proportions, than by its beauty of detail. It would require a volume to do justice to the works of art that enrich this temple; the monuments, the bas-reliefs, the groups of statuary, and the mosaics — from the striking figures which adorn the dome, to the copies of some of the finest works of the great masters, which overhang the various altars. Raphael's Transfiguration glows in the enduring brilliancy and vivid colouring which the finest mosaic could impart to the greatest and last work of that most illustrious of Italian painters.

Few have ever stood beneath the dome of St. Peter's without having felt the enthusiasm which the place inspires. Eustace visited Rome more than half a century since, and, in his *Classical Tour*, he thus describes the impression which it made upon his mind : —

"As you enter you behold the most extensive hall ever constructed by human art, expanded in magnificent perspective before you ; advancing up the nave, you are delighted with the beauty of the variegated marble under your feet, and with the splendour of the golden vault over your head. The lofty Corinthian pilasters with their bold entablature, the intermediate niches with their statues, the arcades with the graceful figures that recline on the curves of their arches, charm your eye in succession as you pass along. But how great your astonishment when you reach the foot of the altar, and, standing in the centre of the church, contemplate the four superb vistas that open around you ; and then raise your eyes to the dome, at the prodigious elevation of 400 feet, extending like a firmament over your head, and presenting, in glowing mosaic, the companies of the just, the choirs of celestial spirits, and the whole hierarchy of heaven arrayed in the presence of the Eternal, whose 'throne, raised above all height,' crowns the awful scene."

A far severer critic, the accomplished but cynical Forsyth, who made his Italian tour somewhat about the same time, indulges in a burst of enthusiasm, as rare as, in this instance, it was fully justified by its object : —

"The cupola is glorious. Viewed in its design, its altitude, or even its decorations ; viewed either as a whole or as a part, it enchants the eye, it satisfies the taste, it exhausts the soul. The very air seems to eat up all that is harsh or colossal, and leaves us nothing but the sublime to feast on : — a sublime peculiar as the genius of the immortal architect, and comprehensible only on the spot. The four surrounding cupolas, though but satellites to the majesty of this, might have crowned four elegant churches."

And Hilliard, whose *Six Months in Italy* * I regretted not having seen till after my return from Rome, writes with no less enthusiasm than his predecessor Forsyth, whom he fully equals in his appreciation of art and his grace of description, without being in any way marred by the repelling harshness of his unsparing censure. The elegant and fair-minded American writer thus treats of this matchless work of human art : —

"The pilgrim is now beneath the dome. The spirit of criticism, which has hitherto attended him with whispers of doubt, goes no further. Astonishment and admiration break upon the mind and carry it away. To say that the dome of St. Peter's is sublime, is a cold commonplace. In sublimity it is so much beyond all other architectural creations, that it demands epithets of its own. There is no work of man's hand that is similar or second to it. Vast as it is, it rests upon its supporting piers in such serene tranquillity, that it seems to have been lifted and expanded by the elastic force of the air which it clasps. Under its majestic vault the soul dilates. To act like the hero — to endure like the martyr — seems no more than the natural state of man."

* John Murray, London.

So majestic, so holy, did St. Peter's appear to Madame De Stael, that she represents *Corinne* and *Oswald* hushed into silence as they enter the temple, and first comprehend its sublimity.*

I had an excellent opportunity of appreciating the vastness of St. Peter's, on the 18th of November, when the Pope attended at High Mass in the Canons' Chapel. The knowledge of the intended presence of the Holy Father had drawn together a considerable number of persons — many of them mere spectators, but more of them devout and earnest worshippers — sufficient in all to form an average congregation for an ordinary church. And yet they seemed a mere handful in that enormous structure, as, at the conclusion of the Holy Sacrifice, they divided at each side of the nave, to make way for his Holiness, who, heading a long and splendid procession of ecclesiastics, proceeded to offer up his prayers before the tomb of the Apostles. In fact, the many hundreds of persons then present only fringed the marble pavement of the mighty nave. How beautiful the piety of the Pope! What an expression of devotion— of sublime, prayerful devotion—lit up his whole face, as he thus knelt before the tomb of the Prince of the Apostles, in " the most glorious church that has ever been applied to the use of religion!" Not the marble figure of his saintly predecessor, Pius VI., which the chisel of Canova has represented in a kneeling posture

* " Là tout commande le silence : le moindre bruit retentit si loin, qu'aucune parole ne semble digne d'être ainsi répétée dans une demeure presque éternelle."— *Corinne, ou L'Italie.*

before the entrance to the tomb, was more replete
with the sentiment of holiness, than were the unconscious attitude and absorbed air of the living Pope.

In company with seven other visitors, I made the ascent of the dome, even to the ball of the cross which
surmounts it. I thought the view down into the church
from the lower gallery, by which the interior of the
dome is encircled, sufficiently trying to the nerves;
but that from the upper gallery, into which a little door
opened from the winding stair, was literally enough to
take away the breath. The eye dived down into a fearful depth, comprehending with difficulty that the mite-
like things that crept over the floor were full-grown
men and women; and that the toy-like decoration, beneath the centre of the dome, was the baldachino which
rose above the high altar to the height of 100 feet !
No building in the world could convey an idea of such
gigantic altitude as St. Peter's, when seen from the
upper gallery in the interior of the dome. I confess
I was happy to exchange this position for the still loftier
but far more agreeable one afforded by the balcony at the
base of the tower from which the cross springs into the
air. And, save from the summit of a mountain, where
can one behold so glorious a prospect as is here
spread out on every side? Rome, living and dead, lies
beneath, expanded like a map, with every line, marked
by nature or by man upon its seven hills, distinct and
legible to the eye — its Christian temples and its Pagan
ruins — its venerable walls, traceable for many miles

z

over the varying surface of the soil — the grand old
Tiber, sweeping majestically by the base of the Castle
of St. Angelo, and gleaming like silver beneath the
noon-day sun, as it winds through the purple brown of
the desolate Campagna — desolate for more than a
thousand years, since the villas and temples of the Republic and the Empire were made the prey of the ferocious Hun, the brutal Vandal, and the scarcely less
savage and ruthless Lombard.*   The eye leaps across
this barrier of desolation, which encircles Rome with its
girdle of ruin, and dwells with delight upon the distant
Apennines, upon whose wooded sides or naked cliffs
beautiful shadows chase each other, as if in sport —
upon the picturesque outlines of the Alban and the
Sabine hills, famous in Roman story — and is caught
by the bright line of light where dance and sparkle the
waters of the Mediterranean.

A dapper little French soldier amused me much by
the eagerness with which, at every stage of our ascent,
he scribbled his name in pencil upon various parts of
the building.   His labours for the benefit of an admir-
ing posterity only terminated in the ball!

To other works I must refer the reader for a description of this great monument of human genius, which,

---

* Nothing can be more unjust, or more untrue to history, than to charge
upon the Popes that which was completed more than a thousand years
since.   Even in the sixth century its ruin was consummated.   Gibbon
says of that time: — " The Campagna of Rome *was speedily reduced to
the state of a dreary wilderness*, in which the land is barren, the waters
are impure, and the air is infectious."

begun by Constantine in the fourth century, and recommenced in the fifteenth, employed the genius of the greatest architects, and the energies and resources of the most vigorous Popes, and consumed, in its erection, nearly three hundred years, and twelve millions of money.

CHAP. XXX.

The Fine Arts. — Why they are specially fostered in Rome. — The Church their uniform Friend. — Pius IX. a liberal Patron. — Discoveries of Ancient Painting. — Valuable Restorations of Works of Modern Art. — Churches restored. — Church of St. Agnes, and Church of St. Paul.

IN Rome, the Fine Arts possess a special importance; and the question of their encouragement is not to be determined on data similar to those on which it is founded in other countries. Many thoughtful men have of late inquired, whether some governments have not devoted too much attention to Arts, which, being but the ornaments of life, have a tendency to distract the mind from the more earnest duties and the more evident realities of citizenship. On the other hand, it has been urged that, in an age evidently utilitarian, and when mankind seems to be devoted to material interests, almost to the exclusion of other con-siderations — in an age when faith has waned, and reason has not grown — it is the duty of the State, by its fos-tering care, to cherish Art, as the power which, next to Religion, has the greatest tendency to elevate the human mind, and preserve men from being made the mere tools of an unresting industry, or the mere slaves of an insatiable greed of gain.

But whatever may be thought of the abstract question, it must be admitted that in Rome there are special circumstances which make the cultivation of the Fine Arts there a matter of peculiar importance; whether we examine the question from a higher point of view, or descend to the level of the most vulgar and merely commercial considerations.

So far as we can judge from what monuments remain to us, the Plastic Arts have had two great developments; the age of Phidias, and the age of Raphael. By a coincidence, remarkable, but not difficult to account for, Rome is especially associated with both eras. It was the sepulchre of the ancient, it was the cradle of modern art. Thither were carried, amidst the spoils of Greece, those marbles which, even by the comparatively rude conqueror, were estimated beyond their weight in gold; and thither strayed, probably, the last students of an art which had in their native land attained a perfection never before approached, never since reached; and which, by a kind of inspiration, seems, in its ideal of the human form, to have surpassed the beauty of Nature herself. In Rome especially, these masterpieces, hidden beneath the *débris* of the imperial city, rested only to be disinterred, and to prove the existence of a perfection which, but for their evidence, would be as little conceived as the proportions of a Megatherium. By an accident, fortunate but not singular, these relics were discovered principally in the age which possessed, of all others, the men the best calculated not only to feel their beauty, but to rival it. Here, then,

z 3

grew up Modern Art—here was formed the greatest of its schools, and here its greatest triumphs were attained.

To Rome there had been transplanted whatever of most value ancient art possessed — in Rome had grown up modern art, there to attain its highest perfection; and, therefore, for centuries, the student has turned his steps to the banks of the Tiber, if he sought to draw some kindred inspiration from the greatest works of painting or of sculpture. And not alone the professional student, but the scholar and the man of taste, sought in Rome the highest types of that ideal perfection to which the schools of Greece and Italy attained.

Again, Rome was the Queen City of the Church, which had always reckoned the arts amongst her handmaids. A religion which recognised sentiment, as well as reason, could never be content with a bald ritual, or a bare temple; and the same principle which introduced music into the ceremonies of the Church, admitted with welcome within her portals sculpture and painting. The principle which gave to the Sistine Chapel the "Miserere," gave also the "Last Judgment"—that principle of sacrifice which bids man to dedicate to the temple of his Creator whatsoever is most precious, not merely gold and jewels, but those gems beyond price, in which the loftiest inspirations of the noblest minds have been stamped in an enduring form, to communicate their refining and elevating influence, not to a day, but to generations.

Thus Rome, from several causes, has become especially the great art-capital of the world.   Thousands of pilgrims flock thither with that object alone; and even the bitterest enemies of the Church must visit her Cathedral City, if they wish to see or to study the greatest monuments of the plastic arts.   For these reasons, the Fine Arts in Rome should command the attention of the State, and their encouragement becomes in its way a matter of industrial importance.   Out of the crowds of pilgrims who come to the Tiber, few leave its shores without some memento of their visit, memorials on which Artists are always engaged; and hence there is a larger proportion of the population of Rome dependent upon the exercise of art, as a profession, than in any city of the world.   In whatever way, therefore, we view the abstract question of government endowment of the Fine Arts in other countries, it must be confessed that in Rome, at least, it is founded on sound economical principles.

And indeed in almost all ages of the Church the same principle prevailed; as well when great wealth and power enabled it to be a munificent patron — the only *patron* which the true Artist should condescend to acknowledge — as when its limited resources allowed it to do little more than manifest its feelings of paternal care.

The present Pope has been eminently remarkable for the zealous care which he has devoted to the preservation of objects of Antique Art, and for the encouragement which he has given to artists of the pre-

z 4

sent day. It would be far too long to enter upon a detail of the many services which he has thus rendered. It will be sufficient if we take as an example the year 1854, and point to some of the objects to which attention was devoted in that year. We select them from the official report of the Minister to whom such subjects were referred.

In this year the Pope established in the Academy of Bologna a new professorship of Elementary Architecture, including the study of Ornament and Decoration; and granted to the Roman Academy of St. Luke ten medals of gold, each of the value of 25 scudi, to be distributed amongst the professors who, besides the stated instruction in the schools, should devote the greatest attention to the progress of the students in the study of the figure and of drapery. He also presented to the Academy a series of casts from the Egina sculptures and the marbles of the Parthenon. These were probably obtained from the British Museum, and were necessary to complete the illustrations of ancient art.

To antiquities, the Pope has devoted special attention; and some fortunate discoveries, which have recently taken place in Rome, have enabled him to make most valuable additions to museums already so rich. Amongst the most valuable and the rarest of the relics of the classical art, are the remains of the ancient painting. The nature of the art itself has necessarily made its works less stable than those of sculpture; but, even making due allowance for this, it is still remarkable how very few of the classic paintings have escaped destruction.

The Egyptian paintings, or picture-writings, can claim a much earlier antiquity than the times of the Roman Empire, and yet many of them have been discovered in a state of almost marvellous preservation; whilst the Greek and Roman paintings that have been rescued are singularly rare.   Indeed, if we were to except those found in Pompeii, they might almost be enumerated from recollection.   Rome itself contained only those called " the Aldobrandini Nuptials," the frescoes of the Baths of Titus, of the Pyramid of Caius Cestius, and those discovered in the Columbaria of the Appian Way.   But Pius IX. disinterred from the Via Graziosa a series of ancient paintings, which are certainly the most valuable that have ever been discovered.   They are seven in number, and represent several scenes in the adventures of Ulysses, described in the 10th and 11th books of the Odyssey.   They are especially interesting for the reason, that some of the scenes are identical with those represented in a celebrated painting by Polygnotus at Delphi, which has been described by Pausanias; and it is conjectured that these paintings may have been copies from some greater original.   They have followed the tradition of probably the earliest artists, by having, like those also of the Byzantine and early Christian schools, the names of the several actors in the scene attached to the figures.   The perspective, the colours, and the composition, are all very remarkable, and the paintings have been greatly improved by careful and judicious restorations.   When first discovered, they were almost hidden by a thick coat of mould, and also much injured by scratches caused by the demolition of the walls above them. This mould was completely removed, and all the scratches carefully filled up with colour, accurately matched with the ancient portion of the pictures. Two out of the number having been found in much better condition than the rest, these greatly assisted the artists in their work, which stopped short at the barest restoration, and avoided that point where a vicious effort at renovation is attempted, which always detracts from the value and authority of ancient monuments. The work was one of great difficulty, and was conducted to the most complete success, as the pictures can now be easily seen and studied. They have been placed in the library of the Vatican, which can boast, in addition to its other treasures, of possessing the most perfect and the most interesting relics of the painting of the classic ages.

The works of the great masters of Modern Art have likewise been the objects of the Pope's solicitude, and especially those earlier works over which centuries have not passed without leaving traces behind.

In the magnificent Duomo of Orvieto important restorations have been made, although only the most urgent of these works were undertaken. The paintings which adorn the Chapel of the Santissimo Corporale, representing the miracle of Bolsena, and subjects connected with it, and which are so remarkable from being representations, in a great part, of contemporary scenes, giving the costumes of the period, and even portraits of those who took part in the ceremonies when Urban IV. translated the relics from Bolsena to Orvieto, have been carefully and delicately restored. These paintings carry us back to the time when the Feast of the Corpus Domini was instituted, and the Office for it composed by Saint Thomas of Aquin, who was then Professor of Theology at Orvieto.

One of the chapels of the Church of Santa Maria sopra Minerva possesses some characteristic pictures of Filippino Lippi, which were threatened with destruction by damp, caused by the bad state of the roof of the church. At a considerable expense, however, the necessary repairs and restorations were made, and some of the most precious works of one of the founders of modern art thus preserved for posterity.

In the Church of the Convent of Monte Falco, in like manner, the paintings by Benozzo Gozzoli, representing scenes in the life of St. Francis, were in danger of being utterly destroyed. The apse of the church, which contained these precious relics of early art, had been shaken by an earthquake, and it was feared would soon crumble into ruin. But the liberality of Pius IX. was exercised in its restoration, and the works of Gozzoli are saved.

Another early work is to be found in the Church of Santa Maria de Toscanella, namely, "the Last Judgment," which is supposed to have suggested to Michael Angelo the picture in the Sistine Chapel; and this, too, has been the object of similar care.

The celebrated mosaics in the churches were in many

places loosened from the walls, and would have suffered serious injury if steps had not been taken for their preservation. Perhaps, of all works of art, there are no others which can be so perfectly restored as mosaics. The mode in which they are put together makes it comparatively easy, although expensive, to replace any portions that are lost, unless the damage extends over a large area of surface. The churches of Ravenna have now those rare and brilliant works restored to all their pristine beauty.

The Church of St. Bernard, at the Baths of Dio-cletian, that of Santa Maria degli Angeli, and that of Saint Mark, at Rome, as well as that of San Girolamo at Forli, have also undergone extensive repairs; and, in a word, there has been no notable work of sculpture, or painting, or architecture, in the Roman States, which has not had extended towards it a saving hand, whenever the lapse of time and the wear of centuries has threatened to deface the characters in which the genius of past ages strove to perpetuate its inspiration for posterity.

It would be an unpardonable omission not to include the restoration of the Church of St. Agnes, and the greater work of the completion of St. Paul's, which is second only to St. Peter's, and, therefore, one of the noblest of existing Christian temples.

The former work was undertaken by Pius IX., in gratitude to God for his marvellous escape, in April, 1855, when the floor of the hall in the adjoining con-vent gave way beneath him and his court. This church, which now exhibits a fine specimen of the richest type of modern decorative art, was re-opened for public worship in the January of the present year.

The latter work — the completion of St. Paul's — may be regarded as one of the most extraordinary efforts of modern times, when the vastness of the undertaking is considered, together with the short time in which it has been accomplished, and the interruptions caused alike by political convulsions and financial difficulties. To this grateful duty Pius IX. has devoted immense sums, and an energy which piety alone could inspire. The magnitude of this glorious edifice may be in some degree appreciated by its measurement; but no figures, no language, can convey an idea of the majestic effect produced by the four rows of lofty granite columns which divide the aisles from the nave. These rows of magnificent columns stretch along the marble pavement for more than 300 feet — the length of the nave — and, in spite of their regularity, impress upon the mind of the beholder the idea of a forest of pillars. The length of this grand church exceeds 400 feet, while the width of the transepts is not less than 250 feet. Had I space at my command, I might well devote more than one chapter to this glorious basilica; but necessity compels me to confine myself to this simple allusion to it, and merely to add that, by his munificence and his energy, Pius IX. has completely identified his pontificate with its splendid restoration.

CHAP. XXXI.

Pius IX. a Preserver of the Pagan Antiquities of Rome. — The
Coliseum and the Popes. — Great Repairs effected by Pius VII.
and Pius IX.— Devotions of Friday and Sunday. — Visit to
the Coliseum by Moonlight.

No one who has visited Rome, and looked around him
even with the most careless glance, but must have admitted that Pius IX. has done much for the preservation
of those Pagan remains which form one of the great attractions of the Eternal City.   Deprived of the care
and protection of the Popes, the monuments of Pagan
Rome would soon cease to exist.   The law of decay is
as inexorable as it is universal ; and the very most that
we can do, is to arrest its progress for a time.   To this
universal law the most sublime creations of the strength,
the skill, and the genius of man must alike submit.   Its
ceaseless tooth eats into the hardest bronze, and crushes
the densest marble.   But while the wisest precaution
can only delay for a time a fate which is inevitable,
neglect precipitates ruin, and ensures the destruction
of even the most gigantic monuments of human pride
and power.

Perhaps man never reared a more stupendous structure than the Coliseum — stupendous, not merely in

its size, but in its materials; and yet, were it not for the taste of successive Popes — Pius VII., Leo XII., Gregory XVI., and Pius IX. — that most striking, most interesting, and most impressive of all the monuments of Pagan Rome would now be a mass of shapeless ruin; indicating, perhaps, by a solitary arch, that here, some seventeen hundred years before, stood the Flavian Amphitheatre, on whose sands the Church of God was baptized in the blood of its apostles, its confessors, and its martyrs. To the Christian, not even the Catacombs, in which the faithful prayed and preached, is more replete with interesting associations, than the arena whereon the persecuted of centuries confronted their tyrants, and died amidst the open mockery or silent sympathy of the Roman people, still masters of the world. Even before a wise and pious policy had consecrated the Coliseum to the purposes of religion — an act for which posterity is indebted to the piety of Benedict XIV., in 1750 — its soil was sacred in the estimation of every human being who believed in the Gospel, and knew that within the encircling walls of this mighty structure was written the grandest page of the history of the Christian Church. Approach it how you may, and enter it at either end of its vast ellipse, you cannot fail to understand your obligation to the Popes, for the preservation of this noble monument, so replete with real and living associations. In other times, and it might be, in some instances, under the pressure of urgent necessity, the Coliseum was treated as a vast quarry, from which the warlike and quarrel-

some baron drew the means of maintaining his power,
or of overawing his neighbours; and from which, in less
remote periods, princely families borrowed ready materials for their sumptuous palaces.   So that, from
actual pillage, as well as from the ceaseless action of
time, a great portion of the mighty structure has been
destroyed; and at one side it has been reduced by more
than a third of its original height.   On the other side
the original line is still almost unbroken.

If you enter at one end, you perceive that Pius VII.
has reared a barrier against further ruin, in the shape
of an enormous mass of splendid masonry, which rises
from the base to the top of the outer wall.   Look again,
and you will at once perceive that, had he not done
so, that rent which, some twenty feet from it, extends
from the very top to the third arch, would have been
certainly fatal to an immense portion of the building,
and probably brought down, or materially endangered,
a vast mass of the majestic outer wall, with all its
wealth of pillar and of arch.   Such was the imminent
peril in which this end of the outer frame, or shell, of
the building was placed, that several arches had to be
built up with brick, in order to afford it sufficient support, notwithstanding the enormous buttress to which
I have referred.   Then, at the other end, Pius IX.
reared another gigantic buttress, thus placing a limit
to further decay — it may be for centuries to come.
Besides this most important undertaking, he has effected
many beautiful restorations — namely, reproducing in
travertine, or in brick, the same colour as the old ma-

terial, several arches, with their simple and chaste but most beautiful decorations — so that you may examine here, in its primitive perfection, in its clear lines and fine detail, what, just next to it, you behold worn and almost indistinct from the tooth of the destroyer. Pius IX. has done much more than this, — he has improved on the example of his illustrious predecessors, and enabled the visitor to ascend the better preserved or loftier side of the building, to within some 20 or 30 feet of the top, or about 125 feet above the present level of the arena. The ascent is easy and perfectly safe, and the view from the platform, or terrace, to which it leads, is superb. The galleries, the many flights of steps, as well as all other parts of the building, are maintained in a state of scrupulous cleanliness, worthy no less of the dignity of the sublime structure, than of the purposes to which it has been dedicated for more than a century.

On the very spot upon which many a martyr stood in the days of the more cruel of the Cæsars, the Cross is now reared aloft, and, following the beautiful outline of the arena, are placed, in niche-like altars, representations, in fresco, of the various stages of the Passion. At half-past three o'clock, on Fridays and Sundays, a procession may be seen winding its way beneath the entrance arches, preceded by a cross-bearer and two acolytes. A Franciscan Friar, clad in the coarse brown habit of his order, with sandalled feet, and the white cord encircling his waist, walks in front, supported at each side by two members of a religious confraternity, whose ordinary dress is completely shrouded in a gown and cowl, which

A A

leave nothing visible save the feet and the eyes. Other members of the confraternity follow. They are succeeded by a procession of women, many of whom are ladies of high position. Three go in front, with a cross-bearer in the centre — and, as they walk, they chant, in simple but not unmelodious tones, the hymns belonging to the particular devotion which they perform. The Franciscan then ascends the platform, from which he delivers a short but most impressive discourse, which is listened to with the greatest attention by the congregation, usually consisting of about one hundred persons of both sexes — the men standing on the one side, and the women on the other. Beside the preacher, is placed the large crucifix, with which he is enabled to produce a powerful effect, in addition to that created by his own earnestness and eloquence. The concluding appeal is invariably heard and responded to by a kneeling audience. The sermon concluded, the procession is again formed, and goes the circuit of the arena, chanting sacred hymns while in motion, and stopping at every altar, in order to recite the appropriate prayers belonging to each Station of the Cross. Even the most indifferent cannot hear those pious strains, echoing between the arches and along the corridors of this great monument of Pagan pride and cruelty, without emotion, certainly not without some association of the past. The gorgeous rites and solemn sacrifices to false gods — the heaving multitude, thirsting for innocent blood — the cruel or the cowardly emperor, the author of relentless persecution, or the slave of a wicked priesthood or a base apprehension — the fearless and holy martyr, sustained alike by the example of those who died before him, and his hope in that immortality which awaits the just ; — these visions of the past acquire a momentary shape and form, as, to the excited imagination, the ruined arches are restored to their pristine beauty, and the myriad benches, which they once supported, again rise, tier above tier, from the reddened sand of the arena, to within a few feet of the lofty cornice. That mind must be barren indeed which may not realise some picture of the past, in such a place, and under such influences.

I had frequently indulged a ramble through the building by day, and had spent hours in the enjoyment of the delicious pictures — of ruin, convent, and vineyard, of dark cypress and tall pine—framed in by some one of the open arches of the building ; and also of the wide-spreading landscape beheld from the highest platform to which the visitor can ascend ; but, like every stranger, I was anxious to afford myself a still greater treat — a view of the Coliseum by moonlight. To this I was by no means impelled by a romantic yearning, but simply because the grand old ruin presents a peculiarly beautiful and impressive aspect when beheld by that solemn and mysterious light.

At length, a more than usually favourable night afforded the desired opportunity, when two friends and myself started on our appointed pilgrimage. As we walked through the silent and almost deserted streets of the city, the moon began to make her wished-for appear-

ance, flooding a solitary piazza with light, or turning
into a shower of silver the spray of some ceaseless fountain, and brightening up house-top, turret, and dome —
everything beyond a strongly-marked line of deep, dark
shadow.   Even our harvest moon shows but a feeble
splendour when compared with the full radiance of an
Italian moon, as she slowly climbs up the dark blue
vault of an Italian heaven.   We passed by the Forum
Trajanum, upon whose lofty pillar the moonlight fell
with grand effect; and in whose well-enclosed space,
at a depth of some twenty feet beneath the level of the
modern highway, the outlines of long extinct temples
are marked by unequal fragments of columns, resting
on marble pedestals.   To this work the present Pope
mainly contributed.   Proceeding through the Via Ales-
sandrina, we passed into one of the vast halls of the
Basilica of Constantine, or Temple of Peace, which,
without the support of a single pillar, lift on high
their enormous arches; and on whose sides and roof,
like flakes of snow on a dark mountain, fragments
of marble still gleam, giving evidence of a once costly
incrustation.   We passed through the three silent halls
of this vast ruin, and thus came out on the Forum
Romanum, in which much of what is yet left of Pagan
Rome is fast mouldering into dust.   The moon lit up
this vast burial-place of the past, shedding a mournful
splendour over shattered porticos and lonely columns,
mutilated fragments of what were once proud temples
— casting a veil of brightness upon ugly mounds and
hideous chaos, that marked the spot on which a palace
once lifted its superb front to the heavens — and

making plain to the eye where the modern so-called
Capitol was joined to the remnant of the venerable
pile, which, in the hour of Rome's greatness, looked
down upon many a glorious structure, then gleaming
in all the pride of its marble beauty. We passed
beneath the Arch of Titus, abhorred by Jews, and so on
to the Coliseum — the increasing light showing clearly
what portions of the Forum had been excavated by the
Pope — what had been railed off — what pillars had been
propped or supported — what monuments were still afforded a lingering existence, for the delight of the artist,
the speculation of the antiquary, or the theme of the
moralist.

As we approached the entrance of the Coliseum, the
clash of arms, and the sharp " *Qui Vive* " of the sentry,
were a guarantee for the safety of a spot which, without such protection, might have furnished unpleasant
materials for an Italian adventure. The moon was
slowly pursuing her way up the blue sky, and gradually
rising, foot by foot, to the height of the unbroken wall
of the building, now and then peeping in through arch
or window, and, while leaving most of the vast interior
in sublime shadow, making all she shone upon nearly as
bright and distinct as if beheld at mid-day. The massive stone, the broken pillar, the jagged column of masonry, which had formerly supported the platform of the
seats — the frayed brickwork, which time had worn
away till one could almost imagine it transparent — the
uneven line of the lesser wall — the bush gently waving
in the night wind — the deep arch and its noble outline,

—every object at which the moon peeped, through opening after opening in the vast side on which she shone, was traced out with exquisite distinctness, decay thus clothing itself in transitory beauty. Patiently we awaited the higher elevation and full splendour of the chaste Dian, enjoying each new effect, as she sported with the venerable ruin, and imparted to its grim antiquity a youthful flush — mocking but delightful illusion. Higher and higher she soared, flinging a fuller light, extending her bright conquest over a wider domain; when, as she topped the giant wall, and exhibited herself to us, prosaic mortals, with somewhat of the splendour which shed its radiance on the sleeping Endymion, a troop of envious clouds, evidently enamoured of her beauty, and that lay as it were in ambush, closed in on her, shrouded her, and took her captive, — at any rate, she was snatched from our longing gaze; and so we made the best of our melancholy way back, considering the clouds to be " no better than they should be."

I have only incidentally hinted at some of the other services which the Pope has rendered to the antiquities of Pagan Rome; and indeed it would occupy more space than I can venture to devote to the subject, to give even a mere enumeration of the monuments which he has preserved by various means. For instance, it is a private house which obstructs the view of an ancient temple, or hides a beautiful frieze, rich with bas-reliefs; and the house is purchased and taken down.

In the town of Cori, there still exist valuable remains of a temple erected to Castor and Pollux; but the frieze and a portion of the columns were partly concealed by a house.   The house has been taken down, and these fine specimens of ancient art restored to view.   At Tivoli, the temple of Vesta and the House of the Sybil are now partly hidden by a portion of the Church of St. Martin ; but the ground is being purchased for a parochial church, in order to have the old church taken down, and these precious remains seen on every side.

It had long been regretted that the beautiful Arch of Trajan at Beneventum, a Papal town in the midst of the Neapolitan dominions, was partly hidden by some mean houses which were built up against its sides, and concealed part of the architecture.   For several years the intention had been expressed of removing these incumbrances from, perhaps, the finest specimens of the later classic art.   It was, however, reserved for the present Pope to carry out this improvement, so long proposed. The adjoining houses were purchased and taken down, and a portion of the arch, which had hitherto been hidden, was discovered to contain some choice bas-reliefs, which were as fresh and sharp as they were in the day when they received the last touches of the sculptor's chisel.   Thus was not only a beautiful example of architecture freed from the mean objects which concealed it, but the operation disclosed some sculptures which have not been exceeded by any belonging to the second epoch of classic art at Rome.

The ancient gate of Perugia and the Theatre of Ferentum have also had considerable sums expended on their restoration.

A A 4

The Pantheon, which owes its almost miraculous state of preservation to its fortunate conversion into a Christian temple nearly a thousand years since, has been freed, in a great measure by the present Pope, from the vulgar incrustation of mean buildings which had been built up against its eastern side. It has been carefully protected from further encroachment, by a wall and iron palisade; the old level has been also exposed by excavation; and the whole building is kept in excellent condition.

Several of the great arches which form so striking a feature in the antiquities of Rome, including those of Constantine and Septimus Severus, have been protected from a most formidable danger, which menaced their safety — namely, the accumulation of water flowing down from the Celian and Esquiline hills. The water has been carefully diverted into safe channels, and the foundations of those grand and striking monuments have been thus effectually rescued from injury.

Then every foot of the Forum Romanum speaks of the solicitude of His Holiness for the preservation of its precious relics. He has undertaken and completed many costly excavations; brought to light the base of several beautiful pillars; adopted precautionary measures to uphold tottering walls and ruined porticos; and, perhaps most valuable work of all, has had collected, and perfectly restored, splendid pieces of the frieze and cornice that once adorned the front of the temple of Castor and Pollux. For greater safety, as well as for the convenience of modern artists, these fragments have been taken to the *tabularium* of the Capitol, there cleaned up, adjusted, and re-arranged — so that the visitor might easily imagine that the whole was the work of yesterday, and intended for a building then in actual process of erection.   No monument, or fragment, that I have seen, presents to the mind so vivid an idea of the splendour as well as the exquisite beauty of the great Pagan temples, or of the genius and wealth lavished on their decoration.   One actually beholds them again gleaming in the sunlight, in all their freshness, in all their rich yet chaste and elegant ornament, with their smallest detail visible to the eye.   These restorations are a noble benevolence to the arts, and far outweigh the value of the more commonplace improvements which the Pope has made in the Forum, by the planting of four rows of trees leading from the Arch of Titus to the Arch of Septimus Severus.

The Pope has also lately unveiled the long-hidden mystery of the Appian Way, which stretches for miles beyond the walls of Rome, and was the famous promenade of the ancients, who beheld, on either side, the proud tombs of their ancestors.   In the process of this great work of excavation, many rare and beautiful things have been discovered, all of which have been carefully placed in the public museums, to enrich still further collections unrivalled in interest, and almost inappreciable in value.   There, as in other places where it exists, the old Roman way has been carefully guarded from destruction.   I cannot say much for the personal comfort to be derived from passing over a quarter of a

mile or so of this particular monument of Roman greatness. It may have been all smooth and pleasant
enough to the chariots that bore the great, the wealthy,
and the beautiful, in the days of the Cæsars ; but, as I
am no fanatical stickler for mere antiquity, I should
prefer a jaunt on a moderately well-repaired county highway in Ireland. At any rate, credit must be given to
the Pope for the preservation of those interesting relics
of the past.

The Consular Way, which conducted to the Temple
of Jupiter on Monte Cave, and was known as the *Via
Numinis*, has been saved from destruction ; so have the
ancient ways in the district of Grotta Ferrata ; and
express orders have been given to the Presidents of the
Provinces to watch over their preservation, and protect
them from injury by every available means in their
power.

The grand circular tomb of Cecilia Metella, which is
about twice the size of one of the Martello Towers
in Ireland, is now fully exposed to view, sufficient of its
marble ornaments and incrustations being left to show
what it was in the days of its pride.

For miles along the Appian Way, each side is
strewn with disinterred ruins ; a very few still exhibiting indications of past magnificence, but the greater
number being only remarkable for their shapeless de-
formity, or melancholy decay.

I should exhaust my remaining space, did I give a
list of the excavations undertaken — of the precautions
adopted in the shape of wall and buttress — of the

valuable ruins actually purchased from private persons — of the restorations accomplished — of the additions made to the collections of Greek and Roman medals — of bronzes and marbles placed in the Vatican and the Capitol; all the work of Pius IX.

The Etruscan Museum was lately enriched with some valuable bronzes, amongst the rest with a colossal torso, which is believed to have been the statue of an athlete. Some of the smaller works are a good deal in the Egyptian manner, and are very valuable contributions to a historical gallery of art.

Water is a dreadful enemy to the old monuments — it saps the foundations of arch, and wall, and pillar; and destroys, by the damp which it creates, every trace of painting in fresco. The tomb of Tarquin has been recently saved from the destroyer, the waters being prevented from penetrating the interior, and injuring the old Etruscan figures which adorn its walls. The gate and the steps by which to descend have also been restored.

Much has been likewise done for the Baths of Diocletian, to preserve portions of them from the utter ruin which has overwhelmed so many of the once famous palaces and temples of the Cæsars.

Amongst the excavations and discoveries lately made, might be mentioned those on the Palatine Hill, where, in the Palatine Garden, other traces of the Imperial Palace have been made visible, together with fragments of richly sculptured friezes, as well as part of the old walls of Romulus brought to light. In the Vineyard of the Jesuits, on the Aventine, there has been discovered and disinterred a fine portion of the old walls of Rome, built by Servius Tullius, and constructed of massive square blocks of *tufa*. To preserve this most singular relic of a remote age from destruction, the area on which it stands has been purchased from the Jesuits, who have been compensated for the expense incurred in the excavation.

Amongst the other discoveries, the result of recent excavations, may be likewise noticed the subterranean passage by which the emperors went from the Celian Hill to the Flavian Amphitheatre, more generally known as the Coliseum.

The Columbaria of the Codini Vineyard are well known. They now present the most perfect examples of the urn-burial of the ancient Romans. They have, as far as possible, been restored to the condition in which it is supposed they might have been seen in the time of the Cæsars. The vaults, which were ruinous, have been rebuilt, the Pope having expended a considerable sum for these works. The cinerary urns have been replaced in their niches, the paintings judiciously restored, the marbles and epigraphs again put in their original places, and the three vaults opened to the visitors, who can now see, at a glance, the mode in which the ancient Romans cared for the ashes of their dead.

In fact, on the mere antiquities alone, not at all including purchases for the galleries, no less a sum than 14,000 scudi was expended in the year 1855. The gross expenditure of the year 1856 on works connected

SUMS EXPENDED ON ARTS AND ANTIQUITIES. 365

with ancient and modern art, including renovations of various kinds, amounted to 244,000 scudi. For the year 1857, a much smaller sum is proposed, because of the pressure resulting from the general failure of the harvests ; but so dear to the Holy Father is the work of restoring and preserving the monuments of Pagan antiquity, as well as of Christian art, that 60,000 scudi have been demanded for the present year.

I feel I have by no means done justice to the subject ; but I venture to think I have stated sufficient to show that Pius IX. has, in his respect for the mouldering but still beauteous remains of ancient art, and for those monuments which help to illustrate one of the most interesting and important pages in the annals of the human race, displayed the enlightened liberality of a princely disposition, and the refinement of a scholar and a man of taste.

CHAP. XXXII.

The Catacombs. — Institution of the Commission of Sacred Archæology by the Pope. — The Catacombs proved to be the Burying-places of the early Christians. — Cardinal Wiseman's " *Fabiola.*"

IT would be an unpardonable omission not to allude to the eminent service which Pius IX. has rendered to the Church, through the successful labours of the Commission of Sacred Archæology ; by which a flood of light has been flung into the inmost recesses of the Catacombs, to the confusion of the scoffer, and the more profound conviction of the conscientious inquirer. This Commission has been established by the present Pope, by whom all its expenses are defrayed.

Their success has realised the most sanguine anticipations ; for not only have they discovered, and opened for inspection, new and extensive catacombs, but their investigations have established, by a variety of the most conclusive proofs, the identity of the Catholic Church of this day, with the Church of the early Christians — the Church of the Catacombs. The paintings, carvings, and inscriptions found in these burial-places of the early Christians, and which bear date as well during as after the persecutions of the Emperors, afford the most eloquent testimony to the Sacraments of the Church, and to its fundamental doctrines, — the Real Presence in the Eucharist — the doctrine of the Holy Trinity — of Prayers for the Dead — the Invocation of Saints — as well as proofs of the honours paid throughout all ages to the Blessed Mother of God.

The correct maps and plans of these subterranean cemeteries demonstrate the utter absurdity of the notion of their ever having been intended for any other purpose than that of affording a place of sepulture, and equally of prayer and sacrifice, to the persecuted Christians. To divest the Catacombs of a dangerous importance, it has been the fashion to represent them as sand-pits, opened for the obtainment of a valuable ingredient for the manufacture of cement. But the plan of the sand-pit and the plan of the catacomb — as shown, for instance, in the splendid work of M. Perret, for which the world is indebted to the imperial liberality of the French Government — are as different as two things could possibly be. The plates in these noble volumes exactly represent what I have myself remarked; for while nothing can be more unequal, irregular, and capricious, than the excavations of the sand-pit — nothing, on the contrary, can be more regular, more precise, and more mathematically correct, than the arrangement of the catacomb. Besides, the catacomb is hewed out of a material too hard for cement, and too soft for building purposes — sufficiently soft to admit of its being worked with facility — sufficiently hard and consistent not to require the aid of props for the sustainment of the roof, and the preservation of the sides. It

is quite true, that the persecuted Christians frequently
made the *entrance* to their cemeteries and places of
worship in some remote recess of a deserted sand-pit;
by which two objects were obtained — seclusion from
the eyes of their enemies, and the facility of disposing
of the produce of their excavations, without the liability
of exciting suspicion.

The thousands of inscriptions already brought to light,
many of which now enrich the Christian Museum of the
Lateran, and also the Vatican, would of themselves be
conclusive testimony to prove that the catacombs were
places of Christian sepulture.   But if any evidence were
required beyond the well known hatred and contempt in
which the Pagan Roman held the Christians, who, according to Tacitus, "were branded with deserved infamy," to prove that no Pagan would suffer a member
of his family to be buried in the same place with members
of an "abominable and impious sect," who were convicted "for their hatred of human kind," it is had in
sufficient abundance in the *columbaria* — which were,
beyond question, devoted to Pagan sepulture, — that is,
to the reception of the *ashes* of those whose bodies had
been previously burned.   One of these latter burying-
places, certainly not much more than twenty feet square,
might contain the ashes of a thousand persons ; for not
only are the urns disposed in small niches, placed in
rows over the entire face of each side, but, through the
means of a solid block of masonry, occupying the greater
part of the centre of the chamber, and rising to the level
of the main walls, four additional faces are presented—

each of which contains an allotted number of niches, or pigeon-holes, for the reception of the urns, with a marble or other slab inserted into the wall, either beside or above it, on which are cut the name or names of the person or persons whose ashes there rest.

I shall not pursue this subject farther, but merely say, that the recent discoveries, for which the world is indebted to the piety and liberality of the present Pope, have been of inestimable service to the cause of truth. Indeed, these irresistible voices, issuing from the tombs of the saints and martyrs of the Church of God, have recently brought many good and pious Christians of other communions to her fold.

With the permission of the distinguished author, I have added to the Appendix of this volume a valuable chapter on this subject, taken from a work of far less pretensions than that of M. Perret, to which I have alluded, but one which has done more than could be well described, to awaken interest in those silent resting-places of the dead. I allude to that admirable work from the eloquent pen of Cardinal Wiseman — *Fabiola*, — a work which, to the most admirable portraiture of the faithful of the early Christian Church — the holiness and heroism of its martyrs and confessors — the purity of their lives, and their fortitude in facing death — has superadded to it the interest of a romance, and the fascination of a poem. With the impressions of this charming volume fresh in his memory, the visitor to the Catacombs needs no guide-book, no chattering cicerone, — his imagination fills the void, and lights up the darkness. He beholds those little chapels crowded with hushed worshippers, and the pastor — perhaps one of the martyr-Popes — offering up the Holy Sacrifice of the Eucharist on the tomb of a predecessor who has already sealed his fidelity with his blood ; or he hears the flying feet of the betrayed congregation, and the shouts of the pursuing soldiery. I certainly confess my obligations to the author of *Fabiola*, for emotions of solemnity and awe which otherwise I could not have experienced, although the Catacombs are necessarily replete with associations of a nature at once tender and sublime.   But this volume imparts, as it were, a living interest — the interest of awakened human sympathy — to their galleries, their crypts, and their altars.*

The extent of the Catacombs already known to exist, may be estimated from the calculation, based upon the measurement of some of the more important ones, that there are about nine hundred miles of galleries in all these burial-places; and that they "may be believed to contain almost seven millions of graves."†

---

* Perhaps no work in modern literature has had such a world-wide circulation as Cardinal Wiseman's *Fabiola*.   It has been reproduced in almost every European language, and has been published in various parts of America.   There are no less than five different Italian translations of it — two French — two German — three Spanish — one Dutch — one Polish — one Hungarian — one Flemish — and one Swedish.   In Milan alone there have been 17,000 copies sold, and in England somewhere about 20,000.   Of all versions of this beautiful book, 100,000 copies must have been sold up to this moment.

† For a most satisfactory account of the Roman Catacombs, I would refer the reader to an admirable little volume, by the Rev. J. Spencer Northcote, M. A., and published by Dolman.   The writer has himself devoted the most patient attention to the subject, and also uses such materials as are supplied from the very best sources.

CHAP. XXXIII.

The Papal Government not opposed to Material Progress. — Railways.—Reasons why they have not hitherto existed.—Four Principal Lines in progress, or projected.—Gas. — The Roman Works.— Gas first started in Rome. — Electric Telegraph, its Use and Success. — Great Public Works inexpensively constructed.

IT has been too much the fashion to attribute to the Papal Government systematic hostility to material as well as to intellectual progress. England, with her network of railways, points contemptuously to the primitive modes of travelling still the rule in the Papal States, and cries out — " Lo! the result of priestly government!" Now nothing can be more unfair or unjust than the inference sought to be drawn from the admitted fact, that, as yet, railway communication does not exist to any extent in the States of the Church. Not many years since, railways were a novelty in England*, the

* At a time like the present, when a railway speed of 30 miles an hour is considered rather " slow," and 50 miles an hour is " nothing wonderful," it is rather amusing to read of the horror with which no less an authority than a writer in the " *Quarterly* " contemplates any rate of progression greater than *nine miles an hour ;* beyond which maximum speed, safety, according to the oracle, was out of the question. This remonstrance, which, however laughable it reads at the present time, must have

country of the largest capital and most resolute enterprise of any in the world; and she must not be surprised if it require a very great effort on the part of
countries with small means and but moderate enterprise
to obtain them. The resources of the Papal States are
not of themselves sufficient to the construction of extensive lines of railway; nor, as yet, is the speculative enterprise of the people equal to the risk of so great an undertaking. So that railways have to be constructed for
Rome, by foreign speculators, and with foreign capital.
And in this very fact lies the explanation of that
seeming want of energy, and that imaginary opposition
to improvement, of which we have heard so much. Now
what is the real state of things? That railway projects
in the States have been made matters of the merest
speculation, as a means of raising sums of money for
their projectors. Thus, companies have been established
— *on paper ;* and concessions have been granted to their
originators. But, while many of these schemes have
broken down, from the inability of the parties to carry
them out; in other instances, those who have obtained

had great effect in its day, is quoted in the *Life of George Stephenson,*
by S. Smiles: —

" What (said the reviewer) can be more palpably absurd and ridiculous than the prospect held out of locomotives travelling twice as fast
as stage-coaches ? We should as soon expect the people of Woolwich
to suffer themselves to be fired off upon one of Congreve's ricochet
rockets, as trust themselves to the mercy of such a machine going at
such a rate. We will back old Father Thames against the Woolwich
railway for any sum. We trust that Parliament will, in all railways it
may sanction, *limit the speed to eight or nine miles an hour, which, we
entirely agree with Mr. Sylvester, is as great as can be ventured on with
safety.*"

concession, have sold it — and thus the project has been handed from one set of speculators to another, to the indignation of the Government, and the disgust of the people. I have proofs before me of this being the fact; but it is not my duty to introduce names in such a case. There is, besides, another and sufficient reason why railways have not been established before this — namely, the Revolution of 1848, and the long time which elapsed before confidence was restored to the public mind, or before speculators of other countries could rely upon the continuance of that tranquillity which is essential to the success of such undertakings. From the first hour of his reign, Pius IX. was desirous of encouraging the introduction of railways, and he adopted such means as were alone in his power, in order to carry his wishes into effect. And, ere long, he will have the satisfaction of beholding important lines of communication connecting his capital with Naples and with Tuscany, with the Mediterranean and the Adriatic. Railways are projected northward, to the Tuscan frontier; southward, to the Neapolitan kingdom; westward, to Civita Vecchia, connecting Rome with the Mediterranean; and eastward, to Ancona, and along the coast of the Adriatic. The railway from Rome to Ceprano, on the Neapolitan frontier, is already finished as far as Frascati; and the Neapolitans are at work on their end of the line, from Capua to Ceprano. The line to the Tuscan frontier is to join that from Sienna to Florence. A considerable number of the shares in the line to Ancona have been reserved, by the Pope's desire, for his people; and stimulated by the example of the Holy Father, whose name heads the list of contributors, prelates, princes, religious orders — in fact, all classes — have entered into this national undertaking with an ardour amounting to enthusiasm.   The same applies to the other lines. Then the works on the line to Civita Vecchia are being vigorously proceeded with ; so that in a short time that port is likely to become one of considerable importance. Between Ancona and Bologna the line of railway is also being constructed.   It is definitely traced between Case Bruciate and Ancona, as well as between Faenza and Bologna.   And, indeed, the Holy Father has had the satisfaction of witnessing the progress of these latter works, during his recent .tour through his dominions. The severity of the weather did not prevent him from quitting his carriage, inspecting the operations, and addressing words of kindness and encouragement to the people employed.

Gas being a dangerous " innovation " upon oil, tallow, and wax, of course the Pope, to be consistent, must have been vehemently opposed to its introduction.   But the fact is quite the other way ; and though there have been many and grave difficulties in the path of the intelligent and energetic representative of the English company by which Rome is now lighted, that gentleman has, to my knowledge, ever found his best resource in the practical good sense and genuine kindness of the Holy Father.

I well remember my first visit to the Roman gas-works.   In company with a friend, I crossed the Tiber for the purpose of seeing some remarkable ruins, not far from the Trastevere side of the Ponte Rotto, including the beautiful little circular Temple of Vesta, with its graceful peristyle of pillars, but most abominable roof of red tiles; the temple of Fortuna Virilis; the Arch of Janus Quadrifrons; and the Palace of the Cæsars. We had clambered up, through tangled path-ways and shattered steps, to an extensive platform, or floor, formed by the roofs of a series of arched halls, then stuffed with hay and straw, but once belonging to the Palace of the Cæsars. From this lofty elevation — perhaps a hundred feet above the main road below—a splendid view was obtained; but on nothing more strange and curious did the eye rest, than upon what lay almost immediately beneath. It was an immense oblong space, half of which was occupied by a thriving and well-stocked cabbage-garden, and the other by the buildings and premises of a gas-works. At the former end, was distinctly traced the semi-circular termination of a circus, with its slanting bank, on which rows of seats had once been constructed. The top appeared to be about six feet above the soil; but, originally, it might have been as high as forty. Indeed, Mr. Shepherd, the manager of the gas-works, told me that, when sinking a foundation for the gas-tank, he had to go down a depth of thirty-five feet, and that it was only at that depth that he came upon the original soil — in fact, to the very sand of the arena. Here, then, were cabbages growing, and a gas chimney smoking, many feet above the ancient level of the Circus Maximus; and vines, fig-trees, and potherbs flourishing in luxuriant vigour above the broken arches and ruined halls of the Palace of the Cæsars!

All was activity in the works, which appeared to be admirably constructed. Amidst the gloom, and vapour, and flame of the retort-house, a number of half-naked figures, swarthy and bearded, were seen hard at work, charging the retorts — drawing out the red coke, and inserting great long scoops, full of fresh coal. These men were all Italians; not more than one foreigner — an Englishman of experience — being employed on the premises. This visit led to an introduction to Mr. Shepherd, who may be said to be the founder of gas in Rome; and from conversations with that gentleman, I learned many interesting particulars with respect to the origin and progress of the undertaking.

Mr. Shepherd obtained the "concession" in 1847, but under disadvantageous circumstances, the result of competition, and of a prevailing idea that gas could be made for something "next to nothing." The Revolution of 1848, however, put an end to all undertakings in Rome, as indeed to every description of continental enterprise. Some difficulties occurred, after the restoration of order, with respect to an arrangement of terms on a new basis; but a personal appeal to the Pope put an end to opposition, notwithstanding that learned men had pronounced against the noxious vapours of the manufacture, and prophesied all manner of frightful results to the health of the city. Even the procurement of a site was a matter of time and trouble — such were the apprehensions entertained of the deleterious and poisonous nature of the foul breath hereafter to be vomited forth into the mild air of Rome, by that modern monster, a gas-house chimney. At length, he succeeded in purchasing the Circus Maximus — or rather the soil that exists some thirty-five feet above the sand on which, some fifteen hundred years ago, the swift chariot was whirled to the goal. This site of ancient magnificence had been for centuries the receptacle of the sweepings and rubbish of Rome; and for years past, its dedication to the more profitable purpose of a market-garden had clothed it with a grateful though humble verdure. After undergoing many difficulties, and conquering many obstacles, Mr. Shepherd ultimately obtained a modified contract, and manfully set to work — being bound to light certain streets within a period of eighteen months. I remember asking him if the Pope were at any time opposed to the introduction of gas; and his answer was in these words: — "No; on the contrary, I found in His Holiness not only a friend to progress, but a patron to the judicious innovator."

The difficulties of the undertaking were greatly enhanced by the immense distance from which a large proportion of the "plant" had to be obtained. However, the purifying apparatus, the lamp-posts, brackets, and such matters, were all cast in Rome. At length, the hour of triumph arrived; and on the night of the 6th of January 1854, the Corso blazed with unusual light, not to say to the rapture, but the actual frenzy, of the Roman populace. Fortunately for the Signor Shepherd, he was not in the way, or he would certainly have received the unwelcome honours of a popular ovation.

But enthusiasm found a safe vent in several poetic ef-
fusions, in which the author of this nocturnal splendour
was compared with a considerable number of the heroes
of mythology.   Still, there were those who entertained
the firm conviction that Rome was to be scourged by
the deadly vapours emanating from the gas-chimney, and
who regarded poor Signor Shepherd as a very dangerous
person.   The fact is, the Romans are peculiarly sus-
ceptible in this respect : and such is the rarity of the
atmosphere, that even perfumes are not tolerated in a
ball-room.   However, all apprehensions were soon set at
rest by the moral courage of Prince Doria, who determined on preparing a surprise for the numerous company expected to attend the annual ball in favour of an
institution for the education of poor children, of which
Princess Doria is one of the directresses.   The Prince
consulted with Mr. Shepherd as to the possibility of
having the riding-school of the palace lit with gas for
the occasion ; and, although gas was only "started" for
the first time on the night of the 6th of January, there
sparkled, on the night of the 14th of February, amidst
the brightest foliage and the loveliest statuary, some
1200 jets of the dreaded light ! Of course, the spectacle of these lights suddenly bursting into bright and
pure flame, was hailed with a simultaneous outburst of
applause ; and as for the *savans* — why they had to give
in.   Mr. Shepherd was in ecstacy, for there was not
the slightest unpleasantness of smell, although the heat
was very great.   To use his own words — " I felt that
evening that gas was a reality in Rome."

From that moment success was certain: orders steadily coming in from all classes, from the noble to the seller of lemonade in the street. The hotels and the cafés at once adopted this brilliant innovation, and the shops gradually abandoned the candle and the oil-lamp. The following figures exhibit the progress which the consumption has made up to the present time :—

		Public Lights.		Private.
Commenced January 1854	with	200	-	525
January 1855	„	247	-	1,510
January 1856	„	280	-	2,379
January 1857	„	393	-	4,227
May 31. 1857	„	456	-	4,642

This progress is in the highest degree satisfactory, and promises speedily to reward the enterprising projectors by a far greater dividend then the 5 per cent which they now receive.

Immediately after the first lighting of the Corso, Mr. Shepherd had an audience of the Holy Father, who received him with marked kindness, and instituted the most minute inquiries with respect to the undertaking, and promised to visit the works ; but without notice and without ceremony. This the Holy Father did in a few days after, when his stay was protracted far beyond the ordinary limits. His inquiries were numerous, and much to the point ; he examined every part of the apparatus minutely, and expressed himself pleased to find that, with the exception of the head workman, all the people employed were natives. He asked Mr. Shepherd how he had managed to make workmen of them

in so short a time — if he found them willing and intelligent — and whether he thought he could depend
upon them permanently ?   The Pope listened attentively
to the characteristic reply — " Your Holiness, I pay
them well, and expect a day's work in proportion.   Having served my time to my profession, I am fully capable
of directing others ; and, lastly, I invariably adopt a
policy which I consider indispensable in the management
of workmen — I unite firmness with kindness ; and if
a man do not appreciate these, I discharge him irrevo-
cably."   " Ah ! " said the Pope, " unfortunately these
two qualities are too seldom united."

The next day, Monsignor de Merode, the Pope's principal Chamberlain, called upon Mr. Shepherd, and, in
the name of His Holiness, presented him with a splendid gold medal, and his son with one of silver.   He
also gave to each of the workmen a golden scudo.

But the Pope was not satisfied with exhibiting personal kindness to the representative of the company ;
he gave orders to have the Quirinal and the Vatican
lit with gas ; which was done as speedily as the requi-
site fittings could be prepared.   Some of these are positive works of art, for which special designs were made,
and models taken.   The lamps on the principal staircase of the Vatican are very beautiful — in fact, worthy
of . the place ; and, considering their great beauty, the
cost of each — £75 — is rather moderate.   The consumption of gas in the Vatican for a single month, in
winter, is somewhat about £40.

As yet, the price is rather high to the consumer ;

but English coal has not cost much under £3 per ton, when laid down in Rome. Fortunately, Mr. Shepherd is enabled to use a certain proportion of Tuscan with English coal; by which arrangement much expense of production is saved, and the consumer is enabled to have his gas even at 11*s.* 6*d.* per thousand feet.

I have introduced this subject merely to show the absurdity of the charges made against the Holy Father, as the alleged foe to progress; and I may conclude with the mention of two facts — the one most creditable to the honourable character of the people — the other full of significance to those who entertain vague notions of "converting" the Italians. When I was in Rome, the "bad debts" of the gas company amounted to *five pence!* — and at this moment I doubt if they exceed that amount. The other is, that in the books of the company, there appears a very considerable item set down to lights "for the Madonna." In every house, in every shop, at every street corner, is to be seen a picture or figure of the Virgin Mother; and in place of the taper, or the oil-lamp, that formerly burned before these most suggestive representations, may now be seen the pretty bracket, with its trinity of brilliant lights.

The great invention of the present age is the Electric Telegraph; and its use, either by a government or a people, is taken as an indication of progress, while its non-use is as freely set down to a blind enmity to all improvement whatever. It has therefore been alleged that the Pope would not consent to its introduction into his States; he being, according to the stupid slander of the

day, necessarily opposed to all modern "innovations."
But this allegation is as true as many more; for not only
has his Holiness established this mode of communication
throughout many parts of his dominions, but he has
set an example to all other governments, by rendering
it the medium of promoting scientific investigation.

To procure meteorological data, an active correspondence has been carried on by telegraph.   At Ancona,
the Commune gave funds to Professor Zazzini to
improve his observatory; and the Government added
the necessary means to erect two magnetic observa-
tories, one at Ancona, the other at Civita Vecchia.
Similar works have been undertaken, or improved
upon, in Urbino and Pesaro; in which latter city
Signor Guidi has constructed a complete meteorological
observatory in his own house.   Professor Respighi at
Bologna, Professor Botter at Ferrara, and other scientfic
men throughout the States, have actively concurred;
so that, in a late statistical work, the Government of
the Pope have been enabled to publish the meteorological observations of the previous six months, with
plans indicating the barometrical changes, and the
currents of the wind.   Very few of the great states of
Europe or America have directed government effort to
these subjects; yet through the whole of Italy — from
the Two Sicilies, the Roman States, Tuscany, and
Lombardy, to Turin — every important town has its
meteorological observatory.

By the latest returns, it appears that four hundred
miles of telegraph have been laid down; but since these

were published, several hundred miles in addition have been projected, or are in course of actual construction. The expense of the four hundred miles then completed had been estimated at 15,000*l.*; but the work was completed for considerably less — a result from which English engineers might derive a valuable hint. As a commercial speculation, the result has been eminently successful; as the revenue obtained from 22,383 messages, sent during the year 1856, produced to the Government a net revenue of 18,780 scudi. Decrees have been issued this year, authorising the erection of lines of telegraph from Rome to various new districts; and the Pope has given orders for the construction of telegraphic stations in all the principal places through which he has passed in his tour, and which had not already had the advantage of this valuable means of communication. So that, in a very short time hence, the subjects of his Holiness are certain to be as well off in this respect as those of any European monarch.

I shall content myself with a very brief allusion to other important works which the Pope has undertaken, as well with a view to the material improvement of his kingdom, as with the immediate object of affording employment to his people.

In the Roman States several of the great roads are not charged immediately on the locality through which they pass, but are classed as National Roads, and are maintained at the expense of the State. Amongst these, the Appian Way is one of the most remarkable; being the main entrance from the south into the ancient city.

Much of this great highway, which has been dignified with the title of *Regina Viarum*, had fallen into disuse, and become in many places almost impassable. The present Pope determined to restore it to its ancient usefulness, and even to improve upon what had been considered the grandest highway ever made by that dominant nation of antiquity, which has left, in all the countries it conquered, enduring memorials of great public works, and, above all, of roads which, for the grandeur of their design, have never been surpassed.

Amongst the improvements which Pius IX. made on the Appian Way, the most remarkable is the great viaduct which he has raised across the deep valley which lies between Albano and Ariccia. This great bridge, which is nearly a thousand feet long, and nearly two hundred feet in height, is composed of three rows of arches —the upper range comprising eighteen, the centre twelve, and the lowest, which is in the valley, but six arches, of an average span of about thirty feet. The lower piers are about twenty-five feet thick, with a depth of nearly sixty feet, and the roadway on the summit is thirty feet in the clear.

But a most remarkable fact with respect to this bridge is the very low cost at which it was executed; the economy of its construction being altogether unparalleled by any similar construction in England, notwithstanding all the mechanical aids for diminishing labour which our engineers have at their disposal. This enormous structure, containing over 100,000 cubic yards of masonry, was executed at a cost of

35,000*l.*, or about 7*s.* the cubic yard — a price which, if compared with the cost of any similar work in this country, will be found wonderfully below our standard.

Other viaducts, on a smaller scale, were also constructed on the Appian Way, beyond Ariccia. On the Aurelian Way and Flaminian Ways, works of a similar character were also executed; being in all cases the completion of works which even the great engineering genius of ancient Rome had left possibly undesigned, but at all events unaccomplished. We may instance, as one of these works, a bridge over the river Metaurus, which was contracted for at somewhere about 20,000 scudi.

Throughout the Roman States, hydraulic engineering is a matter of great importance. In many places the lands are subject to being flooded, unless the banks and beds of the rivers are carefully attended to; and, accordingly, very large sums are devoted to such purposes, as well as to securing an efficient system of irrigation of the low lands. If these works be added to the operations necessary for the partial drainage of the Pontine Marshes, it will be perceived that the public works of this class form an important item in the expenditure of the State. For many centuries the question of the drainage of the Pontine Marshes has occupied the attention more or less of the governors of Rome. And we have often wondered that, among the numerous projects proposed to capitalists by English engineers, one so near home has been neglected. If practicable, and it is hard to say what is impossible for

c c

modern engineering skill and capital to effect, it would
restore to cultivation what would become perhaps one
of the richest districts in the world.   Of course, the
difficulty of the unwholesome climate will present
itself to every mind; but it seems not unlikely that,
by selecting a proper season of the year, and other
safeguards, this great tract may be won from the waste.
The question seems worthy of examination by those
who are competent to pronounce on such matters; and
the works already in existence would contribute much
to facilitate the undertaking.   It is surely not more
removed from probability than the project now so successfully accomplished, of pumping out the lake of
Haarleem, and converting its large expanse into dry
land — a work which would have been impossible
without the aid of the steam-engine.

Some of the navigable canals of the Roman States are
also maintained by the Government; and to works undertaken by the Communal and Provincial authorities,
we find that the Roman Pontiff is ever ready to lend a
helping hand, his contributions being in many cases of
very large amount.

Were it necessary, I might give a long list of works
undertaken by the Pope mainly with a view of affording employment to the inhabitants of districts which
have suffered distress from the failure of the vine or the
olive.   But two instances in point will suffice to exhibit
the paternal solicitude of the Holy Father.   He has
lately given a sum of 50,000 scudi, out of means at his
own disposal, for the formation of a new road from

Castel Gandolfo to Marino. Such a mode of expenditure combines several advantages; it affords relief to a distressed population — it diminishes crime, including brigandage, which is principally caused by poverty—and it improves the country, by adding to the means of its internal communication. The Holy Father has granted a lesser sum, and with similar objects, for constructing a road from Ponte Lucano to Tivoli. He has likewise placed considerable sums at the disposal of the local authorities, with the purpose of employing the labourers of the poorer villages in some work of public utility. Thus, while manifesting the sympathy of a father, Pius IX. also exhibits the practical wisdom of a ruler.

CHAP. XXXIV.

The Pope a Commercial Reformer.—Steady Progress towards Free Trade. — We should not judge a small and feeble State by the Standard of a great and powerful Empire.—Singular Minuteness and Accuracy of Roman Statistics. — Material Progress stimulated by Rewards.—Proportion of Priests to Laymen.— The former preferred to the latter.—The Smallness of the Salaries of Public Officials.

Even in the first year of his pontificate, the present Pope exhibited his anxiety, not alone for political reforms compatible with public safety, but for the relaxation of those laws by which trade and commerce had been hitherto restricted. Accordingly, he then effected considerable changes in the customs tariff, by which the duties payable on a variety of articles were greatly diminished. The results of these wise changes having been sufficiently tested, more extensive alterations were carried into effect last year; and this year, the duties on silk, linen, cotton, and woollen goods, have been considerably reduced. For instance, the 100 Roman pounds' weight of silk textile fabrics, which used to pay by the late tariff an import duty of 269f., will now pay but 161f. The duties on the same weight of woollens have been reduced from 107f. to 80f.; and the duties on cotton cloths, lately at 64f., are now reduced to 32f.;

and on articles of fashionable attire, of which France possesses nearly the entire trade, the duty has been lowered from 400f. to 200f.

The Pontifical Government have been induced to make these further changes in the right direction by the striking results of the alterations effected in the duties on imports, by the new tariff which came into operation on the 1st of June, 1856. The results of the new and old systems were exhibited by returns showing the imports for the last six months of 1855 under the old tariff, and for the corresponding six months of 1856 under the new tariff. As in all countries in which a wise and liberal system has been adopted, the increase in the amount of the imports has been great in proportion to the extent to which the duty has been diminished. Thus, the duties on colonial produce were diminished by one half; and the imports of sugar show an increase from 12,000,000 lbs. in 1855, to 26,000,000 lbs. in 1856; while the imports of coffee were doubled in the same time—from 2,000,000 lbs. in 1855, to 4,000,000 lbs. in 1856. And in many other articles, including machinery, paper-hangings, carpets, &c., a similar improvement is evident.

If we, in these countries, will only look back but a very few years, and remember with what difficulty the friends of Free Trade succeeded in forcing their views even upon the popular branch of the legislature, and what a long and severe struggle it cost them before their efforts were crowned with final success, we must give credit to the Pope's government for its marked progress in the same direction; the more marked and the more creditable, inasmuch as there was in the Roman States no popular element to set in motion, and no powerful press to advocate, to excite, or indeed to overawe.

Much has been said and written of the misery and wretchedness of the population of the Papal States; but any one who will honestly inquire into the true state of the case, will find that industry is making steady progress, and that the material condition of the people is decidedly improving. The increase in the consumption of the two articles just referred to — sugar and coffee — would alone afford an indication of increased comfort. But it is idle for the people of England to contrast the condition of *their* country with that of a small and feeble state, which, moreover, has been terribly scourged, by war and revolution, several times within the present century. They should remember that they inhabit an island on whose free soil no foreign foe has set his foot for many centuries —that for nearly two hundred years they have not heard the voice of civil strife — that the wars in which they have been engaged, have never brought fire to their roof-trees, or steel to their breasts — nay, that not even the boom of a hostile gun has echoed along their shores. Therefore, when they see a government contending against great difficulties, some even chronic in their character, and struggling to bring about social and material reforms, they should not regard such efforts with derision, or thwart them by a reckless sympathy with those whose object is not reform, whether political or social—

but the overthrow of all established order, and the substitution of anarchy for civil government.

I might exhibit the anxiety of the Pope's government to promote industry, to foster manufactures, to stimulate invention, to direct the energies of the people to useful and profitable enterprises; but my allotted space has been already exceeded, and there are yet a few matters which imperatively claim some notice, however brief. I shall therefore merely say, that, in statistical works before me, I have ample proofs of the creditable anxiety of the Pope and his ministers to develope the material resources of the Papal States; and also of the wonderful accuracy and minuteness of detail by which the annual official reports issuing from the various public departments, into which the administration is divided, are characterised.* By these I perceive that useful inventions are rewarded with honorary distinctions and substantial advantages, and that energetic measures are being taken to promote the manufacture of certain staple articles of consumption. For instance, to encourage the manufacture of woollen cloths, premiums to the value of between 800*l.* and 900*l.* were bestowed in the year 1854. This system may be open to objec-

---

* Take an instance in point — the agricultural statistics—which are given with extraordinary precision. The production for every province is given of every kind of agricultural product. They are almost confusing from their minuteness ; and, assuming the details to be correct, they exceed in accuracy the statistical returns of any kingdom. There seems to be scarcely a tree planted of which there is not an account taken. The number of Olives and Mulberries planted have gone on increasing, and the planting of several kinds of trees is stimulated by a bounty. The

tion on some grounds; but, at any rate, its existence is a proof that there is no lack of interest in such purely mundane matters on the part of this " Priestly government."

And here, properly, may be said a word as to the real character of a government which is made the theme of such unsparing animadversion, and on account of which the population of the Papal States are assumed to be entitled to the compassionate sympathy of the rest of the world. A general idea prevails that the Priests absorb all the offices in the State, and that, in a word, they have the entire administration of the country in their own hands. But what is the real fact? One which unthinking revilers of the Papal Government will hardly consent to credit,—namely, that the proportion of ecclesiastics to laymen, taking into account every department of the public administration, is not greater than *one* ecclesiastic to *eighty* laymen! It would be quite unnecessary for me to repeat here the figures which will be found in detail in the Despatch of the French Am-

total number of trees planted, from 1850 to 1854, was 574,880. In 1854 the following are the numbers of trees planted:—

Pines, Firs, and Larch	6,079
Olives	27,720
Mulberries	35,279
Chestnuts	18,341
Elms	5,079
Alders, Poplars, &c.	70,073
Oranges	200
Almonds	100
	162,871

bassador, given in the Appendix; and I shall therefore content myself with asking the attention of the candid reader to the valuable explanation afforded by M. de Rayneval on this head; and quoting the following most significant statement, which effectually disposes of those fine declamations in which it is the custom to indulge with respect to this " monstrous feature" in the government of the Pope.   M. de Rayneval says : —

" But here a curious fact presents itself to our consideration.   *The provinces administered by laymen*, amongst others those of Ferrara and Camerino, *are sending deputation upon deputation to the government for permission to have a* PRE-LATE *appointed*.   The people are not accustomed to *lay* delegates.   *They refuse obedience and respect to these latter. They accuse them of confining their interest to their own families;* and there is nothing, even to their wives, which does not give rise to questions of precedence and etiquette. In a word, the government which, to satisfy this pretended desire of the population to be presided over by laymen, reserved a certain number of places for them, finds this disposition *opposed by the population themselves*."

It is all well to assert that the layman necessarily feels a profounder sympathy with his fellow-man than the ecclesiastic, whose mind is bent in one particular direction ; and that therefore a churchman is unfitted for the administration of public affairs.   Without entering into the abstract question, whether the practice of piety is not rather calculated to stimulate than destroy the best and holiest sympathies of man's nature, let us take, for instance, the administration of his diocese of Imola, or his archdiocese of Spoleto, by Cardinal Mastai

Ferretti (now Pius IX.), in which he combined temporal with spiritual authority ; and how was it possible, I ask, that any mere layman could excel him in his desire to promote the welfare and happiness of his people, or could vie with him in his all-sacrificing generosity ? He founded hospitals, orphanages, schools, asylums for the penitent ; he built churches, promoted public works, and encouraged a spirit of industry in the young of both sexes ; and most of these works were accomplished by the cheerful sacrifice of his own personal income, and the willing surrender of his private means.   However benevolent or munificent a layman may be, he cannot, if he have a family to provide for, attempt to follow such an example as that of Cardinal Mastai Ferretti, while but yet a Prince of the Church.   Therefore, the fact stated by M. de Rayneval does no discredit to the shrewdness and good sense of those who so urgently petition to have an ecclesiastic substituted for a layman.

Independently, however, of the alleged desire of the people to be ruled over by ecclesiastics, it is absolutely necessary, for the government of the Church, that its bishops and cardinals should be versed in public affairs. Besides, it is notorious that ecclesiastics, by choice and from necessity, by training and cultivation, are far in advance of other Italians in education and general knowledge.

If, indeed, it be true, that the priests " have it all in their own hands," it is rather remarkable how very moderately they contrive to pay themselves, even when *they* fill the highest offices of the State.   Thus, for instance, the Cardinal-Secretary of Foreign Affairs has the magnificent salary of 282*l*! Seven Nuncios, or ambassadors to foreign courts, have each, for the support of their respective establishments and their own income and expenses, but 1,480*l*. The Minister and Secretary of the Interior each receive 214*l*. The President of Rome and the Comarcha, 266*l*. The Minister of Public Instruction (a Cardinal) has no salary; but the Minister of Grace and Justice receives one of 222*l*. The Prefect of the tribunal of the Segnatura enjoys what, in Rome, is a considerable income, 468*l*. Twelve Auditors of the Rota, a tribunal of great importance and the highest character, have each 254*l*. The President of the Civil Tribunal, 266*l*. President of the Consulta, 400*l*. Eighteen criminal judges, each 128*l*. The Cardinal-Vicar (Patrizzi), and who, in fact, is the Pope's *alter ego* — 466*l*. The Minister of Commerce, 444*l*. The Minister of Public Works (a Cardinal) has no salary. The Minister of Arms (a secular), 400*l*. Minister of Police, 874*l*. — of Finance, 888*l*. Cardinal Secretary of Briefs, 494*l*. — Cardinal Penitentiary, 440*l*. — Revisor of Marriages (a secular) 600*l*. I must not forget the 128 Prison Chaplains, ecclesiastics of course, who receive salaries ranging from 8*l*. to 10*l*. a year! That there is no attempt on the part of ecclesiastics to monopolise the offices in the State, is tolerably well proved by the proportion of *one* ecclesiastic to *eighty* laymen, as stated by M. de Rayneval; but if further proof be required, it is had in the statistics of the Ecclesiastical Offices, which, without a charge of unfairness, might belong exclusively to ecclesiastics. Thus, while there are but 161 ecclesiastics employed in these offices, at salaries amounting to 36,120 scudi, there are 316 laymen employed, with salaries amounting to 61,836 scudi.   It may also be seen, by referring to M. de Rayneval's despatch, that the term " Prelate " does not necessarily imply a person in holy orders; but that, on the contrary, in many instances, the Prelate is in no respect distinct from the layman, save in the mere assumption of a certain ecclesiastical costume.

CONCLUDING CHAPTER.

Summary of the foregoing Chapters. — The Pope ever merciful.—
Not a single Execution for a purely political Offence.—England
ought not to encourage Anarchists. — Recent Attempts of the
Mazzini Party. — England imitates Russia when she interferes
with the Independence of small States. — The Pope's recent
Tour through his Dominions. — Its Character and Object mis-
represented. — Its real Purpose. — Liberality, Charity, and
Clemency of the Holy Father. — The temporal Sovereignty of
the Popes. — Its Importance to the Dignity of the Papacy,
and Independence of the Church.

I FEEL but too conscious that I have not done anything
like justice to the subject which I proposed to myself
in this volume, and that I have every reason to claim
the indulgence of the reader for the manner in which I
have performed my task. But, on the other hand, I
feel perfectly satisfied that I have done sufficient to
convince the honest and the fair-minded, that calumny
and misrepresentation have been busy with the affairs
of the Papal States; and that there is no justification
whatever for that fierce outcry which has been raised in
these countries against the temporal government of the
Pope.

We have seen, by the history of the first years of the
pontificate of Pius IX., how the liberal intentions of the
Holy Father were frustrated by the machinations of
wicked men, whom no kindness could propitiate, no
concessions could satisfy; but whose sole object was the

overthrow of all existing institutions, and the establishing of a state of things incompatible with the good government of the People, the dignity and even safety of the
Sovereign, and the independence of the Church. We
have seen how the chalice of bounty, presented to his
subjects by the Pope, was dashed to the ground by the
hands of assassins; and what miseries and horrors,
what anarchy and abomination, followed fast upon the
short-lived triumph of the enemies of true liberty. We
have also seen how sedulously the Pope has endeavoured
to heal the wounds which those evil days have inflicted,
and with what paternal care he has been employed in
promoting the material and moral well-being of his
people. And, unless we wilfully shut our eyes to the
truth, we must admit that the future of that people is
safe in the hands of a ruler so merciful, so benevolent,
and so just.

It is true, the assassin was rightly made to pay, with
his guilty life, the penalty of his atrocities; but, save
for the violation of those sacred laws of God, which all
communities reverence, no man's blood reddened a scaffold in the Pope's dominions.* And since the date of

* M. Thiers declared, in his report to the French National Assembly,
13th Oct., 1849, "France has not found the Holy Father less generous
or less liberal than he was in 1847; but circumstances are unhappily
changed."

And on the 18th, Thuriot de la Rosiere spoke the whole truth in these
eloquent words — "To my thinking, the mind of Pius IX. is by nature
so full of clemency, and, if I may say so, so in love with pardoning, that
he needed the example, the experience of the abominable abuse made
of it, ever to be able to bring into a soul so nurtured in sweetness and
clemency, some sense of rigour."

See also the Despatch of M. de Rayneval, in Appendix.

the Revolution, so deeply damning to the personal honour of the amnestied of 1846, the Pope has repeatedly indulged his clement disposition, by restoring to the country which they afflicted, and the position which they forfeited, those who were the prime movers and instigators of rebellion. The fear is not, that Pius IX. will not prove sufficiently merciful and compassionate to those who have raised their armed hands against his authority, but that he may, from an excessive generosity, permit the return of men who are the sworn enemies of rational liberty, and the deadly foes of the Church — who would overthrow the throne and the altar, and substitute in their place a Red Republic, and a Goddess of Reason.

With these enemies of social order the people of this empire ought to exhibit no sympathy whatever; for, to them, sympathy is encouragement, and encouragement is justification. Yet the English Press indulges in the coarsest attacks upon the character and rule of certain Italian monarchs — the Pope and the King of Naples affording a never-failing inspiration to its writers. Thus, by the most culpable misrepresentations and distortions of fact, the public mind of this country is unjustly inflamed against these governments, and an outcry is constantly raised from hustings and from platform. Even the House of Commons is not free from the frenzy of the hour; and statesmen are found wanton and reckless enough to lend themselves to the unworthy task, not alone of exciting the prejudices of their own countrymen against friendly and inoffensive states, but of lashing into

active fury the vindictive passions and deadly hatred of
the lurking conspirator. To the heated imagination and
perverted vision of the Italian refugee, the hour of
fancied emancipation is ever at hand; and, from time
to time, he sharpens with eager haste the dagger consecrated "to the downfall of tyrants"—meaning thereby all who are opposed to his views, and who detest
his principles. Scarcely has magnanimous England
hurled her denunciation against "Italian despots"—
scarcely has some disappointed politician, no longer a
minister, vented his malice from a back bench—scarcely
has a Minister of the Crown given strength to calumny,
and force to falsehood, by their reckless repetition—than
we hear of new conspiracies, new plots, new attempts
at assassination.

It has been too much the custom to slur over the
crime of the assassin, and to palliate attempts at murder, by blackening the character of the intended victim.
For instance, a knife or a bayonet is levelled against the
breast of the King of Naples—one of the most foully
libelled of living men *—and we are at once favoured
with thrilling narratives of his judicial atrocities; yes,
and by the very Press which calls upon England to
crush in blood and ashes the flames of Indian rebellion,
and by which every resistance to the authority of its
own country is characterised as an inexpiable offence.
When the dagger gleams in Naples or in Rome, it is
the sovereign or his government that is in fault. What,
then, shall be said of the late insane and infamous
attempt, not alone upon the peace of the Neapolitan

* See Appendix.

dominions, but upon the tranquillity of the dominions of
the King of Sardinia!   Remember, here was a Model
King and a Model Government—here was a Representative Constitution — here was a bold out-spoken Parliament — here, in fact, was an Italian Great Britain!
Well, I assume, for argument's sake, all this to be true
— that the king, the government, and the institutions
of Sardinia, are all which they are represented to be.
But being so, how can the recent attempt at Genoa be
accounted for, save on this reasonable assumption —
that the party which recognises Mazzini as its leader
are the enemies of all governments and of all institutions; and that the ægis of a free constitution is no
protection against the torch of the incendiary, and the
dagger of the anarchist.   This late evidence of their revolutionary impartiality should open the eyes of people
whose prejudices have hitherto led them blindfold, and
teach them the folly of encouraging, whether by pallia-
tion or approval, these pestilent enemies of true freedom.
Reason seems, at length, about dawning on the public
mind of England; and we now behold the sublime figure
of the Triumvir of the Roman Republic dwarfed to very
mean proportions indeed.   It is by the *Times* of July
23rd, 1857, that Mazzini is thus described: —

" *We regard him as an incendiary, whose murderous
designs expand in proportion to his own sense of security,
but who has no such regard for the safety of his dupes.*"

But, let me suppose the Papal Government, or the
Government of the King of Naples, to be as bad as
the most reckless assertion describes it as being — by

what right, I ask, could we attempt to interfere in the
affairs of either country? Especially, since we have
laid down the rule of non-interference so strictly in the
case of Russia, which sought to meddle in the affairs of
Turkey. Turkey was a weak and semi-barbarous government, whose existence in the midst of Christian
states was somewhat of an anomaly; nor was its internal administration entitled to peculiar respect from
European nations. But, said we, of this weak, decre-
pid, and not well-administered state, " Here is a member of the great family of nations — an independent
state — attempted to be bullied and overborne by a great
power, which assumes the right of interfering with its
internal administration, and dictating to the Sultan
what he shall do, or shall not do, with his subjects.
This gross violation of the independence of a friendly
sovereign we cannot permit : and, rather than endure it,
we are prepared to encounter all the horrors and calamities of war." And England did go to war, and did
sacrifice the lives of thousands of her people, and millions of her treasure, in vindication of this principle —
the supreme authority of Turkey over its own subjects,
and its independence of all external control. This
principle was defined by protocols, vindicated by steel,
and sealed with the best blood of the bravest European
nations. Why, then, is it to be abandoned in the case
of an Italian state? What is there peculiarly sacred
in the Turk that does not exist in the Italian? — what
should excite our sympathy for the Mahometan that
should not also command our respect for the Christian?

When we revile, traduce, and outrage an Italian monarch or government, are *we* not doing that which we reprehended in Russia? When we interfere between a Catholic sovereign and his subjects, and when we attempt to bully and browbeat a small state, are *we* not committing that very offence against the law of nations for which we punished Russia with fire and sword?

Or, is it because the Pope, or the King of Naples, is the sovereign of a *small* state, that we therefore violate our own rule, to the injury of either? Now Russia is a pure despotism, and so is Austria; and certainly the existing institutions of France do not meet with our approval. But do we attempt to interfere with the free action of the sovereigns of either of these *great* empires? Nay, let them rain down all manner of persecutions on the heads of their devoted subjects; let them imprison, scourge, strangle, if they so please; let them inflict any and every atrocity which it has entered into the mind of man to conceive — and yet will we venture to interfere? No; we do not usually violate our principles in opposition to the whisperings of our prudence. But where we have little to fear, our forgetfulness is as extraordinary, as our meddling is rash, insolent, and unwarranted.

Again, do we lash the misdeeds of Protestant Rulers, or continually denounce the misgovernment of Protestant States? The King of Naples is guilty of one grievous sin in the eyes of many in these countries — he is devoted to the Church of his fathers, which is also the Church of his people. And the Pope is the Head of that Church. Now if either happened to be other than he is — were he a Lutheran or a Calvinist — anything but a Catholic — is it not probable that we should commence to recognise virtues where we hitherto beheld defects, and even hold up to public respect the very government which we now so recklessly condemn? Does not the conduct of England, in reference to these two Italian governments, lay her open to the double charge of cowardice and bigotry? And should a great and mighty state risk her honour even by the semblance of a policy which cannot entitle her to the respect of other nations?

No matter what course the Holy Father may adopt, with a view of improving the condition of his people, it is certain to be made the subject of misrepresentation.

As an instance in point, the Pope this year resolved on making the tour of his dominions, for the purpose of seeing with his own eyes, and hearing with his own ears, what were his people's wants. And yet the Holy Father is described, by certain writers, as a mere puppet or tool, whose natural good qualities are rendered pitiable by his weakness, and who is compelled to do just what his cunning advisers require of him, and that alone. Nothing can be more unjust or untrue than what has been written on this head. The journey of his Holiness is no pleasure excursion, no mere holiday trip, no piece of state pageantry, to dazzle by its splendour and distract by its excitement; it is a grave act, deliberately resolved upon, and undertaken with a grave and solemn purpose. Pius IX. has seen too much, experienced too much, suffered too much, to love mere idle display, or to encourage, much less take delight in, fêtes and popular ovations. He has too vivid a recollection of the flowers and felicitations of his early Pontificate, not to estimate at their just value the shouts and rejoicings of an excitable population.

It is true the Pope has offered up his prayers in the cathedrals of the cities through which he has passed — that he has knelt at altars beneath which moulder the bones of the saints and martyrs of the Church — that he has visited holy shrines, and walked through historic cloisters — that he has inspected pictures of world-wide celebrity, and admired sculptures that recal the grace and grandeur of the antique; it is true that he has left a chalice of gold on one altar, and a precious reliquary on another — that he has given so many hundred scudi for the poor in one place, and so many in another; it is true that he has here founded a school, there a convent, and there an hospital; it is true that he has given orders for the completion or restoration of shrines, churches, and even cathedrals. But it is also true that he has left, or ordered to be given, large sums of money for building or improving a prison, for constructing a main road, for defending or deepening a harbour, for erecting a telegraphic station, or for the promotion of some other material object, the utility of which every one must equally appreciate. Thus, for instance, he has given 20,000 scudi towards a new prison in Perugia. At Ancona, he has promised

348,000 towards the arsenal, and the extension of the walls of that city. At Pesaro, he laid the first stone of a new fort, and promised 80,000 dollars for the work. Towards the improvement of the prisons of Faro, Forli, and Pesaro, he promised a grant of 60,000 dollars. He has given orders for the construction of telegraphic stations at Terni, Spoleto, Sinigaglia, and a great number of other places. These items are quoted at random, and merely with a view to illustrate the manner in which the Pope has prosecuted his journey, and the nature of some few of the many public works which he has encouraged by his liberality.

There is not a prison, an hospital, or a school, which has not been inspected, either by himself personally, or by his orders; and it was the first duty of Monsignor de Merode, on his arrival in every city or town, to visit its prison, thoroughly examine into all its details, and specially report upon it to the Pope. Monsignor Talbot is also with the Holy Father, and, by inquiry and suggestion, aids in the good work of laying the foundation of speedy reforms in the charitable, educational, and industrial institutions of the Papal States.

Prince Hohenlohe and Monsignor Borromeo also share in the duty of inquiring into and making reports upon every subject which it is of importance to have thoroughly understood by the Holy Father — to whom personally these reports are given.

Monsignor Berardi is represented as a kind of spy upon the actions of the Holy Father; but this able public servant is one of the most faithful and devoted of the subjects of his illustrious Sovereign, and one of the most zealous of reformers, whose ability and whose intelligence are only excelled by his anxiety to promote the material prosperity, as well as the moral welfare, of his countrymen. The progress of the Holy Father through his dominions has been no holiday work to this most laborious of officials, whose presence and services are besides essential to the due transaction of the public business.

Up to the month of June, no less than 30,000 petitions had been received by the Pope, in the course of his tour; and how many more he will have received before he returns to Rome, it would be impossible to say. But certainly there has been nothing hidden by the people from the eyes of their Sovereign.

To those in prison the Pope has exhibited his characteristic clemency, by granting six months' "grace" to all save the worst characters, whose speedy liberation would be a great evil to the community. To political prisoners he has been equally compassionate. To the middle of June, he had liberated, or "graced," twenty-four of this class of offenders. To four, who were exiles, he granted permission to return to Rome; to three he has remitted part of their punishment; and seventeen he has entirely liberated. Previous to his leaving Rome, the Holy Father had given freedom to two men, who were, to say the least, among the most prominent of the Republican party,—namely, Sturbinetti and Galeotti.

Well might my honourable friend the member for

Dundalk, when writing in answer to some of the many
misrepresentations of this remarkable journey, say—

"That progress has indeed been a glorious triumph, not
like those of the ancient Romans, accompanied by the tears,
the slavery, and the blood of the vanquished; but a triumph
befitting the Vicar of Christ, adorned by universal, unalloyed
rejoicing, unbounded munificence, true Christian charity
and devotion, and the warmest paternal and filial affection."

One other point, and I have done.

There are those who, with the utmost coolness, propose the separation of the temporal from the spiritual
authority of the Pope—who, in fact, ask the Pope to
be content with being Head of the Church, and to
relinquish his dominion as a temporal sovereign. They
say the two characters are incompatible, the one with
the other; and that the spiritual authority being that
which he is alone bound to maintain, he should abandon
the temporal.

In whose hands is the temporal sovereignty to rest?—
or by what possible arrangement is the independence of
the Holy See to be maintained, supposing the Pope
willing to abdicate his authority and functions as a
temporal ruler? Is there to be an authority superior
to his in the Papal States? If so, his freedom is lost,
and the action of the Church is more or less interfered
with. When the Revolutionary Government reigned
in Rome, the Pope was a prisoner in his own palace of
the Quirinal. Or, would it be for the advantage of the
Church—meaning thereby the Catholic Church throughout the world, whether in Protestant or in Catholic

States—that its Head should be the dependant of any
European Sovereign, whether of Naples or of Spain, of
Austria or of France?   Would his removal to Vienna
or to Paris promote his independence, and enhance his
authority?   No, no; it is for the advantage of the
Church, that the Pope should remain what he is, and
what his predecessors have been for a thousand years—
a temporal sovereign, recognised as such, acting as
such, and dealing with other sovereigns as such.   Being
such, his ambassadors represent him, in his double
capacity, in the principal Courts, and protect and promote the interests of the Church in all those countries
to which they are accredited.   The Bishop of Rome
would have as little right to send his representative to
Madrid or Vienna, as would the Archbishop of Paris;
but, as a temporal sovereign, the Pope deals with all other
sovereigns as an equal; and as temporal sovereign and
Supreme Pontiff, he combines a two-fold authority, the
one supporting and enhancing the dignity of the other.

It is true, the Church may be momentarily affected
by convulsions in Rome; but it would be permanently
endangered by any state of things which would place
its Supreme Head as a dependant on any sovereign, or
on any state, Catholic or otherwise.   It is not necessary
to quote instances in point; but not only was it the fact,
that the action of the Church was well-nigh paralysed
while Pius VII. was held in captivity by Napoleon,
but it was insinuated that certain acts of Pius IX., in
his spiritual capacity, were influenced by his residence
at Gaeta, although he was there the honoured guest of

the most delicate of hosts.   It is quite a different state
of things where certain Catholic Powers unite in the
common object of guaranteeing the Pope's temporal independence ; for, in doing so, they assist in securing
his spiritual authority, and thus preserving the freedom
of the universal Church.

What was said of the temporal power of the Papacy,
at the Council of Basle, in the 15th century, applies
equally well in the 19th : — " Virtue without force is
but slightly respected ; *and the Pope, without the patrimony of the Church, would be merely the servant of
kings and princes.*"

But, after all, what proposition is more absurd, than
this of the Pope abandoning his sovereignty as a temporal ruler !   To abandon that which has been transmitted through thirteen hundred years, from the foundation of the Western Empire ; that which has passed
through the barbarism of the dark, and the strife of
the middle ages ; that which has outlived the storms and
convulsions which have shattered so many thrones, up-
rooted so many dynasties, and even scattered so many
races of men !   Nations and empires have risen into
existence, flourished, and passed away, since there
reigned in Rome that Leo whom Gibbon so magnilo-
quently describes ;* or even since Pepin's mailed hand
tore the Exarchate from the clutch of the Lombard,

---

* Of Leo IV., the Saviour of Rome, Gibbon says : —

"This Pontiff was born a Roman ; the courage of the first ages of the
Republic glowed in his breast ; and, amidst the ruins of his country, he
stood erect, like one of the firm and lofty columns that rear their heads
above the fragments of the Roman Forum."

Astolphus; and the ambassador of the French ruler, in his master's name, presented the keys of the liberated cities before the tomb of St. Peter. "Their temporal power," says Gibbon, "is now confirmed by the reverence of a thousand years; and their noblest title is the free choice of a people, whom they had redeemed from slavery." To maintain their power, and preserve their independence—an independence essential to the sacred interests confided to their charge—the Popes have sustained a gallant struggle through long ages of difficulty and of trial; and although mighty powers have been repeatedly arrayed against them, still, thanks to an all-wise Providence, they have succeeded in baffling all their adversaries, beating back all their enemies, and preserving, whole and untouched, to the second half of the nineteenth century, that dominion which a Pepin and a Charlemagne restored to them in the ninth.

The trials and the sorrows of many a sainted predecessor have fallen to the lot of the illustrious Pope who now sits in the Chair of Peter. But though gentle as the lamb, and mild as the dove, Pius IX. is not wanting in that fortitude which calmly endures adversity, and that quiet resolution which encounters and overcomes the greatest difficulties; and in his hands is held, as a sacred trust, that temporal inheritance which he well knows to be essential, not so much to the dignity of the Papacy, as to the freedom and independence of the Church of God.

APPENDIX.

STATE OF EDUCATION IN GREAT BRITAIN.

PERHAPS it is consistent with the imperfection of human nature, that nations should depreciate the exertions made by other nations in the path of improvement, while they exaggerate their own efforts in the same direction. If any nation be more prone to this weakness than another, it is the British nation. But the special objects of its unwise depreciation are the Catholic nations of Italy, and, before and beyond all others, the States of the Church. That England is a mighty, powerful, and progressive country, not her most prejudiced enemy can deny. But while she supplies the world with her manufactures, and she carries her commerce into every sea ; while her railways form a perfect network of intercommunication, and the largest ship ever constructed is now ready to be launched into the Thames — she is *not* progressing equally in other respects. Her material progress is that of a giant — her intellectual and moral progress is that of a dwarf. Education is *not* keeping pace with the manufacturing or the commercial greatness of the country. On the contrary — if the deliberate statements, the official reports, of public officers are to be relied upon — education is retrograding, not advancing. Indeed, the case may be put still more strongly— namely, that unless some vigorous measures be adopted, and speedily, too, we shall behold the increase of England's material prosperity become a source of misery and evil such as wise and thoughtful men regard with the gloomiest apprehensions. The demand for labour — infant labour — thins the school ; and the necessities or the greed of the parent render the " education" which the child receives rather nominal than real. Children stay a shorter time in school, and leave it at an earlier age, than ever; and this evil, which is a fundamental one, is every year *on the increase.* No doubt, the State is not idle ; neither are the friends of education less active than before ; but the fact is, education for the mass of the people is not progressing as it ought, and bears not the most remote approach to the material prosperity of the country. Mr. Marshall, one of her Majesty's Inspectors of Schools, says, in his General Report for 1855, published 1856 : —

" It seems *a kind of unreality* to vaunt the improved qualifications of teachers, however reasonable the boast may be, when we have ascertained the *character of their pupils*, or to enumerate complacently the ' square feet'—a considerable arithmetical calculation—which make up the ever-increasing ' area' of school-buildings, *when we know how fitfully and vagrantly they are tenanted.*"

Such, in fact, is the manifest growth of the evil referred to, that nearly all the Inspectors hint at—if they do not suggest — a *compulsory system of education* for Great Britain.

Mr. Macaulay, in the House of Commons, called attention to the fact that, " from the registers of marriages, we find that out of 130,000 couples married in the year 1844, more than 40,000 of the bridegrooms and more than 60,000 of the brides *could not sign their names*, but made their *marks.* Therefore, one-third of the men and one-half of the women who are supposed to be in the prime of life, and who are destined to be the parents of the next generation, cannot sign their names. What does this imply ? *The most grievous want of education.*"

We shall now see if things have materially improved since then.

That there seems to be no national love of education, the reports concur in showing. Mr. Marshall says, " The children themselves are naturally slow to appreciate the value of education, and their parents often *either profoundly indifferent, or stubbornly hostile.*"

The Rev. D. S. Stewart, in his report for 1855, says : —

" I have no hesitation in saying that in the counties which I have visited in the year to which this report refers, I have *not met any instances of that laudable anxiety for education which is at times so flatteringly ascribed to our working classes.* I have found the *parochial clergy* in many places tending to *relax* their efforts to make schools effective, on account of *their inability to overcome the indifference of the labouring people.* I could also point out examples of schools built in anticipation of a large attendance of children which are almost deserted."

Mr. Marshall gives a striking instance in point of the conflict carried on between material and educational progress — between the factory and the school-room : —

" During the last year more than one very painful example of the inevitable triumph of factories over schools, whenever they come into conflict, has fallen under my observation. Such cases appear to me worthy of record. At Cheadle, in Staffordshire, where there are very beautiful schools erected by the munificent liberality of the late Earl of Shrewsbury, and where two years ago there was a very large attendance of children attracted by teaching of an unusually high order, I found at my last visit that the numbers had dwindled away to less than one half. The explanation will be anticipated. In the interval a *factory* had been established, and the energetic proprietor had gained an easy victory over the devoted but defenceless teachers. Wages had made short work of education. The prospect of a few shillings extra per week was an irresistible bait, and the young scholars, reluctant victims of a cheerless but inevitable lot, had fled *en masse* from the school to the mill. The parents, no doubt, were enriched by the weekly gains of their children, *but the district fatally impoverished by the irremediable loss of all that wise instruction, skilful training, and edifying example would have conferred upon it.* It is only the disciples of a very rigid school of political economy who can exult in such a change as this. I think it may even be doubted whether, in the long run, the *material* well-being of the population will be promoted by it. Augmentation of income is no benefit in itself, if coarse, wasteful, and unthrifty habits accompany it ; and surely where discipline and instruction are banished, the whole troop of *diræ facies, inimicaque numina,* may be expected to come thronging in their place."

Nor, if we are to rely on the authority of the Rev. W. J. Kennedy, in his report for the same year, does the *system* of education appear to be entitled to very high praise. He says : —

"I confess I think there is truth in the statement that *those who leave our National schools deteriorate intellectually rather than improve ;* and I do *not* think this is satisfactorily accounted for merely by the *early* age at which they leave. I think there is a serious defect both in the end (τέλος) and means of our schools. I incline to the opinion that the aim of our National school should be, to give the boy, not knowledge, but power to acquire knowledge ; that we should think more how we can make him, not an educated boy, but a self-educator. We should not load him with facts about common or uncommon things, but develope, by some well-chosen studies, his understanding and his thinking faculties. I fear that at present, even in our better schools, our National school-boy skims over too many things, that all is too superficial with him, and made too easy for him. He is not subjected to those exercises, those wrestlings of the intellect, those trials and struggles and fierce persevering battles of the mind with intellectual difficulties, out of which combats alone issues that intellectual being who thenceforward feels that he has attained a certain elevation from which he can never be displaced ; that he has got a power within himself for coping with and mastering almost any intellectual study. *   *   *   *   *

"The result to which I come is this : that the present course of our elementary schools, being *too superficial,* embracing *too many subjects,* and those *not the best* subjects, does not so develope the minds, *even of those children who stay longest in school,* as to induce and enable them generally to continue their education at their leisure hours ; *but that, in fact, they retrograde as intellectual beings.*"

The Rev. H. L. Jones, writing of the schools inspected in Wales, calls on the four Bishops of the Established Church to unite at once, if they wish to rescue religious education from utter extinction : —

" Before concluding my report, I cannot help alluding to a more important subject, which I have touched on in previous years — the *religious education* given in parochial schools. I wish to allude to it only in a few words, and as delicately as possible, and yet as strongly. It is my deliberate conviction — a conviction which I am bound to express to your lordships—that, *unless religion* in the parochial system of Welsh education *is to fall away*, instead of advancing, the *immediate* and *united* action of the *four bishops* is imperatively necessary. *Anarchy and neglect and incapacity* are not the means whereby the righteous cause of this all-important branch of instruction is to be promoted. Whether the children come of parents who belong to the Church, or of those who belong to the different religious denominations, *the result is the same for all.* These three sources of evil are of more frequent occurrence than they should be ; and some means of obviating them must be found, or religious instruction will suffer greatly from the result."

But it appears that the mill, and the factory, and the workshop, are not to be held accountable for empty schools and bad attendance beyond a certain point : for, even in England, there is a vast proportion of children equally without employment and without education. The Rev. H. Moseley states this with great clearness in his Report for 1854 : —

" It has been customary to assume that the children of the poor are *not sent to school because they are sent to work;* and we find an excuse for this in the poverty of the parents. *There can be no greater error;* and the census has come very opportunely to disabuse our minds of it. It tells us that, of the children between the ages of three and fifteen who are *not at school,* there are 978,179 boys, and 1,283,840 girls *who are not at work,* being *forty per cent.* of the total number between those ages of the *former,* and *fifty-three per cent.* of the *latter.*

" The number between those ages not at school because they are at work, is comparatively a small proportion. It is 381,776 boys, and 218,055 girls, being 16 per cent. of the whole number of the former, and 9 per cent. of the latter. It is difficult to understand that the children of the poor who are not at school, and not at work, should be anywhere else than in the streets, where we know that the ranks of juvenile delinquency are filled up. Out of every 100 children in this country of an age to go to school 57 *remain without education, for no other assignable reason than that their parents are indifferent to it;* and 16 per cent., because the children are required to support themselves at a time when it was intended that they should be provided for by the labour of their parents."

Alluding to the short time during which children remain at school, the same gentleman says : —

" Thus what is gained, on the one hand, by the improvement of the schools, is lost, on the other, by the earlier age at which the children are taken away from them; and your lordships' efforts for the education of the people are practically defeated ; there being probably *as many people as ever in this country, in proportion to the whole population, who are growing up unable to read and write.* Every other impediment appears in process of removal but *this.* We seem to be in the way of getting schools, which if they were duly appreciated by the poor would, perhaps, be adequately maintained, and we are getting excellent teachers; but in *this* respect no progress is being made."

In a note, he thus qualifies the assertion which he makes in the foregoing : —

" I do not mean people who, when they were little children, *began to learn* to read ; but who, as men and women, were capable of reading well enough to be able to derive profit and instruction from reading. I doubt whether the number of these, in proportion to the rest of the community, is increasing."

The Rev. F. Watkins concludes an able and thoughtful report, for 1855, in terms which, if employed by any other than a conscientious public officer, bound to speak the truth, would be set down as a gross libel upon the English people.   Such a statement, coming from such a source, ought, at least, to make those who read it somewhat more merciful to the shortcoming of other nations, even though they happen to be Catholic nations.   The Rev. Mr. Watkins says : —

" But it is impossible for any earnest man to be satisfied with even the most intelligent instruction if it produce no higher results, if it have merely an intellectual or commercial value, and bring forth no fruits *in the moral and religious life.*   The operations of your Lordships' Committee have now been continued for fifteen years. For the last ten years those of your Minutes which have had the most tendency to improve the position of the teacher and elevate both his character and attainments, to form and support a class of efficient assistance to him, and furnish his school with all appliances and means for its great objects, to aid in all those points where assistance is most needful, have been acting upon and penetrating into the elementary education of the country.   In that space of time at least three school-generations have passed away and entered upon their work in life.   We are justified, therefore, in looking for results not instructional only, but educational; — results such as these, *greater steadiness of conduct in young people, more truthfulness both of word and action, more thoughtful obedience to parents and all in authority, more cheerful contentment in the state to which God has been pleased to call them; in short, a more truly religious life in the humble but hearty endeavour to do their duty towards God and towards man.*   If there be

E E

little or none of this higher life, then there is little or no education. And if you ask of those who are best able to judge of the moral and religious state of the rising generation, if you ask of the *clergy*, of *magistrates*, of *manufacturers*, of *official people* whose position gives them information on this important subject, or of those—now not few —earnest men who devote their time and their talents and their wealth to the redress of social evils and the well-being of their fellow-countrymen, the answer is not often satisfactory. You hear of a few isolated cases of improvement, you hear of many going on in the old and broad way. *On all sides you hear of the little regard paid by young people to parental authority, of the great love of dress, and carelessness about running into debt, of pleasure-seeking at cost of time, money, and character; above all, of the increase of drunkenness, that fruitful mother of all other vices.* It is impossible, my lords, to hear all these constantly reiterated statements, and to be convinced of their general accuracy, without feeling that, whatever may have been earnestly and rightly attempted towards the education of the working classes, *there is but little yet really done;* enough, perhaps, to show us the way by which further attempts may be successfully and more speedily made, but altogether insufficient to satisfy any one who does not wilfully shut his eyes and stop his ears to the sights and sounds of the every-day life of the working classes of this great country."

A few extracts from the reports presented to Parliament this Session (1857) will enable the reader to understand whether there has been any considerable improvement within the last year.

The Rev. F. Cook, in his General Report on the Schools inspected in Middlesex, says : ——

"It is, however, obvious, that in no one district is the attendance sufficient, either as regards the age to which the children remain, or the time during which they are under instruction in the same school, to enable a fair proportion of them to receive a systematic education in the elementary subjects, much less in the mental training and moral discipline which are acknowledged to be indispensable. This fact is the more painful, *inasmuch as the returns represent the condition of the* BEST *schools in every part of England.*

"In London, moreover, as I have before remarked, a vast stratum of ignorance, misery, and vice, underlies that portion of the population from which our National Schools are recruited. The evil is *enormous :* so far from diminishing, *it increases steadily.* Every year witnesses the absorption of a *large number of young children into the vortex of crime, or vice and destitution*, which appals the philanthropist, and seems to present hopeless embarrassment to statesmen.

"It cannot be doubted, looking at the returns for the last six years, that the number of boys and girls under instruction to the age of 13 or 14, *is far below a fair standard. It shows no tendency to increase.*"

Rev. H. W. Bellairs, reporting on the schools inspected in the counties of Worcester, Warwick, Oxford, Gloucester, Hereford, and Monmouth, complains that the early removal of children from school *continues in the same proportion as before*; and declares his opinion, that no measures which do not meet the question of early removal from school, will produce a general system of education for the poor. He adds : —

"Juvenile labour, or the indifference of careless and dishonest parents, are the causes of our schools being so imperfectly filled ; and, until some remedy or mitigation of this evil be found, it is hopeless to expect those results for which so many persons are crying out."

He quotes an extract from a letter written by the Rev. G. S. Bull, Rector of St. Thomas', Birmingham, who writes:—

"One of the chief hindrances to education is the mischievously early removal of children—say of *mere infants*—to our workshops, warehouses, or factories. Many leave us before they can do more than spell their Maker's name, and repeat His Ten Commandments, or the simplest truths of the Gospel."

Rev. F. Watkins, writing of the schools of the County of York, states that the number of children in attendance at the schools has *fallen off* within the last, as compared with the previous year ; that while, in 1855, the attendance reached to 63 per cent. of the accommodation provided, it fell off to 61 in 1856. He also complains of the increasing evil, of the early age at which the children leave, and their short stay in, the schools. "The evil," he says, "is not only not arrested, *but it is increasing.*" And he adds, "*It is a radical, deeply seated, and widely spreading evil,* not at all confined to any district, *but nearly, if not quite, as mischievous in* ALL *parts of the country.*"

Yorkshire contains rather more than one-tenth of the whole area of England and Wales, and not quite one-tenth of the population.

Rev. E. Douglas Tinlings, in his report on the schools in Dorset, Somerset, Devon, and Cornwall, says, "The greatest difficulty which we have to combat in the elementary schools, is the early age at which the children are removed from school, an evil which certainly does *not diminish.*"

Rev. W. J. Kennedy, reporting on the schools of Lancashire and the Isle of Man, makes this remarkable statement : —

"This absence of real interest in the education of the people, appears to me to be one of the most real and important facts of our time, and yet one which is not duly perceived. *The truth, as I believe, is, that comparatively few persons in Lancashire feel any real concern to see the people at large educated.* A few persons make a good deal of noise on the subject ; and a still fewer number carry on the work liberally and zealously, though without talk and noise; but the *mass of persons are still hostile*, or *at best indifferent* on the matter. *A public feeling for education has yet to be created.*"

This latter sentence Mr. Kennedy himself marks in italics.

With one more authority, the case is concluded. The Rev. T. Wilkinson, in his report on the Episcopal Schools of Scotland, has the following : —

" It appears to be the general impression, that this evil (the short time during which children stay at school) is *on the increase*. *It is aggravated by every fresh demand for juvenile labour,* AND SEEMS LIKELY TO GROW WITH THE MATERIAL PROSPERITY OF THE COUNTRY ; until parents in general become sufficiently enlightened to purchase education for their children at the cost of some present sacrifice."

The Educational Conference, suggested by some of Her Majesty's Inspectors of Schools in their reports to the Council of Education, was formally opened on Monday, June 23 of this year. It was presided over by His Royal Highness the Prince Consort; from whose address the following passage is taken. Speaking from official sources — the most recent which could be had — he gives a gloomy picture of the boasted juvenile education of England. The Prince Consort, in fact, states that, out of 4,908,696 children between the ages of three and fifteen, *there are nearly three millions who receive no instruction whatever.* Here are his own words : —

" But what must be your feelings when you reflect upon the fact, the inquiry into which has brought us together, that this great boon thus obtained for the mass of the people, and which is freely offered to them, should have been only *partially accepted,* and, upon the whole, so insufficiently applied as to render its use *almost valueless ?* We are told that the total population in England and Wales of children between the ages of three and fifteen being estimated at 4,908,696, only 2,046,843 attend school at all, *while* 2,861,848 *receive no instruction whatever.* At the same time an analysis of the scholars with reference to the length of time allowed for their school tuition shows that 42 per cent. of them have been at school less than one year, 22 per cent. during one year, 15 per cent. during two years, 9 per cent. during three years, 15 per cent. during four years, and 4 per cent. during five years. Therefore, out of the two millions of scholars alluded to, more than one million and a half remain only two years at school. I leave it to you to judge what the results of such an education can be. I find, further, that of these two millions of children attending school only about 600,000 are above the age of nine. Gentlemen, *these are startling facts,* which render it evident that no extension of the means of education will be of any avail unless this evil, which lies at the root of the whole question, be removed, and that it is high time that the country should become thoroughly awake to its existence and prepared to meet it energetically. To impress this upon the public mind is the object of our conference."

I shall only ask, in conclusion, have *we* no glass to repair in our own house, before we venture to throw stones at other people's houses?

HOW LUNATICS ARE TREATED IN SCOTLAND.

THE following extracts from the " Report by Her Majesty's Commissioners appointed to inquire into the State of Lunatic Asylums in Scotland," which has been presented to Parliament this Session, exhibit a state of things that, if it were told of the Papal States, of Naples, or of any *Catholic* country, would draw forth one universal outburst of Protestant execration, and be adduced as a conclusive proof of the baleful effects of Popery.

It would be a gross injustice not to state that the Commission, from whose report the extracts are taken, owes its origin to the benevolent enterprise of an American lady, Miss Dicks, who visited Scotland in 1855. Scotland may thank this female Howard that so terrible a cause of reproach, especially in such an age as this, is about being put an end to by legislation.

The Report deals with chartered asylums, licensed houses, poorhouses, and prisons. It appears that the licensed houses are the worst-managed of all. That they are so will cease to be a matter of astonishment when the following description of the " proprietors " of such establishments is considered : —

" Thus, at Musselborough, we found one proprietor whose previous occupation had been that of a *victual dealer ;* another had been an *unsuccessful baker ;* another had been a *gardener;* and the last person who had obtained the sheriff's sanction for a license, was a *woman keeping a public-house,* who had taken a second house for the reception of lunatics, with the view, as we were told by her daughter, of keeping both for a while, and *continuing that which should prove the most successful speculation.* "

As a specimen of the provision made for the " sick, feeble, and aged," this passage will suffice : —

" *Few or no arrangements are made for the proper treatment of the sick, feeble, and aged inmates.* They share the very scanty and insufficient

E E 3

accommodation provided for the able-bodied, and when, from sickness or debility, they are unable to sit up on the forms without backs that are provided, they are kept in bed, and ultimately die in the dormitories in the midst of the other patients; and, in some cases, after death *the body is carted to the burial-ground, and there interred without any religious ceremony whatever.*"

Ecclesiastical management may be a very bad thing; but in what institution in which monks, nuns, or priests have the smallest authority, would such a state of things as is here described be tolerated? —

" Notwithstanding any regulations to the contrary, we have reason to think that, in *most* of the licensed houses, the *attendants* have the power of applying restraint *at their discretion.* In *almost every house*, we found *handcuffs, leg-locks, gloves, straps,* and *strait-waistcoats,* and these not in the custody of the proprietor or medical attendant, but hanging up in the wards, or in the rooms of the *attendants,* who were evidently without *any check* as to their application, showing that the practice of restraint is still very prevalent."

Instrumental restraint appears to be the grand specific for the treatment of the malady :—

" Instrumental restraint is in very general use *in all the pauper-houses,* and not unfrequently also in the houses for private patients. There are houses in which some of the paupers are *constantly manacled,* either with the view to prevent their escape, or to keep them from attacking the attendants or patients. The strait-waistcoat is in daily use."

The proprietors — for instance the unsuccessful baker, the speculating public-house keeper, or the broken-down gardener — allow to themselves the amplest discretion in the use of their remedial agents : —

" In some houses, two medical gentlemen are in the habit of attending, each taking charge of a certain number of patients; but generally the *proprietor* orders the *shower bath, seclusion, or mechanical restraint,* to be applied *at his own discretion, without even consulting them.* The consequence is, that mechanical coercion is applied *and continued* in these houses to a considerable and *much greater extent than is known to the medical officer.*"

The beauty of the modern treatment for mental alienation is further exhibited : —

" That a certain number of the patients, males as well as females, *were stripped naked at night,* and that in some cases two, and in one case even *three* of them, were placed to sleep in the same bed-frame, on loose straw, *in a state of perfect nudity.*"

Delicacy is thus sufficiently provided for : —

" Frequently, also, there is *no proper separation of male and female patients,* who are placed in adjacent apartments, approached by the same stair or passage, who use *the same airing-courts, and are not even provided with separate water-closets.*"

A kind of democratic impartiality is manifested in the treatment of different classes of patients : —

" We have, in our descriptions of the various houses, noticed several instances where the accommodation was inferior to what the patients *had a right to expect for the sums paid on their account.* As examples, we may here mention two of the worst cases that came under our cognizance. Two male patients were confined in Hillend Asylum, near Greenock; *both had occupied respectable positions in life,* and the payments made for them were respectively 53*l.* 11*s.* and 35*l.* per annum. These sums should have secured them comfortable accommodation ; but at the time of our visit they shared a small bedroom with a *third* patient, and for months had slept together, *entirely naked, in a miserable trough-bed, upon a small quantity of loose straw.*"

The influence of religion is not esteemed of very particular importance, even in workhouses, as a means of assisting the cure of the insane : —

" There are some houses, such as that of the Abbey Parish, Paisley, in which *no clergyman ever visits the insane wards, and in which the patients never attend any religious service.* At Falkirk, also, they have no religious exercises, except when the *governor* reads prayers, which he does, *perhaps,* every second Sunday.*"

Restraint appears to be popular in the poor-houses : —

" As a general rule, the attendants are not in sufficient number to insure the proper treatment of the patients, and the consequence is, that *personal restraint is habitually had recourse to in almost all the houses.* The strait-waistcoat and leather muffs are generally left in the keeping of the *attendants,* to be applied *at their discretion.* The Burgh Parish Poor-house, Paisley, is the only house in which we did *not* find instrumental restraint in use. A practice prevails in some workhouses, as in a few of the licensed asylums, of *fastening the hands behind the back,* by which *much unnecessary pain* is inflicted on the patient.*"

Here is an instance of rough treatment inflicted on a woman, and in one of the Queen of England's jails, too : —

" As an example, may be mentioned the case of a *woman* who was brought from Orkney to the Edinburgh Asylum in March, 1856, in charge of a *sheriff-officer ;* and who, on her arrival, was found to be in a state of great exhaustion, having about *six ribs broken on each side of the sternum.* According to the patient's declaration to the Procurator Fiscal of Edinburgh, the injuries were caused *by the attendant in the jail* at Kirkwall *putting his foot on her breast* to enable him to secure her with straps or ropes. It was said that she had then been very violent and destructive.*"

E E 4

The extracts from the report may be fittingly concluded with the following cases, which it would be difficult to parallel in any country:—

" A case is detailed in the last report of the Perth Asylum. 'Patients,' it is there said, 'have been brought to us tied hand and foot. One *young woman*, who was perfectly quiet and affable on admission, *had been tightly strapped to a window shutter for several days prior thereto.* Her *wrists, fingers, and ancles were œdematous, and covered with unhealthy ulcerations ;* and she has since lost the use of a finger by suppuration into, and disorganisation of, the joint, induced by pressure of the ropes with which she was bound.'

" The report of the Montrose Asylum for 1855 contains similar statements : 'Several cases, as formerly,' it tells us, 'have been brought to the house, under restraint, all of which have had their liberty granted at once, without difficulty or danger. One of them, a married *female,* deserves notice. *A strong piece of wood was inserted bit-wise between the teeth, and firmly secured by a strong cord tied behind the neck.* The reason assigned was that the patient had severely bitten her tongue.

" ' The *instrument of torture* was at once removed, with great relief to the sufferer. On its removal, *both angles of the mouth were ascertained to be in a state of ulceration,* from the pressure of the wood, and *the tongue presented a fetid and sloughing mass to the depth of an inch.* The patient was in so anaemic and exhausted a condition as to render recovery almost hopeless. She has, however, done well. She still labours under a certain degree of mental depression, and some impediment of speech, from the loss of so large a portion of the unruly member.' "

It should be added, as a matter of justice, that the Report, from which these extracts are taken, was most ably used by a Scotch Member (Mr. Ellice) in a speech of great force and deserved effect, delivered in the House of Commons, on the 29th of May, 1857.

The *Times* of the 30th thus concludes a stinging commentary on the debate of the preceding night: —

" Such is the picture which Mr. Ellice, relying on the Report, gives of the present treatment of Lunatics in Scotland, — a country which, *though blest with two Church Establishments, a body of stipendiary sheriffs, and a judicial bench quite out of proportion to the work it has to discharge, seems to have known nothing of these abominations.*"

BRITISH ADMINISTRATION IN INDIA.

If England were to be judged by her administration of her Indian Empire, it would go hard with her ; for, notwithstanding that she is an eminently Christian and enlightened nation, it were impossible that the inhabitants of the different provinces into which that vast empire is divided, could be much worse off, if at all worse off, under their former chiefs and princes, whom it is the policy of our times to describe as everything savage, barbarous, ruthless, and bloodthirsty. How far this misrule—sufficient instances of which shall be adduced—is attributable to the supineness of the British public, it is now unnecessary to inquire; but one thing is pretty certain, namely, that if they devoted the same, or anything like the same, attention to the affairs of India — for the happiness and prosperity of whose inhabitants they are answerable before man and God — that they do to the internal affairs of other countries, such as Naples or the Roman States, it would be better for the millions of India, and more creditable to themselves.

It is not necessary to grope back half a century for evidences of wrong and oppression — nor would it be fair or just to do so ; the more especially, if the wise and vigorous administration of the present time were obliterating the traces of remote disorder. But let the reader judge of the existing state of things in two presidencies of India—Madras and Bengal—as described, not by tourists or romance writers — not by the pen of hostility and prejudice—but in authentic documents, emanating from official sources, and published by order of Parliament.

The application of *torture*, no matter in what country or for what purpose it is applied, is repugnant to the feelings of every humane and enlightened man; but torture is not one whit the less odious and revolting, because it is practised on the person of a wretched and defenceless Indian peasant. Let us see if this inhuman and barbarous cruelty be really practised upon *British subjects!* That torture *is* applied, freely and constantly applied, as a means of collecting revenue, extorting bribes, and eliciting evidence, is placed beyond question by the following evidence taken from the " Report of the Commission for the Investigation of Alleged Cases of Torture at Madras ;" which report was printed by an order of the House of Commons, July, 1855.

This " Blue Book " extends to over 300 pages, and teems with the most startling facts ; but the following selections will suffice to give an

idea of the general character of the entire.   The evidence of two
Protestant Clergymen may be quoted, in the first instance :—

"The Rev. H. A. Kaundinya, missionary of Mangalore, details instances in police cases from his personal knowledge :—

" ' I lived formerly in the neighbourhood of *a police-office*, and saw
daily that the prisoners were *beaten, flogged, and ill treated.*   I know also
for certain that, for the purpose of *extorting confessions from women, a
disgusting application of red pepper is sometimes employed.*'

"The Rev. L. Verdier, of Tinnevelley, heard flogging going on ; he
writes as follows:—

" 'Flogging is used in many places : once I have myself heard it
from inside my house at Callivoolum, in the talook of Vulleyore, *and it
was so severe I could hardly take my dinner on account of the sensation
it caused me.*   It is about five years since the fact I relate now took
place.' "

Mr. A. M. Simpson, a merchant of Tripasoor, mentions a cruel
case, of which he was a personal witness, but which occurred " so long
back" as the year 1845 :—

" I mentioned it, however, to justify my belief that the practice does
exist.   It occurred in the coach-yard attached to the cutcherry of the
tahsildar of Burdwai (in the Cuddapah district), in the presence of the
tahsildar and curnums of the village ; I there saw *at least a dozen ryots,*
who were *in arrears of kist, undergoing the ordeal.*   They were all
ranged in the court-yard, *under a meridian sun,* in the hottest period of
the year (if I recollect rightly, in the month of May).   *They all had
heavy stones placed either on their heads or on their backs between the
shoulders.   Their bodies were bent double,* and several of them were kept in
*that position standing on one leg, the other being raised from the ground
by means of a string going round the neck and round the big toe.*   I was
in the cutcherry probably for *two hours,* certainly more than one, and
none of them were released from this painful position during *that*
time."

It is not necessary to add more than the following evidence, given
by eye-witnesses, in order to prove to the fact of torture being administered to British subjects :—

"Mr. Fischer, the mootadar or proprietor of Salem, writes as follows:—
  "Of the *habitual use of violent and illegal means of more or less severity* by the native revenue servants of Government, in the collection
of revenue in every district of this presidency, with which I have
become acquainted, I am constrained to make of my own knowledge
positive affirmation.   But I am not prepared to depose to specific acts,
and which can be substantiated, of violence or torture ; for this simple

and I submit sufficient reason, that I have not been accustomed to take notes thereof, though accident has *often made me a witness of such doings.*"'

Lieutenant Tireman of the Commissariat, writes that *he heard and saw a native undergoing torture,* but when in the Road Department he was thrown much among natives, whom he frequently questioned, *and one and all spoke of it as a matter of course.*

The Commissioners sum up in these words : —

"Such a body of evidence from *credible, and nearly all European, eye-witnesses,* is to our minds *conclusive.* It has been adduced, it will be observed, from *all* parts of the Madras territories."

The report contains the statements of several natives, who had personally suffered torture, inflicted upon them either with a view of collecting—rather extorting — revenue, or eliciting evidence. *Rungial Chatty* states : —

"'We are treated in this way every year, and occasionally we are made to cross our fingers, when the peons seize the tips and squeeze them together, which gives great pain. Some of the men were kept in a stooping posture, by the peons holding down by the hair lock, whilst others are placed astride on their backs. Occasionally the peons twist their ears, and make them walk backwards and forwards. In the absence of the male branch of the family, they take the female to the cutcherry.'"

The following is taken from the statement of *Subapathy Pillay,* in which he gives an account of the cruelties inflicted on his brother, in his presence : —

"'On his arrival at Doorgum, instead of taking him to the chavady, they took him to the traveller's bungalow, outside the village. I was taken there myself. There they asked him where he got the cloth ; he said he purchased it at Sooboo Chetty's shop ; they then told him that if he would confess that he and Sooboo Chetty stole the cloth they would let him go ; they *tied his legs, hung him up with his head downwards, put powdered chilly in his nostrils, and put an iron wire in his penis ; they passed a strong tape round his waist, and tightened it.* There was a crowd assembled ; this was in the daytime ; the windows were opened ; many people could see ; he called on two or three persons standing by to bear witness : he was then taken to the chavady. At night he was again beaten. I was present.'"

Let the Commissioners now describe the different modes of torture, inflicted, be it remembered, on British subjects, and in the second half of the nineteenth century. The milder system is employed to "collect" the public revenue : —

"The descriptions of violence commonly in vogue for revenue and private extortion purposes which have been spoken to in the course of this inquiry are as follows : keeping a man in the sun ; preventing his going to meals, or other calls of nature ; confinement ; preventing cattle from going to pasture by shutting them up in the house ; quartering a peon on the defaulter, who is obliged to pay him daily wages; the use of the kittee anundal; squeezing the crossed fingers with the hands; pinches on the thighs; slaps; blows with fist or whip; running up and down ; twisting the ears; making a man sit on the soles of his feet with brickbats behind his knees ; putting a low-caste man on the back ; striking two defaulters' heads against each other, or tying them together by their back hair ; placing in the stocks; tying the hair of the head to a donkey's or buffalo's tail; placing a necklace of bones or other degrading or disgusting materials, round the neck, and occasionally, though very rarely, more severe discipline still.

"That the 'anundal' (in Telugu 'gingeri'), or tying a man down in a bent position by means of his own cloth, or a rope of coir or straw passed over his neck and under his toes, is generally common at the present day, is beyond dispute ; and we see no reason to doubt that the kittee (in Telugu 'cheerata') is also in frequent use. It is a very simple machine, consisting merely of two sticks tied together at one end, between which the fingers are placed as in a lemon squeezer; but in our judgment it is of very little importance whether this particular form of compression be the one in ordinary use or not, for an equal amount of bodily pain must be produced by that which has superseded the kittee, if anywhere it has gone out of vogue, the compelling a man to interlace his fingers, the ends being squeezed by the hands of peons, who occasionally introduce the use of sand to gain a firmer gripe ; or making a man place his hand flat upon the ground, and then pressing downward, at either end, a stick placed horizontally over the back of the sufferer's fingers."

But the sublime of atrocity is reserved to further the ends of justice! Such a catalogue is enough to make the blood freeze with horror. Surely, such a damning reproach as this ought to be wiped away from the British name, before we venture to point the finger at any other government or country : —

" Among the principal tortures in vogue in police cases, we find the following : *twisting a rope tightly round the entire arm or leg so as to impede circulation ; lifting up by the moustache ; suspending by the arms while tied behind the back ; searing with hot irons ; placing scratching insects, such as the carpenter beetle, on the navel, scrotum, and other sensitive parts ; dipping in wells and rivers, till the party is half suffocated ; squeezing the testicles ; beating with sticks ; prevention of sleep ; nipping the flesh with pincers ; putting pepper or red chillies in the eyes, or introducing them into the private parts of men and women ; these cruelties occasionally persevered in until death sooner or later ensues.*"

So much for torture ; which, according to Lord Dalhousie, in a letter dated the 22nd of Sept. 1855, is practised " in every native state of India, *and in every British province.*" And now with respect to the state of the police and the administration of justice in Bengal.

On Thursday, the 11th of June, 1857, a debate took place in the House of Commons, on the motion of the hon. member for Perth (Mr. Kinnaird), who proposed the following resolutions : —

"That, from representations made to this House, there is reason to believe that the present administration of the Lower Provinces of Bengal does not secure to the population the advantages of good government, but that the *mass of the people suffer grievous oppression from the police, and the want of proper administration of justice :* that, in the opinion of this House, it is desirable that her Majesty's Government should take immediate steps with a view to the institution of special inquiries into the social condition of the people ; and to ascertain what measures have been adopted in consequence of the oppression under which a large proportion of the inhabitants of the Lower Provinces are now said to be suffering, more especially with reference to the system of landed tenures, the state of the police, and the administration of justice ; and also that such report be laid upon the table of the House."

In the course of his statement, the hon. member laid down this fair proposition, one that must meet with general concurrence : —

"This House would agree with him that a Government that did its duty should at least secure to the subjects of the Government these four things : — 1, the administration of justice ; 2, security to life and property ; 3, protection to all classes, poor as well as rich ; 4, and lastly, exemption from excessive taxation."

Mr. Mangles, Chairman of the East India Company, was on this occasion the spokesman and organ of the Court of Directors ; and he thus admitted the whole case : —

"Bengal, which was perhaps the *oldest British possession in India, was, as regarded the affairs of internal administration, in a very bad condition,* and the East India Company would spare no pains or expence to remedy the present state of things."

But having admitted all that was urged on the other side, he gently pleaded in extenuation of the disgraceful fact, by appealing to the character of the miserable race who were to be ruled. In a word, they were some thirty millions of " monkeys." Mr. Mangles thus heaps up evidence against the Bengalees : —

"With respect to the opinion of Mr. Dorin, he could only say that he was perfectly ready to support the statement that the inhabitants of Bengal were an extremely timid people, and that their want of energy was so great that it was very difficult to provide for them any institutions likely to prove of advantage to them, inasmuch as they had not the spirit necessary to maintain their own rights. Mr. Marshman, who knew Bengal well, represented the task of endeavouring to deal with the people of that province as only to be compared to carving in rotten wood, while Mr. Macaulay described the Bengalee as being devoid of courage, and his physical organisation as feeble and effeminate. There were very few Bengalees in the Indian army, and, indeed, the general impression was, that one might as well enlist *a monkey* as a Bengalee for a soldier. Such, then, was the material upon which the Government of Bengal had to work, and he should appeal to the candour of that House to say whether the task of providing a good government for such a people was not one in which great difficulty was involved."

This miserable apology was thus answered by Lord John Russell, who justly said : —

" Then comes Mr. Dorin, and he, differing from Mr. Halliday, says it is a law of nature in such a population as this, that there should be nothing but tyrants and slaves ; and he seems very tranquilly to make up his mind that there are tyrants and slaves in that community, and that tyrants and slaves there must ever be. I should say, no doubt, that the timid and unwarlike character of the population has been the great means by which we have been enabled to conquer that country and establish over it the government of Great Britain, and that *we* have no right after that to turn round on them and reproach them with their timidity, and say we do not mean to give you that full protection which is necessary and desirable."

It appears from official documents, relied on in the debate, that *the Police committed one-fourth more murders and robberies than the rest of the population.*

I have now before me a "minute" of the Hon. F. G. Halliday, Lieut. Governor of Bengal, on this subject ; and it fully corroborates the description of the state of things given in the statement of Mr. Kinnaird, who mainly relied on the representations of certain missionaries. The Village Watchmen are thus represented : —

" *They are all thieves or robbers or leagued with thieves and robbers,* insomuch that when any one is robbed in a village, it is most probable that *the first person suspected will be the village watchman.*"

Mr. Halliday quotes from the report of the Commission of 1837, and then shows that nothing practical has been done in the way of remedy for the twenty years which have intervened since then : —

" 'The most urgent necessity exists for a thorough revision throughout the country. The establishment (of village watchmen) is described not only as utterly useless for police purposes, but as a curse instead of a blessing to the community. *It is even a question whether an order issued throughout the country to apprehend and confine them would not do more to put a stop to theft and robbery than any other measure that could be adopted.*' "

" Various plans have been proposed for amending this state of things, and a good deal of paper has been covered with written discussions regarding them, but nothing has ever been done ; so that many persons have come to think it a thing impossible to do any good in that direction, and have ceased from all effort accordingly."

Mr. Halliday, in the two following paragraphs of his minute, gives a pitiable picture of the manner in which criminal justice is administered to a population of thirty millions of British subjects, and of the increase of heinous crime in consequence : —

" *That a very small proportion of heinous offenders are ever brought to trial is matter of notoriety.* It now appears that *half* of those brought to trial are *sure to be acquitted.* Is it to be expected, then, that the people should have confidence in our system, or that they should show any desire to assist the police, knowing, as they do, from experience, the miserable results to be obtained?

" I must say that this appears to me the weakest point of our whole system, and that which most loudly calls for an effectual remedy. No doubt the badness of the police and the inefficiency of the tribunals act and re-act on each other, and both are concerned in bringing about the deplorable existing consequences. *But until the tribunals are re-formed, I can see no use in reforming the police,* and I think it will be money thrown away to attempt the latter, unless we are determined vigorously to insist on the former. *We have been hitherto debating about both for many years without much practical effect,* and in the meantime, to take only one crime, and only the seven districts round about Government House, we have seen dacoities increase from 82 in 1841, to 524 in 1851! It is true that under a special agency this has since been reduced to 111 in 1855. But the operations of this agency have shown more than anything else the utter inability of our ordinary institutions to cope with the enormous social evil that is ever rising up in defiance before it."

Comment on the foregoing is unnecessary. Or if it be required, it may be given in one sentence from an article in which the *Times* of Saturday, June 13th, referred to the debate of the previous Thursday : —

" The solid fabric of British power *weighs on them* (the people of India), *but does not shelter them.*"

Since the foregoing was put into the printer's hands, the British Public have had a far more startling commentary pronounced upon the administration of affairs in India — in the revolt of the native troops at Meerut, where they massacred their officers ; and in the subsequent capture of the ancient city of Delhi by the mutineers, and the barbarous slaughter of Europeans which followed. These disastrous events, which certainly are not the most conclusive evidences of wise and paternal government, occurred in the early part of the month of May of the present year.

"REPORT FROM THE COUNT DE RAYNEVAL, THE FRENCH ENVOY AT ROME, TO THE FRENCH MINISTER FOR FOREIGN AFFAIRS.

(Copy.)

"*Rome, May* 14, 1856.

"MONSIEUR LE COMTE,—At this moment the situation of the Pontifical States pre-occupies more than ever the different cabinets of Europe, and particularly the government of the Emperor in the twofold point of view of the interests of Catholicism, and of the armed protection with which France and Austria surround the holy chair. This question is contemplated under so many different aspects, it is so perverted by the spirit of party, it excites in one sense and another such vehement passions, that a truthful and impartial review of the facts appears not inopportune.

"Though the accusations brought against the pontifical government may be greatly exaggerated, it is undoubtedly vulnerable on one side; its territory is occupied by foreign troops, and it is questionable whether it can dispense with this support. Every independent state is expected to suffice for itself, and to be able to maintain its internal security by its own forces. The Court of Rome is reproached with falling short of this reasonable expectation; the cause of its weakness is inquired into, and it is generally believed to be the discontent awakened among its subjects by a defective administration.

"The real cause of the weakness of the pontifical government is a much more complicated one, and is, in fact, connected with quite a different class of ideas; but it is a much more convenient and rapid mode of arriving at a conclusion to complain of the administration, than laboriously to interrogate the history and the tendencies of the Italian race The discomfort and discontent of the populations arise more especially from the fact that the part played in the world by Italy is not that of their visionary aspirations. This sentiment of nationality has been sensitively alive at all epochs, and the temporal power of the Papacy has constantly been considered the main obstacle to its gratification. During the last two centuries the general prosperity of the pontifical system, and the abundant resources which flowed to Rome from all parts of the world, silenced complaint. But the great changes which have taken place in Europe during the last fifty years have dried up the sources of Rome's affluence. The Church has been compelled to remain contented with the revenue derived exclusively from its own territory. Hence discomfort, which, increasing from year to year, leads the minds of men by an easy process to discuss and attack the acts of their government. The Papacy, protected till this time by a great *prestige*, begins to sink in the estimation of the people. The last traces of the ancient ecclesiastical sovereignties have disappeared from the rest of Europe. Our fathers, accustomed to the sight of these sovereignties, saw nothing singular in them. In the eyes of the new generation one government of this kind, left alone in the world, becomes an anomaly. Criticisms on this score multiply. At the same time the constitutional system, which easily seduces the people, has gradually established itself in a majority of states. Men ask themselves whether it is conformable to the genius of the age, whether it is respectable to obey a priest, and perpetuate a superannuated system. Besides, how would it be possible to establish a system of liberty and free discussion, in presence of a power which lays claim to infallibility in spiritual matters, and rests exclusively on the principle of authority? How create a powerful Italy so long as the peninsula is divided into two distinct parts by a state, neutral from the necessity of its nature, and isolated from all European conflicts? How play a great part when the centre of Italy is in the possession of a Sovereign who does not wear a sword? Other causes, not less powerful, have encouraged these hostile tendencies. Italy had always wielded the sceptre, not, indeed, of war or politics, which are not exactly in its line, but at least of civilisation, science, and art. All felt that this sceptre was falling from her hands. The hundred voices of the press daily informed the Italians of the progress of their neighbours, and proved to them that they had been outstripped in many points. If— thanks to the blindness of national self-love — this sentiment has not yet become universal, at least a great part of the population feels itself threatened in the last entrenchments of its legitimate pride — a new and terrible grievance for which to hold the governments responsible. In the meanwhile the loudly avowed tolerance of several cabinets for the complaints made by the populations, was not, it must be confessed, one of their least encouragements. At present it is the most active of all, and the one to which the hopes of all those turn who wish for something different from what they possess. On a soil thus prepared, insurrections and revolutions could not fail to germinate with facility. They turned the country topsy-turvy, and left deep traces. The momentary victory obtained over the Papacy completely stripped it of its *prestige*. It was no longer the sacred ark against which no effort could prevail. In vain it heaped concessions upon concessions; the very principle of its existence was called in question. The idea of its ceasing to exist became familiar. Hostile passions derived new strength from the consciousness of a probable success where, till of late, success would have seemed impossible; more than ever the national vanity attributed its wounds to an administration marked out for attack by the peculiarity of its character. The prejudices against what is called a government of priests reached their culminating point.

"It is necessary at this stage to offer a few remarks on the peculiar genius of the Italians. The most prominent feature of the national character is its intelligence, its penetration, its quick comprehension of everything. This precious gift, which Providence has disseminated over Italy much more profusely than elsewhere, and which still shines with all its pristine lustre, is dearly purchased, except in a few remarkable exceptional cases, by the utter want of such qualities as energy, strength of mind, and true civil courage. It is seldom that the Italians are seen firmly united amongst themselves. Always suspecting each other, they are continually separating; no one has any

F F

confidence but in himself; they remain isolated. Hence they have no commercial or manufacturing associations; no common understanding; no combination either in private or public affairs. With such dispositions they are destitute of the essential element of public power; they are totally devoid of organised strength. Armies — which are knit together by the reciprocal confidence of the soldiers, and obedience to the general — are impossible. The ranks are complete on parade; but in the hour of danger the chiefs are accused of treason, and the soldiers have no reliance on each other. This defective equilibrium of intellect and character of the Italians is the key to their whole history, and explains the state of political infirmity in which they have remained, in comparison with the other peoples of Europe. Left to themselves, they have never been able to do anything but debate in public places; give the victory ultimately to extreme parties; wear themselves out in fruitless agitations; divide and subdivide themselves to infinity; and yield up their country to the first occupants— Frenchmen, Spaniards, or Germans. Every nation pays the penalty of its own defects; but how is it possible to make it comprehend that its inferiority is attributable to itself, and not to its government?

" It is the fashion to take the Piedmontese for Italians, and to quote them as an example of what may be expected from the Italian populations.

" This is a great error. The Piedmontese are an intermediary population, containing much more of the Swiss and French element than the Italian. One fact is sufficient to convince me of this. It is that they possess that true military and monarchical spirit which is unknown to the rest of Italy. The Italian mind with respect to policy and administration is by nature directed towards middle terms, accommodations. The interpretation is considered to be above the law itself. Following religiously the traditions which have been preserved of ancient Rome, jurisprudence is a governing principle. This tendency is met with everywhere. It has occasionally a very happy influence on the progress of great affairs, but in practice it leaves to government a very great latitude, and takes away from the authority of the law in the eyes of the governed, encouraging them in a singular manner in all manoeuvres which may spare them from the rigorous application of rules. An inflexible law would be odious to them; an administration keeping close to the letter of the law, without compromise, would appear in their eyes insufferably harsh. Let us examine the possible wishes and tendencies of the population at this moment. They formalise their complaints much more than their plans. With respect to their plans, it may be said that they are almost as numerous as individuals. In the lower depths of society, Carbonarism is kept up; it still continues to make recruits. The dagger here is still held in honour. The end to be attained is the upsetting of every social hierarchy. The followers of Mazzini form already a class in some degree above these. The universal republic, the unity of Italy, constitutional government, war against Austria, is their programme. They say that they are a numerous body, and are ready to act, but they never keep their word. Directed by the committees of London and Geneva, their watchword for the present is quiet and inaction, until the return of their chiefs by means of an amnesty, and the departure of the foreign troops, give them an opportunity of operating with a chance of success. This section extends to a certain portion of the middle class. This class, and the higher classes in general, are tormented with the desire of taking a part in public affairs.

"The example of Piedmont is turning their heads. A constitution *à l'Anglaise* is in their eyes marvellously adapted both to the manners and wants of the country. They desire for themselves and for their country a great line of action. They look upon themselves as disinherited. Convinced that the presence of the Pope is an invincible obstacle to the realisation of their projects, they earnestly pray for the annihilation of the pontifical power. The greater portion of the members of this party have coalesced with the followers of Mazzini, leaving it to the nation to decide between the two parties after the victory is obtained. Refusing to go as far as the English constitution, there is a certain number of individuals who profess attachment to the pontifical government, and at the same time overwhelm it with their attacks, pretending that they limit their desires to the obtaining of a better administration. They are not able to define exactly what they mean by this. In their eyes everything depends upon government, even to the proper maintenance of their own houses, and the direction of their own affairs. If enterprises everywhere reserved for the efforts of private industry are not developed in the Roman territory, the reason is that the government places obstacles in the way. Attributing all the acts of the administration to motives exclusively personal, and such as are founded on the basest calculations of interest, they believe that public affairs and the profit derived from conducting them, are in the hands of a small number of monopolists, who exhaust the resources of their country for their own advantage. They dream of nothing but dishonesty and collusion. Taxed, as they are, more lightly than the majority of European countries, they complain that they are crushed under the weight of fiscal imposition. At the same time, they complain of the State for not undertaking great works which it is their duty to undertake themselves. Ignorant of the first principles of political economy and administration, they enunciate systems utterly opposed to the lessons of experience, when they are compelled to formalise a project. Finally, they profess to have a great fear of the Mazzinians, and at the same time are opening the door to them.

"Lastly, there is a party which attributes every evil to the abandonment of ancient errors. If we could return, they say, to the ecclesiastical *régime pure et simple*, as it existed formerly, excitement would be appeased, and every difficulty would disappear.

"Between these parties there is a numerous crowd very indifferent to everything else but their own prosperity, fond certainly of grumbling, but friends of order, and living on good terms with the pontifical government. Anywhere else such a party would furnish the government with a good *point d'appui*; but in a country in which the spirit of enterprise, and the energy necessary for any resistance whatever, are absolutely unknown; where the only universal rule is *laisser faire*, with the reservation of the right of complaining when the thing is done, instead of beforehand, how can such friends be trusted, and how can the destinies of the state be placed solely in such hands? Here is the grand difficulty. No government can dispense with material assistance, and this condition cannot be fulfilled in the Roman States. Whichever of the whole number of parties has the luck to triumph, it is an indubitable fact that it will see forming around it, as has already been proved, the same assemblage of complaints which is directed against the present government. The same difficulty which the actual government experiences in finding *points d'appui* in a land which is not able to furnish them, will be experienced by every party which gains power. The party which limits its wishes to reforms when incapable of defending itself, on account of no one being willing to compromise himself in its defence, will give place to the constitutional party ; this will in turn yield to the Mazzinians, which, thanks to measures of violence on their part, and carelessness on the part of others, will remain definitively masters of the situation. This will represent accurately the inevitable march of events whenever the present equilibrium is again disturbed.

" Pius IX. showed himself full of ardour for reforms. He himself put his hand to the work. Every one is acquainted with the catastrophe which ensued. What happened then would be reproduced exactly in our days.

" Here, then, we have a nation deeply divided, animated with burning ambition, without any one of those qualities which make the greatness and the power of other nations, stripped of energy, devoid of military spirit, as well as of the spirit of association, knowing nothing of the respect due to law or to social superiorities: and this nation, being discontented with its lot, accuses its rulers, who are in reality bone of its bone and flesh of its flesh. How can we dare to hope that, to meet the difficulties of so complicated a situation, it is sufficient merely to introduce a few reforms into the pontifical administration ? Verily such a remedy appears little adapted to the disease, and it is not easy to see what alleviation even it might produce. If the populations had a real cause of complaint against the pontifical administration, and if their wrongs were founded upon this single cause, the receipt would be excellent; but I have enumerated at length the true causes of the sad condition of the populations, and I have not been able to see that anywhere these causes were in direct connection with the mere mode of administration. Fundamentally, the very principle of government is the point in dispute, and not the mode of putting it in operation.

" What grave reproaches can be made against the pontifical government, and what an idea is formed of the men who compose it? Is it possible that they are devoid of that intelligence which is so richly scattered over their nation ? Can it be that they have so small a sense of their duties and interests as to place, of their own accord, an obstacle in the way of the prosperity of their country ? It surely would not be just to condemn them blindly, and without a rigid examination of their conduct. It is a general opinion that the pontifical administration is placed entirely in the hands of the priests. It is asserted that the priest, whose lot it is to defend the interests of Heaven, understands nothing of the interests of earth ; that having no family of his own, he is utterly indifferent as to the prosperity of the country ; that, dwelling apart from society, he cannot understand the true wants of society ; that the *esprit de corps* is more powerful with him than the feeling of nationality, and so on. People are unwilling to believe that the priest employed in the civil service by the Court of Rome has no sacerdotal character during the great portion of his time, and that far from monopolising the whole of the administration, he has but a small share in it — he is in a minority. I have often asked ardent opposers of the Roman rule what was their valuation of the numbers of priests employed in the administration. In answer to my question the number was generally stated to be about 3000. No credit was given to me when I showed, with the proofs in my hand, that, putting them altogether, the number did not exceed a hundred, and that the half of these pretended priests were not in orders. It is nevertheless upon data of such falsity that are founded grave charges which are accepted by the public as undeniable.

" At a time when the character of the pontifical government gave rise to no ground of objection, the Church understood thoroughly that the part of the priest destined for the altar, and that of the administrator of public affairs, might possibly clash on some occasions. The Church then opened the door to the lay element, by the institution of the *Prélature*, and reserving for it a certain number of places even in the Sacred College. The *Prélature* increases and receives continual augmentations from a class of men who are specially destined for administration. Certain conditions of education and fortune are imposed upon these men. But lately they have performed their duties entirely at their own expense, and thus lightened the weight of the budget.

" So important a position as this yielded to the incumbent a few years back only 600 scudi annually. Since then, in order to render such offices accessible generally, the emolument has been increased in a moderate degree. The Roman prelates are not at all bound to enter into holy orders. For the most part they dispense with them. Can we then call by the name of priests those who have nothing of the priest but the uniform ? Is Count Spada, brother-in-law of Père Beauveau, a more zealous or more skilful administrator now than when, in the costume of a priest, he officiated as Minister of War ? Do Monseigneur Matteuci (Minister of Police), Monseigneur Mertel (Minister of the Interior), Monseigneur Berardi (substitute of the Secretary of State), and so many others who have liberty to marry to-morrow, constitute a religious caste, sacrificing its own interests to the interests of the country, and would they become all of a sudden irreproachable if they were dressed differently ? If we examine the share given the prelates, both priests and non-priests, in the Roman administration, we shall arrive at some results which it is important to notice. Out of Rome — that is, throughout the whole extent of the Pontifical States, with the exception of the capital — in the Legations, the Marshes, Umbria, and all the provinces, to the number of eighteen, how many ecclesiastics do you think are employed ? Their number does not exceed fifteen — one for each province, except three, where there is not one at all. They are delegates, or, as we should say, prefects. The councils, the tribunals, and offices of all sorts, are filled with laymen. The number of these latter amounts to 2313 in the civil service, and 620 holding judicial employments — in the whole 2933; so that for one ecclesiastic in office we have 195 laymen. Is it possible for the most prejudiced intellect not to recognise that an ecclesiastical power which has reduced to so low a figure the number of the men of its order who are the depositaries of power throughout the whole extent of its territory has already reached its lowest limits? Who will believe that this is an intolerable abuse, and that the danger will cease when this small number of prelates shall disappear from the scene? But here a curious fact presents itself to our consideration. The provinces administered by laymen, amongst others those of Ferrara and Camerino, are sending deputation upon deputation to the government for permission to have a prelate appointed. The people are not accustomed to lay delegates. They refuse obedience and respect to these latter. They accuse them of confining their interest to their own families, and there is nothing even to their wives which does not give rise to questions of precedence and etiquette. In a word, the government which, to satisfy this pretended desire of the populations to be presided over by laymen, reserved a certain number of places for them, finds this disposition opposed by the population themselves.

" In the city of Rome, the centre of government, the number of prelates, whether priests or non-priests, engaged in the administration, is necessarily more considerable than in the provinces. Nevertheless, the numerical superiority in favour of the laymen is still striking, and leads to the same conclusions. These are the statistics reckoning by ministerial departments. The office of the Secretary of State for Foreign Affairs, not reckoning those employed abroad, is comprised of 5 ecclesiastics and 19 laymen. The principal of these ecclesiastics, such as the Cardinal Secretary of State and his substitute, are not priests any more than the greater number of the prefects who are marked here as ecclesiastics. The Council of State reckons 3 ecclesiastics and 5 laymen. The Ministry of the Interior comprises 22 ecclesiastics, including among them the 15 presidents of provinces, of whom I have already spoken, and 1411 laymen. The Ministry of Finance reckons 3 ecclesiastics against 2017 laymen. The Ministry of Commerce and Public Works reckons 2 ecclesiastics to 161 laymen. The Ministry of Police, 2 ecclesiastics to 404 laymen. The Ministry of War has not a single ecclesiastical functionary. The Ministry of Justice, including the superior tribunals, which are of a mixed nature, reckons 59 ecclesiastics to 927 laymen. This number of 59 ecclesiastics is divided in the following manner :

" In the Ministry, 1 ecclesiastic, 18 laymen.

" In the Tribunal of the Segnatura (Cour de Cassation), 9 ecclesiastics, 8 laymen.

" In the Tribunal of the Rota (the superior court of civil jurisdiction), 12 ecclesiastics and 7 laymen.

" In the Civil Tribunal, 3 ecclesiastics and 116 laymen.

" In the tribunal of the Consulta (the superior court of criminal jurisdiction), 14 ecclesiastics and 37 laymen.

" In the Criminal Tribunal, no ecclesiastics and 58 laymen.

" In the Tribunal of the Bishop, 9 ecclesiastics, 17 laymen.

" In the Tribunal of the Apostolical Chamber, 9 ecclesiastics, 16 laymen.

" In the Provincial Tribunals of First and Second Instance, both criminal and civil, 620 laymen, no ecclesiastics.

" In the Archives, Chamber of Notaries, &c., 16 laymen, and no ecclesiastics.

" In different offices, 1 ecclesiastic, 6 laymen.

" Fundamentally the tribunals are the nurseries of the Roman prelates. There it is that they serve their apprenticeship and prepare their career.

" In order both to surround itself with administrators wearing the ecclesiastical dress, and to introduce not only into the administration, but also into the Sacred College, and even to the very throne itself, those enlightened views gained in practice by experience in business, and at the same time, as I have already said, to open the door to the lay element, the Court of Rome has always sought to group around it a certain number of men chosen with care, who have no desire to be priests, and to whom a career is opened. Twelve or fifteen prefects' places in the provinces would not suffice for recruiting, apprenticeship, and recompence of services. The superior tribunals have been reserved to satisfy this imperious necessity. The total number of ecclesiastics employed in the interior of the Pontifical States does not exceed the number of ninety-eight. Against this we find there are 5059 laymen in office. This gives fifty-two laymen to one ecclesiastic.* Leaving out of consideration the superior tribunals of the capital, some of which, like that of the bishop, have exclusively ecclesiastical attributes, we find that there are only thirty-six ecclesiastics employed for the whole administration of the Pontifical States.

" The employments reserved for this small number of individuals are not the merely secondary ones. The places which they fill are the most important, otherwise their influence would be *nil*. It is right to say, also, that in spite of prejudice the ecclesiastical habit still inspires a certain degree of respect, which aids the action of government. The people pay no deference to the lay functionary, and do not forgive him his superiority in rank and office in the same manner as they forgive an ecclesiastic.

" I have seen formerly, and I see still, lay functionaries exposed to personal attacks much more violent than those to which ecclesiastics are liable. This is no doubt a contradiction, but it is nevertheless an incontestible fact.

" Is it possible to believe that the happiness and the repose of the populations are powerfully affected by the presence of such a small number of persons, who, I repeat, have for the most part nothing of the ecclesiastic but the habit? Evidently the question does not lie in this

---

* Since the date of the official summary, from which I obtained all these details, the development in all the ministerial departments has been such that the number of laymen, either actively employed or at the disposal of the government, has risen to about 8560. The Consulta is occupied with the task of reducing it to 6000. The number of ecclesiastics remains the same. The proportion in favour of the laics is now as 80 to 1.

direction, because it is not here that we must seek either for the evil or the remedy. On the side of the opponents, however little they may understand the true situation of things, the secularisation indicated as a remedy is nothing more now than a trap used to introduce opinion from without, and to attack the pontifical government in its very principle. The opponents do not at present dare to say we want no more with the Pope; the expression of such a wish would occasion alarm. They content themselves with saying we want no more with the priests. This mitigated formula has the double advantage of appealing to the sympathies which exist among those populations which know of no other priests than such as preach and say mass, and at the same time to strike a blow in the direction of their end, and to prepare the ruin of the temporal power of the Papacy. It is the duty of those who by conviction and interest are the defenders of the order of things essentially connected with the maintenance of the Catholic unity, and the principle of authority in the world, to be on their guard against appearances, and to estimate at their just valuation the exaggeration of the numerous and ardent adversaries of the greatest and most fruitful of the institutions which the ages have left us.

" After having shown in what consists the pretended exclusively ecclesiastical character of the Roman administration, it is essential to examine how it works; and whether in effect its action is so contrary to the interests of the populations that they have a legitimate cause of complaint, and of invoking the support of other nations, to put a termination to the evils by which they are overwhelmed.

" Formerly the ancient traditions of the Court of Rome were faithfully preserved. Every modification of established customs, every amelioration, was looked upon with an evil eye, and was considered to be full of danger. The administration was confided exclusively to the prelates. The laity were by law forbidden to hold the highest offices in the state. In actual practice the different powers of the state were often confounded. The principle of pontifical infallibility was applied to questions of administration. Society saw the personal decision of the sovereign overturning the verdicts of the tribunals, even in civil matters. The cardinal secretary of state, the premier, in the full force of the word, concentrated in his own hands every power. Under his supreme direction the different branches of the administration were confided to persons who were clerks rather than ministers. The ministers formed no council, and never deliberated together on public affairs. The management of the public finances was carried on in secret. No information was given to the nation as to the expenditure of its own money. The budget was a mystery, and it was often discovered that it was not made out, and that the accounts were not closed. Lastly, municipal freedom, which, above everything else, is appreciated by the populations of Italy, was restricted within the narrowest limits.

" From the very day when the Pope Pius IX. mounted the throne, he made, we are entitled to assert, continuous efforts to sweep away every legitimate cause of complaint against the public administration of affairs. I will not content myself with appealing to the commencement of his reign. Betrayed by the very men whom he had recalled from banishment, deceived in the most flagrant manner by the lay ministers who were placed about him in obedience to a principle of complete secularisation, and who had no hesitation in publishing to the world that their sovereign had given his assent to measures which he had in fact distinctly and formally rejected ; carried rapidly along by a system of pure administrative reform to the establishment of a constitutional *régime*, which being destitute of all real strength, and without the slightest support from the nation, gave way at once to the republic ; threatened even in the very interior of his palace by an armed insurrection, the Pope had no other resource left, if he wished to preserve his liberty and independence, than that of leaving his dominions. We must do him the justice to allow that, in spite of the unfortunate termination of his attempts at reforms, he never abandoned his projects of amelioration, and has been unceasingly occupied with endeavours to put them in practice.   I will give a brief sketch of the principal governmental and administrative acts which have emanated from the Papal government. On his return from Gaeta, Pope Pius IX. proclaimed the principle of the right of admission of the laity to all offices save and except one only, that of Secretary of State.   This was the first time that the spectacle was seen of the pontifical government choosing counsellors of the highest dignity from the ranks of the laity.   This principle has been consecrated by the presence of a certain number of laymen amongst the ministers and the delegates.   Already had civil and criminal law been the object of complete revision.   Different codes of procedure in civil and in criminal cases, as well as a code relating to commerce, all founded on our own, enriched by lessons derived from experience, had been promulgated.   I have studied these carefully.   They are above criticism.   The Code des Hypotheques has been examined by French jurisconsults, and has been cited by them as a model document.   The Roman law, modified in certain points by the canon law, was held as a basis of civil legislation.

" The different powers of the state were carefully separated and defined.   Distinct ministerial boards, differing in authority, were created, each operating within the special circle of its duties. A council of ministers, under the presidency of the Secretary of State, was appointed, and business was always subjected to the test of discussion.   At the same time, the greatest respect for the independence of the judiciary power was proclaimed and practised.   A council of state, for the preparation of laws, composed of men the most intimately versed in administrative matters, comprising Prince Orsini, Prince Odescalchi, the Advocate Stoltz, and Professor Orioli, was appointed for the purpose of enlightening the government, by previously investigating all projects prepared in the ministerial boards.   A council of finance, composed of members nominated by the sovereign, after a free election by the municipal bodies, was specially appointed for the supervision of the expenditure of the state revenues.   This council is only deliberative, or consultative, in the discussion of primary budgets.   Unless this were the case it would be a chamber of deputies.   In respect, however, of past accounts, when the matter is to verify the exact application of the regulations established beforehand by the budget, its decisions have the force of law.   Every year the state accounts, and all the projects which, whether nearly or remotely, are connected with finance, are placed before it by the ministers. For the first time in the history of the Pontifical States, we have seen the head depositaries of power compelled to give an account of their doings to the representatives of the nation. For the first time, the public accounts have been properly published at the commencement of the time of their application, and consequently subjected to the control of the nation itself.

" Municipal organisation has been, at the same time, the object of a complete reform. Local interests occupy much of the attention of the Italian mind, and are the object of marked predilection. It would be difficult to respond more completely to this want than has been the case in the new organisation.

" The most highly taxed inhabitants of the commune, together with those who have acquired high degrees in the university, form together an electoral body, which have the direct nomination of the municipal councillors. The latter in their turn prepare, by the mode of election, a list of candidates, from which the government chooses the members of the provincial council. The latter, in the same way, make a list of persons from which the Holy Father selects members of the Consulta of State for Finance. A great latitude both in the creation and expenditure of resources is left both to the communal and to the provincial councils.

" It is not the representatives of the government who are charged with the administration of the funds of the commune or of the province. This trust is confided to an executive commission elected by the council, which it represents, and which remains *en permanence* during the whole of the interval between one session and another. The delegates or prefect have only the power of supervision, and take no direct part in the management of provincial or communal business. This system has already been the occasion of many ameliorations of all kinds in the Pontifical States ; many roads -- an important benefit— have been made, and many useful improvements instituted. Nevertheless, in certain points the equilibrium between receipts and expenditure has been disturbed. The small towns have taken to building theatres, and a question is now mooted whether it would not be proper to limit the discretion left to the municipal power, and extend the supervision exercised by government authority. At other times, and in every other country, such reforms and institutions would have been accredited to their author. In the interior every new concession has had the effect of creating greater wants. Abroad, these essential changes introduced into the older order of things, these incessant efforts of the pontifical government to ameliorate the lot of the populations, have passed unnoticed. People have had ears only for the declamation of the discontented, and for the permanent calumnies of the bad portion of the Piedmontese and Belgian press. This is the source from which public opinion has derived its inspiration ; and in spite of well-established facts, it is believed in most places, but particularly in England, that the pontifical government has done nothing for its subjects and has restricted itself to the perpetuation of the errors of another age. I have only yet indicated the ameliorations introduced into the organisation of the administration. I must mention the acts of the pontifical government and the results obtained.

" Above all, let us remember that never has a more exalted spirit of clemency been seen to preside over a restoration. No vengeance has been exercised on those who caused the overthrow of the pontifical government, no measures of rigour have been adopted against them. The Pope has contented himself with depriving them of the power of doing harm by banishing them from the land. No imprisonment, no trials even have taken place, except occasionally in consequence of the obstinacy of certain individuals who, insisting on being tried, have been condemned, and punished by being presented with a passport. As to the flagrant conspiracies which followed the return of the Pope, it was his bounded duty to take measures against them, as well as against the assassinations which followed them. These measure were taken in the most regular manner. The Holy Father never failed to mitigate the rigour of the sentences. A large number of individuals, the most compromised, obtained their liberty after a certain time without the condition of exile. At the present moment it is difficult to ascertain the exact number of persons who are forbidden to enter the Roman States for political reasons ; but with respect to the number of those who were the authors of the revolution of 1849, it is considered that it does not amount to a hundred. This extreme mildness of treatment, however, has not availed to prevent the English Parliament from accusing the pontifical government of cruelty.

" I come now to questions of administration. We know the cost of revolutions. The Roman republic met its expenses by creating a paper currency, which soon suffered considerable depreciation. The pontifical government did not hesitate to recognise these assignats, and undertook the task of withdrawing them from circulation by buying them up. The operation was successful, although the sum was very large. It amounted to 7,000,000 scudi, rather more than the annual revenue of the state. The same proportion applied to France would have given from 800 to 900 millions. The assignats now have totally disappeared from circulation, and the notes of the Bank of the Pontifical States, the only notes now current, are of equal value with the metallic currency, and are generally at par. This remarkable result goes for nothing with the detractors of the pontifical administration.

" The Roman bank, originally a French foundation, responded but very imperfectly to the wants of commerce. It was remodelled, and became the bank of the Pontifical States. It has established branches in the provinces, has extended the circle of its operations, has given and still gives great assistance to trade and to the government, and has shown that it stands on a solid basis, by passing with safety through many great crises.

" The pontifical government, directing its attention with great propriety to the means of augmenting the revenue derived from indirect taxation, has revised the custom-house duties. It has lowered the duties on a great number of articles, and is at this moment preparing a new measure more complete and more general in its operations.

" Postal and commercial treaties have been concluded with France and other states upon the widest basis, and in conformity with those principles which are adopted elsewhere as being in unison with the idea of progress.

" The system of farming the indirect revenues has been abolished. The government undertakes the direct management of the salt and tobacco trade. Important profits have been realised, and the success of the management is certain.

" In spite of considerable burdens which were occasioned by the revolution, and left as a legacy to the present government ; in spite of extraordinary expenses caused by the reorganisation of the army; in spite of numerous contributions towards the encouragement of public works, the state budget, which at the commencement exhibited a tolerably large *deficit*, has been gradually tending towards equilibrium. I have had the honour recently of pointing out to your excellency that the deficit in 1857 has been reduced to an insignificant sum, comprised for the most part of unexpected expenses and of money reserved for the extinction of the debt.

" The taxes remain still much below the mean rate of the different European states. A Roman pays the state 22 francs annually, 68 millions being levied on a population of 3 millions. A Frenchman pays the French government 45 francs, 1600 millions being levied on a population of 35 millions. These figures show demonstratively that the Pontifical States with regard to so important a point must be reckoned amongst the most favoured nations. The expenses are regulated on principles of the strictest economy. One fact is sufficient to prove this. The civil list, the expenses of the cardinals, of the diplomatic corps abroad, the maintenance of the pontifical palaces and the museums, cost the state no more than 600,000 crowns (3,200,000 francs). This small sum is the only share of the public revenue taken by the Papacy for the support of the pontifical dignity, and for keeping up the principal establishments of the superior ecclesiastical administration. We might ask those persons so zealous in hunting down abuses, whether the appropriation of 4000 crowns to the wants of the princes of the Church seems to them to bear the impress of a proper economy exercised with respect to the public revenue.

" The organisation of the army has been the object of assiduous care. Not only have the native troops received rewards, and been elevated to the number of 12,000 men, but a body of 4000 Swiss has been raised, and novel regulations founded on those in use among ourselves have been promulgated. The principles of military administration followed in the management of our forces have been adopted and put in practice. The appearance of the Roman soldiers at present elicits praise from all who have seen them. If the government could give them fidelity and energy with the uniform and the musket, there would be no need to apply to foreigners for assistance. Even in this direction, however, the government has performed all that was incumbent upon it to do, and if its success have not been complete, the fault is not in it, but in the very nature of the national mind. At the same time the state finances have been reorganised, and in spite of the limited resources of the budget, numerous sums have been devoted to the encouragement of commerce and arts. A great number of roads have been opened in various parts of the country, the port of Terracina has been enlarged, works of drainage have been executed in the Pontine Marshes. The marsh of Ostia is now in process of being drained, and viaducts of remarkable importance have been constructed in several places. Steam navigation has been introduced on the Tiber; thanks to a good system of towing, the port of Rome has been visited by a larger number of vessels than was formerly the case. The city has been lighted with gas, electric telegraphs have been introduced, concessions of railways have been made. That of Frascati, which is to be extended to Naples, will soon be opened. A negotiation is on foot for an important line, which is to connect Rome with Ancona and Bologna. The construction of the railway to Civita Vecchia has been granted to a Company which will commence operations immediately.

"Agriculture has been equally the object of encouragement by the government. Prizes have been established for the encouragement of gardening and the raising of stock. Lastly, a commission, composed of the principal landed proprietors, is now studying the hitherto insoluble question of draining the Campagna of Rome, and filling it with inhabitants.

"If the Roman people were capable of helping themselves, or even if they were eager for work, if their ambition was not limited to the attainment of a restricted income just sufficient to satisfy the primary wants of nature, without the expenditure of much fatigue, if they were to profit, as is the case elsewhere, by the facilities offered to them for the employment of their energies and pecuniary resources, the country might spring up rapidly to prosperity. But they allow all opportunities to escape them, and abandon to foreigners all useful undertakings. To make progress in the direction alluded to, the government cannot, it is clear, substitute its own action for that of private industry. Nevertheless, there are numerous proofs of public energy to be seen. New buildings, for example, are very numerous; the price of lodgings and food of all kinds is increasing rapidly. Commercial relations are extending. Important profits are being realised in agricultural and financial operations. Considerable fortunes are being made. The condition of the population is that of comparative ease. They rush together in crowds at the first signal of public rejoicing or pleasure. On these occasions their listlessness, usually carried to excess, is laid on one side. An appearance of prosperity strikes the eyes of the least observant. Gaiety of the most expansive kind is to be traced on the faces of all. It may be asked whether this can be the people whose miseries excite to such a degree the commiseration of Europe?

"There is, in truth, misery here as elsewhere, but it is infinitely less heavy than in less favoured climates. Mere necessities are obtained cheaply. Private charity is largely exercised. Establishments of public charity are numerous and effective. Here, also, the action of the government is perceptible. Important ameliorations have been introduced into the administration of hospitals and prisons. Some of these prisons should be visited, that the visitor may admire — the term is not too strong — the persevering charity of the Holy Father. I will not extend this enumeration. What I have said ought to be sufficient to prove that all the measures adopted by the Pontifical administration bear marks of wisdom, reason, and progress; that they have already produced happy results; in short, that there is not a single detail of interest to the well-being either moral or material of the population which has escaped the attention of the government, or which has not been treated in a favourable manner.

" In truth, when certain persons say to the Pontifical government, ' Form an administration which may have for its aim the good of the people ; ' the government might reply, ' Look at our acts, and condemn us if you dare.' The government might ask, not only which of its acts is a subject for legitimate blame, but in which of its duties it has failed. Are we then to be told, that the Pontifical government is a model — that it has no weaknesses or imperfections? Certainly not ; but its weaknesses and imperfections are of the same kind as are met with in all governments, and even in all men, with a very few exceptions.

" The Pontifical government is a government composed of Romans, acting after the Roman fashion. It mistrusts, fears, hesitates at, dreads responsibility : it is fonder of examining than deciding. It likes alterations and accommodations. It is deficient in energy, in activity, in taking the initiative, in firmness, as is the case with the nation itself. But although we may be permitted to attack any one who neglects his duties, it is unjust to impute it as a crime to any one that he has not the genius of a Sixtus V., of a Colbert, of a Napoleon.

" I am perpetually interrogating those who come to me to denounce what they call the abuses of the Papal government. This expression, it must be remembered, is now consecrated, and is above criticism or objection. It is held as gospel. Now, in what do these abuses consist? I have never yet been able to discover. At least, the facts which go by that name are such as are elsewhere traceable to the imperfections of human nature, and we need not load the government with the direct responsibility for the irregularities committed by some of its subordinate agents. I am generally told that the custom-houses ask travellers for a *pour boire*. This is without doubt a very blameable custom, but would the secularisation of the government cure the country of a vice deeply implanted in its nature — would it hinder the people from being always ready to hold out the hand? If this sad tendency was carried out on a large scale, there would be reason for alarm ; but whatever may be said of the venality of the Pontifical administration, it would be impossible to quote a single authenticated and notorious fact, unless we accept as genuine the current coin of calumny. In any case, if we see any one becoming rich it is always a layman. I have never seen a prelate augment his property by illicit means. The fortunes which are made, and which may easily be cited, originate in either banking or agricultural operations. Nothing shows that there is any trading with power, or appropriation of the State funds.

" To pretend that no act of faithlessness is committed would be irrational. No country is beyond the reach of such misfortunes ; but what may be maintained is this, that if they take place in the Pontifical states, they do so on a small scale, and that the public service and public morality are not affected by them in a sensible manner.

" The imperfections of the judiciary system are often cited. I have examined it closely, and have found it impossible to discover any serious cause of complaint. Those who lose their causes complain more loudly and more continuously than is the custom in other places, but without any more reason. Most of the important civil cases are decided in the tribunal of the Rota. Now, in spite of the habitual license of the Italian criticism, no one has dared to express a doubt of the profound knowledge and exalted integrity of the tribunal of the Rota. If the lawyers are incredibly fertile in raising objections and exceptions — if they lengthen out lawsuits — to what is this fault to be attributed except to the peculiarity of the national genius?

" Lastly, civil law is well administered. I do not know a single sentence the justice of which would not be recognised by the best tribunal in Europe.

" Criminal justice is administered in a manner equally unassailable. I have watched some trials throughout their whole details. I was obliged to confess that all necessary precautions for the verifications of facts, all possible guarantees for the free defence of the accused, including the publication of the proceedings, were taken. The sentences are occasionally delayed, the processes are prolonged. These, however, are inconveniences, not unpardonable crimes.

" When Italian witnesses shall learn to give their evidence without being intimidated by the presence of the accused and the fear of his vengeance, the delays will be less. Our French councils of war have the greatest difficulty in obtaining depositions, and are often forced to employ severity for this purpose. Against tendencies of this kind the government can do nothing.

" Much is said of the brigands who, we are told, lay the country desolate. It has fallen to our lot to pass through the country in all directions without seeing even the shadow of a robber. It cannot be denied that from time to time we hear of a diligence stopped, of a traveller plundered. Even one accident of this kind is too many ; but we must remember that the administration has employed all the means in its power to repress these disorders. Thanks to energetic measures, the brigands have been arrested at all points and punished. When in France a diligence is stopped, when in going from London to Windsor a lady of the Queen's Palace is robbed of her luggage and jewels, such an incident passes unnoticed, but when on an isolated road in the Roman States the least fact of this nature takes place, the press, eager for a pretext, prints the news in large characters, and cries for vengeance on the government. On the side of Rome, the attacks which have taken place at distant intervals have never assumed an appearance calculated to excite anxiety. In the Romagna organised bands have been formed, which, taking advantage of the neighbouring Tuscan frontier, easily escaped pursuit, and were for a time to be dreaded. The government declared unceasing war against them, and after several engagements, in which a certain number of gendarmes were either killed or wounded, these bands have been in a great measure dispersed.

" To conclude, we shall be obliged to confess, upon investigation, that the pontifical government has not failed in its task, that it has proceeded regularly in the road of reform and amelioration, and that it has realised a considerable progress. If agitation is still kept up the cause of it will be found in the character of the nation itself, and it ambitious views directed to unattainable objects. We must recognise, lastly, that the remedy for this sad situation of things is not to be found in a crowd of measures which, modifying an order of things perfectly unconnected with the evil, would only make the evil much greater and more dangerous still by exalting its hopes, and by reducing it, already much shaken, to the last degree of impotence and weakness.

" If the sovereign of the Pontifical States were not at the same time Head of the Church, his preservation or his ruin would be of little importance. But the cause of Catholicism is at stake in this matter. For this reason it is that so high a degree of interest is so justly considered by the great Catholic Powers to attach to the interior condition of the Roman States. These Powers have a profound feeling of the dangers which would threaten themselves even in the event of a new revolution, and they understand what a reconstruction of the temporal power of the Papacy on a new basis might cost Europe. Religious passions being unchained simultaneously with political passions, the gravest, perhaps even the bloodiest, conflicts might arise.

" The prudence of statesmen induces them to seek for the means of anticipating and preventing such fatal complications.

" Attention is naturally directed towards the nature of the concessions necessary to satisfy the populations. Unhappily these populations are not to be satisfied. I think I have proved this. By destroying the Pontifical authority, a numerous party, but not the whole nation, is sure to be satisfied. By the establishment of a constitutional *régime*, which would appear, however, to be little in harmony with the power of the Head of the Church, a large number of individuals would be equally satisfied ; but, as I have said, the one party as well as the other would rapidly allow public business to fall into the hands of the most violent section. M. Rossi, who wanted neither the necessary talent nor the good will, had devoted himself to the task of introducing into the Pontifical States a parliamentary *régime*. It might have been believed that he might have reckoned on some support. The event teaches us that he completely failed in obtaining this support. Nobody was found in the moment of danger to support or defend him. No voice was raised to deplore his violent death, still less to invoke vengeance for the deed.

" It is in the highest degree impossible, in the midst of passions which are dividing the minds of men, to create a truly popular administration. But allowing the attempt to be successful, such an administration would find no more defenders at a critical moment than Count Rossi found when endeavouring to carry his undertaking to a successful termination. Simple reforms content no one. I think I have abundantly shown that this is not the question, and that, besides this, the movements of the Pontifical government are far from being such as to give occasion for the populations to consider themselves damaged in their legitimate interests. Reforms would be momentarily granted by certain parties only on consideration of the damage and loss of popularity which they might inflict upon the Pontifical government.

" We cannot even see to what combination we could have recourse. A profound investigation of the true situation of things gives no precise indications as to the course to be adopted in this matter. In what direction are modifications to be employed? How far are they to be carried? With regard to this point the greatest uncertainty exists. Now modifications can bear no good fruit unless they are clearly indicated by the nature of things. This is not the case here. We consequently see the spectacle of the most contradictory views being promulgated according to the nature of individual opinions.

"Certain persons who have already succeeded once in depriving the Holy Father of his tiara, not for their own profit, but for that of the demagogues, are accused of entertaining the project of dividing the Pontifical States into two portions, one of which is to be governed by a delegate of the Holy Father. Such a combination as this, I confess, appears to me to present the greatest dangers. There is no doubt that it would open the door to revolution, and that it would take advantage of the revolution, attracted by the expectations founded upon certain success. The population would have less respect for their lay governor than for the present delegates. They would not risk a crown or a drop of blood to defend him. At the end of a few months the fall of the Sovereign Pontiff would be declared at Bologna, an Italian constituent assembly would be convoked, and war would be declared against Austria. Allowing that the new power would be able to maintain its position, and should succeed in satisfying the populations, what answer could be given to the other half of the Pontifical States, which will complain of being abandoned, and will ask for their equal share? What is to be done if they rise in insurrection to gain their ends, and how can we doubt that they will resort to extreme measures? Thus, then, will the Papacy be plundered, its enemies satisfied, and Catholic Europe become a prey to the most dangerous agitations. In any case, we must expect that the Pope would meet such a project with the most desperate resistance. In reality, if he did not, he would deserve to have a brevet of radical incapacity decreed to him in the presence of all Europe. He will never give his assent to such a plan; but whether he were to resist or yield, the Papacy would be struck with a mortal wound, and this is what the authors of this combination understand very well. There would be but one remedy. The Italians always depend for the completion of their projects on foreign support. If this support were to fail them, they would adopt a proper course much more readily than would be imagined, looking at their actual situation. It would be necessary, however, that in England and Sardinia the organs of the press should cease to excite the passions, and that the Catholic powers should continue to give the Holy See evident marks of sympathy. But how can we hope that enemies, animated with such a spirit as influences the opponents of the Holy See, would put a stop to their attacks when they have been made in so remarkable a manner?

"I do not think that all the questions of this world must necessarily have a definite solution. The Roman question, in my opinion at least, has none. We can only, exercising a benevolent and attentive protection, avert the dangers of a catastrophe, and prolong a provisional state of things which has at least the grand merit of preserving Europe from innumerable evils.

"Any other order of measures would only precipitate events. If his

G G

Majesty's government, from motives easily comprehended, should desire to put a stop to the French occupation of the Roman States after a delay of greater or less duration, it would be better at once to abandon the sluices to the impulse of the torrent than to open them by dealing, either by means of advice openly given, or by forced combinations, the *coup de grace* to the temporal power of the Popes.

"In the presence of the existing agitation of mind in Italy and of the very lively emotion caused by the publication of the protocols, it is impossible to keep down a profound feeling of anxiety as to the future destiny of the Papacy. If care is not taken, Europe will see the most terrible of problems present itself — terrible, in fact, because it is connected with the deepest and the most ardent passions of the human heart.

"The words pronounced by your Excellency in the Conference, the assurance you have given of the interest which the Emperor's government will not cease to take in the safety of the Pontifical power, are certain proofs that the true interests of the Church are in no danger in the present crisis. With such a programme, the most imminent dangers may be removed, and the catastrophe delayed. This is all that can be accomplished at the present moment by human wisdom. Let us continue to give the Papacy the benefit of our protection. Let us decide deliberately only, and after successive diminutions, on complete evacuation, and only after being well assured that it is possible. Calm will come by degrees. Finally, if the political and religious tranquillity of Italy, perhaps even of Europe, should appear to depend solely on the presence at Civita Vecchia and Ancona of a few hundred men, giving a moral, rather than a material, support to the Pontifical flag and establishment, but still a support which is sufficient, is it not a hundred times better to have recourse to this certain remedy than to attempt to obtain similar ends by ways full of peril? If in such circumstances the temporal power of the Papacy should be menaced anew, and if, in spite of our efforts, grave complications should arise, the responsibility would then at least rest wholly and entirely on events which are often stronger than man, and we should not have to reproach ourselves with having contributed to so fatal a result.

" I thought that I was performing a duty in submitting to the high appreciation of your Excellency the results of a tolerably long experience and connected study. The kindness and encouragement with which you have met my proposal to explain my opinions, have emboldened me to do so without reserve.

" I appeal to the indulgence of your Excellency in reviewing my labours, and beg you to accept the reiterated assurance of my high consideration."

THE CHRISTIAN SCHOOLS.

THE *system* of education adopted by the Brothers of the Christian Schools is substantially the same in all countries in which they are established; and, therefore, an account of a Public Examination of their pupils in an Irish city affords a correct idea of the character and success of their teaching in the schools of France or Italy. The following is taken from a newspaper sketch of the Public Examinations of the pupils of the Cork schools, held in the month of June, 1857. It is copied from the " *Cork Examiner* " of the 26th of June : —

" To give some idea of the scope of these examinations, and the training of which they are the evidence, it will be interesting to glance at the several subjects proposed.

" The first class brought forward was a junior class of geometry. The examination embraced the definition and the principal properties of the triangle, parallelogram and square. The young fellows answered with a briskness and accuracy that would put their seniors to shame.

" The geography of America was next introduced. Its physical features, various climat s and colonisation were described. A sketch of the history of each important state was given; and the manners and customs of its inhabitants detailed.

" A catechism class followed; and the principal doctrines of the Church explained in a way that many a Catholic *Littérateur* or merchant might be puzzled to equal.

" Off filed the young divines, and on came another row of youngsters with the geography of Ireland bursting from their eager lips. It would be well if all our Secretaries of State had mastered the *physique* of Ireland so thoroughly.

" Subjects of composition were now proposed to a group with slates and pencils. Those subjects were chosen by the audience by lot. The boys retired a little and set to work. While another class was examined, it was interesting to observe the young heads bent over the slates — the pauses of thought — the rapid rush of words — again the puzzled pause — and once more the vehement flow of ideas. At length the time came to read what they had written; and as each one mounted the platform, bowed to the audience, and read his improvised essay, the room rang with applause. The promptness of composition, the felicity of illustration, the almost invariable purity of diction, and the occasional originality of thought, were rare proofs at once of moral power and intellectual culture.

" A class of ' Christian Politeness ' closed the first day's work. Perhaps nothing could better exemplify the ingenious wisdom of the Brothers than the novelty of thus cultivating even the manners of these poor boys. We looked at the class book upon this subject with some

curiosity.　It is a well adapted translation of a work of the Founder of
the Brotherhood — the Venerable DE LA SALLE.　As might be expected, it is full of good sense and truly 'Christian' spirit.　The boys
had evidently more than a technical knowledge of it.　Their deportment throughout would almost suggest that they were gentlemen;
while, in fact, they were children of poor labourers, and the humblest
class of tradesmen.

" Next day's Examination opened with a class of Arithmetic.　Here
were evinced the complete culture and rapid power that make these
boys sought, and enable them to rise, in almost every counting-house
of the city.

" A class of Sacred History was now rigorously examined, and
proved an affluence of information on the subject.

"Other classes of Catechism, Geometry, Geography, and Composition succeeded as on the previous day, with results even more
gratifying.

" The Laws of Colour and Light, Architecture, Mechanics, the Laws
of Motion, the Mechanical Powers, Mensuration, were amongst the
subjects of this day's examination.　It was evident that the more
difficult the subject the more thorough was the instruction, and interesting to observe how each of these topics was so handled as at
once to exercise the highest reasoning powers of the boys, and to be of
practical use in the lives of the future mechanics.

" A class of well-trained Readers agreeably terminated the Examination, which was also varied at intervals during each day by the per-
formances of the well-known Singing Class of the Schools."

It may be added that the Brothers are established in all the cities
and in the principal towns of Ireland ; and also in many of the cities
and large towns of Great Britain.　In Cork alone, the average attendance of pupils is 1300.　The number of pupils in the schools in
the United Kingdom may be set down at 30,000.　As they never receive, nor would accept, any assistance from the State, they depend
on the voluntary support of the communities in which they are established, as well as upon their own private resources, which are freely
devoted to the education of the poor.

MEASUREMENT OF THE BASE LINE FOR A TRIGONO-METRICAL SURVEY, BY FATHER SECCHI.

IT is now more than a century ago since Benedict XIV. entrusted to Father Boscovich the important task of measuring within
the Roman States an arc of the meridian.　In connection with this
undertaking of so much scientific importance, a trigonometrical survey

of the States of the Church was commenced by Boscovich and his colleague Maine, and continued at subsequent periods by other eminent men of science.

In trigonometrical surveys the operation which is generally first in order, as it is always first in importance, is the measurement of a base line. This line is in every sense the *base* of the whole system, as from it are calculated all the other lines which by their network form the triangulation of a country. Of the great lines of a survey it is the only one which is actually *measured*, except when, at the termination of his labours, the engineer tries the length of another line, in order to see how far the calculated differs from the real length; thus applying the most severe test of the accuracy of his work and of his instruments. Everything therefore depends on the precision with which this base line is measured, as any error in its length infects the whole of the survey; and no matter how exact all the angular measurements may be, still the original and inherent vice of an erroneous base remains multiplied and magnified throughout the whole system. Science, therefore, has exhausted every expedient, and provided every safeguard against error which she could devise in order to insure what, at the first glance, may seem a very simple task — the accurate measurement of a straight line of considerable length. The trigonometrical survey which had been commenced by Boscovich was one which was accounted of remarkable accuracy for the time when it was executed; but it must be recollected that all the scientific instruments of 1751 were very different from, and far inferior to, those which the mechanical skill of the present day can construct. And doubts were entertained whether the survey founded on Boscovich's original measurement was as correct as might be required in the present age. The first step towards the rectification of the survey was the re-measurement of the base. Boscovich had measured his line on the Appian Way. That great highway, running for so many miles in a line almost perfectly straight, presented peculiar facilities for the operation in question, and it was believed that both the terminal points of the line measured in the last century could again be discovered, as that next to Rome was well known. However, unfortunately, all trace was lost of the point near Le Frattocchie. Many attempts were made, by indirect methods, to determine again the southern extremity of the line which Father Boscovich had measured.

Pius IX., not content with opening again that great Appian Way with which so many recollections of Roman greatness are associated ; not satisfied with having recovered from its great storehouses so many monuments of classic art, determined that not only Commerce and

G G 3

Art, but also Science, should reap some of the first-fruits of his work of reclamation; and he commissioned Father Angelo Secchi, the Director of the Roman Observatory, and a worthy successor of Boscovich, again to measure the base line on which the Roman survey was founded, placing at his disposal all the aid which mechanical ingenuity and the scientific knowledge of modern times could render him. And, perhaps, no similar operation was ever carried out with so much care and accuracy. The main objects which it is proposed to acomplish are, — 1st, To rectify and check the several trigonometrical surveys which have been made in the neighbourhood of Rome, and to complete the triangulation of the Southern States. 2ndly, To determine exactly the length of the ancient Itinerary Measures. 3rdly, To settle some important questions which have arisen amongst men of science relative to the length of the meridional degree in Italy, the figure of the earth, and the deviation of the pendulum produced by the attraction of the mountains.

It would be uninteresting to the generality of readers to describe the method in which the measurement of the base line was conducted. Indeed, it would require some acquaintance with scientific instruments to understand the sources of minute errors, and the methods employed to prevent them from occurring, or to eliminate them from the work when they do take place. It is enough to say that it is perhaps impossible to lay down a line mathematically for any considerable length; and in practice, that the man of science has to observe the deviations from a true rectilinear path which must inevitably take place both in a horizontal and a vertical direction, and by the aid of mathematical science calculate, from what may be called the zig-zag which he has really measured, the length of the right line that would connect its two extremities.

The method adopted on the present occasion may be explained in general terms as follows: —

The measurement of the line was commenced opposite the tomb of Cecilia Metella, and its initial point was marked on a small cone of brass fixed to a large block of travertine, which was connected by a solid mass of masonry with the subjacent rock of lava. The cone of brass was placed beneath the surface of the roadway and afterwards covered by a large block of stone. The operation of measurement was commenced by adjusting a vertical microscope over this cone of brass until the spider line bisected the initial point marked on it.

A set of five microscopes was then arranged along the line to be surveyed, at a distance from each other of about 4 metres (13 feet), and the distance from each to the next was noted by means of a very accurately graduated rod, of over 4 metres in length, which was placed beneath each two in succession, and viewed through them. The system was, in fact, to place the microscopes in nearly a right line, and by means of the rod to measure the distance between their spider lines. At each end of the rod was a short vertical staff, and by means of an ordinary level the difference of height between its extremities was observed. Each microscope had attached to it a small telescope, which served to place the succeeding microscope in the right line, or to note its deviation from it. Thermometers were also attached to the apparatus in order that the correction made necessary by change of temperature might be noted. The conclusion of each day's labour was marked by a point connected by measuring into the ground, and the termination of the base line at Le Fratocchie was marked in a similar way with the commencement near Rome. So great was the care taken, that in a whole day, at the beginning of the operation, there were only measured thirty or thirty-five lengths of the 4 metre rod; but after some time the progress was more rapid, in some days exceeding 400 yards. A very useful instrument was employed during the progress of this operation — it was, in fact, invented for the special purposes of the survey. It has been called by the inventor the Meroscope, and is in fact a telescope which, by the introduction of an additional lens between the object and the eye-piece, can be converted into a microscope. It has been employed in the latter character in observing the finely graduated scales of the measuring apparatus, and is capable as a telescope, according to Father Secchi, of showing the belts and the satellites of Jupiter. An instrument with such an extraordinary range of focus is quite a novelty amongst optical apparatus, and is as useful as it is new.

The commencement of this great scientific undertaking, which it will probably take years to accomplish, and which will in all likelihood embrace the triangulation of all Southern Italy, seems to have been carried on in a manner worthy of the great object in view. Indeed, it is remarkable that Italy has in the last half-century produced so many eminent men of science. While the arts and literature are far below the level of her classic eras, science can count perhaps more great names and important discoveries in Italy than at any former period since the time of Galileo.

POVERTY, IN LONDON, TREATED WORSE THAN CRIME.

THE statement of Mr. Alderman Copeland, given in the note at the bottom of p. 297, appeared to some who heard it to be a kind of rhetorical flourish; and yet he only stated that " poverty was regarded as a crime, and treated as a crime." But had he remembered the description of the Casual Ward of the West London Union and its occupants, as given in the *Times* of the 20th of February, 1857, he might have used far stronger language, without the slightest risk of exaggeration. Now here is a picture of the existing state of things in London; that proud capital of the United Kingdom, the seat of its Legislature, and the residence of its Sovereign—whose press and whose people sit in such stern judgment upon the failings and misfortunes, the imperfections and shortcomings, of Catholic peoples, institutions, and governments. It is the *Times* that holds the pencil, not I : —

" On Wednesday night, at ten o'clock, the Lord Mayor, the Recorder, Mr. Under Sheriff Anderton and Mr. Bunning, the City Architect, visited the establishment for the houseless poor, where they found nearly 100 persons, who, after being supplied with food, were accommodated with shelter for the night.

" They afterwards visited the West London Union, near Smithfield, and, upon inquiring for the casual ward, were informed that this establishment was at Battle Bridge, a distance of two and a half miles off.

" They immediately repaired thither, and found the building to consist of a large stable, containing fourteen horse-stalls, the *only* provision for the lodging of the casual poor, some few men being huddled together round a fire. The place was *totally destitute of either straw or bedding of any description whatever*. The poor creatures, in answer to inquiries made of them, stated that, upon entering the building, a small portion of bread had been given them, but that it was the custom to turn them out in the morning *without anything to eat*, unless they first broke a certain quantity of stones, of which there was a large heap in the yard.

" The Lord Mayor and his friends next entered an adjoining *cattle-shed*, where they found *two destitute women huddled together in a rug, lying on the bare ground, almost perished with cold, and without either fire or food*.

" These two persons were relieved by the visiting party with a small sum of money, for the purpose of enabling them to obtain the common necessaries of life in the morning.

" The visiting party next proceeded to the *City Gaol* at Holloway, where they found 455 *prisoners, snugly housed in separate apartments, with an abundance of warm bedding and blankets, and other articles necessary for the personal comfort of mankind.*

" The contrast between the provision for the *criminal* and the *destitute* was *beyond conception.*"

ENGLISH PRISONS NOT YET PERFECT MODELS.

If the following statements, made by two jail chaplains, are to be taken for granted — and there seems no reason why they should not — it must be apparent that the prison system of England is far from being in that perfect state which would warrant her to sit in judgment on other nations.

At the Conference at Birmingham, in December 1851, the Rev. T. Carter, chaplain of the Liverpool jail, said : —

" Liverpool has one of the largest jails in the kingdom.   The commitments during last year were upwards of 9,500.   Of that number, upwards of 1,100 were juvenile offenders under 16 years of age ; and of these the proportion of recommitments amounted to more than 70 per cent.   This one fact must give you some idea of the inefficiency — the utter uselessness — of such institutions as the Liverpool jail for the reformation of criminals.   Indeed — and I say it advisedly — if it had been the object in Liverpool to devise a scheme for the *promotion,* rather than the *prevention,* of juvenile crime, no contrivance could have been hit upon better calculated to accomplish that object than the Liverpool jail.   *And yet that jail has been held up as one of the best regulated in the kingdom !* "

Having described how the several classes of prisoners are mingled together ; how " as many as five persons are crammed into cells, which, when designed and built under the direction of Howard, were intended to hold only one ; " and having stated, from his own observation, what the result of the prison discipline is, he concluded by saying : —

" I think I have established my position that the Liverpool jail, *although singled out for special commendation by the Inspector of Prisons, is the most effectual institution that can be devised for transmitting and propagating crime.*"

The Rev. W. C. Osborn, chaplain of the Bath jail, having spoken of the opportunities he has had of knowing the condition and treatment of the prisons, said : —

" Although the system adopted at Bath is, I believe, as good, if not better, than that adopted elsewhere, yet I must say, that our treatment of these poor, destitute creatures has been, and is, most cruel, unjust, and unchristian. * * * * * * * * *

"I cannot help feeling that our conduct towards them is most unjustifiable, and I trust that God will not visit us with His anger for our treatment of those poor creatures. We give them justice — *justice without mercy — justice without scales, for there has been no measurement of the cruelty of our treatment of them.*"

The same speaker strongly condemned the practice of whipping the prisoners, and very properly remarks, "this system of whipping in our prisons is not calculated to reform, but to harden,"

In August 1856, a paper was contributed by Lord Brougham to the " National Reformatory Union," which was held in Bristol. From that paper, read by the Dean of Bristol, the following passage is extracted: —

"It is our highest duty to rescue the people from ignorance and vice by giving them the inestimable blessing of a sound moral and religious education ; to prevent the growth of crime, while we provide for reclaiming from their vicious courses those who have been led astray — a cure only to be effected by making the punishment of criminals the instrument of their reformation. *That duty we have not discharged.* But if we have planted no schools where habits of virtue may be induced, stretched forth no hand to extirpate the germs of vice, we have kept open other schools where vice is taught with never-failing success, used both hands incessantly to stifle the seeds of virtue ere yet they had time to sprout, and laid down many a hotbed where the growth of crime in all its rank luxuriousness is assiduously forced. The infant school languishes which a paternal Government would have cherished ; but Newgate flourishes — *Newgate, with her thousand cells to corrupt their youthful inmates, seducing the guiltless, confirming the depraved.*"

CRIMINAL STATISTICS OF THE PAPAL STATES.

THE following sketch of the criminal statistics of the Roman States is too necessary to a fair understanding of this important subject to be omitted from a work of this nature. It formed part of a letter which I sent from Rome towards the end of November, 1856, since when the number of political and party offenders has been greatly diminished through the clemency of the Pope : —

"In forming a fair estimate of the state of crime in the Papal States, as represented by the number now actually suffering punishment for their offences, under process, or awaiting their trial, one consideration should be held distinctly in view, —that Rome has no penal

settlements, such as England and France possess, to which she could
deport the worst portion, or indeed any portion, of her criminals.
Thus, if it be said that Rome has so many prisoners in the various
prisons of the Papal States, the number so stated represents the *entire*;
whereas, if the same be said of France or England, it would not represent anything like the truth ; for France has her Cayenne, and
England her Bermuda and her Australian settlements, for the detention
of a large class of offenders. The Pope's possessions are limited to
his own States, and beyond their boundary it is impossible for him to
establish a prison or penal colony. The statistics now before me, and
upon the exactness of which it is impossible to entertain the smallest
doubt, exhibit *a steady decrease in crime*, so far as that can be evidenced
by the number in prison ; and in all countries this is *the* test and
criterion by which the state of a country, in this particular respect,
is judged of. In December, 1854, the number of prisoners — those
awaiting their trial, under process, or actually condemned and suffering
punishment — was 12,140. The next year showed a lesser amount of
crime; the number for December, 1855, being 11,656. In this year
the diminution is even still more perceptible. I take two months of
the present year, August and September ; and not only do I find
that there is a less number in August, 1856, than in December, 1855,
but I perceive that there is a favourable difference between the two
months of the same year. In August, the number was 10,885; and in
September, 10,777. I can only state, what I have reason to know to
be the fact, that the returns for the months of October and November
exhibit a still more satisfactory diminution in their numbers. These
are distributed throughout the Pontifical States ; the proportion in some
of the chief places having been as follows, in September last:—Rome,
1,186—Bologna, 1,338 — Ancona, 787 — Civita Vecchia, 1,591 — Ferrara, 299.

" The returns quoted embrace all kinds of crimes, and all kinds of
accusations ; and, amongst the rest, they comprehend a class of offenders who, in some countries,—for instance, in France,—are under the
control as well as sanctioned by the police authorities, and in others
defy almost all authority or restraint whatsoever. I allude to women
of depraved character, not one of whom is to be met with in the
streets of Rome, which may accordingly be traversed with impunity,
at any hour of the evening or night, by a modest female — without
the risk of having her eyes and ears offended, as they are in too many
cities of our highly civilised empire. Offenders of this class are at
once made amenable to the law, and committed either to the Termini,

or to the institution of the Good Shepherd, where the most effectual
means of reformation are adopted, and in very many instances with
success—both institutions being specially under the care and control
of religious communities.

"In the returns are also necessarily included all those who, having
been sentenced to imprisonment for life, or for a term of 15 or 20
years, before the accession of Pius IX., have not as yet been the objects
of his clemency. So that the 10,777 prisoners who, in September
last, were confined in the prisons of the Pontifical States, give an exaggerated idea of the actual state of crime; these figures in reality
representing the crime, not of one year, but of many years.

"There has been a notion industriously propagated, for obvious
reasons, that the prisons of the Papal States were filled with political
offenders, the victims of arbitrary power and remorseless tyranny.
That there are persons confined for political offences, there can be no
question whatever — I myself saw prisoners of this class in the prison
of San Michele; but that their number has been immensely exaggerated,
the real state of the case distinctly demonstrates. Of 'purely political
offences' there were, two months since, not more than 99, and since that
time the number has been reduced to 70—that is, 29 additional pardons
have since been granted through the clemency of the Pope, in many instances excited by the appeals of those who have since been its objects.
In the early part of October, the number of persons confined for political offences, and offences which are described or classified as those
'arising out of party spirit' — meaning thereby injury to the person,
acts of violence, frequently stabbing, the result of quarrels arising from
party hate or political disputes — did not exceed 338; and of that number, those undergoing sentence, or held in detention, for 'purely political offences' did not exceed 99; which number, as I have stated,
is now reduced to 70, and will be still reduced considerably on the 1st
January, 1857. The gross number has been reduced from 338 to
292. The Pope has granted 47 pardons to 'purely political' offenders, from the 1st of January, 1855, to the 15th of May, 1856
— that is, either remitted the greater portion of their punishment,
or restored them to full liberty; and within the same period he has
exhibited similar clemency to 65 whose offences arose out of 'party
spirit' — making, in all, no less than 112. From May to October
he has granted 82 pardons more, of which 29 have been granted
to 'purely political' offenders, and the rest to persons coming under
the head of offenders from 'party motives.' When the gross number
reached 338 political and party offenders, they were distributed as

follows : — Ancona, 54 — Forte Urbano, 21 — Paliano, 208 — San Michele, 43 suffering punishment, and 12 under process. Now that the number is reduced to 70 'purely political' offenders, and 222 offenders from 'party spirit,' somewhat of the same proportion is maintained in the prisons mentioned.

"These statistics would not exhibit the whole truth, unless they also embraced another class, who are suffering exile in consequence of their connection with the memorable revolution which compelled his Holiness — himself the first as well as the most illustrious of reformers — to fly from Rome to Gaeta. The number of those who were formally excluded from the amnesty of September 1849, was 283 ; and of those, 200 were members of the Triumvirate, the Constituent Assembly, and the Provisional Government ; and 83 were chiefs of the different military corps. Of this number, 21 were strangers, and not subjects of the Pontifical states. Of the 283 mentioned, 59 have received pardon — that is, 35 of the Constituent Assembly, and 24 military leaders. Hence the number of the Pope's subjects so exiled at present is 203. Some of those have since died ; others would not appeal to the clemency of their Sovereign ; and more have exhibited such 'perverse conduct' (*perversa condotta*) that it is not thought prudent to extend pardon to them.

"There is, lastly, another class, who fled from Rome and the Papal States after the success of the French, and whose return to the States is prohibited. These amount in all to 1273; but, as there were no less than 629 foreigners among them, not more than 644 are subjects of the Pope. Subtracting from this number those who were then exiled, as a commutation of a heavier sentence, or who demanded and obtained permission to spend the remainder of their lives in foreign countries, in order, amongst other reasons, to be free from all surveillance, and amounting in all to 152, it appears that the total number of the Pope's subjects to whom return, without permission being obtained, is prohibited, is 492. Many of these have fled from punishment for offences not political ; but there can be no doubt whatever that an appeal made by most of those now in exile, and who could be proved not to have been leagued in other countries against the throne and authority of the Pope, would not be made in vain. The whole career of Pius IX. is in favour of the belief that, could he carry out his own benevolent intentions, and freely obey the promptings of his noble and tender nature, there is not a good or honest subject of his now in exile to whom he would not to-morrow grant permission to return to his home and country. One fact must be mentioned to the honour of Pius IX., as it contrasts so strongly with the vengeance which other sovereigns wreak on their subjects when once rebellion has been crushed, — that *there has not been, during his reign, a single person executed for a purely political offence.* Try this fact by the actual conduct of other European monarchs, and by what that of the English Government would have been, had the affair of 1848 in Ireland been like that of the Hungarians, the Venetians, or the Sicilians ; or had an Irish Secretary of State been shot in the Castle of Dublin, and Lord Clarendon been compelled to fly across the Channel to England for personal safety : test it by such a standard, and then the clemency of Pius IX. will shine the brighter by the contrast.

"But while clemency is a noble virtue, especially in sovereigns, weakness is a folly, and may be as ruinous as a vice ; and thus, though one would ardently desire that every native of the Papal States now in exile, on account of the part which he took in the Revolution of 1848, should be permitted to return to his home and kindred, provided he did not come back in the spirit of a revolutionist and an avenger, no rational person could expect that the Pope would be so insensible to the promptings of ordinary caution and foresight, as to allow men to return to his States who have been openly declaring their determination to accomplish his overthrow, or have been known to be parties and promoters of conspiracies towards the same end. If he did so, he would be more or less than mortal, and would act as no other sovereign has acted, or is ever likely to act, under similar circumstances."

THE CATACOMBS.

(From Cardinal Wiseman's *"Fabiola."*)

"THE history of the early Christian cemeteries, the *Catacombs*, as they are commonly called, may be divided into three portions: from their beginning to the period of our narrative, or a few years later ; from this term to the eighth century ; then down to our own time, when we have reason to hope that a new epoch is being commenced.

"We have generally avoided using the name of catacombs, because it might mislead our readers into an idea that this was either the original or a generic name of those early Christian crypts. It is not so, however: Rome might be said to be surrounded by a circumvallation of cemeteries, sixty or thereabouts in number, each of which was generally known by the name of some saint or saints, whose bodies reposed there. Thus we have the cemeteries of SS. Nereus and Achilleus, of St. Agnes, of St. Pancratius, of Prætextatus, Priscilla, Hermes, &c. Sometimes these cemeteries were known by the names of the places where they existed.* The cemetery of St. Sebastian, which was called sometimes *Cœmeterium ad Sanctam Cœciliam*†, and by other names, had among them that of *Ad Catacumbas.*‡ The meaning of this word is completely unknown; though it may be attributed to the circumstance of the relics of SS. Peter and Paul having been for a time buried there, in a crypt still existing near the cemetery. This term became the name of that particular cemetery, then was generalised, till we familiarly call the whole system of these underground excavations — the Catacombs.

"Their origin was, in the last century, a subject of controversy. Following two or three vague and equivocal passages, some learned writers pronounced the catacombs to have been originally heathen excavations, made to extract sand, for the building of the city. These sandpits were called *arenaria*, and so occasionally are the Christian cemeteries. But a more scientific and minute examination, particularly made by the accurate F. Marchi, has completely confuted this theory. The entrance to the catacombs was often, as can yet be seen, from these sandpits, which are themselves underground, and no doubt were a convenient cover for the cemetery; but several circumstances prove that they were never used for Christian burial, nor converted into Christian cemeteries.

"The man who wishes to get the sand out of the ground will keep his excavation as near as may be to the surface; will have it of easiest possible access, for drawing out materials; and will make it as ample as is consistent with the safety of the roof, and the supply of what he is seeking. And all this we find in the *arenaria* still abounding round Rome. But the Catacombs are constructed on principles exactly contrary to all these.

"The catacomb dives at once, generally by a steep flight of steps, below the stratum of loose and friable sand §, into that where it is indurated to the hardness of a tender, but consistent rock; on the surface of which every stroke of the pick-axe is yet distinctly traceable. When you have reached this depth you are in the first story of the cemetery, for you descend again, by stairs, to the second and third below, all constructed on the same principle.

"A catacomb may be divided into three parts, its passages or streets, its chambers or squares, and its churches. The passages are long, narrow galleries, cut with tolerable regularity, so that the roof and floor

---

* As *Ad Nymphas, Ad Ursum pileatum, Inter duas lauros, Ad Sextum Philippi,* &c.

† The cemetery at St. Cœcilia's tomb.

‡ Formed apparently of a Greek preposition and a Latin verb.

§ That is, the red volcanic sand called *puzzolana,* so much prized for making Roman cement.

are at right angles with the sides, often so narrow as scarcely to allow two persons to go abreast. They sometimes run quite straight to a great length; but they are crossed by others, and these again by others, so as to form a complete labyrinth, or network, of subterranean corridors. To be lost among them would easily be fatal.

" But these passages are not constructed, as the name would imply, merely to lead to something else. They are themselves the catacomb or cemetery. Their walls, as well as the sides of the staircases, are honeycombed with graves, that is, with rows of excavations, large and small, of sufficient length to admit a human body, from a child to a full-grown man, laid with its side to the gallery. Sometimes there are as many as fourteen, sometimes as few as three or four, of these rows, one above the other. They are evidently so made to measure, that it is probable the body was lying by the side of the grave, while this was being dug.

" When the corpse, wrapped up, as we heard from Diogenes, was laid in its narrow cell, the front was hermetically closed either by a marble slab, or more frequently by several broad tiles, put edgeways in a groove or mortice, cut for them in the rock, and cemented all round. The inscription was cut upon the marble, or scratched in the wet mortar. Thousands of the former sort have been collected, and may be seen in museums and churches; many of the latter have been copied and published ; but by far the greater number of tombs are anonymous, and have no record upon them. And now the reader may reasonably ask, Through what period does the interment in the catacombs range, and how are its limits determined ? We will try to content him as briefly as possible.

" There is no evidence of the Christians having ever buried any where, anteriorly to the construction of catacombs. Two principles as old as Christianity regulate this mode of burial. The first is, the manner of Christ's entombment. He was laid in a grave in a cavern, wrapped up in linen, embalmed with spices ; and a stone, sealed up, closed His sepulchre. As St. Paul so often proposes Him for the model of our resurrection, and speaks of our being buried with Him in baptism, it was natural for His disciples to wish to be buried after His example, so to be ready to rise with Him.

" This lying in wait for resurrection was the second thought that guided the formation of these cemeteries. Every expression connected with them alluded to the rising again. The word to *bury* is unknown in Christian inscriptions. '*Deposited* in peace,' ' the *deposition of* —,' are the expressions used : that is, the dead are but left there for a time, till called for again, as a pledge, or precious thing, intrusted to faithful, but temporary, keeping. The very name of cemetery suggests that it is only a place where many lie, as in a dormitory, slumbering for a while; till dawn come, and the trumpet's sound awake them. Hence the grave is only called ' the place,' or more technically, ' the small home,'* of the dead in Christ.

" These two ideas, which are combined in the planning of the Cata-

* Locus, loculus.

combs, were not later insertions into the Christian system, but must have been more vivid in its earlier times. They inspired abhorrence of the pagan custom of burning the dead; nor have we a hint that this mode was, at any time, adopted by Christians.

"But ample proof is to be found in the catacombs themselves, of their early origin. The style of paintings, yet remaining, belongs to a period of still flourishing art. Their symbols, and the symbolical taste itself, are characteristic of a very ancient period. For this peculiar taste declined, as time went on. Although inscriptions with dates are rare, yet out of ten thousand collected. and about to be published, by the learned and sagacious Cavalier de Rossi, about three hundred are found bearing consular dates, through every period, from the early emperors to the middle of the fourth century (A.D. 350). Another curious and interesting custom furnishes us with dates on tombs. At the closing of the grave, the relations or friends, to mark it, would press into its wet plaster, and leave there, a coin, a cameo, or engraved gem, sometimes even a shell or pebble; probably that they might find the sepulchre again, especially where no inscription was left. Many of these objects continue to be found, many have been long collected. But it is not uncommon, where the coin, or, to speak scientifically, the medal, has fallen from its place, to find a mould of it left, distinct and clear in the cement, which equally gives its date. This is sometimes of Domitian, or other early emperors.

"It may be asked, wherefore this anxiety to rediscover with certainty the tomb? Besides motives of natural piety, there is one constantly recorded on sepulchral inscriptions. In England, if want of space prevented the full date of a person's death being given, we should prefer chronicling the year, to the day of the month, when it occurred. It is more historical. No one cares about remembering the day on which a person died, without the year; but the year, without the day, is an important recollection. Yet while so few ancient Christian inscriptions supply the year of people's deaths, thousands give us the very day of it, on which they died, whether in the hopefulness of believers. or in the assurance of martyrs. This is easily explained. Of both classes annual commemoration had to be made, on the very day of their departure; and accurate knowledge of this was necessary. Therefore it alone was recorded.

"In a cemetery close to the one in which we have left our three youths, with Diogenes and his sons *, were lately found inscriptions mingled together, belonging to both orders of the dead. One in Greek, after mentioning the 'Deposition of Augenda on the 13th day before the Calends, or 1st of June,' adds this simple address,

ZHCAIC ENKῶ KAI
EPῶTA YΠEPHMῶN

" ' Live in the Lord, and pray for us.'

---

* That of SS. Nereus and Achilleus.

H H

" Another fragment is as follows : —

```
. . . . . N. IVN—
. . . . . . IVIBAS—
IN PACE ET PETE
PRO NOBIS
```

" '. . . Nones of June . . . Live in peace, and pray for us.'

" This is a third : —

```
VICTORIA . REFRIGERER [ET]
ISSPIRITVS . TVS IN BONO
```

" ' Victoria, be refreshed, and may thy spirit be in enjoyment '
(good).

" This last reminds us of a most peculiar inscription found scratched in the mortar beside a grave in the cemetery of Prætextatus, not many yards from that of Callistus. It is remarkable, first, for being in Latin written with Greek letters ; then, for containing a testimony of the Divinity of our Lord ; lastly, for expressing a prayer for the refreshment of the departed. We fill up the portions of words wanting, from the falling out of part of the plaster.

BENE MERENTI SORORI BON	
VIII KAL NOB	
ΔΕ	ϹΠΙ
ΟΥϹ	ΡΙΤ ουμ
ΧΡΙϹ	ΤΟ Υ ουμ
ΤΟΥϹ	ΡΕΦ φ
ΟΝΝ	ΙΓΕΡΕ τ
ΙΠΟ	ΙΝ ρ
ΤΕϹ	

" ' To the well-deserving sister Bon . . . The eighth day before the calends of Nov. Christ God Almighty refresh thy spirit in Christ.'

" In spite of this digression on prayers inscribed over tombs, the reader will not, we trust, have forgotten, that we were establishing the fact, that the Christian cemeteries of Rome owe their origin to the earliest ages. We have now to state down to what period they were used. After peace was restored to the Church, the devotion of Christians prompted them to desire burial near the martyrs and holy people of an earlier age. But, generally speaking, they were satisfied to lie under the pavement. Hence the sepulchral stones which are often found in the rubbish of the catacombs, and sometimes in their places, bearing consular dates of the fourth century, are thicker, larger, better carved, and in a less simple style, than those of an earlier period, placed upon the walls. But before the end of that century, these monuments become rarer; and interment in the catacombs ceased in the following, at latest. Pope Damasus, who died in 384, reverently shrunk, as he tells us, in his own epitaph, from intruding into the company of the saints.

"Restitutus, therefore, whose sepulchral tablet we gave for a title to our chapter, may well be considered as speaking in the name of the early Christians, and claiming as their own exclusive work and property, the thousand miles of subterranean city, with their six millions of slumbering inhabitants, who trust in the Lord, and await His resurrection.*

"When peace and liberty were restored to the Church, these cemeteries became places of devotion, and of great resort. Each of them was associated with the name of one, or the names of several, of the more eminent martyrs buried in it; and, on their aniversaries, crowds of citizens and of pilgrims thronged to their tombs, where the Divine mysteries were offered up, and the homily delivered in their praise. Hence began to be compiled the first martyrologies, or calendars of martyrs' days, which told the faithful whither to go. 'At Rome, on the Salerian, or the Appian, or the Ardeatine way,' such are the indications almost daily read in the Roman martyrology, now swelled out, by the additions of later ages.†

"An ordinary reader of the book hardly knows the importance of these indications; for they have served to verify several otherwise dubious cemeteries. Another class of valuable writers also comes to our aid; but before mentioning them, we will glance at the changes which this devotion produced in the cemeteries. First, commodious entrances, with easy staircases were made; then walls were built to support the crumbling galleries; and, from time to time, funnel-shaped apertures in the vaults were opened, to admit light and air. Finally, basilicas or churches were erected over their entrances, generally leading immediately to the principal tomb, then called the *confession* of the church.

---

* So F. Marchi calculates them, after diligent examination. We may mention here that, in the construction of these cemeteries, the sand extracted from one gallery was removed into another already excavated. Hence many are now found completely filled up.

† One or two entries from the old *Kalendarium Romanum* will illustrate this:

"iii. Non. Mart. Lucii in Callisti.
vi. Id. Dec. Eutichiani in Callisti.
xiii. Kal. Feb. Fabiani in Callisti, et Sebastiani ad Catacumbas.
viii. Id. Aug. Systi in Callisti."

We have extracted these entries of depositions in the cemetery of Callistus, because, while actually writing this chapter, we have received news of the discovery of the tombs and lapidary inscriptions of every one of these Popes, together with those of St. Antherus, in one chapel of the newly-ascertained cemetery of Callistus, with an inscription in verse by St. Damasus:

"Prid. Kal. Jan. Sylvestri in Priscillæ.
iv. Id. (Aug.) Laurentii in Tiburtina.
iii. Kal. Dec. Saturnini in Thrasonis."

Published by Ruinart,—Acta, tom. iii.

APPENDIX.

The pilgrim, thus, on arriving at the holy city, visited each of these churches,—a custom yet practised,—descended below, and without having to grope his way about, went direct, by well-constructed passages, to the principal martyr's shrine, and so on to others, perhaps equally objects of reverence and devotion.

" During this period, no tomb was allowed to be opened, no body to be extracted. Through apertures made into the grave, handkerchiefs or scarfs, called *brandea*, were introduced, to touch the martyr's relics ; and these were carried to distant countries, to be held in equal reverence. No wonder that St. Ambrose, St. Gaudentius, and other bishops should have found it so difficult to obtain bodies, or large relics of martyrs for their churches. Another sort of relics consisted of what was called familiarly the oil of a martyr, that is, the oil, often mixed with balsam, which burned in a lamp beside his tomb. Often a round stone pillar, three feet or so in height, and scooped out at the top, stands beside a monument : probably to hold the lamp, or serve for the distribution of its contents. St. Gregory the Great wrote to Queen Theodelinda, that he sent her a collection of the oils of the popes who were martyrs. The list which accompanied them was copied by Mabillon in the treasury of Monza, and republished by Ruinart.[*] It exists there yet, together with the very phials containing them, sealed up in metal tubes.

" This jealousy of disturbing the saints, is displayed most beautifully in an incident, related by St. Gregory of Tours. Among the martyrs most honoured in the ancient Roman Church were St. Chrysanthus and Daria. Their tombs became so celebrated for cures, that their fellow-Christians built (that is, excavated) over them a chamber, with a vault of beautiful workmanship, where crowds of worshippers assembled. This was discovered by the heathens, and the emperor closed them in, walled up the entrance, and from above, probably through the *luminare*, or ventilating shaft, showered down earth and stones, and buried the congregation alive, as the two holy martyrs had been before them. The place was unknown at the peace of the Church, till discovered by Divine manifestation. But instead of being permitted to enter again into this hallowed spot, pilgrims were merely allowed to look at it, through a window opened in the wall, so as to see, not only the tombs of the martyrs, but also the bodies of those who had been buried alive at their shrines. And as the cruel massacre had taken place while preparations were being made for oblation of the holy Eucharist, there were still to be seen lying about, the silver cruets in which the wine was brought for that spotless sacrifice.[†]

" It is clear that pilgrims resorting to Rome would want a hand-book to the cemeteries, that they might know what they had to visit. It is likewise but natural that, on their return home, they may have sought to edify their less fortunate neighbours, by giving an account of what

---

[*] Acta Martyr, tom. iii.
[†] S. Greg. Turon, de Gloria Mart. lib. i. c. 28. ap. Marchi, p. 81. One would apply St. Damasus's epigram on these martyrs to this occurrence, Carm. xxviii.

they had seen. Accordingly there exist, no less fortunately for us than for their untravelled neighbours, several records of this character. The first place, among these, is held by catalogues compiled in the fourth century ; one, of the places of sepulture of Roman Pontiffs, the other of Martyrs.* After these come three distinct guides to the catacombs ; the more interesting because they take different rounds, yet agree marvellously in their account.

" To show the value of these documents, and describe the changes which took place in the catacombs during the second period of their history, we will give a brief account of one discovery, in the cemetery where we left our little party. Among the rubbish near the entrance of a catacomb, the name of which was yet doubtful, and which had been taken for that of Prætextatus, was found a fragment of a slab of marble which had been broken across obliquely, from left to right, with the following letters :

" The young Cavalier de Rossi at once declared that this was part of the sepulchral inscription of the holy Pope Cornelius ; that probably his tomb would be found below, in a distinguished form ; and that as all the itineraries above mentioned concurred in placing it in the cemetery of Callistus, this, and not the one at St. Sebastian's, a few hundred yards off, must claim the honour of that name. He went further, and foretold that as these works pronounced St. Cyprian to be buried near Cornelius, there would be found something at the tomb which would account for that idea ; for it was known that his body rested in Africa. It was not long before every prediction was verified. The great staircase discovered ‡ was found to lead at once to a wider space, carefully secured by brick-work of the time of peace, and provided with light and air from above. On the left was a tomb, cut like others in the rock, without any exterior arch over it. It was, however, large and ample ; and except one, very nigh above it, there were no other graves below, or over, or at the sides. The remaining portion of the slab was found within it ; the first piece was brought from the Kincherian Museum, where it had been deposited, and exactly fitted to it ; and both covered the tomb, thus:

---

* Published by Bucherius in 1634.
† (Of) . . nelius martyr.
‡ The crypt, we believe, was discovered before the stairs.

```
┌─────────────────────────────────────┐
│                                    * │
│       CORNELII   MARTYRIS            │
│               EP                     │
│                                      │
└─────────────────────────────────────┘
```

Below, reaching from the lower edge of this stone to the ground, was a marble slab covered with an inscription, of which only the left-hand end remains, the rest being broken off and lost. Above the tomb was another slab let into the sand-stone, of which the right-hand end exists, and a few more fragments have been recovered in the rubbish ; not enough to make out the lines, but sufficient to show it was an inscription in verse, by Pope Damasus. How is this authorship traceable ? Very easily. Not only do we know that this holy pope, already mentioned, took pleasure in putting verses, which he loved to write, on the tombs of martyrs †, but the number of inscriptions of his yet extant exhibit a particular and very elegant form of letters, known among antiquarians by the name of ' Damasian.' The fragments of this marble bear portions of verses, in this character.

"To proceed : on the wall, right of the tomb, and on the same plane, were painted two full-length figures in sacerdotal garments, with glories round their heads, evidently of Byzantine work of the seventh century. Down the wall, by the left side of each, letter below letter, were their names ; some letters were effaced, which we supply in italics as follow :

SCI☩ CORNELI PP   SCI☩ CIPRIANI.‡

"We here see how a foreigner, reading these two inscriptions, with the portraits, and knowing that the Church commemorates the two martyrs on the same day, might easily be led to suppose, that they were here deposited together. Finally, at the right hand of the tomb, stands a

---

* Of Cornelius Martyr Bishop.
† These form the great bulk of his extant works in verse.
‡ "(The picture) of St. Cornelius Pope, of St. Cyprian." On the other side, on a narrow wall projecting at a right angle, are two more similar portraits ; but only one name can be deciphered, that of St. Sixtus, or, as he is there and elsewhere called, Sustus. On the paintings of the principal saints may still be read, scratched in the mortar, in characters of the seventh century, the names of visitors to the tomb. Those of two priests are thus —

☩LEO PRB IOANNIS PRB.

It may be interesting to add the entry in the Roman calendar.
"xviii. Kal. Oct. Cypriani Africæ: Romæ celebratur in Callisti."
"Sep. 14. (The deposition) of Cyprian in Africa : at Rome it is kept in (the cemetery) of Callistus."

truncated column, about three feet high, concave at the top, as before described ; and as a confirmation of the use to which we said it might be put, St Gregory has, in his list of oils sent to the Lombard Queen, 'Oleum S. Cornelii,' the oil of St. Cornelius.

"We see then, how, during the second period, new ornaments, as well as greater conveniences, were added to the primitively simple forms of the cemeteries. But we must not, on that account, imagine that we are in any danger of mistaking these later embellishments for the productions of the early ages. The difference is so immense, that we might as easily blunder by taking a Reubens for a Beato Angelico, as by considering a Byzantine figure to be a production of the two first centuries.

"We come now to the third period of these holy cemeteries, the sad one of their desolation. When the Lombards, and later the Saracens, began to devastate the neighbourhood of Rome, and the catacombs were exposed to desecration, the Popes extracted the bodies of the most illustrious martyrs, and placed them in the basilicas of the city. This went on till the eighth or ninth century ; when we still read of repairs made in the cemeteries by the sovereign Pontiffs. The catacombs ceased to be so much places of devotion ; and the churches, which stood over their entrances, were destroyed, or fell to decay. Only those remained which were fortified and could be defended. Such are the extramural basilicas of St. Paul on the Ostian way, of St. Sebastian on the Appian, St. Laurence on the Tiburtine, or in the Ager Veranus, St. Agnes on the Nomentan road, St. Pancratius on the Aurelian, and, greatest of all, St. Peter's on the Vatican. The first and last had separate *burghs* or cities round them ; and the traveller can still trace remains of strong walls round some of the others.

"Strange it is, however, that the young antiquarian, whom we have frequently named with honour, should have re-discovered two of the basilicas over the entrance to the cemetery of Callistus, almost entire ; the one being a stable and bake-house, the other a wine-store. One is, most probably, that built by Pope Damasus, so often mentioned. The earth washed down, through air-holes, the spoliation practised during ages, by persons entering from vineyards through unguarded entrances, the mere wasting action of time and weather, have left us but a wreck of the ancient catacombs. Still there is much to be thankful for. Enough remains to verify the records left us in better times, and these serve to guide us to the reconstruction of our ruins. The present Pontiff has done more in a few years for these sacred places, than has been effected in centuries. The mixed commission which he has appointed have done wonders. With very limited means, they are going systematically to work, finishing as they advance. Nothing is taken from the spot where it is found ; but everything is restored, as far as possible, to its original state. Accurate tracings are made of all the paintings, and plans of every part explored. To secure these good results, the Pope has, from his own resources, bought vineyards and fields, especially at the Tor Marancia, where the cemetery of SS. Nereus and Achilleus is situated ; and we believe also over that of Callistus. The French emperor too has sent to Rome, artists, who have produced a most magnificent work, perhaps somewhat overdone, upon the catacombs : a truly imperial undertaking."

LETTER FROM NAPLES.

THE following extract of a letter lately appeared in the "Cork Constitution," a highly respectable Protestant journal, of strong anti-Catholic tendencies; and the Editor vouches for the high honour and veracity of the writer, who thus affords a glimpse at the true state of things :—

"13th July, 1857.

"We are perfectly tranquil here at present. The landing of a party of Mazzinisti the other day was repelled by the peasants, before the Government could send troops—a proof that the people here will *not* revolt.

"Yesterday a friend and myself read a most violent tirade in the 'Morning Post' against the Government. Both of us, having much to do in the country with the people, know tolerably their sentiments, and we agreed that the whole was *absolutely untrue.* Would such a newspaper, uttering such virulent falsehoods, and expressing itself so unjustifiably, be allowed to pass through the Post-office in Austria or Russia? No. English papers in those countries are scissored or blotted. Here not an English paper is prohibited or mutilated, not even 'Punch.' Why, then, does Lord Palmerston's paper, the 'Morning Post,' bully the weak Governments, and not attack those powerful ones whose atrocities are a hundred times greater than those of this country?

"Lord Palmerston and the 'Morning Post' know that the statements they publish are false. *They have received counter-statements, but will not publish them, excusing themselves by saying that the parties have been imposed on, &c. ;* but when some infamous account is sent them, so exaggerated, that it may be said to surpass the bounds of probability, then it suits them, and is inserted.

"This country is undoubtedly capable of great improvement — the people are too uneducated, but there is material prosperity. The produce of the country is required abroad, and sells for more than is required in imports; therefore the precious metals come in largely to balance the account, and the country people are rich.

"The total debt is about eighteen millions sterling, on a five per cent. stock, the price of which is now 110 — a tolerable proof of the feelings of the country.

"If the English Government wished really to be informed of the state of this country, let it send an impartial man ; and I am sure that prisons and every source of information would be open to him.

"The King is as different from what he is represented as possible : he is mild, benevolent, painstaking, and a very hard-working man, accessible to everybody. But he commits the great error of thinking that he alone knows how to govern the country. He is his own minister, and governs by means of heads of departments, called directors, who will not take on themselves the least responsibility, and, as a consequence, the movement of the Government is too slow, and every unjust or unpopular act is attributed to the King."

London : Printed by SPOTTISWOODE & Co., New-street Square.

WORKS IN GENERAL LITERATURE.

1.

The HISTORY of ENGLAND, from the Accession of James II. By THOMAS BABINGTON MACAULAY. Eleventh Edition. Vols. I. and II. 8vo. price 32s.; Vols. III. and IV. 8vo. 36s.

2.

Sir JAMES MACKINTOSH'S HISTORY of ENGLAND, from the Earliest Times to the final Establishment of the Reformation. Library Edition. 2 vols. 8vo. 21s.

3.

Mr. MACAULAY'S CRITICAL and HISTORICAL ESSAYS contributed to the *Edinburgh Review*.

1. LIBRARY EDITION, in 3 vols. 8vo. price 36s.
2. Complete in ONE VOLUME, with Portrait. Square crown 8vo. price 21s.
3. Another NEW EDITION, in 3 vols. fcp. 8vo. price 21s.
4. PEOPLE'S EDITION, in 2 vols. crown 8vo. price 8s.

4.

The HISTORY of SCOTLAND, from the Revolution to the Extinction of the Last Jacobite Insurrection (1689—1748). By J. H. BURTON. 2 vols. 8vo. price 26s.

5.

The SAXONS in ENGLAND: A History of the English Commonwealth till the Period of the Norman Conquest. By JOHN MITCHELL KEMBLE, M.A., F.C.P.S., &c. 2 vols. 8vo. price 28s.

6.

SHARON TURNER'S HISTORY of the ANGLO-SAXONS, from the Earliest Period to the Norman Conquest. Seventh Edition, revised by the Rev. S. TURNER. 3 vols. 8vo. price 36s.

7.

SHARON TURNER'S HISTORY of ENGLAND during the MIDDLE AGES: Comprising the Reigns from the Norman Conquest to the Accession of Henry VIII. Fifth Edition, revised by the Rev. S. TURNER. 4 vols. 8vo. price 50s.

8.

HISTORY of the ROMANS under the EMPIRE. By the Rev. CHARLES MERIVALE, B.D. Vols. I. to III. 8vo. 42s.

9.

The Rev. C. MERIVALE'S HISTORY of the ROMANS under the Empire. Vols. IV. and V., *Augustus* to *Claudius*, price 32s.

10.

The FALL of the ROMAN REPUBLIC: A short History of the Last Century of the Commonwealth. By the Rev. C. MERIVALE, B.D. New Edition. 12mo. price 7s. 6d.

11.

HISTORY of GREECE. By the Right Rev. the LORD BISHOP of ST. DAVID'S (the Rev. Connop Thirlwall). An improved Library Edition, with Maps. 8 vols. 8vo. 3l.

* Also, an Edition in 8 vols. fcp. 8vo. with Vignette Titles, price 28s.

London: LONGMAN, BROWN, GREEN, LONGMANS, and ROBERTS.

12.

ESSAYS in ECCLESIASTICAL BIOGRAPHY; from the Edinburgh Review. By the Right Hon. Sir JAMES STEPHEN, K.C.B., LL.D. *Third Edition.* 2 vols. 8vo. 24s.

13.

COMPENDIUM of CHRONOLOGY: Containing the most important Dates of General History, Political, Ecclesiastical, and Literary, from the Creation of the World to the end of the Year 1854. By F. H. JAQUEMET. Edited by the Rev. JOHN ALCORN, M.A. *New Edition.* Post 8vo. 7s. 6d.

14.

BLAIR'S CHRONOLOGICAL and HISTORICAL TABLES, from the Creation to the Present Time: With Additions and Corrections from the most authentic Writers. Under the revision of Sir HENRY ELLIS, K.H. Imperial 8vo. price 31s. 6d.

15.

An ATLAS of HISTORY and GEOGRAPHY, from the Commencement of the Christian Era to the Present Time: Containing a Series of 16 coloured Maps in Chronological Order, with Illustrative Memoirs. By the Rev. J. S. BREWER, M.A. *New Edition.* Royal 8vo. 12s. 6d.

16.

CALENDAR of VICTORY: A Record of British Valour and Conquest by Sea and Land, on Every Day in the Year, from the Earliest Period to the Battle of Inkermann. By Major JOHNS, R.M., and Lieutenant P. H. NICOLAS, R.M. Fcp. 8vo. 12s. 6d.

17.

HISTORY of GUSTAVUS ADOLPHUS, and of the THIRTY YEARS' WAR to the KING'S DEATH. With some Account of its Conclusion by the *Peace of Westphalia* in 1648. By B. CHAPMAN, M.A., Vicar of Letherhead. 8vo. with Plans, price 12s. 6d.

18.

The LIFE and EPISTLES of ST. PAUL: Comprising a Complete Biography of the Apostle, and a Translation of his Epistles inserted in Chronological Order. By the Rev. W. J. CONYBEARE, M.A., and the Rev. J. S. HOWSON, M.A. *Second Edition*, with several Maps and Woodcuts, and 4 Plates. 2 vols. square crown 8vo. price 31s. 6d.

19.

EGYPT'S PLACE in UNIVERSAL HISTORY: An Historical Investigation, in Five Books. By C. C. J. BUNSEN, D.D., D.C.L., D.Ph. Translated from the German, by C. H. COTTRELL, Esq., M.A. With many Illustrations. Vol. I. 8vo. 28s.; Vol. II. 8vo. 30s. —Vol. III. is in the press.

20.

CHRISTIANITY and MANKIND: Their Beginnings and Prospects. By C. C. J. BUNSEN, D.D., D.C.L., D.Ph. Being a New Edition, corrected, remodelled, and extended, of *Hippolytus and his Age.* 7 vols. 8vo. £5. 5s.

21.

MAUNDER'S HISTORICAL TREASURY: Comprising a General Introductory Outline of Universal History, Ancient and Modern, and a Series of Separate Histories of Every principal Nation. New Edition; revised throughout, with a new Index. Fcp. 8vo. 10s.

22.

HISTORY of GREECE, for the Use of Schools and Young Persons, from the Earliest Times to the Taking of Corinth by the Romans, B.C. 146; mainly based upon Bishop Thirlwall. By Dr. L. SCHMITZ, F.R.S.E., Rector of the High School of Edinburgh. *Fourth Edition;* with Chapters on the Literature and Arts of Ancient Greece, and 136 Woodcuts from the Antique designed by G. Scharf, F.S.A. 12mo. price 7s. 6d.

London: LONGMAN, BROWN, GREEN, LONGMANS, and ROBERTS.

23.

ESSAYS from the **EDINBURGH** and **QUARTERLY** REVIEWS, with Addresses and other Pieces. By Sir JOHN F. W. HERSCHEL, Bart., K.H., M.A. 8vo. 18s.

24.

The **CHINESE EMPIRE**: A Sequel to *Huc* and *Gabel's* "Journey through Tartary and Thibet." By the Abbé HUC. *Second Edition*; with Map. 2 vols. 8vo. 24s.

25.

CHRISTIANITY in **CHINA, TARTARY**, and **THIBET**. By M. l'Abbé HUC, formerly Missionary Apostolic in China; Author of *The Chinese Empire*, &c. 2 vols. 8vo. 21s.

26.

TRAVELS and **DISCOVERIES** in **NORTH** and CENTRAL AFRICA: Being the Journal of an Expedition undertaken under the auspices of Her Britannic Majesty's Government in the Years 1849-1855. By HENRY BARTH, Ph.D., D.C.L. Maps, tinted Illustrations, and Woodcuts. Vols. I. to III. 8vo. 63s.—Vols. IV. and V., completing the work, are in the press.

27.

The **DISCOVERY** of the **NORTH-WEST PASSAGE** by H.M.S. INVESTIGATOR, CAPT. R. M'CLURE, 1850, 1851, 1852, 1853, 1854. Edited by Captain S. OSBORN, C.B., from the Logs and Journals of Captain ROBERT LE M. M'CLURE. *Second Edition*; with Map, Portrait, and 4 tinted Views. 8vo. 15s.

28.

The **EVENTFUL VOYAGE** of **H.M.** Discovery Ship RESOLUTE to the Arctic Regions in Search of Sir John Franklin and the Missing Crews of H.M. Ships *Erebus* and *Terror*, 1852, 1853, 1854. By GEORGE F. M'DOUGALL, Master. With Chart, tinted Illustrations, and Woodcuts. 8vo. 21s.

29.

TRAVELS in the **FREE STATES** of **CENTRAL** AMERICA: NICARAGUA, HONDURAS, and SAN SALVADOR. By Dr. CARL SCHERZER. With coloured Maps and Sections. 2 vols. post 8vo. 16s.

30.

PERSONAL NARRATIVE of a **PILGRIMAGE** to EL MEDINAH and MECCAH. By RICHARD F. BURTON, Captain Bombay Army. *Second Edition*, with numerous Woodcuts and coloured Plates from Drawings by the Author. 2 vols. crown 8vo. 24s.

31.

FIRST FOOTSTEPS in **EAST AFRICA**; or, an Exploration of Harar. By RICHARD F. BURTON, Captain Bombay Army. With Maps and coloured Plates. 8vo. 18s.

32.

MEMOIRS of **REAR-ADMIRAL SIR W. E. PARRY**, the Arctic Navigator. By his Son, the Rev. EDWARD PARRY, M.A., Domestic Chaplain to the Bishop of London. *Second Edition*; with Portrait and Map. Post 8vo. price 10s. 6d.

33.

QUEDAH; or, Stray Leaves from a Journal in Malayan Waters. By Captain SHERARD OSBORN, R.N., C.B., Officier de la Légion d'Honneur. With a Map and 4 tinted Illustrations. Post 8vo. 10s. 6d.

London: LONGMAN, BROWN, GREEN, LONGMANS, and ROBERTS.

34.

ENGLAND'S GREATNESS: Its Rise and Progress in Government, Laws, Religion, and Social Life; Agriculture, Commerce, and Manufactures; Science, Literature, and the Arts, from the Earliest Period to the Peace of Paris. By JOHN WADE, Author of the *Cabinet Lawyer*, &c. Post 8vo. 10s. 6d.

35.

The **PROPHECIES** relating to **NINEVEH** and the ASSYRIANS. Translated from the Hebrew. With Historical Introductions, and Notes Explanatory and Critical, exhibiting the principal Results of the recent Discoveries in their relation to these Prophecies. By the Rev. G. VANCE SMITH, B.A. Post 8vo. with Map, 10s. 6d.

36.

CHRISTIAN RECORDS: A Short History of the Apostolic Age. By L. A. MERIVALE. Fcp. 8vo. 7s. 6d.

37.

MAUNDER'S TREASURY of GEOGRAPHY, Physical, Historical, Descriptive, and Political: Containing a succinct Account of Every Country in the World. Completed by WILLIAM HUGHES, F.R.G.S. With 7 Maps and 16 Steel Plates. Fcp. 8vo. 10s.

38.

MEMOIRS and **LETTERS** of the late **COLONEL** A. S. H. MOUNTAIN, C.B., Aide-de-Camp to the Queen, and Adjutant-General of Her Majesty's Forces in India. Edited by Mrs. MOUNTAIN. Post 8vo. with Portrait, price 8s. 6d.

39.

The **FRANKS**, from their First Appearance in History to the Death of King Pepin. By WALTER C. PERRY, Barrister-at-Law, Doctor in Philosophy and Master of Arts in the University of Göttingen. 8vo. 12s. 6d.

40.

MEMORIALS, SCIENTIFIC and **LITERARY**, of ANDREW CROSSE, the ELECTRICIAN. Edited by Mrs. CROSSE. Post 8vo. 9s. 6d.

41.

COLONEL MURE'S CRITICAL HISTORY of the LANGUAGE and LITERATURE of ANCIENT GREECE............3 vols. 8vo. 36s.
VOL. IV. comprising Historical Literature to the Death of *Herodotus* ....8vo. 15s.
VOL. V. containing *Thucydides, Xenophon,* and the remaining Historians of the Attic Period ....8vo. 18s.

42.

The **ECLIPSE** of **FAITH**; or, a Visit to a Religious Sceptic. The *Eighth Edition*. Fcp. 8vo. 5s.

43.

DEFENCE of the **ECLIPSE** of **FAITH**, by its Author; Being a Rejoinder to Professor Newman's *Reply*: Including a full Examination of that Writer's Criticism on the Character of Christ; and a Chapter on the Aspects and Pretensions of Modern Deism. *Second Edition*, revised. Post 8vo. 5s. 6d.

44.

SELECTIONS from the **CORRESPONDENCE** of R. E. H. GREYSON, Esq. Edited by the Author of *The Eclipse of Faith*. 2 vols. fcp. 8vo. 12s.

London: LONGMAN, BROWN, GREEN, LONGMANS, and ROBERTS.

Check Out More Titles From HardPress Classics Series In this collection we are offering thousands of classic and hard to find books. This series spans a vast array of subjects – so you are bound to find something of interest to enjoy reading and learning about.

Subjects:
Architecture
Art
Biography & Autobiography
Body, Mind &Spirit
Children & Young Adult
Dramas
Education
Fiction
History
Language Arts & Disciplines
Law
Literary Collections
Music
Poetry
Psychology
Science
…and many more.

Visit us at www.hardpress.net

Im The Story

personalised classic books

"Beautiful gift.. lovely finish. My Niece loves it. so precious!"

Helen R Brumfieldon

☆☆☆☆☆

UNIQUE GIFT

FOR KIDS, PARTNERS AND FRIENDS

Timeless books such as:

Kids

Alice in Wonderland · The Jungle Book · The Wonderful Wizard of Oz
Peter and Wendy · Robin Hood · The Prince and The Pauper
The Railway Children · Treasure Island · A Christmas Carol

Adults

Romeo and Juliet · Dracula

| Highly Customizable | Change Books Title | Replace Character Names with yours | Upload Photo for inside page | Add Inscriptions |

Visit

Im The Story .com

and order yours today!

CPSIA information can be obtained
at www.ICGtesting.com
Printed in the USA
BVHW061239160819
556068BV00020B/1995/P